THE SPIRITUAL LOGIC OF
RAMON LLULL

IP93 79-

75-

40

The Spiritual Logic of Ramon Llull

MARK D. JOHNSTON

B
765
. L84
J64
1987

West

CLARENDON PRESS · OXFORD

1987

Oxford University Press, Walton Street, Oxford OX2 6DP

Oxford New York Toronto
Delhi Bombay Calcutta Madras Karachi
Petaling Jaya Singapore Hong Kong Tokyo
Nairobi Dar es Salaam Cape Town
Melbourne Auckland
and associated companies in
Beirut Berlin Ibadan Nicosia

Oxford is a trade mark of Oxford University Press

Published in the United States
by Oxford University Press, New York

© Mark D. Johnston 1987

All rights reserved. No part of this publication may be reproduced
stored in a retrieval system, or transmitted, in any form or by any means
electronic, mechanical, photocopying, recording, or otherwise, without
the prior permission of Oxford University Press.

British Library Cataloguing in Publication Data

Johnston, Mark D.
The spiritual logic of Ramon Llull.
1. Llull, Ramón
I. Title
196'.1 B765.L84
ISBN 0-19-824920-9

Library of Congress Cataloging in Publication Data

Johnston, Mark D. (Mark David), 1952–
The spiritual logic of Ramon Llull.
Bibliography: p.
Includes index.
1. Llull, Ramón, d. 1315—Contributions in logic.
2. Logic, Medieval. I. Title.
B765.L84J64 1987 160 86–21857
ISBN 0-19-824920-9

Set by Katerprint Typesetting Services, Oxford
Printed in Great Britain
at the University Press, Oxford
by David Stanford
Printer to the University

FOR DIANE

Acknowledgements

THE material presented in this study is part of a larger project devoted to Llull's handling of the trivial arts in general; with luck and diligence, I hope to produce further studies of his rhetorical and linguistic theories as well. All of this work had its genesis in my doctoral dissertation, written in 1977 at the Johns Hopkins University. That I was able to study Llull at all I owe to the indulgence and encouragement of my thesis director, Elias L. Rivers; I am also grateful for much advice and direction from my other graduate professors at Johns Hopkins, especially Harry Sieber, the second reader of my dissertation, and Nancy Struever, whose own work on the history of rhetoric I have often and profitably consulted.

The work on this study has required consultation of various manuscripts and scarce printed sources, which I have only been able to obtain through the dedicated services of the interlibrary loan staffs at Johns Hopkins, the University of Puget Sound, Washington University, and Illinois State University; to Helga Whitcomb of Milner Library at Illinois State I owe a truly profound debt of gratitude for her unflagging diligence, peerless efficiency, and ready sympathy. I did much of the early research for this study during the summers of 1979 and 1980, thanks to grants from the American Council of Learned Societies and National Endowment for the Humanities. This assistance afforded me not only the time, but also the materials essential to my work. An initial, and much longer redaction of my researches received the benefit of thorough and critical readings by Curt Wittlin of the University of Saskatchewan and R. D. F. Pring-Mill of Saint Catherine's College, Oxford. Without their honest evaluations and detailed recommendations I would have laboured much longer with much less to show for my efforts. Finally, I owe not only my success in this work but in all else to the support and empathy of my wife, Diane Urey, who has assisted me at every stage even while pursuing her own career as a scholar and teacher. The best expression of my thanks to everyone who has aided or encouraged me is to offer them in return a work of potential value to their own studies and permanent witness to their generosity.

Bloomington, Illinois   M.D.J.
August 1985

Contents

x   *Contents*

List of Tables

List of Illustrations

Note on References and Quotations

BECAUSE this work includes hundreds of short references to passages in Classical and medieval authorities, it has seemed expedient to offer all such references in parentheses within the text itself. This procedure not only saves the reader from the tedium of glancing at columns of brief footnotes, but also allows a much more economical presentation of the work's argument. Each reference generally follows the mention or citation of an authority's text, indicating in parentheses the pages or textual divisions from the edition cited. The editions used appear in the List of Works Cited at the end of this study, which gives the abbreviations employed (if any) as well as the pages or textual divisions (book, part, chapter, etc.) designated by the reference numbers. The reader should note that, for the sake of brevity, clarity, and uniformity, the references use only Arabic numerals to indicate textual divisions; Roman page numbers or Greek and Roman letters of textual divisions remain as given in the edition cited. Moreover, abbreviations appear only when necessary to distinguish between the several works of one author; where the study cites only a single work from any author, no abbreviation appears with the reference numbers. The reader should understand that the numbers indicate pages or textual divisions in the single work listed for that author in the List of Works Cited. For example, all mentions of Isidore accompanied by the reference '(1.1.1)' refer to book, chapter, and paragraph in his *Etymologiae*. References to anonymous works use their titles only. All long quotations set apart from the text include page or folio numbers from the edition or manuscript cited. Some references consist of or include the abbreviations 'Prol.', 'Intro.', or 'Proem.', as necessary to identify portions of a text, especially if they are not otherwise labelled as such in the edition cited. The reader should bear in mind that not every work, especially those of Llull, uses all of its textual divisions fully: that is, not every distinction has parts, not every part has chapters, and so forth.

All passages or phrases quoted from other authors within the running text of this study appear translated into English, with problematic or unusual words from the original indicated in parentheses, and this writer's own editorial interpolations in brackets. Because this study assumes a reader familiar with Scholastic Latin, long quotations of Latin passages set apart from the running text remain in Latin. Many readers, however, are undoubtedly less familiar with Old Catalan, and hence all long quotations in that language appear translated into English, with the original Catalan text given in footnotes. Unless otherwise indicated in the List of Works Cited, all translations into English are this writer's own.

Introduction

GORDON LEFF has observed that 'no phase of Scholasticism, certainly in terms of our present knowledge, remains more confused than the events in the decades immediately each side of the year 1300'.[1] No figure from this phase better justifies Leff's claim than that of the Catalan theologian and philosopher Ramon Llull (1232–1316). This extraordinary nobleman-turned-evangelist wrote almost 300 works in Latin, Arabic, and Catalan, and travelled the entire Mediterranean in pursuit of his life's goal of promoting the Christian Faith. (The reader unfamiliar with this remarkable career will find a brief review of Llull's life and work in the second half of this introduction.) His wide-ranging activities engendered an equally great, though often un-warranted, reputation as polymath, martyr, and even alchemist. This reputation rests especially on the estimation and diffusion of Llull's unique dialectical system, the so-called Great Universal Art, which attracted numerous practitioners in later centuries. In 1639 Bishop John Prideaux included it as one of the seven great systems of Logic in his *Heptades logicae*.[2] Despite this historic celebrity, Llull's *Art* has continued to puzzle and even repel modern scholars of medieval and Renaissance philosophy. E. J. Ashworth declares that Renaissance Lullists offer nothing to those interested in formal logic, semantics, or scientific method.[3] While one might question the historiographical soundness of a judgement that so radically separates these fields, conceived in a narrowly modern sense, from the broader context of Renaissance intellectual culture, Ashworth's claim does rightly, if negatively, point to the non-formal character of Llull's system. In a different way, Philotheus Boehner excludes Llull's *Art* from consider-ation in his survey of Scholastic Logic, pleading unfamiliarity with its

---

[1] *The Dissolution of the Medieval Outlook: An Essay on Intellectual and Spiritual Change in the Fourteenth Century* (New York: Harper & Row, 1976), p. 32.

[2] Cited in Wilber Samuel Howell, *Logic and Rhetoric in England, 1500–1700* (1956; repr. New York: Russell & Russell, 1961), p. 311.

[3] *Language and Logic in the Post-Medieval Period* (Dordrecht: Reidel, 1974), p. 20.

'peculiar' method, but suspecting that 'it is much better than the usual evaluation by historians would lead us to believe'.[4]

Purpose and perspective of this study

Now the purpose of this study will not be to contend judgements such as these, but rather to make more informed ones possible by defining more exactly the position of Llull's work in that very agitated situation of Latin Scholasticism around the year 1300. In order better to accomplish this end, it takes as a subject an aspect of Llull's work, his treatment of Scholastic Logic, whose examination most directly reveals the operative tenets of his own system. This is so because to study Llull's accounts of Logic is to adopt the comparative perspective established by his own conception of his *Art* as a programme of theological demonstration alternative to Aristotelian Logic, and basis for redefining Scholastic methods of argumentation. Moreover, Llull always treats other subjects in his own terms; his accounts of Logic are therefore examples of his own method at work. To investigate his treatment of Logic is to investigate his use of his own system. The results of this investigation, as conducted in this study, will certainly gratify scholars perplexed or frustrated by the unclear relationship of Llull's *Art* to contemporary Scholastic logical doctrine. The present study concludes that Llull's conception of Logic—and by extension of the demonstrative methods employed in his own *Art*—owes very little to either the theoretical or practical foundations of Aristotelian Logic; instead it adapts, in a largely superficial way, received Scholastic terminology and forms of argument as analogies for his own fundamental theological and metaphysical values. As a system of argument, the *Art* of Ramon Llull is neither material nor formal in any recognized logical sense, but rather spiritual in a broadly theological sense of 'speaking about God'. This conclusion will certainly disquiet those scholars of Llull's work who have sought to specify carefully its connections with the most sophisticated logical and philosophical issues animating the medieval schools around 1300. Yet it does not in any way detract from the value of Llull's work as an example—and perhaps the greatest—of the basic spiritual preoccupations current not only in the *studia*, but also in the courts and cloisters, and not simply in a few generations around 1300, but throughout the later Middle Ages.

---

[4] *Medieval Logic: An Outline of Its Development from 1250 to c.1400* (Manchester: Manchester University Press, 1952), p. xiv.

In order to suggest what these preoccupations are, and in order to introduce the basic perspective adopted in the much more detailed analyses that follow, it is advisable to describe here three features of Llull's treatment of Logic that this study considers fundamental, and broadly characteristic of his entire *Art* as well. These three features are its popularizing design and goals, its natural ontology, and its moralizing procedures of argument.

First, its doctrines and teachings are popular and non-academic in the extent demonstrated forty years ago by Tomás and Joaquín Carreras y Artau.[5] All scholars of Llull's work since then have necessarily acknowledged, despite attempted qualifications, this popular character. Llull possessed a limited, and usually superficial knowledge of not only Latin, but also Arabic philosophy and science, as Dominique Urvoy has lately shown.[6] His *Art* includes an explicit popular orientation simply by virtue of its use for directly converting non-believers, redaction in the vernacular, and frequent claims to offer a facile knowledge of all the arts and sciences. The fact that Llull began his intellectual career in middle age, apparently received little formal training, and always pursued his work as an instrument for mass proselytizing necessarily limits the scope and depth of his ideas to the surface of received doctrine, usually in the traditional and syncretic form of medieval encyclopedias or compendia, genres that Llull himself cultivated. Juan Tusquets has attempted to show that Llull's knowledge of medieval natural science depends directly on Vincent of Beauvais' *Speculum naturale*.[7] Among Arab authorities, the widely disseminated *Rasā'il* of the Islamic Brethren of Purity may have served, but more indirectly, the same purpose.[8] The content of Llull's teachings is neither profound nor original, and his few truly innovative ideas, such as his proposal of speech as a sixth sense called *affatus*, are derivations or extrapolations of his other basic theological or metaphysical values. Llull shared the general intellectual inheritance of his

[5] *Historia de la filosofía española: filosofía cristiana de los siglos XIII al XIV*, 2 vols. (Madrid: Asociación Española para el Progreso de las Ciencias, 1939–43), 1. 339. Though superseded in many regards by more recent scholarship, this is still the best full-length survey of Llull's doctrines available.

[6] *Penser l'islam: les présupposés islamiques de l'"Art" de Lull*, Études Musulmanes, 23 (Paris: J. Vrin, 1980), pp. 158–61. This study replaces all previous scholarship on Llull's relationship to Islam and Arab culture.

[7] *Ramón Lull, pedagogo de la cristiandad* (Madrid: Consejo Superior de Investigaciones Científicas, 1954), pp. 175–82.

[8] See Urvoy, *Penser l'islam*, pp. 144–7 and 380–1.

Christian and Muslim contemporaries: his fundamental notions on any subject derive from the texts of ancient or medieval authorities such as Aristotle, Porphyry, Augustine, Boethius, the Pseudo-Dionysius, Avicebron, or Avicenna. The degree to which he depends on any of these directly is a special problem considered in more detail below; it is impossible to determine whether Llull knew the works of other authorities at first hand or merely through florilegia and compendia. Llull's knowledge of more recent writers in the Latin West is also difficult to judge. Many of his doctrines are, however, typical of the schools of the twelfth century. The circumstances that might have contributed to this somewhat antiquated character in Llull's intellectual formation are still obscure. None the less, it is necessary to insist here that claims regarding Llull's special access to arcane or esoteric writings from Classical or Islamic philosophy reflect an imperfect understanding of the circulation of those writings or their doctrines in the Middle Ages; there is no reason to suppose that Llull had access to materials not already widely known among his Latin and Muslim contemporaries, and many better reasons to suppose that he knew considerably less than they.[9] This study will attempt to show, moreover, that many of his most unusual, idiosyncratic, or unconventional pronouncements are typically products of his methods of argument, especially the 'moralizing' procedures explained below.

Second, Llull's logical method assumes a 'natural' ontology that is extremely Realist and extremely 'essentialist' in an ultra-Avicennian fashion. All beings exist for Llull as the concrete realizations of real universal substantial and accidental essences or natures. This aspect merits mention here because it determines Llull's conception of both rational and real beings. All these form a hierarchy of existence that culminates in the Godhead. For Llull, Logic and indeed all philosophical discourse must reflect the natures of things, and hence he deliberately applies the label 'natural' to his own logical programme. Logic is never a *scientia sermocinalis* for Llull, and this explains in itself his disregard for some of the most elementary logico-linguistic distinctions of his contemporaries. Llull's Logic is always a *scientia realis*, to a degree probably unimaginable for even his most Realist colleagues in the schools, as E. W. Platzeck has explained.[10]

---

[9] See ibid., p. 64.

[10] 'Raimund Lulls Auffassung von der Logik (Was ist an Lulls Logik formale Logik?)', *Estudios Lulianos*, 2 (1958), 5–36 and 273–96 and his masterwork, *Raimund Lull. Sein Leben—Seine Werke. Die Grundlagen seines Denkens (Prinzipienlehre)*, 2 vols. (Rome: Editiones Franciscanae & Düsseldorf: Verlag L. Schwann, 1962–4), I. 393–445.

Finally, Llull's procedures of argumentation are 'moralizing'. This term appears throughout this study and is fundamental to understanding its explanations of Llull's methods and doctrines. It embraces two related senses. First, it designates the 'ethico-ontological' duty of every being to acknowledge God, according to Llull's doctrine of 'intention', explained in detail below. In so far as this acknowledgement indistinctly embraces both faith in, and understanding of, God, the relationship between these two modes of knowledge becomes one of the great problems in Llull's development of his *Art*. Second, this 'moralization' designates Llull's effort to explain the status, function, or understanding of any real or rational being according to that duty, and these explanations thus constitute a kind of tropological exegesis of creation; Llull offers a 'moralized *liber naturae*' to set alongside the moralized Ovid. This procedure is not analytical or formal. Faced with a body of received doctrine on any subject, Llull's moralizing method does not attempt to investigate it using its own proper terms and methods, but instead applies to those terms his own understanding of that subject's intention or duty to God, argued through the terms and methods of his *Art*. Thus his procedure typically takes the discursive form of analogy, and many eminent scholars of Llull's work, from the brothers Carreras y Artau to E. W. Platzeck to R. D. F. Pring-Mill have argued the fundamentally analogical character of the Lullian *Art*. This study attempts to carry their insights still further and to explain Llull's entire treatment of Scholastic Logic as an analogical interpretation of its received doctrine, and to identify the handful of discursive or conceptual strategies that he uses in doing so. These strategies, and the basic theological or metaphysical values that they realize, comprise the fundamental working principles of the entire Lullian *Art* as a model of argumentation and as applied to any other body of knowledge. Llull's moralization produces not only a new definition of received doctrines, but new 'knowledge' about a subject in its analogical association and reassociation of received doctrines with Llull's own principles. Since the latter are themselves derivations from traditional or established concepts, the knowledge produced is often a curious collocation of properly unrelated notions and commonplaces, based on verbal or conceptual affinities; the following chapters offer scores of examples.

This view of the role of analogy in Llull's work as a procedure of moralization differs sharply in several respects from the view of that role suggested by E. W. Platzeck, whose special interest in Llull's Logic made him one of its most subtle interpreters. This difference does not diminish the great debt of this study to Father Platzeck's many learned researches, but it does reflect another conception of the historical position of Llull's work. Platzeck argued that Llull's use of analogy manifests a determined 'form of thought' common to the entire Western philosophical tradition from Plato to modern mathematical logic; this interpretation reflects his own conviction that analogy could serve as a master logical method that 'follows more faithfully the transcendental properties of objects'.[11] This master logic includes Aristotelian demonstration as a more limited sub-type.[12] Hence Platzeck devotes considerable attention to such general issues as the relative formal and material bases of Lullian Logic and its value as a programme of transcendental knowledge, often defined in specifically Platonic terms. His approach thus tends toward a very idealistic and trans-historical critique of Llull's method, which typically concludes by proclaiming him one of the great minds of Western thought.[13] This study prefers, on the other hand, to consider Llull within the narrower historical context of thirteenth-century Scholastic theology and philosophy, and to trace both his doctrines and his methods to values and practices current in the Latin and Arab intellectual life of that era. Moreover, where Platzeck develops his own superb definition of Llull's Logic as the 'art of separating the gnoseologically true and false'[14] by emphasizing the 'forms of thought' fundamental to that art, this study develops that same definition by emphasizing the primacy of the spiritual values that constitute truth for Ramon Llull. In this task Platzeck still offers invaluable assistance. His characterization of Llull's pretended 'natural Logic' as a sort of 'Christian phenomenology'[15] is tremendously suggestive of the direction that any analysis of his *Art* should take. This study attempts to pursue that direction in order to show that Llull's analogical method is not simply 'adequate' to his spiritual values, as Platzeck suggests at one point, but rather, as he elsewhere remarks, that it assumes the divinely guaranteed likeness of all beings and knowledge.[16] Llull's *Art* does not so much employ the

---

[11] *La evolución de la lógica griega en el aspecto especial de la analogía (desde la época de los Presocráticos hasta Aristóteles)* (Barcelona: Consejo Superior de Investigaciones Científicas, 1954), p. 117. In part his argument is based on an adaptation of the theory of 'thought-forms' of Hans Leisegang.

[12] 'La combinatoria luliana', *Revista de filosofía*, 12 (1953), 575–609 and 13 (1954), 125–65; at p. 162.

[13] e.g. *Evolución de la lógica griega*, p. 135.

[14] 'Raimund Lulls Auffassung von der Logik', p. 36.

[15] 'La combinatoria luliana', p. 164.

[16] *La evolución de la lógica griega*, p. 125 and 'La combinatoria luliana', p. 155.

'forms of thought' whose classification Platzeck adapts from Leise-gang, but instead requires that 'onto-theo-logical' constitution of metaphysics described by Heidegger.[17]

Method of this study

The three features of Llull's Logic just described comprise broadly the argument of this study. The details of their realization in Llull's logical theories are certainly too numerous and diverse to review here, and even the few operative principles of his moralizing method resist adequate description outside the context of their discursive use in specific arguments. These difficulties in fact point to one of the great advantages of Llull's moralizing procedure: it does not require systematic coherence of a deductive nature among its arguments; it is endlessly capable of offering yet another analogical explanation of the same idea or concept, or of restating the same truth in different terms. This explains both the volume and exhaustively repetitive character of nearly all Llull's 240 extant writings. Many of the shorter works among these are scarcely more than excerpts from his longer ones. The scholar who sets out to analyse Llull's treatment of any question faces a troubling dilemma: where one well-chosen example might adequately represent Llull's analogical method, the range of possible positions generated by that method can be staggeringly broad, with little internal consistency, but many slight variations. If there is one fault common to many of the existing accounts of Llull's work, it is their over-zealous synthesis of his often divergent positions, without regard for their chronological or ideological order. The careful selection and organiz-ation of material thus becomes a prime consideration for anyone who seeks to expound Llull's work. As regards organization, this study attempts to respect the chronological order in Llull's writings by treating them in two parts, corresponding to what it presents as two periods in Llull's attention to logical doctrine. The detailed justifi-cations for this division properly appear in the analyses of each part. Here it is appropriate simply to note that this division helps draw attention to changes in Llull's arguments and thereby reveals some of the new interests or knowledge that must have precipitated those changes. Tracing these changes also establishes a trajectory in Llull's intellectual development whose backwards extrapolation can some-times lead to some approximation of the original values and doctrines

---

[17] 'The Onto-theo-logical Constitution of Metaphysics', in *Identity and Difference*, tr. Joan Stambaugh (New York: Harper & Row Torchbooks, 1974), pp. 42–74.

that Llull evidently assimilated in his early and still obscure training. On the other hand, this study prefers to respect the ideological order of its subject, logical doctrine, by employing the received divisions of Scholastic theory as the framework for each part of this study; these examine Llull's remarks on the predicables, categories, propositions, syllogism, fallacy, and demonstration, in that order. While this sequence has the advantage of displaying very clearly Llull's relative handling of various branches of received doctrine, it admittedly does not correspond to the relative importance of these divisions in Llull's own programme, nor does it indicate which areas embrace the special techniques that he develops. None the less, the need to explain exactly how Llull's views relate to received doctrine ultimately justifies using the latter's own internal order as a framework for analysing Llull's treatment. Finally, in order to avoid too reductive a synthesis of Llull's diverse views, this study relies heavily on the explication of actual passages from his works, rather than paraphrase or summary of his views. This procedure has the advantage of revealing the specifically literary mechanics of his moralizing method at work, and his sometimes highly idiosyncratic or simply superficial expressions of commonplace doctrines.

The desire to define Llull's understanding of received teaching requires a very extensive use of comparative analyses. Consequently, this study commonly evaluates Llull's views on any point by comparing them to those found in the authorities of contemporary Scholastic doctrine. Such a comparison unfortunately runs foul of one of the great difficulties in Llull's work, already noted above, and perhaps most simply called the 'problem of Llull's sources'. Llull regularly recasts received ideas in his own peculiar jargon, sometimes misrepresents or drastically simplifies their import, and very rarely refers to any authorities except his own writings. This anonymity is perhaps a consequence of the popular origins of his knowledge, which he may have obtained from encyclopaedic works that did not distinguish their own sources. Most of the references that Llull does provide are to individuals, not to their writings, and these probably number no more than a few hundred in his whole mammoth *œuvre*. Hence only a tiny fraction of the authorities cited in this study appear as 'sources' of Llull's own views. Nearly all of them serve instead as 'parallels' for Llull's positions, and the doctrines that they offer are better understood as 'objects' of Llull's interest and consequent moralizing treatment.

Foremost among the logical authorities cited as parallels stands Peter of Spain, later Pope John XXI, whose *Summule logicales* remained a standard school text for over three centuries; Ockham serves as a representative of the fuller *logica moderna*.[18] The basic texts of Porphyry and Boethius, the chief components of the early medieval *logica vetus*, also appear frequently. Around all these stand the works of Aristotle's Organon, which define either directly or indirectly the theoretical and practical foundation of Scholastic Logic, even while it is unnecessary and improbable that Llull knew any of the Philosopher's texts in their medieval Latin or Arabic translations. Constant references to these standard authorities should show that Llull does not attempt to reformulate received doctrine in a consistent manner, but moralizes it, point by point or structure by structure, according to his own theological and metaphysical values.

These values are so basic (for example, universal hylemorphism) that their parallels or sources must be a whole school or tradition, rather than any specific authority. Thus one could classify Llull as an 'Augustinian' or 'Franciscan' thinker with respect to his Latin masters, and as a representative of 'Almohadism' or 'zahirism' with respect to his Arabic guides;[19] each of these labels in fact has only a limited application to Llull's programme as a whole. Because this study pursues the comparison of Llull's texts with other authorities as a means of comprehending his moralization of existing doctrines, it is expedient to refer his basic values to the account of them found in some Scholastic authority, and Aquinas fulfills this function frequently throughout the chapters that follow. Aquinas is the easy choice for this purpose not simply because well-commented editions of his works are readily available, but precisely because Saint Thomas typically covers a range of subjects, and of opinions on those subjects, rarely exceeded by any writer of the period. This is tremendously useful in understanding the polemical value of Llull's own views in the decades around 1300. Gordon Leff has suggested that 'from about 1265 all thinking bears witness to Thomism and the growth of heterodoxy'[20] and the

---

[18] Since Llull's views are, as will become clear, wholly antithetical to those of the terminist *modernistae*, and especially of the 'nominalist' Ockham, the Venerable Inceptor serves as a contrast in all instances.

[19] See Urvoy, *Penser l'islam*, pp. 55-70 on the cultural milieu of Majorcan Islam for an account of these movements.

[20] *Medieval Thought: St Augustine to Ockham* (Harmondsworth: Penguin Books, 1958), p. 232.

testimony of Ramon Llull is loud and vehement. His anti-Averroist campaigns at Paris and extreme Realism make the contrast between his arguments and those of Aquinas especially instructive, particularly because of the very different character of their methods. Llull does show clear affinities on specific questions with many past authorities from Algazel and Avicenna among the Arabs to Anselm, the Victorines, and Bonaventure among the Latins. In every case, Llull's views deserve more scrutiny from specialists knowledgeable in the relevant primary literature; the identification of Llull's 'sources', difficult though it might be, still aids significantly in understanding the relative contribution of his moralizing method to the formulation of his positions. The comparison of his views to the various parallels or antitheses noted in this study does suggest that his moralizing procedure has an almost overwhelming impact on any body of doctrine that it interprets.

Life of Ramon Llull

The reader unfamiliar with Llull will undoubtedly feel by now the need for some fuller orientation regarding his career. The following brief account of his life and works attempts to satisfy that need, but necessarily ignores many interesting details and passes over several controversial questions of chronology; for a fuller account, the reader should consult J. N. Hillgarth's fine study.[21]

Ramon Llull was born on the island of Majorca, probably in 1232. He was the only child of a wealthy French-descended merchant from Barcelona who settled on Majorca with James I of Aragon after the king conquered the island from the Moors in 1229. Llull was raised and educated at court during the latter part of his early years, about which little is known. He was eventually appointed seneschal to the young James II of Majorca, who received the island from his father in 1253. Traditional accounts have left colourful stories about Llull's gay life at court, especially his amorous exploits and cultivation of the troubadour lyric. He married one Blanca Picany in 1257, and had two children.

Sometime in 1263 or 1264, however, Llull underwent a profound religious conversion, induced by repeated visions of Christ crucified. At this time Llull is said to have conceived the three great goals of his life's work as a missionary and proselyte; these form the indispensable

---

[21] *Ramon Lull and Lullism in Fourteenth-Century France* (Oxford: Oxford University Press, 1971), pp. 1–134.

context for any understanding of his doctrines and activities. They were: (1) the founding of schools to teach missionaries the oriental languages, (2) the writing of a book to prove Christian doctrine, and (3) the propagation of the Faith among the infidels. Inspired by a Franciscan sermon, Llull renounced his life at court, sold all his goods, and went on pilgrimages to Rocamadour, Compostela, and other shrines. Returning to Barcelona in 1265, he met Ramon de Penyafort, the redoubtable former Dominican Master-General, who approved Llull's goals, but urged that he prepare himself adequately in advance. Consequently Llull returned to Majorca for nine years of study, which included learning Arabic from a Muslim slave. He seems to have acquired the rudiments of a traditional medieval arts curriculum education, and acquainted himself with the literature of Augustine, Anselm, the Victorines, and Franciscan authorities, perhaps by reading materials available at the Dominican and Franciscan churches then existent in Palma de Majorca.[22] Similarly he acquired some knowledge of traditional Islamic theology and philosophy, apparently from their more popular manifestations among the various schools or sects of Majorcan Islam, and from versions (perhaps excerpted) of the works of great Arab authorities such as Algazel. Dominique Urvoy has noted, however, that it is unlikely that Llull would have found any Islamic teachers capable of expounding Arab philosophy to him in a very sophisticated way.[23] During these years Llull produced the Arabic versions (now lost) of his first works: a compendium of the *Logic* of Algazel, the *Libre del gentil e los tres savis*, and the *Libre de contemplació en Déu*, a seminal work and the first of Llull's encyclopaedic compilations. In 1274, Llull received an intellectual 'revelation' on Mount Randa near Palma, which effected the transformation of his nascent doctrine of Divine Dignities or attributes of the Godhead into a global metaphysical system. The first *Ars magna*, or *Ars compendiosa inveniendi veritatem*, completed shortly afterwards, was the first redaction of this system, the famed Lullian *Art*.

In 1275 Llull left Majorca to seek the patronage of his former associate James II, now ruler of Majorca, Roussillon, Cerdanya, and Montpellier. He thus began a life of nearly continual peregrination. Llull's works were approved by a friar minor appointed to inspect them

[22] See J. N. Hillgarth, 'La biblioteca de La Real: fuentes posibles de Llull', *Estudios Lulianos*, 7 (1963), 5–17.
[23] *Penser l'islam*, pp. 152–3.

by James II. Llull then received approval for establishing a monastery at Miramar on Majorca; this was founded in 1276 with thirteen Franciscans who were to study the Liberal Arts, Theology, oriental languages, Islamic doctrine, and Llull's own *Art*. Its foundation was confirmed later that year by Pope John XXI, Peter of Spain. Very little is known about the subsequent ten years of Llull's life, except that he continued to produce works in Latin, Arabic, and Catalan. These included tracts advocating his missionary plans and perhaps his literary masterpiece, the *Libre de Blanquerna*.

The death of Pope Honorius IV (3 April 1287) and Llull's lack of academic credentials frustrated his attempt to obtain a papal hearing at Rome that year for his proposals. He went then to Paris, where he was licensed by one of the Chancellors, Bertaud de Saint-Denis, and authorized to teach his *Art*. This licence indicates that Llull must have possessed some academic qualifications, but their source or nature is uncertain, and licensing requirements were still flexible at this time.[24] In Paris he began his long conflict with the Latin Averroists and found a new and powerful patron in Philip the Fair of France, nephew of James II; James was now weakened by the loss of Majorca in 1285 to nephew Alfonso III of Aragon. Returning to Montpellier in 1289, Llull wrote several works and composed a second, more simplified, redaction of his *Art*, the *Ars inventiva veritatis*.

About 1290 Llull began an association with the Spiritual Franciscans, whose unorthodox millenarian doctrines were commonly associated with him, even during his own lifetime, although he rejected their views and wrote several anti-Spiritual works. Llull knew well the notorious Arnold of Vilanova who, since the death of Peter John Olivi, was the leading Spiritual of the time. The Franciscan Minister-General Ramon Gaufredi, deposed by Boniface VIII in 1295 for his tolerance of the Spirituals, met Llull in 1289 during the Chapter-General of the Order at Rieti, and authorized Llull to teach his *Art* to Franciscan houses at Apulia and Rome (26 October 1290). In 1290 Llull visited Genoa, where he completed an Arabic translation of the *Ars inventiva*, and then Rome, where he presented to Pope Nicholas IV his first treatise advocating a crusade, the *Tractatus de modo convertendi infideles*. Llull's proposals were not received favourably, despite the

---

[24] On these requirements, see Gordon Leff, *Paris and Oxford Universities in the Thirteenth and Fourteenth Centuries* (New York: John Wiley & Sons, 1968), p. 155.

eventual fall of Acre in 1291 and a renewed crusading fervour in Europe; he returned to Genoa, whose citizens welcomed him and his plans.

In Genoa Llull suffered some kind of spiritual crisis: he vacillated with anguish between joining the Dominican or Franciscan orders; the former had already rejected his *Art*, but a revelation indicated that it was his only path of personal salvation; he eventually joined the Franciscans, whose vows he took at the rank of tertiary. Deciding ultimately on an overseas mission, Llull enlisted the support of James II of Aragon, who recommended him to King Abu Hafs Omar I of Tunis, where Llull arrived in mid-1293. Adopting a common Dominican tactic, Llull challenged local Islamic scholars to a debate on the relative truth of their faiths, which led to his speedy banishment from Tunis and return to Naples. He visited Majorca briefly again in 1294.

Llull continued to entreat the Papacy. After the renunciation of the Holy See in 1295 by the hermit Pope Celestine V, Llull directed his recently composed *Disputació dels cinc savis* and *Petitio Raymundi* (which urged missions to the Tartars) to Celestine's successor, Boniface VIII. At Rome between September of 1295 and April of 1296, Llull completed the greatest of his encyclopaedic works, the *Arbre de sciència*. After visiting James II of Majorca at Montpellier, Llull returned to Paris for three years, where he disputed with the 'Averroists' and sought the aid of Philip the Fair. Llull supported Philip's campaign against the powerful Templar Order as a means of achieving his own goal, the unification of all the military orders for a general crusade. At Rome once more in 1299, his views were heard with little enthusiasm, and he went from there to Barcelona. At the court of James II of Aragon, Llull received permission to proselytize the Moors within James's realm, and dedicated more works to him and his wife, Blanche of Anjou, before returning to Majorca.

After 1300 Llull's original literary production diminished considerably; he turned instead to the revision and amplification of earlier works in order to complete the envisaged universal scope of his *Art*. He also abandoned—temporarily—the advocacy of further crusades and undertook a missionary journey to the eastern Mediterranean. In Cyprus King Henry de Lusignan II refused Llull's request to proselytize the Eastern monophysites; he held disputations with Orthodox theologians, but quickly departed after an attempt on his life. While at Limassol Llull met the last Master of the Temple, Jacques de Molay (burnt at the stake in 1314), who obtained permission for Llull to visit Armenia, a Templar ally. Llull travelled to Armenia, and perhaps to Jerusalem, during 1301 and 1302.

From 1302 to 1308 Llull lived alternately in Genoa and Montpellier, centres of support and patronage for him, and wrote a number of works. These included especially the *Liber de ascensu et descensu intellectus* (March 1304), the most refined statement of Llull's contemplative programme, and the *Liber de fine* (April 1305), the most complete expression of his missionary and crusading plans.

Llull failed in new attempts to interest Clement V, the first Avignon Pope, and the Genoans in a crusade. Only James II of Aragon responded to Llull's proposals with the ill-fated seige of Almería in 1309. In 1307 Llull embarked from Majorca to Bougie for his third overseas mission. There he was immediately imprisoned, but then exiled by its king at the request of James II of Aragon. On the return voyage, Llull was shipwrecked and rescued by vessels from Pisa, whose citizens supported him generously. At Pisa in 1308, Llull completed his *Ars generalis ultima* (begun in November of 1305), and its epitome, the *Ars brevis*.

Llull made another round of visits to the Pope at Avignon, the Pisans, and the Genoans in order to promote unsuccessfully the crusading proposals set out in his *Liber de acquisitione Terrae Sanctae* (March 1309), which supported the French campaign against the Byzantines. In 1309 Llull made his last visit to Paris, where, despite 'Averroist' opposition, he publicly read his *Art* and received the commendation of forty masters of the university (February 1310), Philip the Fair (August 1310), and the Chancellor (September 1311). This was Llull's last appeal for support to his powerful patron of nearly twenty-five years. In 1311 an account of Llull's life, known as the *Vita coetanea*, was composed, perhaps from his own recollections, at the Carthusian house of Vauvert outside Paris; a large collection of Llull's works was kept there and it remained a major centre of Lullism after his death. That same year Llull wrote several short tracts in preparation for attending the Ecumenical Council of Vienne. *Lo concili* set forth his three goals: conquest of the Holy Land, writing books to prove the Faith, and establishing language schools. The Papacy fulfilled this last proposal with the creation of language chairs at major European universities in 1312. *En route* to Vienne, Llull composed the *Disputatio Raymundi phantastici et clerici* and at the Council presented his *Petitio Raymundi in concilio generali ad acquirendam Terram Sanctam*.

The portrayal of himself as a *phantasticus* or as 'Ramon the fool' in the *Blanquerna* (82. 6) is an entirely probable representation of how his contemporaries regarded him. They never did consider his proposals worthy of their material support, and after 1311 Llull appears to have abandoned entirely the idea of a crusade. He returned to Majorca, where, nearly eighty years old, he dictated a will on 26 April 1313. In it he provided especially for the posthumous disposition and dissemination of his writings. Finally Llull went to Messina to appeal to Frederick III of Sicily, a friend of the Spirituals with an interest in overseas missions, but Llull received no support from him either. After completing various short works there, Llull undertook one last mission to Tunis, arriving there in November 1315. His last work, the *Liber de maiori fine intellectus, amoris et honoris*, is dated at Tunis in December 1315. Llull died early the next year, martyred at Bougie according to one probably apocryphal tradition, or more likely upon returning to his native Majorca, where he was buried in the convent of Saint Francis.

The Art *of Ramon Llull*

The preceding sketch of Llull's life is necessarily cursory, but also inherently incomplete, because it fails to describe his philosophy as well. Many scholars have affirmed, with J. N. Hillgarth, that 'Llull's life, superficially extraordinarily picturesque, is intimately linked to his philosophy' or that 'Llull's philosophy is his autobiography'.[25] It would be impossible here to mention every facet of Llull's work, or to describe certain stages in its evolution from the *Libre de contemplació* and *Ars compendiosa inveniendi veritatem* of the 1270s to the *Ars generalis ultima* of 1308. Some of these developments that relate to Logic are the subject of subsequent chapters; the rest await the interested reader's attention in other studies.[26] Among these, a long-neglected

[25] *Ramon Lull and Lullism*, p. 1.

[26] There is an extensive bibliography on Llull, comprising many works of diverse value. Besides the above-mentioned studies of the brothers Carreras y Artau (n. 5), Platzeck (nn. 10–12), Tusquets (n. 7), and Urvoy (n. 6), the following are also especially important: Robert D. F. Pring-Mill, *El microcosmos lul·lià* (Oxford: Dolphin, 1961); 'The Trinitarian World-Picture of Ramon Lull', *Romanistisches Jahrbuch*, 7 (1955–6), 229–56; 'Ramon Lull y las tres potencias del alma', *Estudios Lulianos*, 12 (1968), 101–30; and 'The Analogical Structure of the Lullian Art', in *Islamic Philosophy and the Classical Tradition. Essays presented to Richard Walzer* (Columbia, SC: University of South Carolina Press, 1973), pp. 315–26; Frances A. Yates, 'The Art of Ramon Lull', *Journal of the Warburg and Courtauld Institute*, 17 (1954), 115–73. The recent study by the eminent Arabist Miguel Cruz Hernández, *El pensamiento de Ramon Llull* (Madrid: Castalia, 1977) is to be avoided because of its uncritical reliance on secondary studies and numerous factual inaccuracies, especially in its critical apparatus.

series of articles in the old *Revista Luliana*, written by the Neo-scholastic Lullian apologist Antonio Raymundo Pascual, deserve notice as one of the most penetrating and lucid expositions of Llull's philosophy as a specifically Scholastic system of thought;[27] frequent references to it appear below. For the purposes of this study, the summary offered here treats the major features of Llull's philosophy in three broad categories—the spiritual, metaphysical, and dialectical.

Among the spiritual principles of Llull's thought stands one that is absolutely primary to all others, as Pascual recognized long ago,[28] because it defines the status of everything in the world. This is Llull's doctrine of 'intention', which embraces a dense confection of Classical and Christian commonplaces regarding the teleology of the good. In his *Doctrina pueril* of the 1280s, a primer written for his son, Llull summarizes them thus:

There are two intentions, son, in the rational process (*moviment*), first and second. Hence, if you know the nature and property of these two intentions, you will know many things: and if you know how to order them in your soul, you will have many virtues.

The first intention is the final cause; the second is the material and formal: and the form is a first intention with respect to the matter . . . because the form is nearer to the final cause than matter.

. . . because man is nobler than the trees or beasts or other beings beneath him in nobility, God has decreed that man be for the first intention, and . . . the less noble for the second.

God is, son, nobler than man or any creature, and therefore God wishes that one act to serve, love, and know in Him the first intention, and in other things the second. Hence, if you hold God as first intention, you should love Him because He is good, because He created you, not because He will give you Paradise.[29] (92. 4–5, 7–8)

---

[27] 'Comparación del arte luliana con la Lógica de Aristóteles y la de los otros', *Revista Luliana*, 3, No. 25 (Oct. 1903), 251–60; 'Comparación de la lógica luliana con la aristotélica', *Revista Luliana*, vol. 4, No. 29 (Feb. 1904), 13–16; 'Comparación de la metafísica luliana con la aristotélica y la de otros', *Revista Luliana*, 4, No. 30 (Mar. 1904), 23–6; 'Del sistema del Arte Luliana y la solidez e infalibilidad de sus principios de discurrir en todas las cosas', *Revista Luliana*, 4, No. 31 (Apr. 1904), 39–43; 'De las definiciones de los principios universales', *Revista Luliana*, 4, No. 32 (May 1904), 51–5; 'De las condiciones universales', *Revista Luliana*, 4, No. 33 (Jun. 1904), 69–73; 'De las reglas generales', *Revista Luliana*, 4, No. 34 (Jul.–Sept. 1904), 102–11.
[28] 'Comparación del arte luliana con la Lógica de Aristóteles y la de los otros', p. 255 and 'De las reglas generales', p. 103.
[29] 'En moviment racional son, fill, dues entencions: primera e segona. On, si tu sabs la natura el propietat d estes dues entencions, moltes coses sabríes: e si les sabs ordonar en ta anima, moltes vertuts aurás.

As metaphysics, these claims assume Aristotle's identification of a being's ultimate good or perfection with its final cause and of the first mover as the ultimate good and end of all things (*Metaph.* 5. 16 1021b20–5 and 11. 1 1059a36–7); for a Christian thinker such as Aquinas, of course, this is God (1a. 5, 4). As theology, Llull's claims recall Augustine's distinction between use and enjoyment (*Doc. christ.* 1. 3. 3) and Anselm's arguments that the first principle of human existence is to love, know, and serve God, because man resembles God as created in His image (*Monol.* 68). Llull repeats this same argument in his *Libre de meravelles* (3, 46, 68) and describes man's orientation to God in the *Libre de intenció* (1. 1) as his Will's natural desire for the good, in the manner of Aristotle's axiom (*Eth.* 1. 1 1094a1). Aquinas acknowledges that man has a more immediate orientation towards God than plants or beasts, but adds that love of God is still only possible through grace (2a. 2ae. 2, 3). Llull tends to view this natural intention as a universal desire of the creature for the Creator, and it is fruitless to attempt to understand his work without recognizing the constant assumption of this principle. In a broad sense, Llull's missionological concerns derive from his doctrine of intention, as expressions of his own obligation to know, love, and remember God. Even the arguments of his *Art* serve this first intention: as he notes in the *Libre de meravelles* (63), it is better to honour God than to convert men. The range of physical and metaphysical relationships that Llull correlates with this intention in the *Doctrina pueril* suggests how it constitutes in man a kind of natural sympathy of the soul, and the Intellect's necessary attraction to its own proper object is a major tenet of his gnoseology. The naturalistic character of this attraction is especially evident in the *Introductorium magnae Artis generalis* of 1306, when he refers to the Divine Dignity of *Voluntas* as the '*pondus naturalis*' in any creature.[30] Such a broad conception of the desire or Will active in Llull's intention

---

'Primera entencio es la cosa final; segona es la materia e la forma: e la forma es primera entencio a esguardament de la forma: ¿e sabs per que? per so car la forma es pus prop a la causa final que la materia.

'. . . car home es pus noble cosa quels arbres ne les besties ne les altres coses que son dejús home en nobilitat, per assò ha Deus volgut que hom sia per la primera entencio, e les coses qui no son ten nobles sien per la segona.

'Deus es, fill, pus noble cosa que hom ne nulla creatura; e per assò Deus vol que hom age en ell a servir, amar e conèxer, la primera entencio, e a les altres coses la segona. On, si tu has a Deu la primera entencio, amar l as més per so car es bo, que per so car t a creat ne per so que t don gloria.' (*Obres Originals*, I. 179–80.)

[30] Cited in Platzeck, 'La combinatoria luliana', p. 604.

makes it unlikely that any single authority, such as Algazel or Richard of Saint Victor, suggested this doctrine to him.[31]

The metaphysical principles of Llull's work all serve to define this relationship between Creator and creature, and thus propound the exemplarism that Van Steenberghen has declared basic to all medieval Christian thought.[32] For Llull, as for Hugh of Saint Victor, 'all nature bespeaks God' (*Didasc.* 6. 5); Llull's conception of all creation as an expression of God places him squarely in the tradition of Bonaventure and Saint Francis, as Leff has noted.[33] God imposed this likeness of himself upon the world in order for man to recognize and honour him (*LM* 4).[34] All being is thus a univocal sign of God.[35] Llull conceives this exemplary relationship on the basis of an ontology of participation that reveals itself in resemblance; he refuses the Aristotelian metaphysics and physics of causality, and regularly interprets the four causes participationally as relations of greater to lesser, usually by appealing to the axiom 'every agent causes something like itself'.[36] Even though Llull explicitly recognizes that there is no proportion of Creator to creature,[37] it is always preferable to regard his exemplarist arguments as dynamically proportional, rather than statically analogous, definitions of an active participation. Llull himself never uses the term 'analogy'.[38] The specific instruments of this participation are the nine Divine Dignities that Llull fixes as the uncreated, essential attributes of God's being; these are *Bonitas, Magnitudo, Aeternitas* (or *Duratio*), *Potestas, Sapientia, Voluntas, Virtus, Veritas,* and *Gloria.* These Absolute *Principia,* as he also calls them, are in effect 'relational concepts' that signify God with reference to the created world.[39] Along with these

---

[31] As Platzeck considers, *Raimund Lull*, 1. 103–4.

[32] *The Philosophical Movement in the Thirteenth Century* (Edinburgh: Thomas Nelson, 1955), Ch. 3–4. Cf. Pascual, 'Comparación del arte luliana con la Lógica de Aristóteles y la de los otros', p. 258 and 'Comparación de la metafísica luliana', p. 30.

[33] *Medieval Thought*, p. 238.

[34] Cf. Pascual, 'Del sistema del Arte luliana', p. 42.

[35] See the excellent discussion by Louis Sala-Molins, *La Philosophie de l'amour chez Raymond Lulle* (Paris and The Hague: Mouton, 1974), pp. 207–12.

[36] As Platzeck rightly stresses, 'La combinatoria luliana', p. 598. Louis-Bertrand Geiger discusses many of the participational axioms invoked by Llull in *La Participation dans la philosophie de S. Thomas d'Aquin* (Paris: J. Vrin, 1953).

[37] e.g. *Liber de inventione maiori* 3. 9 (p. 302).

[38] Platzeck himself notes this, but insists on speaking of analogy, and thereby neglects the dynamic character of participation through resemblance, and its expression in an active discursive process of moralization ('La combinatoria luliana', pp. 595–600).

[39] Platzeck emphasizes this relational aspect, 'La combinatoria luliana', p. 593.

Llull posits nine Relative *Principia* by means of which the Dignities mutually communicate their natures and diffuse them throughout all creation. These form three triads of *Differentia*, *Concordantia*, and *Contrarietas*; *Principium*, *Medium*, and *Finis*; and *Maioritas*, *Aequalitas*, and *Minoritas*. These Relative *Principia* define the 'participation and mutual disposition' of all created beings among themselves, too.[40] *Contrarietas* and *Minoritas* are in fact only fully applicable to created beings, since such qualities cannot pertain to the perfection of Divine Being. Llull claims that these 'substantial and accidental principles of all things', as he often terms them, are the foundation of the inspired doctrine revealed to him on Mount Randa. The writings of John Scotus Erigena, Algazel, the Jewish *sephiroth*, and Islamic *hadras* (Divine Attributes), have all been proposed as direct sources for Llull's scheme of Dignities. Of course, he may also not have followed any one model, but rather—and perhaps more probably—devised such a scheme precisely because he recognized its broad affinities with various Christian, Jewish, and Islamic precedents.[41]

Llull also adds in the later versions of his *Art* the three 'innate correlative principles' of agent, patient, and act. These correlatives are a metaphysical reality in every entity and apparently replaced similar distinctions originally listed among the sixteen Absolute and Relative *Principia* of the early versions of his *Art*. Emanating from the Dignities and the triune nature of God himself, these three innate correlatives impose a trinitarian image on every created being. For example, the possession of *Bonitas* yields in any being the capacity to be *bonificativum* (or *bonificans*), to be *bonificabile* (or *bonificatus*) and *bonificare*. The correlatives are the chief manifestation of the trinitarianism present throughout Llull's philosophy, which probably derives from the examples of Augustine and Richard of Saint Victor in their treatises *De trinitate*, while the particular triple scheme of participial terms has parallels in various Latin and Arab authorities.[42] These schemes do not seem to have any necessary formal value as expressions of fixed grammatical or logical relationships, however.[43] The sort of broadly 'transitive' relation that the correlatives do define is best understood as Llull's means of expressing his fundamentally 'activistic' interpretation

---

[40] This is Pascual's felicitous comment, 'De las definiciones', p. 54.

[41] See Urvoy, *Penser l'islam*, p. 67.

[42] Platzeck reviews these, 'La combinatoria luliana', pp. 136–40.

[43] Platzeck makes this claim in several studies: 'La combinatoria luliana', p. 138; 'Raimund Lulls Auffassung von der Logik', p. 296; *La evolución de la lógica griega*, p. 126.

of the nature of being,[44] which attempts to generalize the Neoplatonic dictum that 'the good diffuses itself' to all the *Principia* and hence to every aspect of every being's existence.[45] It formalizes a good operation as the sort of natural sympathy that must link a good cause and its good effect.[46] This strongly activist emanationism gives Llull's metaphysics and his arguments from it a marked determinist cast that contrasts to the new emphasis on God's freedom among his Scholastic contemporaries.[47]

Llull also advocates many other more conventional metaphysical positions: an extreme Realism, universal essences for all substantial and accidental forms, plurality of substantial forms, and universal hylemorphism. While these positions evidently correspond to so-called Augustinian and Franciscan schools of thought around 1300, Llull's adherence to many positions that were almost anachronistic in his day makes it difficult to identify satisfactorily his real affiliation with any current movement or posture in the schools. Llull's greatest affinities seem to lie, as noted already, with the Prescholastic authorities of the twelfth century, some of whom, such as Anselm and Richard of Saint Victor, figure among his predilect sources.

The dialectical principles of Llull's philosophy include the symbolic devices that made his Great Universal Art especially notorious, even though their connection to the spiritual and metaphysical principles already mentioned is almost entirely incidental or extraneous. Llull designates the nine Absolute and Relative *Principia* with the letters B to K of the Alphabet (A is reserved to indicate the totality of all nine in the Godhead). By inscribing these letters about the peripheries of circular figures, or enclosing them in the chambers of matrix-like tables, he mechanically generates their permutations and combinations. Thus he creates an *ars combinatoria* of all the possible manifestations of the Dignities in creation (see Illustrations 1–4). The Figure

[44] By far the best account of this feature of Llull's system is Louis Sala-Molins, *La Philosophie de l'amour chez Raymond Lull*, but his attempt to interpret every element of the *Art* from this perspective is excessive and unconvincing.

[45] This study has unfortunately been unable to benefit from consultation of the new analysis of Llull's correlatives by J. Gayà Estelric, *La teoría luliana de los correlativos. Historia de su formación conceptual* (Palma de Mallorca, 1979) (cited in *Opera Latina*, 10. x). On the doctrine of the Good and others from the Christian Neoplatonic tradition to which Llull pertains, see the superb study of Stephen Gersh, *From Iamblichus to Eriugena* (Leiden: E. J. Brill, 1978).

[46] As noted by Pascual, 'De las definiciones', p. 52.

[47] Compare Llull's views to those of Scotus or Ockham, reviewed by Leff, *The Dissolution of the Medieval Outlook*, pp. 13–14 and 55.

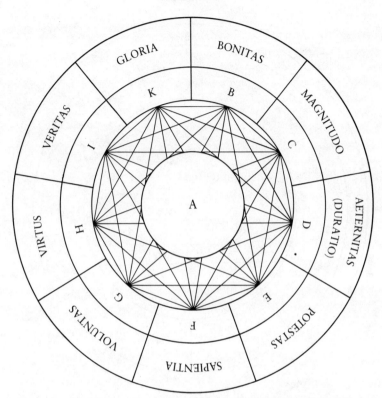

1. Figure A. The lines between the letters symbolize the convertibility of Llull's *Principia.*

A shows the coessential interrelations of the Absolute *Principia*, the Figure T the triads of Relative *Principia*, the Table possible pairs of B and K, and the Combinatory Figure possible triple combinations of the letters (by means of three rotating concentric circles). Jewish cabbalistic speculation, as represented in the monumental *Zohar*, flourished in Spain during Llull's lifetime, and has often been considered an immediate model for the Lullian *ars combinatoria*. Platzeck has rightly argued, however, that popular cabbalistic works like the *Yezirah* emphasize the exegesis of individual letters rather than the significance of their combinations. Moreover, the illustrations from the well-known *De natura rerum* of Isidore, as well as others from the works of Boethius and certain authors of the Chartres school, offer ample precedents for the use of geometrical or mathematical schemes such as Llull

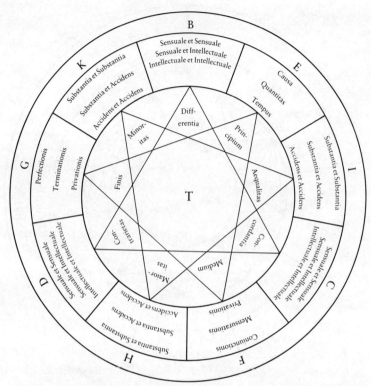

2. Figure T. The points of each triangle indicate necessary relationships for all beings.

devised.[48] Recently, Dominique Urvoy has suggested that the poetic hermeneutics of the *trobar clus*, which Llull evidently knew, perhaps conditioned his exegetical practice,[49] and this possibility certainly finds confirmation in the quasi-rhetorical functions of moralization examined in this study. As is often the case, Llull's doctrines or ideas are too generalized to admit a single source, or bear only a superficial resemblance to a specific work, which proves to be more dissimilar than similar in the particulars of the doctrines that it offers. The use of such a simple mechanical scheme as the *ars combinatoria* is, finally, one of the signally popularizing features of Llull's *Art*.

[48] See the very good discussion by Hillgarth, *Ramon Lull and Lullism*, pp. 19–20.
[49] *Penser l'islam*, pp. 72–90.

BC	CD	DE	EF	FG	GH	HI	IK
BD	CE	DF	EG	FH	GI	HK	
BE	CF	DG	EH	FI	GK		
BF	CG	DH	EI	FK			
BG	CH	DI	EK				
BH	CI	DK					
BI	CK						
BK							

3. Combinatory Table. Each chamber combines two letters from Llull's Alphabet.

The purpose of these combinatory methods is to find all the relationships joining the nine Absolute and Relative *Principia* and other sets of nine categories designated by the letters B to K (see Illustration 5). Identification of these relationships is facilitated through Llull's nine *Regulae* or questions, which function as topics of invention, as Platzeck explains,[50] and imitate similar schemes from ancient rhetoric,[51] the Scholastic *introductio ad artes*,[52] and Llull's Muslim contemporary Ibn Sab'in (d. 1270).[53] Llull's arguments seek 'the metaphysical reduction of all created things to the Dignities . . . and the comparison of particular things in the light of the Dignities'.[54] It is essential to recognize that Llull always saw the Dignities as

[50] 'La combinatoria luliana', p. 147.

[51] e.g. Fortunatianus, *Ars rhetoricae* 2. 1; Pseudo-Augustine, *De rhetorica*, 7–8; Boethius, *De differentiis topicis*, 4 (1205D) and *In Isagoge Porphyrii* 1. 1.

[52] See R. W. Hunt, 'The Introductions to the "Artes" in the Twelfth Century', in *Studia Mediaevalia in honorem admodum Reverendi Patris Raymundi Josephi Martin* (Bruges: De Tempel, 1948), pp. 85–112.

[53] Urvoy discusses Llull's 'remarkable' affinities with the theories of Ibn Sab'in, pp. 381–6, drawing on a paper by Charles Lohr not available for consultation in preparing this study: 'Ibn Sab'in of Murcia and the Development of the Lullian Art', presented at the Segundo Congreso Internacional de Lulismo (Mallorca, October 1976), and to appear in the *Acta* of that conference.

[54] Hillgarth, *Ramon Lull and Lullism*, p. 10.

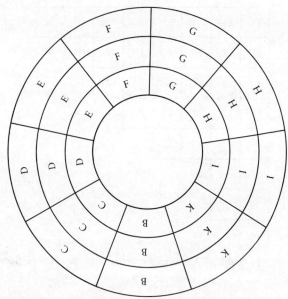

4. Combinatory Figure. The two inner circles revolve, providing triple combinations of letters.

'principles of being and knowing' alike. Hence the *Art* also seems universally applicable to philosophical argument, and Llull apparently 'believed that he had discovered, or had had revealed to him, an art of thinking which was infallible in all spheres because based on the actual structure of reality, a logic which followed the true patterns of the universe'.[55] Thus Llull calls his programme an 'art of finding truth' (*ars inveniendi veritatem*). Robert D. F. Pring-Mill has succinctly observed that the 'search for truth by means of the Lullian Art is always a search for congruence with God'.[56] Llull's *Art* is thus a programme for recognizing the agreement between a thing and Supreme Truth that is the thing's truth or *rectitudo*, in Anselm's view (*De ver.* 13). Pring-Mill suggests that a graphic means of charting this agreement is to imagine a grid in which the nine Absolute and Relative *Principia* (along with their correlatives) are set horizontally above the hierarchically and vertically arranged nine *Subiecta* (levels of being from God and Angel to Elements and 'Instruments'). The analogical

[55] Yates, 'The Art of Ramon Lull', p. 117.
[56] 'Trinitarian World-Picture', p. 255.

	PRINCIPIA ABSOLUTA	PRINCIPIA RELATIVA	QUAESTIONES	SUBIECTA	VIRTUTES	VITIA
B	Bonitas	Differentia	Utrum ?	Deus	Iustitia	Avaritia
C	Magnitudo	Concordantia	Quid ?	Angelus	Prudentia	Gula
D	Aeternitas	Contrarietas	De quo ?	Coelum	Fortitudo	Luxuria
E	Potestas	Principium	Quare ?	Homo	Temperantia	Superbia
F	Sapientia	Medium	Quantum ?	Imaginatio	Fides	Acidia
G	Voluntas	Finis	Quale ?	Sensitiva	Spes	Invidia
H	Virtus	Maioritas	Quando ?	Vegetativa	Charitas	Ira
I	Veritas	Aequalitas	Ubi ?	Elementativa	Patientia	Mendacium
K	Gloria	Minoritas	Quomodo ? Cum quo ?	Instrumen- tativa	Pietas	Inconstantia

5. Llull's Alphabet. Specialized applications of his *Art* to other fields include appropriate additional values for each letter.

descent and ascent of such a grid, the contemplation of the chain of being by tracing the differential diffusion of the Lullian *Principia* throughout creation, provides the plan for works such as the *Libre de meravelles*, *Arbre de sciència*, and *Liber de ascensu et descensu intellectus*, whose rubrics form summaries of the stages in this process.[57] Llull conceives this process as being performed by the three faculties of the human mind—the Intellect, Will, and Memory—whose primary tasks are, respectively, to know, to love, and to recall God. In fulfilling these tasks, they most truly exist and most truly know, love, or remember. In this way Llull's *Art* serves to help the human soul achieve its first intention, and thereby perfect its nature by attaining its proper natural object, God.

The mechanics of Llull's *ars combinatoria* does nothing more than to collate the values symbolized by the letters combined. The Lullian artist must then construct an argument about those values that 'correctly' relates them. In this respect, all the combinatory relations reduce to *Concordantia* or *Contrarietas*, that is, to separation or combination, negation or affirmation, as Pascual recognized long ago.[58] This discursive elaboration of identity and difference in Llull's arguments is one of the chief features examined in this study. As regards the form of this discourse, Urvoy has rightly noted that Llull's very simple conception of his combinations as propositional structures merely projects the basic view of phrase structure accepted in the West since Aristotle.[59] As regards the content of this discourse, Llull expects the mind naturally to distinguish true from false combinatory relationships, according to its natural proportion and attraction to its proper object, as explained more fully in Chapters 7 and 19 of this study. But the correctness that the mind perceives obviously depends on the whole mass of Llull's proportionally conceived spiritual and metaphysical principles, their corollaries, and consequences. Pascual well observed that the move from any universal principle to its particular realization in one of Llull's arguments inevitably requires introducing one of these

[57] This scheme, and Llull's other notions of the hierarchy of being, are magnificently represented in the illustrations to the *Breviculum* compiled by Thomas Le Myésier, a French disciple of Llull; Hillgarth discusses the significance of Le Myésier's work at length in *Ramon Lull and Lullism*, pp. 135–268.

[58] 'De las condiciones', pp. 70–3; cf. the similar conclusions by Platzeck, 'La combinatoria luliana', p. 132, and Sala-Molins, *La Philosophie de l'amour*, p. 210, where he renames them 'difference' and 'movement'.

[59] *Penser l'islam*, p. 164.

other principles in order to explain, or moralize, the homology of universal and particular.[60] Some of these principles he regularly includes in his redactions of his *Art* as the 'Hundred Forms', or definitions of one hundred essences ranging from the *Principia* themselves to the four Aristotelian causes to the powers of the soul. Still, the relevance of these to any argument is rarely immediate, and instead requires the exegetical work or moralization already described. Thanks to his manifold arguments from analogy, congruence, proportion, or resemblance, Llull is always able to 'find' the truth in any relationship of terms generated by the combinatory mechanism of his *Art*. His attempt to revise Aristotelian propositional and syllogistic structure using the same procedure imparts to them his own basic theological and metaphysical values, creating the peculiarly 'spiritual logic' that is the subject of this study.

[60] 'De las condiciones', pp. 71–2.

PART ONE

Early Writings to 1303

I

Llull's First Summa of Logic: *Logica Algazelis*

ALMOST the whole range of Llull's logical learning, including its popular, natural, and moralizing character, appears in his first logical writing, the *Compendium logicae Algazelis* (1275?). Llull's treatise is of paramount importance because it reveals, at the very outset of his career, the range of logical doctrine known to him and his selection of particular topics for special development in his later writings. It serves thus as a gauge for measuring Llull's individual intellectual development and as a pre-calculated balance sheet of his debt to contemporary Scholastic teachings. It does not, however, show that Llull had an aboriginal interest in formal logic that continued from this early work throughout his career.[1] The *Logica Algazelis* remains Llull's only specifically logical work for almost thirty years. This period constitutes the first phase in his attention to logical doctrine; its distinguishing characteristics are the limited and idiosyncratic treatment of only the most elementary logical doctrines, usually in a popularizing manner as part of larger encyclopaedic works, or as incidental contributions to the larger problems of theological argumentation, demonstration, or disputation that concern him most. His remarks on Logic in some works from this period do show his developing awareness of Scholastic Logic as a system of argument in need of wholesale reform, which becomes the dominant concern of his later period; similarly, they occasionally display his efforts to assimilate the Scholastic precepts surveyed in his own *Logica Algazelis*, but more often ignore or barely acknowledge them. This first period in Llull's cultivation of Logic is, in effect, a prelude to the eventual confrontation between his own *Art* and Aristotelian demonstration.

---

[1] As Charles Lohr suggests in his introduction to the *Liber de novis fallaciis* (*Opera Latina*, 11. 3).

Llull's adaptation of Algazel

The *Compendium Logicae Algazelis* is nominally an adaptation of Algazel's account of Logic in his *Maqāṣid al-falāsifa* ('Meanings of the Philosophers') composed at Baghdad between 1091 and 1095.[2] The *Maqāṣid* is a survey of philosophical and theological doctrines, based on Avicenna's *Dānish Nāmeh* ('Book of Science'), and presents the background for Algazel's critique of those doctrines in his *Tahāfut al-falāsifa* ('Incoherence of the Philosophers'). The *Maqāṣid* alone was translated into Latin, probably between 1151 and 1166, by Dominicus Gundissalinus and other scholars working at Toledo. The Latin version then circulated widely in the West, and was later revised. Llull made a compendium in Arabic directly from an Arabic version of Algazel's work, perhaps with the aid of the Moorish slave who taught him that language.[3] Llull then translated this Arabic compendium into Latin while at Montpellier later, as the opening lines of the Latin version indicate:

Deus ad laudem tue clemencie a qua singule gracie emanantur et consolationem scolarium afectantium suscipere pabulum sciencie logicalis, presens libellus continens partem logice Algazelis ac etiam de theologia et phylosophia paululum comprehendens, in Montepesulano illo anuente qui regnat ubique, translatus est de arabico in latinum, cuius titulos est: incipit logice Algazelis. (Intro.; p. 94)

The circumstances that these lines describe have puzzled scholars of Llull's work. The students in the Arts Faculty at Montpellier already possessed Latin versions of Algazel's text. Llull's work would probably not have been especially pertinent to their studies anyway: the phrase 'a little bit from Theology and Philosophy' understates the amount of extraneous material, some from other sources, some from Llull's own invention, that his compendium includes. Miguel Cruz Hernández has suggested that this phrase describes the text of Algazel as Llull found it, in one of the manuals common among the schools of Islamic Spain, which offered somewhat free summaries of philosophical classics such as the *Maqāṣid*. Llull's version would thus be a sort of notebook based

---

[2] On Algazel and his work, see Margaret Smith, *Al-Ghazali, the Mystic* (London: Luzac & Co., 1949); Arent Jan Wensinck, *La Pensée de Ghazzali* (Paris: Adrien-Maisonneuve, 1940); and Charles Lohr, 'Logica Algazelis. Introduction and Critical Text', *Traditio*, 21 (1965), 223–90.

[3] So suggests Miguel Cruz Hernández, *El pensamiento de Ramon Llull*, p. 370. Urvoy argues in *Penser l'islam* (pp. 62, 152) that this slave would have been too unlearned to expound the text's doctrine to Llull.

on such a summary, compiled during his period of study from 1265 to 1275.[4] The mixing of topics perhaps reflects the eclectic philosophical culture of Majorcan Islam.[5]

Llull's Arabic and Latin versions of Algazel evidently are products of different circumstances of time, place, and purpose.[6] Dominique Urvoy characterizes Llull's entire adaptation of Algazel as 'precipitous' and not the work of an academic scholar.[7] In the introduction to the Latin text, the phrase 'consolation of students striving to comprehend the pablum of logical doctrine' has a pejoratively polemical ring that recalls Llull's later customary denunciations of the verbose inanity of Scholastic Logic and view of his own *Art* as a simpler, non-sophistical alternative to contemporary doctrines. This function of the *Logica Algazelis* led Jordi Rubió to assign its Latin translation to the second of the two visits made by Llull to Montpellier in 1275 and 1289. Because Llull had just returned from an unsuccessful attempt to promote his *Art*, at Paris he may have translated the Arabic version as part of a new effort to attract an audience at the Provençal university. On the other hand, the *Doctrina pueril*, composed sometime between 1282 and 1287, tells Llull's son that 'before you learn Logic in Latin, learn it in the vernacular, with the verses that are after this book' (73. 8). This possible allusion to the vernacular versified abridgement of the *Logica Algazelis*, analysed below, would of course place the date of translation at Montpellier in 1275. Tomás and Joaquín Carreras y Artau also argue that the probable origin of Llull's treatise in his earliest studies, which is obvious in similarities between the theological arguments of the *Logica Algazelis* and those of the *Libre de contemplació en Déu* of 1271–6, strongly favours the earlier date of 1275.[8]

The Catalan Lògica del Gatzel

The Latin *Logica Algazelis* and Catalan *Lògica del Gatzel* are not sufficiently different to merit individual analysis; because the latter displays somewhat better the basic features of Llull's method, it will

---

[4] Cruz Hernández, *El pensamiento de Ramon Llull*, pp. 67–8.

[5] Urvoy, *Penser l'islam*, p. 62.

[6] Charles Lohr analyses these exhaustively, if somewhat inconclusively, in *Raimundus Lullus' Compendium Logicae Algazelis. Quellen, Lehre, und Stellung in der Geschichte der Logik* (Freiburg im Breisgau: Albert-Ludwigs-Universität, 1967), pp. 28–39.

[7] *Penser l'islam*, p. 62.

[8] For their arguments, see 'La Lògica del Gazzali, posada en rims per En Ramon Lull', *Anuari de l'Institut d'Estudis Catalans*, 5 (1913–14), 319 and *Historia de la filosofía española*, 1. 349–50.

serve as the basis for subsequent references to his compendium of
Algazel, with the Latin version used chiefly for clarification. The verse,
vernacular, and slightly abridged form of the *Lògica del Gatzel* reflects
one of the most important features of all Llull's work—its popularizing
function—which he asserts in its very first lines:

> God, in order to honour You,
> we treat Logic briefly,
> which is a new compendium
> where my Intellect has recourse,
> and which translated from Latin into the vernacular
> in verses and plain words,
> so that one can demonstrate
> Logic and philosophizing
> to those ignorant of Latin
> or Arabic, so that you will
> direct me, Lord, in knowing
> and having a good intention.[9]   (lines 1–12)

It is especially curious that Llull treats both Arabic and Latin as
possible learned languages for his Catalan-speaking audience. Moreover, if the Arabic and Latin versions to which he refers are his own, it
is possible that he was not aware of the existence of any others. These
lines assert not only the popularization, but also the moralization of
Logic, according to the mediate and immediate intention of all creatures toward God. Llull's dual focus here on knowledge and good (i.e.,
his first) intention repeats his usual insistence on the separation of
Philosophy and Theology. The former is subordinate to the latter, and
Llull's whole project is directed towards making 'Logic and philosophizing' serve the pursuit of theological 'knowledge and good intention'. Thus Llull concludes the 'new compendium' with this claim:
'since my intention concerns something else, we wish to finish this

---

[9] Deus, per far a vos honrament
de lògica tractam breument,
lo qual es compendi novell,
en mon enteniment appell
que translat de latí en romanç
en rimes en mots qui son plans,
per tal que hom puscha mostrar
lògica e philosoffar
a cels qui no saben latí
ni aràbich: per que vos mi
endreçats, Sènyer, en saber
e n bona·entenció haver.

(*Obres Originals*, 19. 3)

discourse. We will speak briefly of Logic, since we should speak of God.' (lines 1603–6.)[10] Rubió observes that 'secret affinities of temperment' may have led Llull to choose Algazel as his guide in Logic.[11] The lines just cited suggest an even more concrete correspondence between their works, however. Platzeck has noted that Algazel also seeks to subordinate the knowledge of things human to that of things divine,[12] as he states in the introduction to his account of metaphysics. He explains that

Usus fuit apud phylosophos preponere naturalem scienciam. Nos autem eligimus preponere divinam eo quod magis necessaria est et maioris diversitatis est; et quoniam ipsa est finis omnium scienciarum et inquisicionis earum. Unde ipsi propter difficultatem et obscuritatem suam postposuerunt eam; et quia difficilius est eam scire ante naturalem. Nos autem interponemus aliqua de naturalibus sine quibus non potest divina intelligi. (1a. 1; p. 1)

The heterogeneous character of Llull's adaptation, which treats theological and metaphysical, as well as logical, doctrine, thus has a warrant in the programme that Algazel defines for his own *Maqāṣid*. In so far as the *Logica Algazelis* circumscribes the fundamental theological and philosophical topics that concerned Ramon Llull, it expresses the project of his entire career's labour. With respect to Logic itself, the *Logica Algazelis* fixes, either fully or *in embryo*, almost all the particular doctrines that Llull develops in his later writings. Not all of that development arises from this compendium, and its comprehensive character makes it difficult to appreciate exactly which doctrines these are, except where they are allied to some of the other theological or metaphysical principles that the treatise includes. In any case, the subsequent chapters in the first part of this study will deal with each of those doctrines in turn, noting, where relevant, their initial presentation in the *Logica Algazelis*. As to the other aspects of received doctrine that do not figure prominently in Llull's early logical writings—the syllogism, topics, and fallacies—it is sufficient to note their appearance in the *Logica Algazelis* as proof of Llull's exposure to them.

Contents of the Lògica del Gatzel

Turning now to the contents of Llull's treatise, it is expedient to group them into four basic categories: (1) an adaptation of Algazel's account

---

[10] The Carreras y Artau also note this orientation, *Historia de la filosofía española*, 1. 353–4.
[11] 'La Lògica del Gazzali', p. 313.
[12] 'La combinatoria luliana', pp. 589, 591.

of Logic; (2) elements of Theology and Metaphysics perhaps adapted from Algazel's other accounts of these subjects; (3) elements of logical doctrine adapted from the logical manuals of Llull's Scholastic contemporaries; and (4) theological arguments similar to those advanced in Llull's own *Libre de contemplació en Déu*, whose doctrines often derive from the works of Anselm and other twelfth-century theologians. Jordi Rubió and Charles Lohr have identified some of the sources or parallels for this material in their editions of the vernacular and Latin texts; Table 1 (pp. 39 ff.) gives a synopsis of the correspondences between Llull's text and that of Algazel or others. The list does show one striking difference between the Latin *Compendium* and its Catalan abridgement: the vernacular work transposes the sections from the Latin text devoted to the fallacies, syllogism, categories, and Tree of Porphyry (lines 1080–602) with those devoted to theological and metaphysical topics (lines 605–1079). Although this arrangement obviously splits the account of Logic, there is no indication in the verse text whether this transposition is deliberate or not. It is tempting to consider lines 1603–6, quoted above, as a transitional passage between the logical material and the theological and metaphysical material, since these lines express Llull's intention of turning from the treatment of Logic to a discussion of Theology. This would require postulating some mis-copying in the transmission of the text, however, and this accident is not supported by any detectable internal evidence.

Llull's presentation of logical doctrine in the *Lògica del Gatzel* is, for the most part, too brief to display very many peculiarities in its views, although many of its expressions and phrases are unusual. Llull's interpolation of material from Scholastic logical literature is perhaps noteworthy precisely as a reflection of the work's effort to follow conventional doctrine in both scope and exposition. Thus he offers accounts of the five predicables, ten categories, and Tree of Porphyry, since these elements are the foundation of the *logica vetus*, which had come, by the fourteenth century, to comprise the introductory portions of the logical *summulae* of the moderns. Llull could have encountered them in any work on Logic. He does not, however, treat the post-predicamental categories (*Cat.* 10–15 11b15–15b31), and his enumeration of the categories itself does not correspond to Peter of Spain's (3. 6–28), but rather to that of the traditional Isidore (2. 26. 5–10) or modern Ockham (1. 41–62). Llull also inserts a discussion of the enthymeme in his exposition of the types of argumentation. Algazel does not discuss the enthymeme, so Llull must have learned of it from some Latin or Arab text more faithful to Aristotle. Finally, Llull prefaces Algazel's treatment of the thirteen types of fallacies with another treatment of these same types that corresponds to Peter of Spain's. The comprehensive scope of Llull's account of Logic in the *Logica Algazelis* is therefore somewhat misleading; neither the vernacular text nor its Latin model offers a very coherent plan of logical doctrine, although each expounds specific doctrines or rehearses specific arguments very concisely.[13] Unlike Scholastic commentators such as Albert the Great or Aquinas,[14] Llull never explicitly states the rationale underlying his selection and organization of doctrine, probably because his concept of intention already fulfils that role. As indicated already, the apparently comprehensive character of the *Logica Algazelis* is also misleading with respect to Llull's subsequent logical production up to 1303. His writings rarely cover any areas beyond the predicables, categories, and formation of propositions taught by the *logica vetus*, and the concentration of his attention on these most traditional rudiments in fact corresponds to the scope of his own *ars combinatoria*, which simply pursues the formation of propositions for analysis according to the values of his *Art*.

Jordi Rubió has suggested that Llull's accounts of sensation and psychology may be derived from Algazel's exposition of these topics in his treatise on metaphysics (2a. 2. 3–4).[15] Their accounts are so different that any direct connection seems very unlikely, however. Llull's description of the five senses includes details not mentioned by Algazel at all, while he introduces the psychology of the soul's functions chiefly in order to explain how the Imagination deceived ancient philosophers regarding the truth naturally known to the Intellect, in the manner described in Chapter 7. Moreover, Llull's quasi-personification of the powers of the soul is equally notable as an example of an allegorical moralization of Scholastic scientific (in this case, psychological) discourse.

Llull's treatment of such relationships as part to whole, similarity and dissimilarity, or perfection and imperfection in this treatise on Logic and philosophizing is also perhaps noteworthy as a tacit

[13] See Lohr, *Raimundus Lullus' Compendium Logicae Algazelis*, pp. 40–66 for a comparison of Llull's programme to the plans of compendia by Arabic and Latin authorities.

[14] On their classifications, see Thomas McGovern, 'The Division of Logic', *Laval philosophique et théologique*, 11 (1955), 157–81.

[15] 'La Lògica del Gazzali', p. 322.

acknowledgement of the topical function that these relationships serve in Llull's other works. His explanations of them here are certainly much more concise than those found in the *Libre de contemplació*, which more often applies them as general arguments from proportion to specific problems. They underlie many of the 'necessary reasons' that Llull claims to offer, and Chapter 7 will examine their demonstrative value more carefully. Here it is simply relevant to observe that Llull's moralization of logical doctrine most often consists precisely in the reformulation of conventional propositional or syllogistic relationships according to these proportionally conceived topics from the *Logica Algazelis*. In this respect the latter comprehend almost all the methods of demonstration that Llull elaborates more extensively in his later logical writings, and this anticipation of his subsequent efforts in the early *Logica Algazelis* does ultimately suggest a certain continuity of interests that illuminates the very tangential and adversarial position of Llull's *Art* with respect to contemporary Scholastic learning. How this position manifests itself in Llull's treatment of specific logical doctrines is the subject of the following chapters. These will treat first his general remarks on the status of Logic as an art, and then his particular expositions of the predicables, categories, propositions, syllogistics, demonstration, and logical disputation.

Table I. *The Contents of the* Logica Algazelis

The first column indicates line numbers from the Catalan text, with section numbers from the Latin in parenthesis; the second lists section titles from the Latin version; the third indicates corresponding passages from Algazel's treatise on Logic, in Lohr's edition; the fourth column indicates parallels in other authorities, along with an explanation, if necessary, of the doctrines treated in the section. In the references to other authorities, *SL* indicates the *Summule logicales* of Peter of Spain, *M* indicates Algazel's treatise on metaphysics, and *LC* Llull's own *Libre de contemplació*. The Aristotelian passages indicated are the ultimate bases for doctrines or terms that do not appear in Algazel; Llull may have encountered them in contemporary logical *summulae* or in encyclopaedic accounts such as Vincent of Beauvais'. This list gives a somewhat different estimation of Llull's possible 'sources' than Lohr does, and the reader may wish to consult his suggestions as well.[16]

Lines in the *Lògica del Gatzel*	Section titles from the *Compendium Logicae Algazelis*	Parallel passages in Algazel's *Logic*	Parallel passages in other authorities and doctrines treated
1–12			Introduction
13–96 (1. 01–9)	De universalibus		*SL* 2. 1–19: predicables and Tree of Porphyry
97–134 (1. 10–15)		2. 72–93	Types of accident
135–9 (1. 16)	De comparatione universali	2. 186–8	Three substantial and two accidental predications
140–53 (1. 17)	De diffinitionibus generalibus		*M* 1a. 1. 5 and *SL* 5. 19–22: definition through the four causes
154–63 (1. 18)	De cognitionibus esse rei	2. 15–33	Three conditions of essential predication
164–81		2. 34–56	essential and non-essential predication
182–212 (1. 19–23)	De demonstratione speciei per genus et differentiam	2. 15–139	cf. *SL* 1. 8–14 and *LC* 106
213–26 (1. 24)	De comparationibus universalibus	2. 5–11	Natural or essential and accidental predication
227–40 (1. 25)	De cognitione quod quid est	2. 140–8	Three responses to 'quid?' through genus and species

[16] *Raimundus Lullus' Compendium Logicae Algazelis*, pp. 8–39, 124–5.

Lines in the *Lògica del Gatzel*	Section titles from the *Compendium Logicae Algazelis*	Parallel passages in Algazel's *Logic*	Parallel passages in other authorities and doctrines treated
241–7 (1. 26)	Qualiter differentia demonstrat quod quid est	2. 149–59	Response to 'quod quid est?' through one and many
248–51 (1. 27)	De ostensione per differentiam quale quid est	2. 124–39	Response to 'quale quid est?' through genus and species
252–65 (2. 1)	De propositionibus	3. 1–92	Disjunctive or conjunctive and conditional types
266–75 (2. 2–4)	De propositionibus determinatis	3. 93–123	Universal, particular, affirmative, and negative types
276–325 (2. 5)	De contradictione que videtur inter propositiones et non est contradictio	3. 148–86	8 types: from equivocation, or diverse laws, particulars and universals, act and potency, relation, place, state, or time
326–51 (2. 6–9)	De propositionibus convertibilibus et non convertibilibus	3. 187–211	Universal negatives and affirmative particulars convert, universal affirmatives and negative particulars do not
352–7 (2. 10)	De modis conversionis	3. 188–211	Simple, accidental, and contra-positional types; cf. *SL* 1. 15
358–99 (2. 11)	De modis tredecim propositionum	4. 531–675	Primary, sensible, experimental, ['famous'], self-proving, opinative, public maxim, received, granted, simulative, apparent maxim, putative
400–27. (2. 12–15)	De divisione predictarum propositionum	4. 676–740	Demonstrative, dialectical, sophistical, rhetorical, and poetical types

Lines in the *Lògica del Gatzel*	Section titles from the *Compendium Logicae Algazelis*	Parallel passages in Algazel's *Logic*	Parallel passages in other authorities and doctrines treated
428–35 (2. 16–17)	De possibili et impossibili et necessario	3. 124–47	[As three types of proposition]
436–57 (3. 1–3)	Sequitur de argumentis	4. 1–51	[Structure of syllogism]
458–67		4. 111–63	
468–85 (3. 4)	De materia argumenti	4. 494–530	Demonstrative, dialectical, rhetorical, sophistical, 'sumic' arguments
486–505 (3. 5)	Sequitur de sillogismis	5.70–153	Subject, accident, question, first truth
506–17 (3. 6)	De conditionibus syllogismi	5. 154–231	True, necessary, primary, and essential
518–27 (3. 7–11)	De speciebus argumentationis	4. 1–10	Syllogism, exemplum, induction
528–34		4. 333–49	
535–40			*SL* 5. 3: enthymeme
541–4		4. 350–71	
545–50 (3. 12)	De obscuratione argumenti		*SL* 5. 3: enthymeme
551–67 (3. 13–14)	De inquisitione syllogismi	5. 37–65	Demonstration *propter quid* and *quia*
568–92 (3: 15–20)	De modis interrogandi	5. 1–36	An, quid, quale, quare est?
593–605 (3. 21)	Sequitur de opositione		cf. *M* 1a. 1. 5 and *SL* 5. 27: relative, contrary, privative, and contradictory types
606–11 (8. 2)	Sequitur de principio numeri		cf. *M* 1a. 1. 2. 2 and *Cat.* 6 5a30–3: discrete and non-relative quantity
612–22 (8. 3)	Sequitur de diferencia inter esse et essentia		cf. *M* 1a. 1. 2. 3

Lines in the *Lògica del Gatzel*	Section titles from the *Compendium Logicae Algazelis*	Parallel passages in Algazel's *Logic*	Parallel passages in other authorities and doctrines treated
623–39 (8. 4)	Sequitur de appetitu universali		cf. *LC* 31 and Avicebron 2. 5 and 5. 4: primary matter and the individual
640–73 (8. 5)	De investigatione veritatis	3. 69–147	cf. *LC* 173 and 175: *credo ut intelligam*
674–708 (8. 6)	De investigatione secreti		cf. *LC* 166–206, esp. 174. 21: cognition from sense to sense, sense to Intellect, and Intellect to Intellect
709–71 (8. 7)	Sequitur de demonstrationibus		cf. *LC* 174. 4, *M* 1a. 1. 3, *SL* 5. 11–18 and Avicebron 2. 10:[17] composite whole, finite simple whole, infinite simple whole
772–99 (8. 8)	Sequitur de subiecto, obiecto et medio		cf. *M* 1a. 1. 3 and *De an.* 3.10 433b13–14: media and objects of sensation
800–6 (8. 9)	De investigatione rei nobilioris		cf. *Phys.* 1. 8 191b15, *Metaph.* 10. 4 1055a33 and Avicebron 5. 31, 33: being, non-being, perfection, imperfection, greater and lesser
807–51			cf. *LC* 100–2 and 106, *Metaph.* 10. 3–8: diversity and contrarity of the perfect and imperfect

[17] It is interesting that Llull's three degrees of demonstration—the whole greater than its parts, the undivided finite whole, and the undivided infinite whole—are similar to three Neoplatonic categories of universals noted by A. C. Lloyd, 'Neoplatonists' Account of Predication and Medieval Logic', in *Le Néoplatonisme* (Paris: CNRS, 1971), p. 358.

Lines in the *Lògica del Gatzel*	Section titles from the *Compendium Logicae Algazelis*	Parallel passages in Algazel's *Logic*	Parallel passages in other authorities and doctrines treated
852–927 (8. 10)	De investigatione eius quod est		*LC* 106; cf. *Metaph.* 5. 9 1018a15–19: similarity and dissimilarity
928–87 (8. 11)	Sequitur de sensibus particularibus		*LC* 151 and *De an.* 2. 5–12 passim: five senses
988–1044 (8. 12)	De representatione sensuum particularium intellectui		*LC* 151; cf. *De an.* 3. 3–9 passim: Imagination and fantasy
1045–80 (8. 13)	Sequitur de prima et secunda intentione		*LC* 45 and *Libre de intenció*
1081–176 (4. 1–33)	Sequitur de fallaciis		*SL* 7. 24–278
1177–258 (4. 34–43)	De cautelis evitande decepcionis fallaciarum	4. 741–807	Algazel's ten errors of sophistical argument
1259–89 (5. 2–7)	Sequitur de modis prime figure	4. 71–163	[First syllogistic figure]
1290–328 (5. 8–12)	Sequitur de modis secunde figure	4. 164–221	[Second syllogistic figure]
1329–74 (5. 13–20)	Sequitur de modis tercie figure	4. 222–61	[Third syllogistic figure]
1375–414 (6. 1–5)	Sequitur de predicamentis		cf. Vincent, *SD* 3. 16
1415–38 (6. 6–8)	Sequitur de predicamento quantitatis		cf. Vincent, *SD* 3. 17
1439–54 (6. 9)	Sequitur de predicamento relationis		cf. Vincent, *SD* 3. 18
1455–80 (6. 10–11)	Sequitur de predicamento qualitatis		cf. Vincent, *SD* 3. 19
1481–90 (6. 12)	Sequitur de predicamento accionis		cf. Vincent, *SD* 3. 22
1491–502 (6. 13)	Sequitur de predicamento passionis		cf. Vincent, *SD* 3. 23

Lines in the *Lògica del Gatzel*	Section titles from the *Compendium Logicae Algazelis*	Parallel passages in Algazel's *Logic*	Parallel passages in other authorities and doctrines treated
1503–10 (6. 14)	Sequitur de predicamento situs		cf. Vincent, *SD* 3. 26
1511–20 (6. 15)	Sequitur de predicamento quando		cf. Vincent, *SD* 3. 24
1521–35 (6. 16–17)	Sequitur de predicamento ubi		cf. Vincent, *SD* 3. 25
1536–41 (6. 18)	Sequitur de predicamento habitus		cf. Vincent, *SD* 3. 27
1542–65 (7. 1–6)	Sequitur de arbore Porphirii		cf. *SL* 2. 11
1566–602 (8. 1)	Sequitur de afirmatione et negatione	3. 68–210	cf. *SL* 1. 9–15; 4. 1–14
1603–12			Conclusion

2

Logic as an Art

As noted already, the *Logica Algazelis* offers no definition of the art of Logic or explanation of its relationship to the other arts or sciences. In part this is because the application of Llull's General *Art* to all the particular arts and sciences renders their various interrelationships unimportant; his definitions of them tend to distinguish them according to their subject-matter alone, since their methods, principles, or procedures will all come from his own *Art*, and the all-embracing principle of Llull's first intention applies indifferently to any subject. In the case of Logic, however, Llull does face the problem of whether to regard the predicables, categories, propositions, and syllogisms of Aristotelian logic as its subject-matter or its method. His insistently Realist or natural conception of Logic as a science of being obviously favours the latter possibility, while the pre-eminent role of his own methods would demand the former. This dilemma is only one way of confronting the broad conflict between Scholastic Logic and Llull's *Art*. To consider it explicitly would require acknowledging the metaphysical value of all logical distinctions, an issue that Llull's search for 'principles of being and knowledge' cannot even recognize. Two particular aspects of Scholastic doctrine, the traditional view of Logic as the art of separating the true from the false, and the logician's use of second intentions, help to understand better the relationship of Logic to Llull's own *Art* and the status of Logic as a separate art.

In early works from the *Doctrina pueril* (73. 4) of 1282–7 to the *Arbre de sciència* (Hum. 5. 5. i) of 1296 and *Aplicació de l'Art General* (lines 424–7) of 1301, Llull regularly proffers the traditional definition, repeated since Isidore (2. 22. 2) that Logic is the art of separating the true from the false. His remarks from the *Doctrina pueril* are typical: 'Logic is the demonstration of true and false things, through which one learns to speak correctly and sophistically and Logic is the art through which the human Intellect is refined and exalted.' (73. 4.) The distinction between 'correctly and sophistically' speaking may simply restate that between true and false things; or perhaps it echoes the distinction between syllogism and fallacy; or it may well recall the designation of Logic as the member of the trivium that 'teaches to speak correctly', as William of Sherwood indicates in his *Introductiones in logicam* (1. 1). Llull's claim that Logic refines and exalts the mind recalls commonplace praises of Logic from Augustine (*De ord.* 2. 13. 38) to Ockham (Proem.). It is typical of Llull's early accounts of Logic that he does not denounce its sophistical subtleties, but rather proposes to improve its efficacy, as several passages from the *Compendium artis demonstrativae* discussed below will show. This corresponds in part to the popularizing function of his *Art*; Llull frequently claims that it allows mastery of any art or science in short time. The same popularizing function is obvious in the *Doctrina pueril* when Llull tells his son to learn Logic in the vernacular first in order to understand it better (73. 8). It is possible that Llull so often repeats the traditional identification of Logic as the art of distinguishing the true from false, because affirmative and negative propositions are the foundation of the procedures of his own *Art*. The weight of traditional formulae from the encyclopaedists or other compendia of Logic may account for its perpetuation in his work: the *Logica nova* of 1303, which opens his later period, still offers it, even while denouncing the sophistry of Scholastic practice. This ambivalence reflects the two conflicting orders that Llull's *Art* pretends to harmonize: the truth and falsity in things and the truth and falsity in words.

Llull's effort to impose the order of things upon that of words is clear in his conception of another, more technical logical tenet, the Scholastic distinction between first and second intentions. Ockham defines them thus: 'Nouns of second intention are those that absolutely are imposed for signifying the intentions of the soul, or in short the intentions of the soul that are natural signs, and the other signs conventionally instituted or things consequent upon these signs . . . but nouns of first intention are all others than these, which namely signify some things that are not signs, nor things consequent upon such signs.' (1. 11.) Logicians are commonly said to deal only with second, rather than first, intentions, a view that apparently came from Avicenna (*Metaph.* 1. 2), and which many Scholastics repeat, as Aquinas does (e.g. *In* 11 *Metaph.* 3. 2204). In his *Arbre de sciència* of 1296, Llull offers one of his few explicit references to the doctrine of logical first and second intentions. It is noteworthy that in his definitions of intention from the *Proverbis de Ramon* (96) of the same year, he says nothing about this doctrine. In the former text, he explains that the 'logician has second intentions, which are the meanings (*significats*) of real things, of which the natural philosopher treats, and from which the logician takes the names (*noms*) and likenesses of natural activities' (Hum. 5. 5. i). Thus Llull mentions only the second, but not the first intentions, and ignores the difference between them. His statement obviously reflects awareness of the importance of second intentions for Logic, but these are not, as he claims, the 'meanings of real things'; these meanings, as well as the 'names and likenesses of natural activities' correspond instead to the logical first intentions. The same confusion is apparent in his *Libre de Blanquerna* of 1284, when he notes that one should learn Logic 'in order to understand and learn natures' (56. 5). It is not obvious whether these 'natures' (of things) would be first or second intentions, although subsequent developments in Llull's doctrine of a 'natural logic' based on immediate abstraction of universal natures make the former more likely.

In the Tree of Questions of the *Arbre de sciència*, Llull asks 'why logicians are nearer to being crazy (*fantàstics*) than other men?' and responds 'No one uses intentions as much as the logician, nor has as much pleasure in sophisms.' (5. 5. i. 179.) This question identifies the logician's use of second intentions as one of the grounds for Llull's increasing criticism of Scholastic Logic toward the end of his early period up to 1303. It is an especially important reason because it directly concerns the putatively natural character of Llull's new Logic. When, in his later works, he proposes to use only first intentions in Logic, he does so because these first intentions are the mind's immediate apprehensions of the true natures of things.

Such a conception of a natural Logic effectively identifies cognition and ratiocination, and this is implicit in Llull's remarks on Logic in the *Arbre de sciència*, when he explains how the logical disposition of the soul is able to consider the 'real forms' of all the entities from all the lower trees in the hierarchy of being, 'as it comes from potentiality into actuality, by the artificial agent who seizes likenesses from other trees in the Tree of Imagination, so that from these likenesses it can furnish and arrange the art of Logic, and have knowledge of real things' (Hum. 5. 5. i). Intelligible species thus compose logical discourse concerning real beings. Llull's conflation of logical, metaphysical, and physical knowledge refuses some of the basic distinctions recognized by his Scholastic contemporaries. Avicenna explicitly differentiates forms received through the senses from the logical intentions (*De an.* 1. 5) as does Aquinas (1a. 78, 4; 85, 1–2). Llull's *Arbre de sciència* attempts to define exhaustively all the interrelationships among the various orders of material and spiritual being through its scheme of corresponding trees. One important consequence of this project is the extreme simplification of the metaphysical relations that explain intellection, as this passage on Logic implies. Llull's Realist account of intellection founds his natural Logic by asserting the direct apprehension of universals, a feature that becomes clear in later works.

So, where Llull continues to identify Logic as one of the traditional arts and sciences in his encyclopaedic works, and regularly ascribes to it the function of separating the true from the false, his further comments on this art develop the conception of a natural Logic that is in fact nearly indistinguishable in purpose from his own General *Art*. This development reaches its fulfilment only in Llull's later works, and may be regarded as the inevitable result of his claims for the general validity of his own system. He does make one attempt to respect the discrete scope of Logic and to distinguish it from his own *Art* in the *Compendium artis demonstrativae* of 1277–83. The last three of the many questions posed and answered in the work's Third Distinction show how Llull's *Art* is general, inventional, and adds something above and beyond all other arts and sciences. The generality of Llull's *Art* derives directly, of course, from the universality of its *Principia*, which are necessary for investigating or judging the truth of any thing because 'as every creature is a likeness of God, just as through the *Bonitas* of God every *Bonitas* is revealed (*monstratur*), so through the *Veritas* of God is revealed every *Veritas*' (p. 150). Llull's choice of *Bonitas* and *Veritas* as examples is not arbitrary: these *Principia* are transcendentals that bridge the realms of being and knowledge. Since they join God and His creatures, Llull's *Principia* also join divine and human knowledge, and thus his *Art* 'adds these common *Principia* beyond Theology, from whence it concludes from them under Theology, just as under other common sciences' (p. 154). Llull's *Art* is, none the less, only potentially universal because of the 'defect and smallness of the Intellect' (p. 146). The contribution of his *Art* thus comes to be chiefly a quantitative extension of the mind's abilities. Llull declares that his *Art* adds to any other, considered by itself, a 'mutual disposition (*habitudinem*) and combination of principal terms in any thing . . . adding in that combination other universal terms that are not simply from speculation in that art'; likewise it adds to all other arts, considered jointly and at once, 'what is barely available, namely an artful (*artificiatum*) mode of functioning though the combined acts of the Memory, Will, and Intellect, and artful mode of universalizing and particularizing by mixing terms of the *Principia*'; in short, 'no other art can multiply the disposition to knowledge' as much as Llull's; it offers the greatest wealth of arguments and reasons for one conclusion or many (pp. 154, 155).

As regards Logic, Llull's *Art* does not add more power to the syllogism as a 'means of probability and demonstration', but rather 'the greatest material compendiously, for forming many syllogisms . . . and adduces from reason many reasons for the same or different conclusions for forming thence a syllogism, and from a syllogism many syllogisms for the same or different conclusions' (p. 156). Likewise, the affirmative, negative, and dubitative consideration of the combined *Principia* of his *Art* provides 'such a multitude of affirmative and negative demonstrations or proofs that the Memory and Intellect satisfy the acts of the Memory, Will, and Intellect so that oblivion, ignorance, and hate suppose from the combined acts of recollection, oblivion, understanding, ignorance, love, hate, not loving, and not hating, that in any faculty the acts of the Memory, Will, and Intellect will be replete with a wealth of relevant working material' (p. 157). According to the *Compendium artis demonstrativae*, then, Llull's *Art* offers no qualitatively new methods to those of received logical doctrine, with the exception of his demonstration *per aequiparantiam* (p. 156), discussed in more detail in Chapter 7. This suggests that he sees no differences between the reasons and proofs offered by his *Art* and those commonly employed by his contemporaries, and likewise regards the material provided by his *Art* as acceptable stuff for the construction of syllogistic arguments in accepted Scholastic fashion. Perhaps Llull's emphasis on the purely quantitative contribution of his system reflects his perception that existing means of proving Christian doctrine to non-believers merely suffered from a dearth of adequate proofs and reasons, which his *Art* would supply. His insistence on the qualitative differences between his system and Scholastic Logic, and consequent criticism of the latter's efficacy, certainly increases in later years. One might suspect that Llull's criticism reflects his own increasing dissatisfaction, and even irritation, with the resistance of contemporary logical doctrine, especially when used against him, to reformation according to the tenets of his *Art*. The failure of a merely quantitative reform in the scope of Logic urges the attempt at a complete qualitative reform, as he eventually seeks to impose. Such a qualitative reform necessarily diminishes, however, the status of Logic as a separate art. This problem is not peculiar to Logic; the reformulation of any art or science according to Llull's *Art* inevitably requires the likeness that for him founds all relationships of particular to universal, even among branches of knowledge.

This likeness is most obvious in Llull's *Aplicació de l'Art General* of 1301, a text that effectively marks the transition between his earlier and later periods of work. The *Aplicació* is noteworthy as one of Llull's last major verse vernacular works, and thus indicates a real decline in this mode of pursuing the popularizing function of his programme. The *Aplicació* expounds the application of Llull's system, as presented in the *Art amativa* of 1290 and *Taula general* of 1292, to the arts of Theology, Philosophy, Logic, Law, Medicine, and Rhetoric, and is probably the collective expression of various other works, such as the *Logica nova, Rethorica nova, Metaphysica nova, Liber novus physicorum* and so on that attempt the same end. The term 'application' is singularly ironic, since what Llull proposes is either to substitute his own *Principia, Regulae*, and so forth for the particular principles and categories of those other arts, thereby creating a sort of Rhetoric or Physics of the Divine Dignities, or to derive their particular principles and categories from his own *Principia* and other distinctions, thereby bringing their subjects within the scope of his own *Art*. The discussions of the predicables, categories, and other logical doctrines in the following chapters will show exactly how he attempts to achieve this with them. Here it is instructive to observe how he derives the art of Logic as a whole from his own. One remark from the last lines of his treatment of Logic summarizes his entire argument: he urges study of the universal more than the particular, 'since it is naturally right that truth come from the greater to the lesser' (lines 555–6). This claim correlates the relationships of universal to particular, greater to lesser, and full truth to partial truth in a single hierarchy that explicitly displays the Neoplatonizing character of Llull's whole system. Llull does not say that greater beings embrace a greater truth than the lesser, but this seems to follow from his claims. Thus, in the *Taula general*, he replies to the question whether one truth is greater than another by arguing that because man has a greater number of constituent powers than an irrational creature, he has a greater truth, and thus the irrational animal has a greater truth than a plant for the same reason (5. 5. 16). Llull assumes that each being has a differential capacity to receive his *Principium* of *Veritas* in the same manner that the

Neoplatonic *Liber de causis* posits its differential ability to receive goodness from the One (158, 179–80).

This hierarchy of truth includes both the elements of logical doctrine and those of Llull's *Art*. The former, as particulars, must derive from the latter, as universals. The *Taula general* summarizes Llull's view very neatly:

All these principles are bound (*enplegats*) in the principles of this *Art*, because they are all good, great, and so on; and therefore this *Art* is general to those with its general principles, and it inclines to the other sciences according as the principles of those others are bound up (*enplegats*) in its principles, and it is above them, just as genus is above species, and it uses the principles of those sciences according to the order and usage that it makes of its own principles, and the practice of this usage is given in this science.[1] (8. 6. 25)

This implication, binding up, or employment of the principles of every individual art or science in those of Llull's *Art* follows a universal law: every real or conceptual being, including those individual principles, is good, great, true, and so forth because it participates in the *Bonitas*, *Magnitudo*, *Veritas* and so forth that Llull posits as his general principles. But the verb 'bind up' and the simile of genus and species do not explain the diffusion of Llull's *Principia* so much as they describe it. This is in part the fundamental indistinction of any metaphysics of participation through resemblance: resemblance describes the participation that explains it. The Relative *Principia* and *Regulae* do help to differentiate various specific elements, but in so far as they serve the derivation of particular from universal, they cannot escape the bonds of resemblance. The autonomy of particular principles or elements in other arts and sciences often compels their replacement with the *Principia* of Llull's *Art*, but more often he must argue their derivation, authorizing this with the order and usage mentioned in the passage cited above. This usage is the moralization that Llull carries out, submitting all beings to definition of their first intention.

---

[1] 'Totz aquestz comensamens son enplegats en los comensamens d aquesta art, quar totz son bons e grans e los altres; e per asò aquesta art es general a aquells ab sos comensamens generals, e enclina s a les altres sciencies segons que ls comensamens d aquelles estan en los seus comensamens enplegats, e està desús a aquelles, enaxí com genre qui està sobre especia, e usa dels comensamens d aquelles sciencies segons l orde e l ús que à de sos propis comensamens, la pràtica del qual ús es donada en esta sciencia.' (*Obres Originals*, 16. 490–1.)

Thus the application of Llull's system to Logic according to the *Aplicació de l'Art General* is really an attempt to rectify that discipline to investigation and recognition of the same truths as the Lullian *Art*. The derivation of logical doctrines from the *Principia* of his Art is above all a definition of their theological and ontological value and only secondarily explains their eristic or demonstrative functions as a result of that status. Llull brings Logic to serve the mind's apprehension of its proper object, according to the principles described below in Chapters 7 and 19. In this respect, Llull attributes to Logic the same fusion of material and formal aspects that his own *Art* achieves in its use of *Principia* that are foundations of being and knowledge alike. Llull's subsequent attempt to define a natural Logic represents a shift from merely asserting the theological and ontological community of his *Principia* and logical principles to defining the cognitive and ratiocinative consequences of that community. From this arises the great concern in his later period for the formal structures of Logic and their redefinition according to his own system. That this concern has its origin in the aboriginal values and convictions of Llull's philosophy should be evident even from the few passages examined in this short chapter. The following analyses of Llull's accounts of the predicables, categories, propositions, and other elements of logical doctrine will show in detail how his treatment of them both applies and defines those values from the earliest stages of his career, and thus achieves the moralization of these elements.

3

Predicables

THE five Scholastic predicables or universals—genus, species, difference, and accident—enjoy a broad primacy in Llull's *Art* that is not simply due to their role as the most basic distinctions of medieval logical doctrine, but depends also on their value as the primary types of the relationship between the One and the Many that founds his entire system. Llull's is not a logic of classes, but of transcendence.[1] His Neoplatonic foundations are clearly manifest in his unvarying treatment of the five universals as real, rather than simply mental, stratifications of the hierarchy of being. He tells his son in the *Doctrina pueril* that 'through this knowledge you can descend from general to specific things, and you will know how to lift your Intellect up from specific to general things' (73. 5). These two modes of inquiry, which Llull's fellow Scholastics so often invoke from Aristotle (*An. post.* 1. 24 85a10–b31) are for him the pre-eminent, if not in fact only, ones worth pursuing, since they inevitably trace the path between God and his creatures. Because the relationship of universal to particular corresponds better to that between genus and species than to those indicated by difference, property, or accident, the latter predicables play a largely indistinct role in Llull's metaphysics as names for universal essence.

Llull's presentation of the five predicables in the opening lines of the *Lògica del Gatzel* is not especially remarkable, although he does omit defining genus and species in favour of briefly describing the famous Tree of Porphyry, a choice that underscores his debt to the Neoplatonizing tendencies of the *Isagoge* and its notorious claim that 'the genus is a kind of whole, the individual a part' (p. 14). Still, he uses only commonplace examples in illustrating each universal, and the definitions that he does provide are very conventional, as when he states that property is 'a universal particular that is the sign of its species and the individuals in it' (lines 57–60). Llull's use of the term 'sign'

---

[1] As suggested by Platzeck, 'La combinatoria luliana', p. 594.

suggests well his habitual treatment of any logical, metaphysical, or physical relationship as a semiotic connection, and the arguments of his writings, from the early *Libre de contemplació* to the later *Liber de significatione* consist above all in the reading of such signs. Llull also notes that difference and property are convertible (lines 78–9), a view that reflects the frequent uncertainty about their distinction in Scholastic doctrine. The fact that he offers in lines 37–139 several unsynthesized definitions for difference, property, and accident foreshadows his typically arbitrary use of these terms as names for universal essence in all his later works.

The single most important feature in all Llull's accounts of the five universals is, as already noted, his absolutely unwavering advocacy of their real existence. Llull appeals to or defends the real existence of the predicables so often throughout his work that it would be impossible even to classify here all the arguments that he uses. This passage from the *Liber chaos* of 1277 is exemplary in its brevity and simplicity:

Quoniam proprietas in primo gradu Chaos est quoddam commune, aliquid vero specificum in tertio, est proprietas universalis sive communis in primo gradu Chaos praeter sua particularia, quae habet in tertio gradu, et ideo patet universale naturae esse ens reale in communitate. ('De proprietate chaos'; p. 24)

This passage defines two metaphysical corollaries of Llull's Realism that merit mention because of their basic importance. The first is the plurality of substantial forms, which his *Principia* necessarily exemplify as substantial constituents of every being. The second is the essentialism that typically attributes an essence to any specific difference, property, or inseparable accident in a being, with the result that the being possesses numerous 'co-essential' attributes, which Llull's own innate correlatives render active in the being's existence and operation.

Llull's Realism, advocacy of multiple substantial forms, and essentialism can create difficulties in explaining various aspects of received logical doctrine, most notably predication, as subsequent sections of this study will show. It also complicates explanation of the nature of the predicables themselves, and these problems become apparent in those works from the end of Llull's early period where he most vigorously seeks to apply his *Art* to Logic. These works show very well how Llull's own handling and use of the received doctrine found in his *Lògica del Gatzel* extends or modifies it in various peculiar ways.

Thus, in the list of One Hundred Forms from the *Arbre de sciència*,

Llull defines both genus and species. His definitions display an emphatically material or even physical orientation that becomes explicit in the natural Logic of his later works. Llull begins his account of genus by declaring that substance is a genus with many species, but he does not call it a *genus generalissimum*, as the categories are designated in standard authorities such as Peter of Spain (2. 7). Llull instead calls being (*ens*) the *genus generalissimum* (Elem. 7. '100 formes'. 99), a view denied by Aristotle (*An. post.* 2. 7 92b14), but variously received by Llull's Scholastic contemporaries.[2] More unusually, Llull places essence as a genus between being and substance. The genus of substance itself must be real, he declares, in order to stand as first substance to many specific substances, just as a tree trunk to its limbs and branches. Although appeals to tree symbolism are hardly unusual in medieval literature, Llull's use of it in his *Arbre de sciència* in order to expound his extremely Realist views inevitably recalls the Tree of Porphyry, and the famous part-to-whole interpretation of species and genus in the *Isagoge*. Llull concludes:

Thus genus is a real being (*ens*) in the Elemental Tree; and if it were not real and substantial, and were only intentional, the way the logician considers it, all the general principles would be lost in the Elemental Tree, so that the first causes would not be real beings (*ents*), and in their loss the Elemental Tree, which could not be a real being, would be lost; and in its loss no secondary cause could be from the first, and all individuals would be from themselves, and not from another, which is impossible.[3] (Elem. 7. '100 formes'. 7)

The last lines explicitly show how the direct participation and procession of being is the axiomatic ontological basis of Llull's system. His subsequent remarks on species rehearse the same argument, adding that 'it is impossible for the good not to be from *Bonitas* or the great

---

[2] This issue is bound up with the question of the univocity of being, which Llull addresses only rarely. On this question, see Leff's comments, *Dissolution of the Medieval Outlook*, pp. 44, 71, and 76–7 as well as the context for Llull's position offered by the studies of Stepehen F. Brown, 'Robert Cowton, O.F.M. and the Analogy of the Concept of Being', *Franciscan Studies*, 31 (1971), 5–40, and Noel A. Fitzpatrick, 'Walter Chatton on the Univocity of Being: A Reaction to Peter Aureoli and William Ockham', *Franciscan Studies*, 31 (1971), 88–126.

[3] 'Es doncs gendre ens real en l Arbre elemental; e si no era ens real e substancial, e que fos entencional tan solament segons que l lògic lo consira, seríen perduts los generals començaments en l Arbre elemental, enaxí que no seríen ents reals les causes primeres, e en lur perdiment se perdría l Arbre elemental qui no poría esser ens real; e en lo seu perdiment neguna causa secundaria no sería de primera, e seríen tots los individuus cascún de sí meteix e no d altre, la qual cosa es impossible.' (*Obres Originals*, II. 49.)

from *Magnitudo*, and just as that is impossible in the species of *Bonitas* and *Magnitudo*, so it is impossible that the individual be from no species' (ibid. 8). The many must come from the one, the particular from the universal, the individual from the species, the species from the genus.

The necessity of this ontological order among genera, species, and individuals does not, however, necessarily correspond to their cognitive or logical order, as Aristotle argues (*Metaph*. 5. 11 1018b30–7). The lack of homology between these orders motivates this query in the Tree of Questions of the *Arbre de sciència*:

QUESTION. The hermit asks if the logician considers genus before species and species before individuals and substance before accident. SOLUTION. The final ends are naturally prior to the first in speculative understanding, and in practical understanding the first are prior to the final, just as in the art of ironworking in which the Will desires a nail before a hammer, and the smith makes the hammer before the nail.[4] (Quest. 5. 5. i. 180)

Llull's question and answer offer a quadruple analogy regarding the distinction between prior and posterior ends in knowledge and in actions. As regards knowledge, Llull basically follows the Aristotelian axioms that substance is prior in knowledge (*Metaph*. 7. 1 1028a32), but that speculative or scientific understanding is always of universals (1. 1 982a1; 11. 1 1059b26). His example of the hammer and nail parallels one that Peter of Spain offers: 'the end is always prior in intention, but posterior in operation; for first we intend a house and then the beams and walls and foundation; in operation however it is the other way round, because first the walls and foundation are set and then beams, in order to set up the parts of the house, and finally a house results' (7. 22). The Will's desire for the nail and having a complete house function like speculative understanding for Llull, while the desire for a hammer and constructing a house function like practical understanding, at least in respect to their pursuit of proximate and ultimate ends. Llull leaves the moral of this analogy unexpressed probably because it is for him self-evident: the logician, like the Lullian artist, can reason either from general (ends) to particular

---

[4] 'QUEST. Demanà l ermità si lògic consira enans genre que especia e especia que individuu e substancia que accident. —SOL. Les derreres fins son enans en natura que les primeres en l enteniment especulatiu, e en lo pràtic son enans les primeres que les derreres, així com en la art de ferrería en qui la voluntat desira enans clau que martell, e l ferrer fa enans lo martell que l clauell.' (*Obres Originals*, 13. 250–1.)

(ends) or vice versa. His use of the adverb 'naturally' implies the necessity with which these ends define all logical and real relationships. These natural ends assume the teleology that Llull's maxims regarding genus and species in the *Proverbis de Ramon* state very neatly:

Without genus, there would be no species.
Many specific *Bonitates* are sown in a general *Bonitas*.
If genus were not substantial, there would be no substances from it.
Without genus there would be no general end in nature.
Genus is a confused being, like *hyle*.
Genus is the font of species.
Without species, there would be no individuals.
If being were not real in species, it would not have some thing in which to be.
The influence of species is in their production from potentiality to actuality.[5]
(122. 3, 9, 10, 14, 17, 19; 123. 7, 12, 18)

These relations are fundamental to the whole process of Llull's *Art*, and the *Arbre de sciència* illustrates in its trees the natural and organic necessity of this teleology for Llull. It represents the necessary orientation of all individuals in creation toward their one Creator, in fulfilment of the ends for which he created them, as Llull explains in the Prologue to his *Art amativa*. Since this order is also that of knowledge, Llull effectively moralizes the logical relationships of individuals to species and of species to genera by defining man's apprehension of them as means for him to fulfil his own ends. All real and conceptual relationships, including those of Logic, conform to the telic order defined by Llull's doctrine of intentions.

Where Llull globally reorders the real and conceptual relations of the universals by defining them in a theocentric structure of creation, he attempts to define those relations themselves as consequences of the metaphysics of the Godhead, described by his own doctrine of Divine Dignities. This is the project of the *Aplicació de l'Art General*.

---

[5] 'Sens genus, especies esser no pogren.
  'En general bontat estàn sembrades moltes bontats específiques.
  'Si genus no fos ens substancial, no pogren esser d ell substancies.
  'Sens genus no pogra esser en natura general fi.
  'Enaxí es genus ens confús, com *yle*.
  'Genus es font de species.
  'Si specie no fos, individuu no fóra.
  'Si ens no fos reyal en especie, no hagra en que fos.
  'Influencia de especies està en producció d elles de potencia en actu.' (*Obres Originals*, 14. 125–7.)

Llull's bluntly direct statement of his argument in this work makes it
an excellent example of his method. He begins by declaring that 'Logic
is of universals and with the Figures one knows which they are, and in
their combination the things from which one makes the argument.'
(lines 428–31.) Thus, *Bonitas* is a genus, and 'great *Bonitas*' a species
(lines 432–3). The fact that the five predicables are universals makes
them analogous in function to the *Principia* of Llull's *Art*: they are both
'universals, under which are the particulars in question', as he asserts
in the chapter of the *Art amativa* that explains how 'the whole procedure of this *Art* consists in seeking and finding the particular in the
universal' (2. 9. 1–2). This universalizing import of Llull's *Art*, and
above all of its *Principia*, makes *Bonitas* a paradigmatic example of
genus, and 'great *Bonitas*' of species. It is interesting that his accounts
of the Figures in the contemporary *Art amativa* (1. 1–4) and *Taula
general* (1. 1–4) do not, however, treat the *Principia* in these terms. Llull
none the less pursues this argument in the *Aplicació*, where subsequent
lines explain the predicables of property, difference, and accident,
whose distinctions are not necessarily clear with Llull, by arguing that

> And you can divide them
> through properties, and behold how:
> the *Bonitas* of *Voluntas*
> is a property to it;
> and *Bonitas* is a property
> by itself and a quality;
> and *Bonitas* is an accident
> through colour and through motion.[6]
>
> (lines 434–41)

These explanations are very problematic, and require some elucidation
from Scholastic doctrine and Llull's other writings. In Aristotelian
theory, the division of genera into their constituent species is accom-
plished by a specific difference. That is, the combination of a genus

---

[6] E pots ne far divisió
per proprietat, e veus co:
la bonea de volentat
es a ela proprietat;
e bonesa's proprietat
per sí matexa e qualitat;
e bonea es accident
per color e per moviment.
(*Obres Originals*, 20. 225.)

and a specific difference defines a species, just as 'rational animal' defines man, and signifies its essence or *quid est esse*, according to Aristotle (*Top*. 1. 5 101b38–102a1) and Peter of Spain after him (2. 14). The property pertains to one species alone, according to Porphyry (pp. 19–20), but does not signify its essence, according to Aristotle (*Top*. 1. 5 102a18). Therefore it provides only a description, or 'comprehensive statement composed of accidents and properties', as Ockham calls it (1. 27). In his own *Proverbis de Ramon*, Llull avers that property is natural to a creature and pertains to no other, and also is 'the instrument' with which difference divides a genus into species (137. 11, 18). Similarly, he defines property in the glossary appended to the *Art amativa* as 'that through which the thing is defined and known, just as laughing is a property of man'. The example of man and his capacity to laugh is that of Porphyry (p. 20). Llull calls *Bonitas* a quality, perhaps attempting to distinguish between the functions of *Bonitas* as a specific difference and as a property (or proper quality, as he terms it). Or, he may refer to a specific difference alone, since this answers the question *Quale?* regarding a substance, according to one of the views noted by Peter of Spain (2. 12). The reference to the functions of *Bonitas* as an accident either 'through colour or through motion' alludes to examples of separable accidents (or common differences) and inseparable accidents (or proper differences) as explained by Peter of Spain: the former include sitting, standing, or white skin in general, while the latter include the shape of the nose, blackness in a crow, or whiteness in a swan (2. 12, 15). Although these lines from the *Aplicació* seem to conflate specific difference and property, Llull does recognize some distinctions between them in the third *Regula* of his *Art amativa*, where he posits two ways of defining entities from each level in the hierarchy of being:

The essential definition of fire is when it is defined through its proper ignivity and ignibility, for to ignite pertains to nothing but fire. Accidental definition is when the fire is defined by a proper quality alone, just as the property of heat (*propia calor*) does not pertain to any of the other elements, but only to fire.[7] (2. 3. 2)

Since Llull's indistinct treatment of property, difference, and accident renders very difficult the creation of Aristotelian definitions in the

---

[7] 'Diffinició essencial de foch es com es diffinit per propria ignitivitat e ignibilitat, car a negú dels altres no s pertany ignir, mas al foch. Diffinició accidental es com lo foch tan solament es diffinit per propria qualitat, axí com a negú dels altres elements a qui no s pertany propria calor, mas al foch solament.' (*Obres Originals*, 17. 33.)

manner described above, it is not surprising that he offers his own broader variety of essential definition, which simply asserts, as Pascual recognized,[8] the proper act of each being that best corresponds for Llull to its fundamentally active nature. These essential definitions become an explicit component of his later programme for a natural Logic. The distinction in the passage just cited between essential and accidental definitions illustrates a recurrent difficulty in Llull's metaphysics: the uncertain separation of substantial and accidental forms. Since they both comprise an essence, Llull treats them as equally essential and substantial in the sense that they both contribute to the ontic determination of an individual as a particular derived from a universal. Here, essential definition is definition in the strict sense, which signifies the essence of fire through the specific difference of proper ignivity and ignibility (its essential correlatives). The accidental definition, on the other hand, is a description, which signifies the accidental aspects of fire through the property of heat. None the less, when Llull states in the *Aplicació* that the '*Bonitas* of *Voluntas* is a property to it', he is not, strictly speaking, defining his *Principium* of *Voluntas* with either a specific difference or a property peculiar to it alone, since all the *Principia* are mutually and coessentially predicable of each other. The logic of coessentiality sacrifices difference to identity or likeness. Llull seems, at best, to predicate of *Voluntas* what Porphyry (pp. 15–16) would call a proper difference or inseparable accident, which inheres either essentially (as rationality does in man) or accidentally (as snub-nosed does in man). Ultimately, however, Llull's essential definitions serve to remove his accounts of essence from any basis in the structures of formal logical predication, and contribute to his general disregard for Scholastic logico-linguistic distinctions.

In lines 431–5 of the *Aplicació de l'Art General*, Llull distinguishes between individuals that differ in number (*per comtar*) and in species; this is the standard distinction, found in Peter of Spain (2. 4). In his *Art amativa*, Llull relates it to the metaphysical and physical derivation of individuals from universals:

In this chaos there exist simple species sown and sustained in it, and these descend from the simple *Principia* of this *Art*; and there exist in it moreover the four simple elements that are powers (*potències*) of the chaos, and from which come the compound elements, in which are composed the individuals of the

---

[8] 'De las definiciones', pp. 52–5.

species, and these individuals are simple with respect to universal existence, just as man, lion, apple, which in so far as each one is an individual substance, is a simple unity (*nombre*).[9] (2. 1. 4)

This passage illustrates very well how Llull's extreme Realism includes physical and metaphysical distinctions in a single system. Here he apparently draws on, in the phrase 'simple with respect to universal existence', the doctrine of the non-numerical simple unity of universals, which he invokes in several of his other writings as well. This doctrine, which appears in Avicenna (*Metaph.* 5. 1), is one of the major arguments in favour of real universals rejected by Ockham (1. 14). It is perhaps one of the most sophisticated conventional arguments that Llull adduces.

As a final conclusion to this survey of Llull's treatment of the predicables, it is sufficient to recall that all his arguments concerning them in the *Aplicació de l'Art General* appeal to the mutual participation and convertibility of his *Principia*. This relationship is hardly receptive of expression according to the distinctions of genus, species, difference, property, or accident, and Llull ultimately must simply assert, rather than prove, their derivation from those *Principia*: he ends his discussion in the *Aplicació* by reiterating that the combination of his *Principia* in the Figures comprehends the predicables, and that they are all equally primary principles (lines 442–7). Thus the foundation of his entire presentation is simply the procession of the many from the one, of particulars from universals. In a broader historical context, it is interesting to contrast Llull's application of his *Principia* to the Scholastic predicables with contemporary debates over the status of universals. The Nominalist solution reached by his peers in the schools recognizes a distinction between real and rational being that is almost incommensurable with the extreme Realism of Llull's natural Logic. Llull's reduction of all particulars to universals comprehends both real and rational beings in a single theocentric hierarchy. The application of his *Principia* to the predicables, as to any thing, moralizes them as elements embraced by this hierarchy, which orders all existence to its proper end.

---

[9] 'En aquest chaos estàn simples species semenades en ell e sustentades, qui devallen dels començaments simples d esta art; e encara estan en ell los .iiij. elaments simples qui son potencies del chaos, de les quals son los elaments compostos, en los quals son compostos los individuus de les species, los quals individuus son simples en quant esser universal, axí com home, leó, poma, qui en quant son cascú substancia individua, es simple nombre.' (*Obres Originals*, 17. 26.)

4

Categories

WHERE the predicables enjoy a broadly fundamental position in Llull's philosophy as divisions of his universalist ontology, the ten Aristotelian categories or *praedicamenta* enjoy a less fundamental role because they do not directly serve to order the procession of particular from universal. This is especially true of the accidental categories, whose arbitrary order is a basic objection to Aristotle's original conception of them. In Llull's *Art* the categories also overlap with some of his own *Regulae*, which very probably derive from them, in any case. This common ground does underscore, however, their common function as topics for pursuing the manifold relations of the many to the one, and rising from knowledge of particulars to knowledge of universals.[1] Thus Llull typically ignores the logical function of the categories as terms of predication in favour of defining their role as real genera. In this way they serve his natural Logic as divisions of the essences that are the natures of things.

His natural orientation is evident even in his rather sketchy summary of the categories in the *Lògica del Gatzel*. This text's prescriptions are often quite conventional, but several of Llull's comments on the categories clearly display a moralization of received doctrine, as in these lines on the category of place (*ubi*):

> One must seek place in two ways.
> The first I will name first:
> it is the captive of this world;
> to all those who are in this world;
> you are in the city, or the road,
> or in a castle, or seated.
> The second is set amidst the world
> in triangular or round:

---

[1] This moralizing interpretation of the categories tends to mitigate the critical value of determining the source for Llull's account of them in the *Logica Algazelis*, which Lohr argues in relation to the previous views of Jordi Rubió, the Carreras y Artau, and Platzeck in *Raimundus Lullus' Compendium Logicae Algazelis*, pp. 27–8.

and if you wish to pass beyond the world,
your Intellect can remember
that God is by Himself in place,
for I believe there is never any place to Him.[2]

(lines 1521-32)

The apparent reference to sitting suggests a confusion between the
categories of place and position (*situs*) that also appears in other works.
Overall, this passage offers a sort of tropological interpretation of place
that would not be inappropriate to contemporary sermon practice. In
contrast to this ethico-theological moralization, Llull's remarks on the
category of quantity and relation simply and clearly state the standard
divisions of each. This collocation, rather than synthesis, of theological
and logical materials in the *Lògica del Gatzel* suggests Llull's incomplete assimilation of the former, and confirms judgements regarding
the occasional or precipitous composition of the work.

Perhaps this is why Llull does not define the categories as a group in
the *Lògica del Gatzel*, nor discuss any question concerning Logic as an
art. However, his general comments from other early works clearly
display the contribution of the categories to the long-standing medieval difficulty regarding the conception of Logic as an *ars sermocinalis*
or *ars realis*.[3] In the *Doctrina pueril* he declares:

Son, every created thing goes through . . . the ten categories, of which you will
learn through Logic; through this learning you will understand how to have
knowledge if you know how to correlate and compose (*concordar e compondre*)

---

[2]   Ubi en dos lo cové sercar.
Lo primer, primer vull nomnar:
so es, hostatge d aquest mon
a tots aquells qui n lo mon són;
estats, en ciutat, en carrer,
o en castell o en seder.
Segon es stat enfre l mon,
en triangle o en redon.
E si part lo mon vols passar,
ton entendra porà membrar
que Deus està per sí sens loch,
car hanc a sí no crec loch . . .

(*Obres Originals*, 1. 59)

[3] In so far as this means an art of the concepts of things, it is interesting to speculate
that Llull's views may represent a somewhat simplistic rendering of Avicenna's conception of Logic as an art of mental concepts, which Scholastics such as Albert the Great
understood very differently than Llull did; see Richard F. Washell, 'Logic, Language,
and Albert the Great', *Journal of the History of Ideas*, 34 (1973), 445-50.

the five aforesaid universals with the ten categories; for through the composition of one word (*dicció*) with another, you will have the signification that you seek.[4] (73. 7)

On the one hand, Llull treats Logic as a science of being, 'of every created thing', as Isidore does in various definitions (2. 21. 1 and 24. 3). On the other hand, Llull's references to the composition of words treats Logic as a science of words, as Boethius declares it to be (*In Cat.* 1; 161). This fundamental ambiguity was one of the first problems of logical doctrine to attract attention in the early schools, and twelfth-century treatises such as the anonymous *Introductiones montane minores* (Intro.) confront it explicitly. In Llull's era the rise of Nominalism obviously provides one clear solution. Yet the examination in Chapter 2 of Llull's comments on Logic as an art have shown that his conception of a wholly real or natural Logic completely refuses any consideration of its specifically verbal elaboration. Still, the truth of things that this natural Logic seeks leaves the way open for a discursive art devoted not to formal logico-linguistic structures, but to hermeneutic analysis, and this analysis is the 'signification' quoted above. These 'significations' play a capital role in Llull's arguments.

In Chapter 219 of the *Libre de contemplació*, Llull resolves the ambivalently real or verbal value of the categories suggested in the *Doctrina pueril*, and completes the moralization of them begun in the *Lògica del Gatzel*, precisely through appeal to their significations. The numerous chapters of the *Libre de contemplació* devoted to teaching the correct apprehension of the significations of things represent one of Llull's most exhaustive and thorough moralizations of received physical and metaphysical lore. The cognitive character of this apprehension is clear in Llull's general comments on the ten categories:

Since all human knowledge is comprehended and bound within the ten categories, so, Lord, human wit must be comprehended and contained and finished and bound within the limits and confines (*compreniments*) of the ten categories. Since the wit of man cannot attain nor be adequate to anything outside the ten categories, thus it must reach its end and limit within the things subject to the ten categories; and since Lord, the things subject to the ten categories are so many and diverse, therefore human wit cannot attain nor be

---

[4] 'Totes quantes coses creades van, fill, per . . . los .x. predicaments, dels quals auras conexensa per lògica; per la qual conexensa sabrás aver sciencia, si ab los .x. predicaments sabs concordar e compondre los .v. universals damunt dits; car per la composicio de la una diccio ab altra, aurás la significacio que demanes.' (*Obres Originals*, 1. 131.)

adequate to all the ends and limits where the created categories are bound in their subjects or the created subjects in the categories.[5] (219. 1–2)

Llull's praise of the categories as the bounds of human knowledge recalls Isidore's claim that all discourse employs them (2. 26. 1, 15). The categories are obviously of things for Llull, and his Realist understanding of them as universals, and of categorized subjects as particulars, is implicit in the last lines of this passage. This view of the categories serves, however, the moral lesson of the insufficiency of human knowledge, and his exposition of each category concludes with this same thesis. In discussing the first category, substance, Llull reprises the traditional view, found in Aquinas,[6] that any substance is unknowable in itself, and this doctrine may well be the point of departure for his entire moral lesson in this chapter.

The ultimately moralized import of his whole exposition of the categories motivates his reduction of their sub-types to the simplest

TABLE 2. *Subdivisions of the Categories in the* Libre de contemplació

Category	Subdivisions	Parallels
Substance	incorporeal, corporeal	Boethius, *In Isag.* 3. 4
Quantity	simple, composite	cf. *Cat.* 6 4b21
Relation	intellectual, sensual	cf. Aquinas, 1a. 28, 1
Quality	essential, accidental	*De gen. et corr.* 2. 3–5
Action and Affection	intellectual, sensual	*De gen. et corr.* 2. 3–5 and *Sex prin.* 29
Position	up, down, through, around	*Phys.* 3. 5 205b33
Habit	potency, act, sense object, intellectual object	*Metaph.* 5. 20 1022b3–14
Time	past, present, future	*Sex prin.* 33–7
Place	diverse, singular	*Sex prin.* 54?

[5] '[C]om tota sciencia d ome es compresa e termenada dintre los .x. predicaments, enaxí, *Sènyer*, subtilea d ome cové esser compresa e contenguda e fenida e termenada dintre les termenacions els compreniments dels .x. predicaments. Car en nulla cosa qui sia fora los .x. predicamens no pot atènyer ni bastar subtilea d ome, enans cové que prena fi e termenacio dintre les coses qui son sobjects als .x. predicamens; e car les coses qui son, *Sènyer*, sobjects als .x. predicaments son tantes e tan diverses, per assò la subtilea humana no pot atènyer ni bastar a totes les fins ni les termenacions on les predicaments creats son termenats en lurs subjects ni los subjects creats en los predicaments.' (*Obres Originals*, 5. 424.)

[6] On Aquinas's position, see the remarks by Paul T. Durbin in *Summa Theologiae*, vol. 12 (New York: McGraw-Hill & London: Eyre & Spottiswoode, 1968), pp. 170–1.

and most suitable for arguing his lesson. These sub-types, with their parallels in traditional authorities, appear in Table 2. The very eclectic and extraneous character of these divisions illustrates very well Llull's conflation of natural and logical science, which results from his moralizing pursuit of analogies, comparisons, or parallels between different doctrines or concepts in his arguments. The *Liber chaos* gives, of course, a completely natural and physical exposition of the categories ('De decem praedicamentis'), arguing in each case for their real existence as universal forms in the primordial chaos.

Llull's increasing naturalization of the categories is one of the important developments in his treatment of Logic throughout his career. He progressively develops a view of the categories as primarily physical characteristics of things at the same time that he insists on their metaphysical status as real universals. This redefinition of them consists principally in correlating metaphysical and physical functions from Aristotelian doctrine that appear, to modern eyes, certainly, to be the same in any case. Still, as a response to received doctrine, Llull's treatment creates some very heterogeneous collocations of distinct elements from Scholastic philosophy, and these are very evident in Llull's *Proverbis de Ramon*. For example, he begins his account of the first category, substance, with the wholly Aristotelian definition (*Metaph.* 7.1 1028a30–4) of 'the being that exists by itself, without which accidents would have nothing to be in', while also declaring that 'plant is a specific substance, and thus lives from the general, as man from air and fish from water' or 'every substance is invisible' (127. 1, 9, 14), which seem to offer very simplistically naturalistic notions of substance. Likewise, he displays an understanding of habit that matches Aquinas's (1a. 2ae. 49, 2 and 51, 1) when he declares that 'habit is the disposed vestment of a power' but other declarations such as 'if there were no substantial habit, no substantial part would be vested with another' (133. 1, 8) reveal both his advocacy of multiple substantial forms and confusion between Aristotle's qualitative 'habit' (*Cat.* 8 8b27) and the 'having' of clothing or vestments (*Cat.* 15 15b17–31).

Various of Llull's works from the end of his early period attempt to explain this naturally physical or metaphysical status of the categories, especially by deriving them from Llull's own *Principia*. The *Aplicació de l'Art General*, which one might expect to accomplish this, does not, although it appeals frequently to the derivation of the categories from the *Principia*, *Regulae*, and other Lullian divisions (e.g. lines 448–56 and 490–502). In the latter passage Llull even asserts that the definitions of his *Art* allow definition of the categories, which is strictly impossible for Aristotle, since only species can be defined (*Top.* 1. 8 103b15) and the categories, as *genera generalissima*, are not species of anything. None the less, Peter of Spain frequently employs the noun 'definition' or verb 'define' when discussing the categories (3. 6–28). The account of them in the Seventh *Regula* of the *Art amativa* surveys the categories, offering Llull's typical conflation of natural physical and metaphysical notions, but the best explanation by far of their character and derivation from Llull's *Principia* appears in his *Arbre de sciència*, where they constitute an integral part of its arboreal structure.

In the Elemental Tree the roots are the Absolute and Relative *Principia*. The trunk is the 'adjustment of all these . . . from which arises the confused body called "chaos", which fills all the sublunar space, and in which are sown the species of things and their habits and disposition, so that there is in it a confused substance underlying the accidents of elemental things' (Prol.). Llull's version of the chaos cosmogony here clearly invokes the Augustinian seminal reasons, and these frequently serve to explain the potential existence of the particular in the universal throughout this work. The branches are the four simple elements. The limbs are the four compound elements. The leaves are the nine accidental categories. The flowers are the instruments of all things' activities, and the fruits are the things themselves. The chaos of the trunk is the 'first body' to all things, composed of prime matter and prime form, following the theories known from Avicebron (3. 45–58). This first body is the 'general substance' to its substantial parts and underlies all their accidents, and thus 'there is made in it an accident from many accidents', which 'passes' the accidents in individuals through natural agents by means of generation (Elem. 2. 1–2, 6–7). Thus Llull posits a natural universal substance and accident. His account of the latter begins with this precious analogy:

By 'leaves' we understand the natural accidents: for just as leaves turn in whatever direction the wind comes, so the accidents turn and are held in the conditions of the natural substances and just as the leaves exist in order to conserve the flowers and fruits against great heat and against great cold and even against great winds, so the accidents exist in order to conserve the substances in which they are sustained.[7] (Elem. 5. Prol.)

---

[7] 'Per les fulles entenem los accidents naturals: car en axí com les fulles se giren al vent de qual que part vinga, enaxí los accidents se giren e s an a les condicions de les substancies naturals; e enaxí com les fulles son per conservar les flors els fruyts contra gran calor e contra gran fredor e encara contra gran vent, en axí los accidents son per conservar les substancies en que on sustentats.' (*Obres Originals*, 11. 35.)

Llull invokes the Scholastic distinction between logical and natural accidents, as defined in the *De natura accidentis,* and his general conception of the relationship between a substance and its accidents parallels that suggested by Aquinas (1a. 3, 6). However, Llull's extreme Realism necessarily leads him to argue that 'these accidents are general in the Elemental Tree, which is general to the other natural trees derived from it' (ibid.). He explains each of the nine accidental categories in order, and his argument concerning quantity is exemplary of his method.

According to Llull, because all *Principia* are different in essence, they must have quantity in order not to be infinite and numerically the same in creatures, even though they are so in God. Therefore quantity exists so that the *Principia* might exist, and this ulterior purpose makes it an accident, because it is not created for itself, as the *Principia* are. This argument combines distinctions between the relative value of immediate and remote ends, of finite and infinite being, and of instrumental and self-serving existence in a characteristically Lullian moralization. Because the *Principia* display discrete and continuous quantity, these accidents also 'extend' throughout the Elemental and other Trees, just as iron is continuous as an indivisible species, even while existing in the discrete shapes of a nail, hammer, or knife (Elem. 1. 5. 1). It would be pointless to object here to the organic metaphors of the Tree and of the iron and implements that support Llull's Realist and essentialist assertions in this passage; the kind of part-to-whole argument that these metaphors comprise is a favourite Realist apology, raised and dismissed in Llull's era by authorities from Aquinas (1a. 77, 1 ad 1) to Ockham (1. 14–18; 2. 2).

Llull's arguments for deriving the other categories from his *Principia* or *Regulae* are various, and not always fully convincing. Quality exists, for example, in the *Principia* in order to keep them qualitatively distinct by conserving their 'proper number'. As usual, he explains quality with examples drawn solely from the four elemental qualities. By virtue of this quality, many others exist in the Elemental Tree, underlying the species so that each of these exists potentially in its 'proper number, until drawn into actuality by their proper qualities and natural agents' (Elem. 5. 2).

Llull derives the relations double and triple first from his innate correlatives, and then again from the actualization of species out of genera and individuals out of species, and finally from the generation or production of individuals by natural agents. This allows Llull to declare that 'there is a disposition in the species for individuals disposed to being drawn into actuality', since there is a natural appetite for the beginning to seek its end through a means (middle point). This relationship of beginning, middle, and end is, Llull concludes, the primary one extended throughout the Elemental Tree, and from which all other relations among individuals and species derive (Elem. 5. 3). His presentation of it as a kind of appetite suggests the importance of natural sympathy as a means of introducing telic order into the relations that his arguments must describe. It is difficult not to see also in this argument a sort of discursive meander among examples of relationships, which Llull collects and identifies one with another in order to assert a jointly metaphysical and physical paradigm of the many's natural attraction to the one. This collection of examples creates the moralizing analogies that Llull applies to any subject, without necessarily proving the adequacy or pertinence of the examples adduced.

In some cases it is difficult not to appreciate the priority of the categories themselves to the Lullian elements from which Llull derives them. Thus, action and affection derive from the correlative and essential transmission of each *Principium*'s nature to the others. From this coessential participation of the substance of each *Principium*, Llull concludes his curious doctrine of substantial action and affection, which 'produce' the accidental actions and affections in a substance, so that 'substances move the accidents to the perfection of the substances' (Elem. 5. 4). By 'substantial action' Llull usually means a being's actuality, and in effect he conflates the meanings of the Scholastic terms *actus* and *actio* under the latter. Thus he recognizes a connection between them, in the manner suggested by Aquinas (1a. 45, 8; 76, 1; 115, 1), but Llull's advocacy of multiple substantial forms makes it much easier for him to confront the problem that Saint Thomas faces of explaining how the one substantial form that gives a being actuality is connected to its various accidental actions.

In some cases Llull's explication of a category confuses its distinction from or relationship to another. This occurs in his account of habit. He begins by describing it in terms that recall the Aristotelian classification (*Cat.* 8 8b27) of habit as a type of quality: 'the primary habits are in the first things, like the habit of *Bonitas*, which is from the likeness of *Magnitudo* in so far as *Magnitudo* has the capacity (*hàbit*) of magnifying *Bonitas*, and *Bonitas* has the capacity of bonifying *Magnitudo*; and these habits extended through the tree are the primary natural habits in which exist potentially the secondary habits with which the elemental individuals are vested' (Elem. 5. 5). At the very end of his account he lists virtue and knowledge as examples of the qualitative habit, following Aristotle (*Cat.* 8 8b28). Llull's use of the term 'vested' shows, however, confusion with the category of 'having', which includes clothing or vestments, as noted above; Aristotle clearly distinguishes 'habit' and 'having' in the *Metaphysics* (5. 20 1022b3–13), but Aquinas still finds it necessary to separate them (1a. 2ae. 49, 1), which suggests that some confusion between them was commonplace. Still, it is important to see how Llull's conflation of the two categories allows him to pursue his naturalistic account of habit in particular. His example of this category reveals how he accomplishes this:

> The species sown in the tree are primary habits with which are vested . . . all its parts; the natural agents of the primary habits, through generation, vest the elemental individuals, just as the lion that engenders another lion from what it takes from the Elemental Tree, converting into its species what it takes; and what it takes, habituated according to its species, it puts into potentiality so that from that habit, which it gives to the lion that it engenders, another lion can be vested, and thus successively, one habit under another and from another, the species lion is conserved, just as many particulars that are conserved in their universals and one part in another and the whole in its parts.[8] (Elem. 5. 5)

The purpose of this passage, as of all those on the categories, is obviously to postulate a real universal category of habit, from which all particular instances of habit derive, because they exist potentially in it. This existence itself is 'habitual', according to Llull, as his comments on other categories show. In arguing thus Llull identifies species as habits or dispositions to produce other members of the same species, apparently recalling the Augustinian *rationes seminales*, while none the less attempting to adapt Aristotelian doctrine concerning the perpetuation of individuals by other individuals alone (*Metaph.* 7. 8 and 12. 5 1071a20–3). It is typical of Llull's wholesale subordination of Aristotelian to Neoplatonic theory that he concludes his account of this process by comparing it to the hierarchy of descending habits, to particulars maintained in their universal, and to parts of a whole.

---

[8] 'E per açò les especies sembrades en larbre, son primers hábits d on son vestides les rayls del arbre e totes les sues parts; els agents naturals dels primers hàbits, per manera de generació, vesten los individuats elementats, axí com lo leó qui engenra altre leó de ço que pren del arbre elemental, convertent en la sua especia ço que n pren; e ço que n pren, habituat segons sa especia, posa en potencia com d aquell hàbit que dona al leó que engenra pusca esser vestit altre leó, e enaxí succesivament, un hábit sots altre e un d altre, es conservada la especia del leó, enaxí com molts particulars qui son conservats en lurs universals e una part en altra e tot en ses parts.' (*Obres Originals*, 11. 41.)

Some of Llull's accounts display confusion of different accounts of different categories. Thus, Llull defines position (or situation—*situs*) in two ways: one 'simple' being is situated in itself, as the coessential correlatives of *Bonitas* are in it; or, in another, as *Bonitas* is great by *Magnitudo* (Elem. 5. 6). He then equates the first mode with the arrangement of a being's parts or members, according to definitions of position from Aristotle (*Cat.* 7 6b6, 12–14; *Metaph.* 5. 19 1022b2) and the *Liber sex principiorum* (60), but stressing that these are parts of a whole, as limbs are of a tree, since this analogy for the derivation of particulars from universals is his favourite. He equates the second mode with the relationship of container to contained, which is not situation at all, but place, in Aristotelian doctrine (*Phys.* 4. 3 210a32), but may have attracted Llull as a suitable analogy, since Aristotle describes the combination of container and contained as a whole. He concludes by invoking another mode of position that again includes types of place (a man in a room, bones in flesh, or wine in an amphora, all mimicking Aristotle's examples in the *Physics*) and types of position as well (lying down, straight, curved, and circular), which he offers without the qualifications explained in the *Liber sex principiorum* (62–8).

Llull's account of place itself displays a similar confusion among Aristotle's eight senses of 'being in' (*Phys.* 4. 3 210a14–34) and argues first that there must be a universal place by virtue of which any particular is in place, just as it is good by virtue of universal *Bonitas*, coloured by universal colour or hot by universal heat (Elem. 5. 8). This argument explicitly contradicts Aristotle's assertion that place is strictly not an accident 'in' a subject (*Phys.* 4. 3 210a32–b31). Llull then proposes a second mode of place, derived from the collocation of one thing in another, as innate correlatives in a *Principium*, or one *Principium* in another, and from these relationships he adduces that of container to contained, even though his examples again contradict Aristotle's dictum that a thing cannot be in itself primarily (*Phys.* 4. 3 210b23). Here, as so often, the demands of Llull's doctrine of coessentiality override rigorous respect for received theory. Llull compares the actualization of potential 'placements' from universal place to the 'collocation' of the tree in its branches. When Llull claims that 'species are collocated actually in the [Elemental] Tree', and individuals potentially in them, it is not clear whether he means all species and individuals, or merely those of place, since he gives only the examples of 'the man placed in the room and the room in the air' (Elem. 5. 8). The confusions that exist in Llull's account of position and place arise precisely from his attempt to fuse the naturalistic and material examples of Aristotle's *Physics* with his own Neoplatonizing account of the origin of particulars in universals.

The inadequacy of the analogies with which Llull moralizes Aristotelian doctrine is patent in his remarks on the category of time. He begins by noting the basic Peripatetic tenets regarding time: it is indivisible in itself (*Phys.* 4. 10 218a3–30), but divisible as a measure of change and motion (*Phys.* 4. 11 220a24). He then compares this to the iron that is undivided as a species, but divided among different implements made from it. Of course, this comparison between a whole composed simultaneously of coexistent parts and a continuum of discretely terminate parts is precisely the one that Aristotle rejects (*Phys.* 4. 10 ibid.). Llull offers this analogy of part-to-whole instead of defining a universal time from which particular times would derive, but he manages to postulate a corollary derivation by asserting that the *Principia* provide the first changes or motion for time to measure in their mutual participation, and that all secondary changes or motion that time measures derive from those first ones. This is an extraordinary alternative to the Aristotelian deduction of all terrestrial from heavenly motion (*De gen. et corr.* 2. 10–11) which Aquinas also presents (1a. 115, 3). Despite Llull's reluctance to posit a universal category of time, he does note that, as a simple indivisible form, time is invisible and insensible to man. The ambiguous mutual implication of Llull's *Principia* and the Aristotelian categories is apparent when he observes that the Elemental Tree and all its parts must exist in time, just as they exist in *Veritas*, place, and *Potestas*. Likewise, he avers that time exists in his Relative *Principia* of *Principium*, *Medium*, and *Finis* in order to be sustained in motion, a view peculiarly inconsonant with the Aristotelian conclusion that 'time is number of movement in respect of the before and after' (*Phys.* 4. 11 220a24). Assertions such as these show how completely Llull simplifies, revises, and restates conventional doctrine under the pressure of his own moralizing effort to represent them as allegories of the truth of his own system.

Llull's physical and metaphysical accounts of the categories as natural accidents and real universals effectively remove them from the realm of Logic as a verbal art, and makes their study or use an entirely real one. Both the predicables and categories become, like the Lullian *Principia* and *Regulae* themselves, principles of being and knowledge. Their assimilation to Llull's own *Art*, either derivatively as consequences of his *Principia*, or virtually as the evident precedents for the

Principia or *Regulae*, would seem to make any further exposition of Logic as a separate discipline superfluous for Llull. Yet it is a measure of both the traditional, popularizing character of his work that he still perpetuates received doctrine and lore from the arts, and of its evangelical, reforming purpose that he still attempts to restate or moralize them according to his own system. In the case of the predicables and categories, the treatments of them from his early period come to establish a real and natural value for all terms of logical discourse. In his later period Llull recognizes that this ontological language of things requires a corresponding epistemology in order to bring those terms into logical discourse as a specifically human activity caused by the soul's own attraction to its final perfection.

5

Predication and Proposition

JUST as Llull redefines the predicables and categories of Scholastic Logic to correspond in value to the *Principia* and *Regulae* that found his *Art*, so he redefines predication and the construction of propositions to correspond to the combinatory mechanics of his *Art*. These two areas remain the foundation of his accounts of Logic, just as they are the foundation of his Great Universal Art. The fact that the predicables, categories, and propositions comprised most of the logical doctrine offered by the Scholastic *logica vetus* suggests, in the correspondence between these elements and Llull's own, the very traditional theoretical basis of his *Art*. Moreover, where the predicables and categories establish the natural character of Logic for Llull, so propositions support its moralized character. For this reason Llull never treats all the forms and modes of propositions, but only those aspects most tractable in his moralizing method; these are affirmation and negation, antecedence and consequence, possibility and impossibility, and contradiction. All but the second ultimately express the basic role of identity and difference in Llull's analogical method; the second serves more typically to express relationships of proportion or participation among the greater and lesser. Llull's special attention to these modes is not necessarily apparent in the *Lògica del Gatzel*, where they receive only their due attention (some 216 lines out of 1622) and display none of the peculiar uses or applications found in his later works.

One striking feature of Llull's treatment of predication and proposition is the complete absence of any references to the theories of supposition of terms that distinguished the Scholastic *logica moderna* of his contemporaries. Although the 'conversion of subject and predicate' becomes one of the special concerns of his later accounts of Logic, he nowhere considers the nature or function of the subject or predicate in themselves. Any consideration of their verbal status as terms of logical discourse would deviate from Llull's insistently Realist interpretation of the predicables, and from the role of his own *Principia* as the most universal and effective terms of inquiry. Thus, in his *Compendium artis demonstrativae* (pp. 79–80) he avers that the Lullian artist must know what the subject and predicate in any question are, and refers them immediately to his own *Principia*. Likewise the *Libre de demostracions* (2. Prol.) takes the *Principia* as the subjects and predicates of logical argument, which thus becomes simply the discourse of his own *Art*. On the other hand, the Glossary appended to the *Art amativa* does define a predicate as 'what is said about a thing, like man, of whom animal is said, or rock, body, because every man is an animal and every rock a body', but at the same time it defines a subject metaphysically as 'what underlies an accident'. One of Llull's very few references to conventional logical doctrine regarding the verbal terms of propositions appears in the *Arbre de sciència*, when he declares that the logician 'considers falsehood and truth under the form of the noun and verb: under the form of a noun, in order to have knowledge of the things that are and of what they are, and therefore he defines nouns, and he considers and defines the verb in order to have knowledge of the operations that substances do; and in these two principles all things exist, that is, existing and operating' (Hum. 5. 5. i).

Aristotle's *On Interpretation* (2–3) distinguishes nouns and verbs as the terms of a proposition and Peter of Spain develops these distinctions, adding the Scholastic designation of the other words in a proposition as auxiliary 'consignificative' or 'syncategorematic' terms (1. 5). Ockham, writing some thirty years after Llull, rejects verbs as terms of a proposition (1. 2). Llull's remarks represent, typically, the most traditional conception possible, without any evidence of using more recent authorities or acknowledging contemporary debates. In this case he applies to nouns and verbs the distinction between existence and activity or operation derived from Priscian's definitions of these parts of speech in his *Institutiones grammaticae*: 'the property of the noun is to signify substance and quality'; 'the property of the verb is to signify action or affection or either one with moods and forms and tenses but without case' (2. 18). Since Llull refers to 'substances' his claim that nouns show 'things that are and what they are' corresponds to Priscian's definition of the noun as the sign of substance and quality. Peter of Spain does not, as it happens, draw on Priscian in his initial definition of nouns and verbs (1. 4–8), although he does later when explaining certain aspects of the fallacies (7. 83). However, the synthesis of Aristotle and Priscian's definitions appears at least as early as

1100[1] and Llull would have found it in many texts, except Aristotle's
or Priscian's own. The whole import of Llull's comments, finally,
focuses on the logician's knowledge of aspects of real beings through
the verb and noun. For Llull, Logic is always an *ars realis*, and the
linguistic or semiotic concerns of the terminist logicians are wholly
antithetical to his system.

Affirmation and negation

Perhaps for this reason Llull typically focuses on the distinction
between affirmation and negation as the most important and indeed
only one among propositions. The manipulation of affirmative and
negative statements is the basis of all Lullian argumentation, as Pascual once declared,[2] because it serves the expression of the identity or
difference between creature and Creator that is the analogical method
of Llull's *Art*. The divisions of universal, particular, indefinite, and
singular defined by Peter of Spain, and his treatment of these types as
verbal constructs created by the terms or signs 'all', 'none', 'every', and
so forth (1. 7–8) again deviate too far from Llull's view of things
themselves and their truths as universal or particular. Llull's presentation of affirmation and negation correlates metaphysical, ethical, and
theological tenets concerning the distinction of truth from falsehood,
being from non-being, and good from evil, as well as possibility and
impossibility and doubt. It is preferable to consider the former group
first, in order to show how they directly reflect some of the most basic
axioms from the great authorities of medieval thought; then it will be
possible to examine their correlations with the second group according
to Llull's somewhat peculiar conception of these.

Among Llull's earliest works, the *Libre de demostracions* echoes
Aristotle (*Metaph.* 4. 7 1011b25–30) in the opening lines of its account
of affirmation and negation:

It is a true thing that an affirmation that affirms what is, is good, and if it
affirms what is not, is bad; and a negation that denies what is not, is good, and
if it denies what is, is bad; and if this were not so, it would follow that truth was

---

[1] On these developments, see Lambertus Marie De Rijk, *Logica Modernorum. A
Contribution to the History of Early Terminist Logic.* Vol. 2, pt. 1: *The Origin and Early
Development of the Theory of Supposition* (Assen: Van Gorcum, 1967), pp. 95–263.
[2] 'Del sistema del Arte Luliana', p. 41 and 'De las condiciones', p. 70; Platzeck also
acknowledges this fundamental role, though more weakly, in 'La combinatoria luliana',
p. 131, and 'Descubrimiento y esencia del Arte del Beato Ramon Llull', *Estudios
Lulianos*, 8 (1964), 137–54; at p. 152.

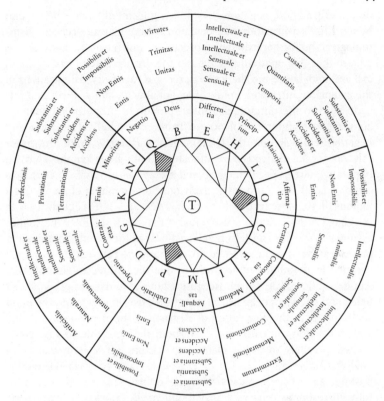

6. Figure T from the *Ars demonstrativa* of 1272–6. This early version of Llull's *Art* uses fifteen alphabetical letters, grouped here in five triangles: Blue (BCD); Green (EFG); Red (HIK); Yellow (LMN); and Black (OPQ), shaded here.

not good and falsehood not evil, which is impossible. Thus . . . affirmation and negation can be converted into good or into evil.[3] (2. 26. 1)

Likewise, this is the method of the entire early *Art demostrativa*, as stated in opening lines of its *Regles introductories* and argued throughout the work itself (e.g. 2. 2. 14. 5; 2. 2. 24. 5; 3. 13). It is the basis of the black triangle in its first Figure T (see Illustration 6), which correlates

---

[3] 'Vera cosa es que affermació qui aferma so qui es, es be, e si afferma so qui no es, es mal; e negació qui nega so que no es, es be, e si nega so que es, es mal; e si assò no era enaxí, seguirsia que veritat no fos be ni falsetat no fos mal, e assò es inpossibol. On . . . afermació e negació se pusquen convertir en be o en mal.' (*Obres Originals*, 15. 126.)

doubt, affirmation, negation, possibility, impossibility, non-being, and being. Llull's affirmation and negation are not logical, or even epistemological, but rather axiological processes, which serve to show and to ensure that 'the good and being and the greater agree (*convenen*) and evil and non-being and the lesser agree' (*LD* 2. 26. 4). All questions of the extension, intension, implication, entailment, and so forth of terms cede here to the ubiquitous Lullian pursuit of proportional analogy, convenience, and resemblance to truth. For Llull, affirmation and negation in Logic, like the combination of *Principia* in his *Art*, never rely on formal dialectical relationships, but rather on the spiritual imperative of certain theological and metaphysical values. It is easy to see that Llull's position rests firmly on the foundation of Augustine's famous dictum 'the true is that which is' (*Sol.* 2. 5). It is equally easy to see that Llull's position must refuse Aristotle, since the Philosopher assumes that truth and falsehood exist only in the mental combination or separation of terms (*Metaph.* 6. 4 1027b17–35); neither can Llull accept the definition of 'conformity between thing and mind' that Aquinas follows (1a. 16, 1). Because Llull's *Principia* are principles of being and knowledge, he insists that truth exists in things and the mind similarly. As to the correlation of affirmation and negation with being and non-being, or truth and falsehood, it is possible to find some limited parallels for such claims in Aristotle's *On Interpretation* (9 19a33), *Categories* (5 4b9–10), or *Metaphysics* (5. 7 1017a31–4), and his position superficially recalls that of Aquinas (1a. 17, 4), but most fully corresponds only with that found in the *Summa* (1. 101) attributed to Alexander of Hales, and which Saint Thomas rejects. Ultimately, Llull's correlations of affirmation, being, and truth with the good and of negation, non-being, and falsehood with evil must require imposition of a very rigidly telic axiology—or more simply, a moralization—that brings all intellection and reasoning within the command of the supreme values defined in his basic doctrine of intention. Llull's moralization of affirmation and negation is perhaps the most fundamental in all his *Art*. With respect to Logic itself, his treatment of affirmation and negation as modes of logical discourse progressively reveals, in his earlier and later periods, the profoundly spiritual motive of his entire programme.

   An early example of Llull's attempts to accommodate this moralization of propositional modes as cognitive or intellective acts of judgement appears in two final chapters of the *Libre de contemplació*, which seem to deal with conventional logical doctrine, although the terminology employed in them does not make this obvious. This ambiguity perhaps reflects Llull's still non-adversarial posture toward conventional Logic at this early stage of his career, and uncertain application of his *Art* to its doctrines. The title of Chapter 362 announces that it will explain 'How by adoring and contemplating one's glorious God, one receives the knowledge and means by which one knows in the disputation whether the affirmation or the negation is true'. The notion that the disputation determines 'which of the affirmation or negation is true or false' (362. 1) joins these basic types of proposition to his favourite traditional definition of Logic, perhaps following formulas similar to Isidore's 'It teaches how the true and false in many classes of questions may be distinguished.' (2. 22. 2.) Since Llull has much more to say about the disputation, Chapter 8 of this study will discuss it more fully. This chapter of the *Libre de contemplació*, as a treatment of affirmation and negation, ought to deal with the proposition, but Llull never uses that term. He proposes instead to recognize the true and false through certain 'intellectual figures', which in turn derive from certain 'sensual figures' (362. 1), a division that repeats the fundamental dichotomy of sense and intellectual knowledge that the *Libre de contemplació* exhaustively develops. Llull uses the term 'figure' in various senses, as when he speaks later in this chapter of the 'true figure' and 'chimera or empty figure' that the Imagination conceives (362. 24). He also uses the Catalan verb *afigurar*, meaning to shape, figure, imagine, or perceive (362. 29), and the verb *transfigurar*, meaning to transform or transmute (362. 22). At the outset of this chapter, however, the term 'figures' designates the eight abbreviations that Llull subsequently uses as a kind of shorthand in expounding his arguments: A = truth; B = signification of A; C = affirmation; D = signification of C; E = negation; F = signification of E; G = Memory, Will and Intellect; H = signification of G (362. 1). These figures obviously name the fundamental hermeneutical function of signification, mentioned above. He also calls figures the three possible combinations of true and false affirmations and negations concerning any disputed position: (1) a true affirmation and a false negation; (2) a true negation and false affirmation; and (3) a true affirmation and true negation (362. 2). These permutations perhaps recall the Scholastic square of opposition, based on Aristotle's presentation of contrarity and contradiction (*De interp.* 7–14) and the term 'figures' even the three figures of the syllogism, but the arguments with which Llull illustrates them are not syllogistic.[4] Each argument instead turns upon the apprehension of the moral or theological values symbolized or 'signified' in the letters A to F by the faculties of Memory, Intellect, and Will. Llull's three figures of affirmation and negation do not define any of the relationships of contradiction or contrarity established by Aristotle, but instead create relationships of correspondence and proportion, in which one fixed point of comparison is always the first intention of God's being and knowledge of that being. Llull's first intention provides the axiological telos of his method; he avers that

the figure where one best receives the meanings (*significats*) of Your virtues and of creatures in order to display the perfection of Your glorious essence, that figure is better than the other figure that is not as capable (*aparellada*) of receiving these meanings, and that figure is worst that most hinders the human Intellect in receiving the meanings that signify Your divine essence.[5] (362. 3)

This is the basis for Llull's response to all the questions raised in this chapter, as one extended example will adequately show.

This example is the question whether God is the Creator of all beings. Llull introduces the contradictory positions thus:

Intellectually we understand that when the C affirms that You are Creator of all things and the E denies a creator, then the D and the F conflict about the A: hence, the E thus demonstrates to the G how the H receiving the B signifies the G, which is better when it receives the B, than when it refuses the D and receives the F; for just as a truthful man is worth more than a lying one, so the G is worth much more when it receives the D, than it is when it receives the F and disbelieves the D.[6] (362. 13)

In virtually all the arguments from Chapters 362 and 363 of the *Libre de contemplació*, Llull appeals to comparisons or analogies like that of

---

[4] Platzeck argues that these figures are the genesis of Llull's combinatory method in 'Descubrimiento y esencia del Arte del Beato Ramon Llull'.

[5] '[A]quella figura on hom mills reeb los significats de vostres vertuts e de les creatures a mostrar l acabament de vostra gloriosa essencia, aquella figura es mellor que l autra figura qui no es tan aparellada a reebre los dits significats, e aquella figura es pijor qui pus fort embarga l umà enteniment a reebre los significats qui signifiquen la vostra essencia divina.' (*Obres Originals*, 8. 571.)

[6] 'Entellectualment entenem que com la C aferma que vos sots creador de totes coses e la E nega creador, adoncs la D e la F se contrasten sobre la A: on, per assò la B demostra a la G com la H reebent la B significa la G que mellor es com reeb la D, que no es com rebuja la D e reeb la F; car aitant com un home vertader val sobre un home mentider, d aitant val la G molt més com reeb la D, que no fa com la F reeb e descreu la D.' (*Obres Originals*, 8. 575–6.)

the liar and the honest man that he introduces here as a truly literal example of the moralizing method that is his *Art*; such examples easily recall the moral or tropological interpretations of medieval sermons and biblical exegesis. Llull's argument here defines the greater value that the Memory, Will, and Intellect incur by receiving the signification of the affirmative proposition that God is Creator. In a statement that is largely an allegory of faculty psychology, Llull explains that 'the G wishes to know and learn in what the A exists, whether in the C or the E, and to know with which letter the B and H agree most' (362. 13). Llull effectively combines an argument from proportion with one regarding the ultimate standard or goal that measures the proportion in a dynamic relationship that imputes to the soul a natural attraction to that goal. The three faculties of the soul perform their functions most 'nobly' when they remember, desire, and understand a Creator, and therefore the affirmation of God as Creator best allows them to attain their own perfections. Hence that affirmation must be true. The denial of God as Creator, on the other hand, would not allow the faculties to attain that perfection, and therefore must lack truth.

Thus Llull attempts to draw epistemological consequences from a function of the soul from which Anselm draws only the eschatological ones of eternal reward or punishment (*Monol.* 66–73). The 'agreement and concord' (362. 15) that Llull posits between truth and affirmation of God as Creator assumes his doctrine of intention, which implicitly makes the remembering, desiring, and understanding of a Creator a purpose or function of the three faculties indistinguishable from the truth of that proposition. The assumption of Llull's intention becomes explicit in his explanation that to consider the denial of God as Creator a more efficacious signification than the affirmation of God as Creator is just as impossible as to consider irrational beings to possess more nobility than rational, and vegetable more than irrational (362. 14–15). Such a comparison again suggests the pervasive role of Llull's ethico-theological intention as a natural function of any creature.

These appeals to natural perfection and deductions of correspondingly proportional realizations of that perfection sustain the interpretative work that arranges the significations of beings, the affirmation or negation of positions about them, and the functions of the faculties of the soul that apprehend them as 'demonstrative' arguments or 'necessary reasons', in the manner considered more fully below in Chapter 7 on demonstration. Here it is sufficient to recognize that they are fundamentally arguments from proportion and resemblance and that each signification proposed by Llull articulates analogically the proportional relations among the various perfections that are spiritual truth for Llull. In these earlier works the structures and rules of Logic are almost entirely incidental to these arguments; in his later writings, Llull attempts to accommodate logical doctrine to them. Thus, in the present chapters Llull mentions only those logical arguments that 'sophistically' deny the truth of the resurrection and advises that the best defence against this deception is the seven theological virtues (362. 22–4). Faith founds understanding in Llull's *Art*, whose putative demonstrative value always observes Anselm's *credo*, even when completely redefining the status of belief, as Chapters 7 and 19 will show. The title of this chapter in fact implies the role of faith when it promises to derive knowledge of the truth in disputed questions from the contemplation of God's being. In his later writings on Logic, Llull also takes Anselm's dictum as the point of departure for various revisions in the received logical rules regarding valid syllogisms and true propositions, thereby moralizing them just as thoroughly as if he were to express them in arguments such as those from these last chapters of the *Libre de contemplació*.

Several of the later works in Llull's early period make the moralization of affirmation and negation especially clear. The role of his intention is obvious in the Prologue to the *Art amativa*, one of the best statements of Llull's entire programme from anywhere in his writings. There he explains how the world, which God created in order to be known and loved, has become disordered because the creatures are known and loved more than the Creator. Llull's debt to the Anselmian principles of *deordinatio* and *rectitudo* is, as usual, very profound.[7] Llull proposes to remedy this evil by composing the *Art amativa* as a corollary to his *Art inventiva*, so that 'science is attained through love, and love is attained through science', since one is defective without the other. Affirmation and negation are the basic recourses of this procedure:

For just as truth is the proper object of the Intellect, that is, a proper cause (*rahó*) of affirmation, so the good is the proper object of the Will, that is, a proper cause of loving the good, and the contrary of the good is thus a proper object to the Will for hate, just as a false object is to the Intellect a cause of

---

[7] Jaroslav Pelikan summarizes Anselms's concepts very well in *The Growth of Medieval Theology (600–1300)* (Chicago: University of Chicago Press, 1978), pp. 139–40.

negation. And these two properties . . . are equally necessary, because God is equally worthy of being known and loved by his people, through which equality there follows that other things be equally affirmable and lovable, deniable and hateful.[8] (Prol. 3)

The true and good are the respective proper objects of the Intellect and Will for Aquinas (1a. 16, 1), but for Llull they also correlate with being and non-being, greatness and smallness, and so forth, as more proper objects of knowledge and desire. It is tremendously important that Llull does not name knowing as the proper activity of the Intellect, but rather affirmation, in correspondence with the loving that is the proper activity of the Will. For Llull the knowable or intelligible is also the affirmable. In the *Taula general* he notes that 'being is more memorable, intelligible, and lovable than non-being' (5. 6. 3), and thus he establishes a range of necessarily affirmable objects or values. The intelligibility of being is presumably a consequence of its status as the *primum cognitum*, in the manner explained by Aquinas (*De ver.* 1. 1), but for Llull this is more a relative status, graduated according to the hierarchy of being that culminates in God. As the last lines of the passage quoted above suggest, all other beings must be affirmable or deniable, lovable, or hateful as steps toward the affirmation and love of God; as always, it is better to say that being is proportional, rather than analogous, for Llull. In practice, Llull's procedures of affirmation and negation work very simply; for example, he explains his 'conditions' as 'a universal where many particulars are found, concluding them in such a way, either affirmatively or negatively, that they always agree with the conditions, which are self-evident (*per si apparexent*)' and 'if a particular contradicts its universal, affirmatively or negatively, it is best to take its opposite as the conclusion, and this is a general rule for the entire practice of this *Art*' (4. Prol. 3). This is the mechanism of the General Universal Art of Ramon Llull in brief. Now the theological and metaphysical values that any true statement must somehow affirm are the real basis of Llull's discourse. Affirmation and negation serve primarily a critical—or better, criteriological—function only:

---

[8] '[C]ar enaxí com veritat es propri object al entendiment, ço es propria rahó d affirmació, enaxí bondat es propri object de volentat, ço es propria rahó de amar la bondat, e lo contrari de bondat es enaxí propri object a volentat sots odibilitat, com es fals object al enteniment sots rahó de negació. Aquestes dues proprietats damunt dites de sciencia e amancia son necessaries egualment, per ço cor Deus es egualment digne de esser conegut e amat per son poble, per lo qual egualment se seguexen les altres coses, com sien egualment affirmables e amables, negables e ayrables.' (*Obres Originals*, 17. 6.)

they propose the comparison between a given proposition and Llull's values, and must be manipulated in order to maintain the primacy of those values as the proper objects of knowledge or desire.

Affirmation, negation, possibility, impossibility, and doubt

In the last works of his early period, Llull fully correlates his moralizing discourse of affirmation and negation with several further distinctions: possibility, impossibility, doubt, and certitude. This correlation appears in embryonic form in the *Lògica del Gatzel* (lines 640–73), alongside his references to possibility, impossibility, affirmation, and negation as modes and divisions of propositions in the conventional sense (lines 1560–602 and 428–35). The Latin *Logica Algazelis* entitles this section 'On the investigation of truth', and its opening lines in Catalan suggest its basis in the Anselmian *credo*:

> If you wish to understand the truth,
> you need faith and understanding.
> With faith you begin to work
> on what you wish to find
> affirming possibility;
> because impossibility
> you do not affirm at first,
> because if you did, the Intellect
> could not advance any further.[9]
>
> (lines 640–8)

This integration of the discursive affirmation of possibility with faith and understanding is tremendously important for Llull's conception of the demonstrative value of his logical programme and *Art* as a whole, as subsequent consideration will show. Here it is necessary to recognize that Llull is not treating possibility and impossibility as two of the six modes of 'composition' of a proposition, as defined by a terminist contemporary such as Peter of Spain (1. 20–1). His perspective, as

---

[9]   Si tu vols entendre lo ver,
    fe e'ntendre t auran mester.
    Ab fe comença a obrar
    en ço que volràs encercar,
    affermant possibilitat;
    car la impossibilitat
    no afferms al començament,
    cor si ho fas, l enteniment
    no porà mays avant anar.
    (*Obres Originals*, 19. 28)

Predication and Proposition

always, focuses immediately on the fact described by the proposition. The infidels commit the error of affirming the impossible and thereby exclude knowledge of the true facts:

> Because they disbelieve at first,
> their Intellect in the end
> has nothing with which to seek
> what it can find,
> but instead its power (*virtut*) is blocked
> by the impossible, which was believed
> at the start of the dispute;
> in this doubt would help them more,
> because doubt demonstrates
> what is possible.[10]

(lines 658–67)

Llull's programme for disputation, his conception of demonstrative proof, and the relationship between faith and reason eventually elaborated in his later works all assume the principles outlined in this extremely fundamental passage. The spiritual import for Llull of all these concerns is evident in his claim that the choice to affirm possibility is an ethical, rather than a logical, one, and involves the proper disposition of the faculties of the soul, as Llull recognizes in passages examined in Chapter 8 of this study. Here again it is sufficient to note that the recommendation of doubt apparently recalls its traditional definition, found in Aquinas (*De ver.* 14. 1) as the inability to choose between the affirmative or negative of a proposition. Llull's concern is not so much to distinguish states of knowledge in the manner of Aristotle (*An. post.* 1. 33) or of conviction, in the manner of Aquinas (2a. 2ae. 4, 2), but to define a sequence of psychological acts that will necessarily lead the mind to accept revealed truth as reasoned fact.

Llull also proposes the interrelation of affirmation, negation, doubt,

---

[10]   [E] cor descreon en primer.
lur enteniment en derrer
no ha ab que vaja cercar
so qu'ell pogra atrobar
si no li embargàs sa virtut
l inpossíbol, qui es creüt
a comensar del esputar;
a qual los valgra mays duptar;
car per duptar es demostrat
so que es possibilitat . . .

(*Obres Originals*, 19. 28–9)

possibility, and impossibility in Chapter 173 of the *Libre de contempla-ció*, where his remarks provide a few more clarifications of the principles supporting this interrelation. He begins by noting that some things are 'deficient in being subjects for the perception of truth', and thus engender doubt, while others are more complete (*an acabament*) in this regard and thus engender certitude (173. 1–2). This again refuses the Aristotelian position that truth or falsity exist in the mind alone, and offers instead the Anselmian view of a thing's truth as participation in the Supreme Truth (*De ver.* 7). Llull's explanation is much less sophisticated than Aquinas's of how some things naturally tend to produce a false impression of themselves by virtue of their physical representation to the Senses (1a. 17, 1). Llull attributes all doubt to inadequate knowledge of the 'concord or discord' between sense objects and intellectual objects (173. 5), following the fundamental dichotomy expounded throughout the *Libre de contemplació*. In this chapter he opposes doubt to affirmation in the sense of 'assent' or certitude (e.g. 173. 22) and eventually he declares that doubt arises from the Senses 'by reason of sin', while affirmation arises from the Intellect, presumably as its natural operation (173. 14–15). In another chapter he simply declares that affirming possibility before impossibility is as natural to the Intellect as falling is to a stone (291. 9); that is, just as a stone is naturally attracted to the earth, so the Intellect is to the existence of being, perhaps because it is the Scholastic *primum cognitum*, following the dictum of Avicenna (*Metaph.* 1. 6) already noted. Llull's entire conception of the Intellect's proper objects and proper operation assumes the sort of natural sympathy or attraction suggested in these passages. Llull's notion that doubt arises from the senses alone is a traditional view that Aquinas qualifies when explaining to what degree pre-lapsarian man was never mistaken (1a. 94, 4). Finally, Llull avers that doubt and affirmation occur because possibility ambivalently signifies being and privation in things (173. 19), but affirmation and certitude occur because possible things signify their possibility and impossible things their impossibility in opposition to each other (173. 20). Obviously, these significations are not oppositions of logical contrariety or contradiction in propositions, as described by Peter of Spain (1. 25), but rather something more like the comparative interpretation of one with another. His concluding example illustrates this in a somewhat confused manner:

Since man, Lord, is certain by reason of the meanings demonstrated by impossible things, which are not signified by possible things, thus man apprehends in possible things those properties and that nature (that are to those possible things impossible properties and nature and qualities) from impossible things, like man flying; for the impossibility of flying is not perceived in man through the possibility of man moving.'' (173. 21)

His argument seems to be that impossible things define their own meanings, and hence need not be apprehended as the opposite of a possible thing, but rather the comparison of one possible and impossible thing reveals their incompatibility, even when this is not logically deduced. Where Aquinas approaches deduction of this impossibility as a broadly intensional understanding of subject and predicate terms (1a. 25, 3), Llull's meanings or significations more exactly concern the complete definition of a being's properties, but involve discrimination between substantial and accidental predication in a generally Aristotelian sense (*An. post.* 1. 22 83a19–23); his example of man moving may echo Aristotle's (*An. pr.* 1. 15 34b15). Llull suggests elsewhere: 'every subject in its properties gives signification of the truth in it and its works' (193. 25). Llull describes, in effect, the assessment of propositions of 'relative' possibility, as Aquinas calls it (1a. 25, 3), that is, what is possible with respect to some particular power. The fideist basis for Llull's correlation of affirmation, negation, doubt, certitude, possibility and impossibility is explicit at the end of this chapter when he notes that the infidel 'affirms that there is no Trinity', and thus lacks 'at the outset faith in possibility', and 'no one can find if anything is true or false, if he at the outset does not consent whether there can be truth or falsehood' (173. 28–30). For Llull, then, this attempt is necessary because 'doubt is closer to faith than to reason and certitude is closer to reason than to faith' (173. 30). In this respect, faith is inferior to reason, which for Llull is able to attain certainly those supernatural truths, such as the Trinity, that Aquinas demarcates as the province of faith alone (1a. 1, 8). Chapter 7 on demonstration in this study will consider how Llull reconciles his fideist principles with this excellence of reason. These final paragraphs from the *Libre de contemplació* suggest the degree to which Llull's concern for affirmation, negation, possibility, impossibility, doubt, and certitude com-

---

¹¹ 'Com home, *Sènver*, es sertificat per raó de los significats que demostren les coses impossibols, les quals coses impossibols no son significades per les coses possibols, adoncs aperceb hom en les coses possibols aquelles proprietats e aquella natura qui son ad aquelles coses possibols proprietats e natura e qualitats impossibols de les coses impossibols, así com a home volar; car impossibilitat de volar no es apercebuda en home per la possibilitat que home ha de esser movable.' (*Obres Originals*, 5. 45.)

prises a spiritual, rather than logical, account of the central problematic of Llull's *Art* and its entire project, the proof of Christian revelation.

In the *Libre de demostracions*, Llull offers two chapters of arguments that deal with the affirmation of possibility, but employ largely appeals to proportion, rather than the natural attraction of affirmation to truth. Thus Llull invokes the absolute possibility of God's existence in claims such as 'it is true that whatever has greater nobility than whatever has less, has a greater possibility of existing' (2. 26. 2) or 'the greatest impossibility in a creature is that the creature by its own power approach and join its Creator' (4. 46. 6). Elsewhere in this work, his accounts of affirmation, negation, and doubt invoke various claims regarding relative or absolute impossibility, but do not correlate them consistently with affirmation, negation, or doubt (3. 17). They evidently represent a somewhat early stage in his development of this correlation, although the chronology of Llull's first works from the 1270s is too obscure to offer any guesses about the date of composition of the *Libre de demostracions*, based on this feature alone. This example is typical of the still imperfect correlation that Llull offers there:

Because it is a greater impossibility that corruption exist in what has infinite generation through *Bonitas*, *Magnitudo*, *Aeternitas*, etc. than that it not exist in what has no generation or has terminate and finite generation, it is necessary that in the Highest Good there exist that through which it is more impossible to have corruption; and if this were not so, you could not truly affirm that corruption was more impossible in the highest good than in the lowest, according as it agrees with the high impossibility of corruption.[12] (3. 17. 2)

The eventual conclusion that it is true to affirm the impossibility of corruption in the Highest Good effectively appears to repeat tautologically the two preceding premises, rather than to be a consequence of the contrast between the greater and lesser possibilities invoked by Llull.

The *Art demostrativa* of 1272–6 fully expresses the correlation of affirmation, negation, doubt, possibility, impossibility, being, and non-being in the Black Triangle of its First Figure T (see Illustration 6).

---

[12] '[C]or es major inpossibilitat que corropció sia en so on ha generació infinida en bonea granea eternitat etc., que no es en so on no ha generació o en so on ha generació termenada e finida, per assò cové de necessitat que en lo subiran be sia so per que sia pus inpossíbol cosa aver corropció; e si assò no era enaxí, no puries afermar segons veritat, que en lo subiran be fos pus inpossíbol cosa corropció, que en lo jusan be, segons que s cové a la subirana inpossibilitat de corropció.' (*Obres Originals*, 15. 291–2.)

Llull evidently recognizes this correlation, even if all of his arguments do not fully exploit it, and conceives it as fundamental to his system. The *Regles introductories* that serve as a sort of preface to the *Art demostrativa* state that the latter operates by 'discoursing, affirming and denying, destroying doubt' (lines 1–2), and they do in fact appear throughout the many questions analysed in that work. For example: 'God and creature and operation are affirmable beings: hence, not deniable; and if they were deniable and not affirmable, it would follow that being and affirmation would agree with privation, and that non-being and negation would agree with being, which is impossible, and this impossibility does not fall within doubt' (2. 2. 14. 5. 1). In this and the other passages cited thus far, it is not difficult to see the sequence of associations that Llull has elaborated among various received doctrines: doubt is lack of inclination towards either of two contradictory propositions, as Aquinas declares (2a. 2ae. 2, 1); these two propositions must be equally possible, as Aristotle asserts (*An. pr.* 1. 13 32a36–9); from these Llull concludes that doubt can never be of the impossible.

Finally, towards the end of Llull's early period he offers a very clear statement of his doctrine in the maxims from several chapters of the *Proverbis de Ramon* of 1296. Even though the correlation of affirmation, negation, doubt, possibility, and impossibility was obviously a developing concern of his career, and has an especially extraordinary impact on certain logical doctrines of his later period, at least two works of the decade 1291-1301 scarcely acknowledge it: the *Arbre de sciència* gives no special attention to this correlation (perhaps because of its exclusive focus on developing its arboreal schemes), while the *Aplicació de l'Art General* merely notes (lines 466–9, 476–9) that the correlated elements of affirmation, negation, and so forth derive from his *Regulae* (again perhaps because of its special emphasis on this derivation). The *Taula general* does explain very concisely that possibility engages affirmation, doubt, and negation, because one must begin by affirming the possibility of one of the two contradictories, and thus allow doubt about both of them; otherwise the Intellect is a 'captive' of the affirmation or negation, and should not even undertake 'the process of this *Art*', Llull declares (3. 1). The latter view figures in his accounts of disputation, examined in Chapter 8 below. Llull's relative neglect of his fundamental procedure in some of his major works from the 1290s perhaps indicates that he had developed it as far as possible, without introducing some entirely new considerations; these in fact present themselves in his later works, when he attempts to reformulate Scholastic syllogistic and sophistic according to his procedure. The *Proverbis de Ramon* offer the best, if somewhat diffuse summary of the various logical, psychological, theological, and even physical or metaphysical considerations that contributed to Llull's development of his procedure in his early period. The order of the chapters that discuss it seems to suggest the context of these considerations. Thus, the two chapters (141–2) on possibility and impossibility follow those on the categories, property, conversion (of subject and predicate), question, and solution—which are all evidently logical concerns—but precede those on potency, object, act, and generation and corruption—which are clearly physical and metaphysical topics. In this regard possibility and impossibility apparently reflect the natural orientation of Llull's programme for argumentation. In fact, Llull's remarks on possibility and impossibility describe them almost entirely in metaphysical terms in relation to potency, act, and privation, following Aristotelian doctrine (*Metaph.* 5. 12 1019b20–20a5). Llull does imply the specifically propositional value of impossibility in his claims that 'impossibility is from contrary ends' and 'the subject of impossibility is contrarity' (142. 15–16), while his own doctrine of affirming the possible apparently justifies the claims that 'impossibility in itself is not desirable' and 'whoever considers impossibility is sad' (142. 17, 20) because impossibility is contrary to the soul's natural perfection and satisfaction.

The chapters on doubt and affirmation and negation (172–3) follow those on the discursive, deliberative, perceptive, doctive or apprehensive, and opinative powers and precede those on the communicative, factive, instrumentative, adjudative, and obstructive powers. The psychological and even broadly anthropological concern of these is patent. Even though Llull illustrates several of these powers with very naturalistic examples based on the elements—such as 'fire deliberates in winter the act that it will have in summer' (168. 3) or 'the sun does not communicate its clarity to fire, but a likeness of it' (174. 6)—it is obvious that they all deal with properly human powers and activities, and the chapters on 'doctive and apprehensive' powers through those on affirmation and negation include no such naturalistic examples. The precise precedents for this particular list of human powers that Llull offers are not immediately obvious, although many of these divisions appear in the authorities collected by Vincent of Beauvais (*SN* 25–7) and especially recall the doctrines of Avicenna's *De anima*. Whatever their rationale, Llull's collocation of doubt, affirmation, and negation among them clearly underscores his psychological, rather than simply logical, treatment of them. His aphorisms regarding doubt display a real conflict in its value, however. On the one hand, it is obviously the indecision regarding two possible alternatives whose resolution leads to apprehension of the truth:

Doubt is the equal confusion of affirmation and negation.
Doubt is the confused matter of affirmation and negation.
Every doubt is a material principle.
If doubt were a formal principle, it would not stand in the middle of affirmation and negation.
Opinion brings deliberation from doubt.
Whoever induces doubt in his adversary, draws him toward truth.
In doubt there occurs first the conversion of error into truth.[13] (172. 1, 4, 6–8, 18)

The last maxims express Llull's identification of doubt and possibility, which the infidel should adopt in disputing about Christian doctrine in order to be open to accepting its truth. Where Aquinas distinguishes doubt from opinion as assenting to neither alternative from assenting to one with fear that the opposite may be true (*De ver.* 14. 1), following Aristotle's definition of opinion (*An. post.* 1. 33 89a2–b5), Llull associates doubt and opinion more closely, as his remarks on the 'opinative' power also indicate (*PR* 171). There he calls it 'Supposition about something with doubt' and 'of the affirmation or negation', but 'if it had equal inclination towards the affirmation and negation, it would be convertible with doubt' (171. 1, 7, 5). Now, on the other hand, Llull also views doubt as an evil and source of ignorance:

Through doubt all powers of the soul are sick.
In doubt the Intellect is sicker than in any other power.
The power most sickened by doubt is most contrary to it.
Nothing is more perilous than doubt.
Doubt is privation of the habit of understanding, as blindness is of vision.
It is a grave thing to destroy an ancient doubt.[14] (172. 9–11, 15, 16, 20)

---

[13] 'Dubitació es egual confusió d afirmació e negació.
  Dubitació es confusa materia d afirmació o negació.
  Tot dupte es material començament.
  Si dubitació fos formal començament, no fora en lo mig d afirmació e negació.
  Opinió trau de dubitació deliberació.
  Qui son enversari [induu] a dubitació, acosta aquell a veritat.' (*Obres Originals*, 14. 181–2.)

[14] 'Per dubitació son malaltes totes les potencies de l ànima.
  Dubitació pus prop es a posició, que a demostració.
  En dubitació es pus malalte l enteniment, que altra potencia.
  Neguna cosa es pus perillosa que dubitació.
  Enaxí es dubitació privat hàbit d entendre, com ceguetat de visio.
    Greu cosa es destruir antiga dubitació.' (*Obres Originals*, 14. 181–2.)

Llull's obviously ambivalent conception of doubt parallels his equally ambivalent view of faith or belief, as Chapter 8 on demonstration will show. It is noteworthy that Llull no longer attributes doubt to the influence of the senses, as in the *Libre de contemplació*, and here refers to the habit of understanding, in the manner of Aquinas (1a. 2ae. 50, 4), although Saint Thomas flatly denies that the intellectual dispositions in themselves have contraries capable of causing their privation by replacing them; particular beliefs or known facts have contrary assertions that could replace them, however (1a. 2ae. 53, 2). Llull's comments may imply none the less that the affirmation or negation of such assertions are mental habits capable of replacement.

Hence in his chapter on affirmation and negation (*PR* 173), he includes various maxims regarding their psychological status: 'One affirmation exists through the Senses and another through the Imagination'; 'No affirmation is as great through Imagination as through understanding'; 'Affirmation through the Will inclines to a position, and affirmation through the Intellect to demonstration' (173. 9–11). Just as Aquinas distinguishes doubt, opinion, knowledge, and belief, according to the Intellect's degree of commitment to a proposition (*De ver.* 14. 1), so Llull distinguishes levels of affirmation through the Senses, Imagination, Will, and Intellect, identifying the latter with the demonstration that both Logic and his *Art* provide. Others of his maxims refer more explicitly to this demonstrative function:

Affirmation is a word (*vocable*) signifying ostensive necessity and negation a word signifying the inconvenient or impossible.

It is truer to say that 'God is *Aeternitas*' than 'God is not an ass.'

A greater affirmation comes from a greater truth, and a greater negation from a greater falsehood.

All negation is a consequence of affirmation, but no affirmation is a consequence of negation.

Ostensive affirmation enlightens negative necessity.

Doubt is farther from, and opinion closer to, affirmation.[15] (173. 1, 4, 6, 7, 13, 14)

---

[15] Affirmació es vocable qui significa ostensiva necessitat, e negació es vocable qui significa inconvenient e inpossíbol.

Major veritat es dir: Deus es eternitat, que dir: Deus no es ase.

De major veritat, major affermació, e de major falsetat, major negacio.

Tota negació es consequencia de affirmació, e neguna affirmació es consequencia de negació.

Affirmació ostensiva es lum a necessaria negativa.

Dubitació es pus luny a affirmació, e opinió pus prop.' (*Obres Originals*, 14. 182–3.)

The second of these maxims shows Llull's habitual preference for the *via affirmativa*; the third clearly reveals his conception of participated truth. His precepts also present a very simplified and moralized fusion of several Aristotelian doctrines: true or false judgements about a thing's essential, as opposed to accidental, nature are most true or false (*De interp.* 14 23b17–27); affirmative is superior to negative demonstration because the latter must assume both what is not and what is (*An. post.* 1. 25 86b7–10, 34–5); the distinction between ostensive and *ad impossibile* syllogism (*An. pr.* 1. 23 40b23–7; 2. 14); and the nature of opinion (*An. post.* 1. 33).

One peculiar feature of his moralization of conventional doctrine in these maxims is his correlation of affirmation and negation with antecedent and consequent: 'doubt does not decide (*declara*) between antecedent and consequent'; 'because affirmation is of antecedent principles and negation of consequent, the Intellect works more through the ostensive than through the impossible' (172. 2 and 173. 12). At least in the second maxim it is clear that 'antecedent' and 'consequent' refer to primary and secondary, or non-derivative and derived, beings in the hierarchy of existence, rather than to parts of a hypothetical proposition and this is typically how Llull understands them in other works as well.

This long and detailed review of Llull's correlation of affirmation, negation, possibility, impossibility, truth, falsehood, being, non-being, and doubt is necessary in order to show how absolutely fundamental it is to his system of argument. It is not merely a formal dialectical trick or purely rhetorical device of exegesis, but instead organizes a wide range of logical, psychological, theological, metaphysical, and even physical principles. It is impossible to understand Llull's method without understanding this wide appurtenance of affirmation and negation. Subsequent chapters in this study will show how some of these principles define his treatment of demonstration, disputation, or, in his later period, syllogistic and sophistic. They bear an especially critical relationship to his conception of the roles of faith and reason. As the discursive expressions of identity and difference, of the fundamental dynamic of *Concordantia* and *Contrarietas*, affirmation and negation are the Lullian *Art*. Llull's constant effort to make them achieve the goals of his project reflect his basic task of establishing formal dialectical procedures, in Logic or his own system, whose validity will always correspond to the material truth of the Christian revelation that they express.

Conversion

Before leaving Llull's accounts of predication and proposition, it is necessary to mention several other aspects that also appear frequently in his writings and that likewise display his efforts to moralize logical doctrine. One of the most important of these, by virtue of its special development in Llull's later period, is the conversion of subject and predicate. The basis for Llull's treatment of this aspect is Algazel's account of it in his *Logic* (2. 5–88; 3. 188–211; and cf. 5. 178–229), which Llull of course summarizes in the *Lògica del Gatzel* (lines 154–81, 213–26, 326–57). Algazel begins his account by defining all 'comparisons' of subject to predicate as either essential or accidental, following Aristotle (*An. post.* 1. 19 81b23–9). This distinction, especially the value of essential or natural predications, is a commonplace in Llull's *Art* and hence in his programme for Logic as well. It provides a discursive expression for the metaphysical doctrines of plural substantial forms and essentiality that are so basic to Llull's system.

The passages from Llull's *Lògica del Gatzel* that treat the conversion of subject and predicate give no hint of the tremendous importance that this aspect will hold in Llull's later work. It is interesting that he perpetuates throughout his career the term 'comparison' used frequently by Algazel; Peter of Spain, among contemporary authorities, uses the term in only one context (7. 102–19), when describing the fallacies of accident where 'anything is assigned as belonging in the same manner to the subject and accident'. Llull uses 'comparison', however, in other less specialized senses as well that have no bearing on the conversion of subject and predicate. His interest in this aspect largely develops with his progressive refinements in the methods of his own *Art*, and hence extensive references to it only appear toward the end of his early period.

The early *Libre de demostracions* does offer, none the less, this very clear illustration of Llull's awareness of the importance of the conversion of subject and predicate:

It necessarily happens that greater concord and greater likeness of nature exist where propositions convert, than where they do not; just as when one says that every animal is mobile, but not everything mobile is animal, for if it were so, plants and the heavens would be animals; and everything alterable has a beginning and an end, and everything that has a beginning and an end is alterable; therefore, a greater agreement and likeness exist between alteration and beginning and end, than between animal and mobility; because if not, it would follow that all movement converts with animal, and this is impossible.[16] (2. 22. 2)

The example of animal and movement appears in Llull's *Lògica del Gatzel* (lines 219–22), and he uses it here to draw a conclusion that is fundamental to his eventual conception of conversion, namely, that greater convertibility involves greater 'agreement and likeness' in nature, according to his customarily Neoplatonic view of the hierarchical participation of being.

The most complete conversion of course exists among Llull's own *Principia*, and thus he explains in the later *Taula general*: 'Time is in *Bonitas* as *Bonitas* is in *Magnitudo*, namely, that just as *Magnitudo* is good by reason of *Bonitas*, so time is in *Bonitas* by reason of *Bonitas*; and this converts, *Bonitas* being in time by reason of it [time].' (3. 7.) So, where Scholastic doctrine, following Aristotle (*An. pr.* 1. 2–3), treats conversion as a function of the various modal and quantifying terms employed in propositions, Llull refers it to the natural physical or metaphysical relationships between subject and predicate, in a manner that very broadly applies Aristotle's dictum that predication be guided by the real connections of subjects and their attributes (*An. post.* 1. 19 81b23); where these connections for Aristotle are causal, for Llull they are participational.

In the chapter on conversion in the *Proverbis de Ramon* (138), the breadth of Llull's application is apparent in the examples of conversion that he cites:

God converts with infinity and eternity.
Only the principles (*raons*) of God convert.
From the conversion of *Potestas*, Intellect, and Will, there follow infinite acts.
If a power and an object converted, there would be no act from them.
If concordant things could convert, contrary things could convert.

[16] 'De necessitat se cové que major concordansa e major semblant de natura sia en so on les preposicions se convertexen, que no es en so on no s convertexen; axí con qui diu que tot animal es mouable, mas tot mouable no es animal, cor si ho era, la planta e lo firmament serien animal; e tota cosa qui sia alterable ha comensament e fi, e tot so qui ha comensament e fi es alterable: doncs major conveniencia e senblansa ha enfre alteració e comensament e fi, que no ha enfre animal e moviment; cor si no ho havia, seguirsia que tot moviment se convertís en animal, e assò es inpossíbol.' (*Obres Originals*, 15. 115.)

Essence and its own existence (*propi esser*) convert.
No essence converts with compound existence (*esser compost*).[17] (138. 2, 3, 9, 13, 20, 17, 18)

The first three maxims effectively describe Llull's notorious *demonstratio per aequiparantiam*, the special argument from equivalence in God's attributes, which Chapter 7 on demonstration will treat more fully. The last three maxims suggest the basic ontological tenets that inform Llull's conception of conversion. Contrarity and concordance are, of course, the Relative *Principia* of Llull's *Art* that are most basic to its elaboration of the identities and differences among things. Llull's Realist understanding of essences founds his typical postulation of the convertibility of any coessential features. The only strictly logical doctrine regarding conversion that Llull offers in this chapter is its first maxim—'definition and the thing defined convert because of conversion'—which recalls Aristotle (*Top.* 1. 5 102a7–14). This implies a cognitive value for conversion that seems apparent in Llull's brief comments from the *Aplicació de l'Art General*, where he avers that 'with the *Regulae* you can give knowledge of the predicate with the subject; and if it's turned around, you can know the subject with the predicate' (lines 457–61). Despite the paucity of Llull's remarks on conversion in his early works, its function is obvious and clearly anticipates his special development of 'natural conversion' in his later works.

Other propositional modes

Llull also names various other aspects of predication and proposition in his early works, but in almost all cases these are mere mentions only, and in those cases where he treats them in any detail, his comments usually moralize them rather heavily.

This is certainly so with the basic distinctions between antecedent and consequent in hypothetical propositions. Llull rarely recognizes them in the conventional fashion defined by Peter of Spain (1. 16–17), and even his terminology is unorthodox. In his *Aplicació de l'Art General*

---

[17] 'Deus se convertex ab infinitat e eternitat.
'Solament les raons de Deu se convertexen.
'De conversió de poder enteniment e volentat, se seguexen actus infinits.
'Si potencia e obgect se convertissen, no fóra actu d ells.
'Si coses concordants se podíen convertir, poríense convertir coses contraries.
'Essencia e son propi esser se convertexen.
'Neguna essencia se pot convertir amb esser compost.' (*Obres Originals*, 14. 143–4.)

(lines 488–9), he mentions their division into conjunctive and disjunctive types. Peter of Spain specifies the types of hypothetical proposition as conditional, copulative, and disjunctive, and his nomenclature reflects Priscian's claim that the copulative and disjunctive are two types of conjunction (16. 1. 1), a division repeated by Peter (7. 75). Llull's two terms follow the account of Boethius alone (*De syll. hyp.* 1; 385). Algazel uses the same division in his *Logic* (4. 263–314), but Llull does not translate Algazel's remarks into his *Lògica del Gatzel*. The fact that Llull does occasionally deal with the divisions of antecedent and consequent is probably due to their possible parallels to distinctions between primary and secondary beings. Thus, in the *Arbre de sciència*, he explains how 'in the Intellect there is a first thing from *Principium*, and through this first thing it attains antecedent things, just as maxims are antecedents of conclusions; and it attains secondary things because it is from *Medium* and thus it attains the minor maxim that is a consequent of the major maxim' (Hum. 3. b. 2 [16]). Llull's derivation of ratiocinative acts from his *Principia* is an extraordinary application of his view of the participation of truth, and one that he develops often in his later works. His reference here to a 'maxim' perhaps recalls its definition as 'a proposition than which no other is prior or more known', as in Peter of Spain (5. 4). Llull's remarks suggest that he regards major and minor maxims as major and minor premisses in a syllogism.

Llull's most extensive account of antecedent and consequent, in Chapter 153 of the *Proverbis de Ramon*, clearly shows his analogically moralizing correlation of this logical distinction with metaphysical, epistemological, and physical relationships, all conceived participationally:

An antecedent is what posits in necessity what follows because of it.

A consequent is what shows necessity anterior to itself.

From the lover there follows love, the lovable, and the beloved.

In love the lover exists formally and the lovable materially.

Love is a consequent of the lover and lovable.

The necessity is greatest that in one species is from antecedent and consequent.

Every appropriation is a consequent of a property.

Antecedent and consequent cannot be divided.

From a greater antecedent comes a greater consequent.

To the heat of water fire is the antecedent as a proper [quality] of heat, and to air as appropriate [quality].

The *Bonitas* that the Intellect understands, is an antecedent for the Intellect that [*Bonitas*] might be understood.[18] (153. 1–10, 14)

The range of examples shows well the scope of the necessary relationships that Llull regards as consequences: these include his innate correlatives and the mind's apprehension of the *Principia*. Even the proportionality suggested in the ninth precept does not mitigate the sheer determinism of this consequential necessity, which often makes Llull's arguments about the obligation of Divine activity so antithetical to conceptions of God's absolute freedom. With respect to his logical programme, the range of Llull's examples is a reminder that a topic from antecedence and consequence figures in Boethius's scheme (*De diff. top.* 3; 1202), which follows Cicero's divisions (*Top.* 12. 53–13. 55). Llull's precepts really show, though, only a nominal connection with the logical treatment of antecedents and consequents as parts of propositions. His examples recognize instead the sort of broadly 'consequential connections' between subject and predicate described by Aristotle in his *Posterior Analytics* (1. 4 73b10–24) or *Sophistical Refutations* (5 167b1–20; 6 168b28–169a5). Llull's handling of these relations never concerns the formal features of their logico-linguistic function; he would refuse the account of them offered in the treatises *De consequentibus* by terminists such as Ockham (3-3 and cf. 3–4. 12).

Llull's analogical use of logical distinctions such as antecedent and consequent to name a range of physical or metaphysical distinctions is certainly one of the most typical features of his moralizing adaptation of Logic. It serves to blur the line of demarcation between purely analogical accounts of these formal structures and his redefinition of them, also moralizing in its reference to his doctrine of intention, as

---

[18] 'Antecedent es ço qui posa en necessitat ço qui per ell se seguex.
'Consequent es ço qui mostra necessitat denant sí matex.
'D amant se seguex amar, e d amable, amat.
'En amar està amant per forma, e amable per materia.
'Amar es consequent de amant e amable.
'Aquella necessitat es major qui en una matexa especie es de antecedent e consequent.
'Tot apropiament es consequent de propi.
'Antecedent e consequent no s poden partir.
'De major antecedent, major consequent.
'A la calor de laygua es lo foc antecedent per propia calor, e làer per apropiada.
'La bontat que lenteniment entén, es antecedent per lenteniment que sia entesa.'
(*Obres Originals*, 14. 159–60.)

recourses of argumentation in later works such as his *Logica nova*. Yet, as functional elements in his logical programme, distinctions such as antecedent and consequent play a very limited role. Even his doctrine of the conversion of subject and predicate, developed much further in his later works, is far less important than his correlation of affirmation and negation. It is difficult to insist too strongly on the absolutely central role of this correlation. It is the direct expression of the soul's necessary pursuit of its first intention, as Llull conceives it. Supported by his insistence on the mind's natural attraction to its proper object, affirmation becomes the naturally proper activity of the mind, as several passages quoted above suggest. Nearly all Llull's subsequent attempts to reformulate logical discourse ultimately consist in assimilating demonstrative argument to the mind's use of affirmation.

6

Syllogistics and Sophistics

GIVEN the overwhelming importance of the predicables, categories, and predication for Llull's presentation of Logic—a status that reflects their correspondence with the *Principia* and *ars combinatoria* of his own *Art*—it is not surprising that Llull says much less in his early period about the major structures of argumentation from Scholastic doctrine, the syllogism, topics, or fallacies. He certainly knew about them, since he treats both syllogistics and sophistics in his *Logica Algazelis*, but no special concern for them appears until his later period, when his new attention to the formal recourses of Aristotelian argument becomes the distinguishing characteristic of that era in his career.

Nearly all of his references to these structures in his early work are broad characterizations, as in his comments from the *Doctrina pueril*: 'through Logic you will learn to begin, and sustain, and conclude what you say, and through Logic you will keep guard lest anyone deceive you with sophistical words. And through Logic you will be subtle in all the other sciences' (73. 6). Here the three distinctions of beginning, sustaining, and concluding probably correspond to the premisses, proof of premisses, and conclusion in syllogistic argument, or perhaps simply to the two premisses and conclusions themselves; his comments remotely recall the broad characterization of syllogistic proof given by Peter of Spain (5. 1–2). Where the encyclopaedist Vincent of Beauvais recommends the study of sophistics in order to avoid error in one's own ratiocinations (*SD* 3. 3), Llull recommends its study in order to avoid being deceived by others, presumably in matters of the Faith. In his *Compendium artis demonstrativae* (p. 147) Llull declares that the syllogism is the subject of Logic, as God is of Theology or being of metaphysics; this view recalls Vincent's denomination of Logic as the 'syllogistic art' (*SD* 2. 1–3). Llull adds that the syllogism suffices for all proof and demonstration (*CAD*, p. 155), as seen already with respect to his view of the relationship between his own *Art* and Logic. In the *Libre de contemplació* (155. 22–3), he notes that syllogisms arise from the concord of Senses and Intellect, while paralogisms of sophistry arise from discord between them. Among Llull's later works from his early period, his references to the topics and fallacies from the *Arbre de sciència* are noteworthy because they imply a correction of Scholastic practice: the logician, Llull claims, 'places the maxims before the conclusion, and has a means of arguing and of signifying false things to be true and true things to be false, in order that he might have better knowledge of truth and falsehood' (Hum. 5. 5. i). This somewhat sanguine assessment of the logician's purpose in employing fallacies becomes the basis for Llull's justification of his 'new fallacy' in his later period; it is basically an inversion of Aristotle's definition of sophistry as 'merely apparent wisdom' (*De soph. el.* 11 171b28), that is, false-hoods that appear true. The fact that Llull still recognizes some prophylactic value in study of the fallacies perhaps explains why he includes them among the elements of Logic that derive from his *Regulae* (although he does not explain how) in his *Aplicació de l'Art General* (lines 480–1). As a generalization, Llull's broad references to the syllogism, topics, or fallacies in his early period never give any obviously conventional definition of them from received doctrine, but instead display Llull's broad appreciation of them as 'necessary reasons', a designation that best identifies his predilect arguments from proportion and resemblance, as the following chapter on demonstration will show.

This chapter will focus on the participational interpretation that Llull gives of syllogistic structure itself. In Chapter 291 of the *Libre de contemplació*, he classifies the syllogism, along with Memory, Intellect, Will, possibility, Imagination, conscience (*seny*), order, actuality, conti-nuity, and signification as the 'roots and subjects of wisdom' (291. 1). In two remarkable analogies, he asserts that man's wisdom exists in and his thought proceeds through these eleven elements, just as 'the splendour of the sun is in the orbit (*roda*) of the sun', and 'air receives from fire its heat because it participates with it, and 'air receives from fire its heat because it participates with it' (291. 2). Although Llull subsequently explains the function of each element more exactly, this broadly participational definition of their role in human intellection represents his normative view of their status, which he underscores by equating their efficacy with the soul's relative approximation or near-ness to them (291. 3).

Llull begins his remarks on the syllogism in this chapter by describ-ing how one must first form and shape in the mind the thing to be known as the conclusion to be sought; then, if necessary reasons do not signify this conclusion figurally (*afiguradament*) to the mind, one must 'set before that conclusion two propositions that demonstrate through necessary reasons to the mind the shape (*figura*) of the conclusion manifestly' (291. 10). He then illustrates this process by explaining how someone seeking to know the truth or falsity of the Incarnation through necessary reasons 'must set before this question two extremes (*termenacions*), that is two propositions' (291. 11). These passages make clear Llull's view of the syllogism as a necessary reason on the one hand, and his knowledge of the standard Scholastic vocabulary regarding syllogistics, as found in Peter of Spain (4. 2 and 5. 2) on the other. Since he uses the terms 'proposition', 'extreme', and 'question' in the second passage in a conventional manner, his identification in the first passage of the conclusion with the thing to be known makes equally clear how his own practice of affirming possible truth and being at the outset attempts to anticipate the conclusion in a very determinate manner. Although Llull regards his *Art* as inventive because it finds truth, in practice it finds arguments to support truths whose possibility it already affirms. Thus, Llull explains his example of a syllogism regarding the Incarnation as an approximation to the 'necessary conclusion' through an elaborate proof of the premises, which are not assertoric, but still questions in themselves: first one determines 'whether God has the power to be God and man at once', and then one 'passes' on to determine 'whether God has the occasion or reason of becoming man'. He concludes that 'if one finds these two shapes shaped (*figures afigurades*) in the mind, then one should shape in the mind the shape of the necessary conclusion' (291. 11). If the second premiss were not shaped thus, he adds, the conclusion would not be 'shaped from the two propositions by truth demonstrated through necessary reasons'. He does not say that it would be rejected as invalid or untenable. Instead, he continues: 'since the two propositions are not contrary to the conclusion, then the conclusion is shaped through them in the mind from an intellectual shape (*figura*) derived and issued from both propositions through necessary reasons, just as materially (*sensualment*) the body is shaped through the corporality derived [from the combination of] matter and form' (291. 12). This last analogy perhaps parallels Aristotle's famous suggestion that premises are the matter of a syllogism (*Phys.* 2. 3 195a18), but his allusion to the form of corporality disputed by Aquinas (1a. 76, 4) tends to confuse the value of this hylemorphic analogy. Or, Llull's view of syllogistic structure may instead take the conclusion as a final cause, as Avicenna suggests (*Metaph.* 6. 5) and treat the premisses as means to that end, which may of course include a middle involving causal connections as defined by Aristotle (*An. post.* 2. 11 94a20). The difficulty in determining the exact function of Llull's hylemorphic analogy arises chiefly from his participational conception of the relationship between the premisses and conclusion. What he seeks is some form of necessity that is coessential to the premisses and the conclusion. The mind finds this form, a participated essence, when it discovers the relationships of analogy, congruence, proportion, and agreement that correctly link the premisses to the intention of the conclusion, which expresses one of Llull's fundamental theological or metaphysical values.

He describes the same general process of harmonizing propositions with a conclusion in this passage from the *Arbre de sciència*, where he suggests using the Scholastic topical maxims, codified in Peter of Spain's fifth tractate, to solve questions:

The second method is to solve questions with maxims conditioned according to the natures of the Trees, harmonizing that maxim with the conclusion of the question, affirming or denying; and if the maxim is obscure to some people, we advise that they recur to the natures of the Trees and their places [i.e. topics] with which the maxim has agreement, just as if one wishes to draw a conclusion from this maxim: Every principle is nobler by being and doing good works, than by being only.[1] (Quest. Proem.)

One might take this proposal of a sample maxim from Llull's *Art* as a broad explanation for the almost total absence of references to the topics in his work: his entire *Art* is itself a great compilation of topics, all of which are real or natural, because they all derive from the real structure of being defined in it. More specifically, this passage shows how he incorporates topical maxims into the same format of argumentation described above and thereby includes them in his repertoire of necessary reasons.

In the passages quoted from the *Libre de contemplació*, the shaping in the mind of each premiss and the conclusion broadly corresponds to the formation of images in the Imagination or of combinations and divisions in the Intellect, which Aquinas describes (1a. 85, 2 and 5).

---

[1] 'La segona manera es solvre les questions per màximes condicionades segons les natures dels Arbres, concordant aquella màxima ab la conclusió de la questió affirmant o negant; e si la màxima es a alguns escura, consellam que recorren a les natures dels Arbres e dels locs daquells ab los quals la màxima ha concordança, axí com si vol traure conclusió de aquesta màxima: Tot començament es pus noble per estar e obrar bones obres, que per estar tan solament.' (*Obres Originals*, 13. 4–5.)

For Llull, it designates the mind's search for the form or essence of a relationship between terms or concepts. However, Llull uses the verb *afigurar* to explain both how the agreement of the propositions with the conclusion is shaped or shown *to* the mind, and how the propositions shape the conclusion *in* the mind, and thus his explanation cannot bear close analysis as a causal account, with a distinct agent and effect, of the intellectual powers and their objects. Several other passages from the *Libre de contemplació* do suggest that Llull tends to view the syllogism as both an instrument and an object of intellection. The following analogy offers an ethico-psychological definition of that instrumentality and objectivity:

But when [the soul] remembers and understands and desires things near in nature and property, then it happens with some that it is possible to remember, understand, and desire them together, just like the two propositions and conclusion of which a syllogism is composed, which two propositions and conclusion one can remember, understand, and desire at one time because they are similar to the Memory, Intellect, and Will in generation and procession: for just as the Intellect is engendered by the Memory, so the second proposition is engendered by the first, and thus as the Will issues from the Memory and Intellect, so the conclusion issues from both propositions.[2] (227. 21)

Aristotle declares that a conclusion follows necessarily from the premisses as its cause (*An. pr.* 1. 1 24b18–21; *An. post* 1. 2 71b19–72b4), and Scholastics such as Aquinas (*In* 1 *An. post.* Proem. 2) and Albert the Great (*De praedicabilibus* 1. 7) do broadly identify syllogistics with the analytical operations of reason, but the model for Llull's remarks is obviously the generation and procession of the Three Persons of the Trinity; the image of this process is a capital assumption of the trinitarian arguments in thirteenth-century natural theology.[3] Llull's usual definition of the three Augustinian faculties and of their interaction generally follows the Bishop of Hippo faithfully

---

[2] '[M]as com membra e entén e vol coses acostades en natura e en proprietat, adoncs se seguex en alcunes que es possíbol cosa que ensemps les membre e les entena e les vulla, axí com les dues preposicions e la conclusió d on es compost argument, les quals .ij. proposicions e conclusió pot hom remembrar e entendre e voler en un temps per so car son semblants ab la memoria et ab lenteniment e ab la volentat en generació e en processió: car axí com lenteniment es engenrat per la memoria, enaxí la segona proposició es engenrada de la primera, e enaxí com la volentat es ixent de la memoria e del enteniment, enaxí la conclusió es ixent de abdues les proposicions.' (*Obres Originals*, 6. 10.)

[3] See Pelikan, *The Growth of Medieval Theology* (600–1300), pp. 262–3.

(*De trin.* 14. 2. 5 and 7. 9–10), and thus his account of their functions is necessarily different from that of the more Aristotelian Saint Thomas (1a. 79, 7; 82, 4). Llull's addition of the syllogism to this trinitarian analogy of psychology is probably not original, yet is no less a contribution to his moralization and naturalization of logical doctrine.

Another perspective on Llull's understanding of the syllogism as an instrument and object of intellection appears in the *Art amativa*, where he states that 'the human Intellect, in moving its understanding through both of the propositions from which it draws a conclusion, binds itself in the conclusion to true understanding, which it forms from the likenesses of the propositions when it understands those likenesses in its "proper intelligible" and ordering them to an end, which is the conclusion composed of those likenesses' (2. 8. 7). The general relationship that Llull suggests between intellection and syllogistic reasoning assumes Aristotle's doctrines regarding the demonstrative or necessary syllogism (*An. post.* 1. 2 71b8–82b4; 2. 19 99b15–100b17), and Llull's correlative passive proper intelligible refers both to the possible intellect, where propositions are formed according to Aquinas (1a. 85, 2 ad 3), and to its ethically determined *recta conceptio* of the Highest Truth, which Llull implies in the term 'true understanding'. It is interesting that Llull here refers to the 'likenesses' rather than shapes, of whole propositions. He never employs the analysis of the suppositional functions of a proposition's component terms, in the manner of contemporary terminist logic. His terminology suggests instead a possible debt to the logical doctrines that treated propositions synthetically as significant wholes. In the decades following Llull's death this approach became the issue of the controversy involving Buridan and Gregory of Rimini over the 'complex signifiable' or total significate of a proposition.[4] One of the old authorities for such an approach was Boethius, who declares that the proposition is a meaningful statement signifying the true or the false (*De diff. top.* 1; 1174B); the doctrines of Boethius ultimately remit to those of the Stoics.[5] Since Boethius was, moreover, a basis of the *logica vetus*, which seems to comprehend most of the logical doctrine of interest to Llull, the latter's own claims about the likenesses of propositions may derive from simple Boethian axioms.

---

[4] On these, see Leff, *The Dissolution of the Medieval Outlook*, p. 88.

[5] On the development of these theories, see Norman Kretzmann, 'Medieval Logicians on the Meaning of the *Propositio*', *Journal of Philosophy*, 67 (1970), 767–87.

Despite the fact that the *Doctrina pueril* proclaims the sufficiency of the syllogism for demonstration and Chapter 291 of the *Libre de contemplació* describes its correct use in theological argument, Chapter 363 of the latter work proposes to supplement Aristotle's three syllogistic figures (*An. pr.* 1. 4–6) with a fourth that will better serve Llull's own purposes. This passage uses the same verb *afigurar* to describe conception of this new figure:

Hence, just as in Logic one has an art and means of knowing which conclusion is true or false, thus, Lord, we through Your Grace and aid shape (*afiguram*) the fourth theological figure and add it to the three figures of Logic and imagine it in a new way and with a new art and demonstration; this fourth figure is composed of nine figures, which are the letters shaped (*afigurades*) above and said of the Divine Dignities. Hence, the reason and the cause why we have newly invented this fourth figure, is so that we might demonstrate in what way the creatures and Your Virtues give a demonstration of the perfection of Your Glorious Divine Essence.[6] (363. 2)

It is worth noting that this passage summarizes either implicitly or explicitly virtually all the claims that Llull makes for his *Art* in its various versions: it is an alternative and supplement to existing arts and sciences; it proves Christian dogma; it offers new methods of demonstration; it is divinely inspired or revealed; and it argues both the exemplary relation of the creation to its Creator as well as the necessary attributes of the Godhead. It is difficult to resist Platzeck's explanation that these final chapters of the *Libre de contemplació* mark the genesis of Llull's *Art*,[7] and equally tempting to regard all of its features as a comprehensive challenge to the Scholastic art of Logic. The exact nature of Llull's new fourth figure, the earliest of his many attempted additions to conventional doctrine, is somewhat unclear here. It is similar in function to the three existing figures, yet derives

---

[6] 'On, enaxí com en lògica ha hom art e manera de conèxer qual conclusió es vera o falsa, enaxí, *Sènyer*, nos per gracia e per ajuda vostra afiguram la quarta figura theological e afigim la a les tres figures de lògica e afiguram aquella de novella manera e de novella art e demostracio, la qual quarta figura se compòn de .ix. figures les quals son les letres damunt afigurades e dites de la K dentrò a la T. On, la raó e la occasió per que nos avem atrobada novellament aquesta quarta figura, es per so que demostrem en qual manera les creatures e les vostres vertuts donen demostració del acabament de la vostra essencia gloriosa divina.' (*Obres Originals*, 8. 585.)

[7] In 'Descubrimiento y esencia del Arte del Beato Ramon Llull'; still, one must bear in mind the qualifications and counter-arguments that Platzeck himself mentions, in order not to accept too uncritically a monogenetic explanation of the development of Llull's devices.

from very different principles of participation, rather than of causality. He goes on to explain that:

Just as the figures of Logic are figures from which all syllogisms are formed, so in the fourth figure composed of the nine figures, one has in each one an art and means whereby one can solve any question that goes though the nine figures; for the fourth figure has nine modes just as the three figures have thirteen.[8] (363. 24)

As presented by Llull, his fourth figure can hardly be regarded as a formal structure of argumentation. He none the less equates its heuristic value with that of the thirteen modes of Aristotelian syllogistics, whose standard enumeration, as in Peter of Spain (4. 6, 8, 11), he obviously seeks to emulate. This comparison in itself lends a certain formalistic appearance to his arguments, just as do his references to the effects of one letter upon another (e.g. 363. 13). He also observes that 'one can give an example in this fourth figure of all the things in which one treats of truth, and through the art of the above-mentioned letters one can give a solution to every question to which some one or many of Your works might be subject' (363. 15). The special subject-matters of this fourth figure, God and—as it derives from him—truth, necessitate the special ethical and psychological responses defined by his doctrine of first intention, just as his procedures of affirmation and negation do in manipulating single propositions. Ultimately, the whole import of his fourth figure rests in its comparison to the three figures of Aristotle, as a retrospective moralization of the latter and claim for the demonstrative value of his own new device.

Finally, a few lines from the *Aplicació de l'Art General* show how Llull attempts both a comparative moralization of Aristotelian practice as a whole and a redefinition of the mechanics of its formal structures, conceived in their own terms. He states in this work that one must 'measure' the middle term in order to define the three syllogistic figures, and likewise 'measure' the 'matter of the argument' (lines 482–7). This joint reference to the figures and matter of argument parallels Algazel's divisions of the form and matter of proof in his *Logic* (4. 5) and thus suggests Llull's continued dependence on that text. More importantly, it shows his new interest in the 'middle', which is

---

[8] '[E]naxí com les figures de la lògica son figures d on se formen tots los silogismes, enaxí en la quarta figura composta de les .ix. figures, ha en cascuna art e manera com hom pusca solvre tota questió qui vaja per les .ix. figures; car axí ha .ix. mous la .iiij. figura, com an les tres figures .xiiij.' (*Obres Originals*, 8. 595.)

probably not Aristotle's syllogistic middle term, but rather the causes set forth in demonstration as 'middles' (*An. post.* 2. 11 94a20). The participational definition of this middle, especially as an object of intellection, becomes the special subject of several of Llull's later works, and so this reference to it here aptly testifies to the development of his new technical interests from this date.

In conclusion, from Llull's few extended comments on the syllogism, topics, or fallacies in his early period, the most important features to recognize are his apparent tendency to treat the relationship between a syllogism's premises and conclusion as an object, as much as an instrument, of intellection and to explain that relationship participationally. This conception supports his doctrine of affirming possible truth and being, in so far as it describes the constitution of a syllogism as a procedure for bringing the Intellect into full participation with the truth expressed in a conclusion, which thus stands as the end or intention of the Intellect's activity. However, the premises of such arguments often require considerable proof through necessary reasons, and the resulting connections can hardly respect Aristotle's formal rules of valid inference according to causal relationships. Thus Llull inevitably moralizes syllogistic structure by making the attainment of an ethico-psychological *rectitudo* its chief function, and in this respect Lullian syllogistics are neither formal nor material, but thoroughly and profoundly spiritual.

7

Demonstration

SINCE Llull's early treatments of Logic do not extensively develop syllogistics, the question might arise whether his system affords any explicit theory of demonstration, in the Aristotelian sense that defines demonstration as use of syllogistic reasoning (*An. post.* 1. 2 71b18). Llull's interest in demonstration is, however, patent from his original concern to prove Christian doctrine and from its expression in the series of works with titles such as *Libre de demostracions*, *Art demostra-tiva*, and so forth. Indeed the nature of Llull's system of demonstration is perhaps the most important question regarding his *Art*, since it covers such fundamental features as its combinatory method and necessary reasons. Moreover, an answer to this question is not difficult to establish because of Llull's reluctance or obfuscation in discussing his notions of demonstration, but rather the opposite: nearly all his writings are, in one respect or another, attempts to restate and refine his particular and peculiar conceptions of proof. It is no exaggeration to say that Llull has a greater interest in demonstration than in Logic. The comments in this study isolate for examination and review several typical passages and texts that bear on demonstration conceived speci-fically as a function of logical discourse, and then consider the general character of Llull's necessary reasons as means of attaining the true understanding that he seeks. This trajectory of study must inevitably cross the problem of Llull's conception of the relationship between faith and reason, which stands at the very centre of the theological values that make his logical programme and the method of his *Art* spiritual enterprises.

Demonstration

One feature of Llull's ubiquitous concern for the nature and structures of demonstration that quickly becomes apparent from any page of his writings is his broad application of the verb 'to demonstrate' and its nominal and adjectival derivations. This broad application is one of the

most common tactics of his moralizing method, and is evident in some
of the very first passages from his *Lògica del Gatzel*:

> Universal property
> is a particular that is
> a sign (*senyal*)
> of its species
> and of the individuals of it,
> and thus since it is in them,
> property demonstrates them;
> just as a dog, which by barking
> and a horse, which by whinnying
> demonstrate their property.[1]

(lines 57–65)

This kind of demonstration is the natural display of a being's essential
or proper (in so far as Llull distinguishes these) characteristics, and
concerns the jointly metaphysical and epistemological immanence of
the being's identity. Llull usually treats this immanence of identity as a
kind of signification; his use of term 'sign' (*senyal*) here implies this
significative function and it eventually becomes one of the foundations
of his natural Logic. Another passage illustrates very concisely his
treatment of demonstration as a sort of immanence in its use of an
etymologically related term:

> Accident cannot demonstrate (*demostrar*)
> genus or species, it seems to me,
> just like whiteness or illness,
> that do not show (*mostra*) what the subject is like.[2]

(lines 93–6)

---

[1] Proprietat universal
particular es, qui senyal
es de la sua specia
e dels individus d ella;
e per ço con en ells està
proprietat los demostra,
axí com cà, qui per ladrar,
e cavall, qui per aniar
demostren lur proprietat . . .

(*Obres Originals*, 19. 5–6)

[2] Accident no pot demostrar
genre ne specia, so m par,
sí com blancor e malaltia,
qui no mostra l subjec qual sia.

(*Obres Originals*, 19. 7)

Here the collocation of the Catalan verbs *demostrar* and *mostrar* suggests the indifferently logical, cognitive, and metaphysical functions of demonstration in Llull's arguments. Another passage shows his use of the term to describe the relations between predicative classes:

> Genus and difference
> demonstrate the species
> when one puts the genus first
> and the species afterwards.[3]

(lines 182–5)

Further examples would be tedious; this is Llull's habitual manner of speaking. It is perhaps unnecessary, yet relevant, to note that his use of 'demonstrate' in this last sense does not appear in the Latin texts of Porphyry (pp. 14–19), Algazel's *Logic* (2. 125–39), or Peter of Spain (2. 12–13). It is exemplary of Llull's very loose adaptation and application of conventional terminology.

The one section of the *Lògica del Gatzel* devoted specifically to demonstration shows clearly just how far Llull's original conception of it extended, and how deliberately this extension served his moralizing method from the outset of his career. Lines 709–71, entitled 'De demonstrationibus' in the Latin version, distinguish three 'degrees' of demonstration: a whole composed of integral parts, a finite simple whole, and an infinite simple whole, which only God can be. Now these distinctions evidently recall commonplace ones of Scholastic metaphysics, like those summarized by Aquinas (e.g. 1a. 77, 1). They concern Llull chiefly in so far as they organize a hierarchy culminating in the one infinite simple whole that is God. In this regard they comprise together one connected topical argument. The degrees of demonstration are degrees in the knowledge of God and the Absolute *Principia* of the Godhead; this theosophic value is clear in Llull's concluding lines:

> The first degree is easily understood,
> because it has no mediator.
> The second degree is understood with effort

---

[3] Genus e differencia
demostren la especia
cant hom met lo genus primer
e l especia en derrer.

(*Obres Originals*, 19. 10)

because you must understand it
by the senses first.
The third degree, where there is the most truth,
has many means that are exalted,
you must know, if you
wish to know God necessarily.
And may He in His Mercy
illumine your Intellect
without which no one understands.[4]

(lines 760–70)

The inclusion of this moralized scheme of demonstration in Llull's
epitome of Algazel is a typical example of that text's heterogenous
character, discussed above, and an evident indication of the primacy
that Llull's moralizing procedure holds for even the most fundamental
elements of logical theory. This is even more obvious when he
rehearses the same scheme in his *Libre de demostracions* (2. 13), adding
numerous analogical examples, and distinguishing the three degrees as
demonstration of composite being through the Senses, of finite being
through the Intellect, and of infinite being through the Intellect. At the
outset of his presentation he avers that 'necessary demonstration' must
be good, because it reveals truth to the Intellect. This occurs best in
demonstration through the Intellect, rather than the Senses, just as an
animal uses Taste and Touch more than the other Senses, and hence
demonstration through the Intellect is superior (2. 13. 4). Also, there
must be a mode of demonstrating infinite being through the Intellect
because there is an infinite being, and it surely merits such demonstration more than the finite beings that also have it (2. 13. 5). It is
instructive to recall that these proportional arguments regarding the

---

[4] Lo primer grau s entén leuger,
per so com es sens mijancer.
Lo segon grau s entén greument
cor ab mijà sensualment
l auràs a entendre primer.
Lo terç grau, on ha mays de ver,
ha molts mijans qui són leu:
saber lo te cové, si Deu
vols saber per necessitat.
E qu'ell per sa gran pietat
enlumén ton entendiment,
sens lo qual null hom no entén.
(*Obres Originals*, 19. 32)

relative nobility and perfection of levels of demonstration are themselves necessary demonstrations for Llull, as subsequent examples will make clear. Here they serve to intimate Llull's broad conception of demonstration as any argument capable of revealing the Supreme Truth to the Intellect. Several passages considered below list all the different types of argument that Llull regards as demonstrative; for the purposes of this study it is most useful only to review a handful of his comments on demonstration that express his conception of its specifically logical or epistemological foundations.

A fully analogical moralization of demonstration appears in Chapter 363 of the *Libre de contemplació*, entitled 'How by adoring and contemplating one's glorious God, one learns to have an art and means by which one knows when the Intellect receives a correct or incorrect figure in a conclusion'. This chapter may bear on the formation in syllogistic reasoning of the necessary connections that constitute demonstration for Aristotle (*An. post.* 1. 6 75a12); since Chapter 362 treats 'affirmations and negations' (see Chapter 5), and Chapter 363 'conclusions', together they apparently refer to the premises and conclusion of Aristotelian syllogistics. As in Chapter 362, Llull employs his series of abbreviational 'sense figures through which one rises to the intellectual figures' in order to offer multiple expressions of a single argument: each of the nine Divine Dignities intrinsically implies all the others, so that any doctrine based too exclusively on the function of one attribute alone will invariably incur some deviation in need of redress. Llull makes this argument entirely through analogical and exemplary proofs, one of which explains how the signification of God demonstrates to the Intellect that God possesses the attribute of perfect patience: 'just as the sun demonstrates its brightness and a rose its red colour and a lion its strength and a man who uses reason his rationality, so Lord, the signification of God demonstrates to the Intellect that perfect patience is in God' (363. 25, with abbreviations resolved). Logical demonstration thus parallels a being's active demonstration or display of its accidental and substantial natures through its 'proper acts'. Llull effectively ignores Aristotle's distinctions between sense and reasoned knowledge (*An. post.* 1. 2 71b33–72a5; 2. 19 100a35–b15) and seeks a mode of demonstration that distantly recalls the Philosopher's intuition instead (*An. post* 2. 19 100b7–16). The significations that effect this demonstration are the special subjects of Chapters 234–7 of the *Libre de contemplació*, which show amply how they constitute a moralization of immediate sense or intellectual perceptions and thus support Llull's natural Logic and claims for the direct apprehension of the universals that organize his theological and metaphysical values.

Demonstration per aequiparantiam

A more notable and notorious refinement in Llull's account of demonstration, and one directly bearing on received Aristotelian theory, appears in the Prologue to the *Art demostrativa*, where Llull explains that:

There are three species of demonstration. The first is from *aequiparantia*, that is, when demonstration is made from equal things: like demonstrating that God cannot sin, because His *Potestas* is one same essence with his *Voluntas* that does not wish to sin, and the *Voluntas* is one essence with *Iustitia* that is against sin, which converts with injury; and because the Divine Dignities are equal in essence and in nature, thus one can demonstrate *per aequiparantiam*, and likewise it follows in the powers (*vertutz*) and properties and entities of the creatures. The second species of demonstration is when one proves the effect through the cause: as when 'if there is no sun, it should be day'. The third species is when one demonstrates the cause through the effect: as when 'if it is day, there should be sun'. Through these three species of demonstration this *Art* discourses; and the first species is stronger than the others because it is of the Divine Dignities; and the second species is stronger than the third.[5] (Prol. 2–3)

Now the second and third types of demonstration indicated are, of course, the Scholastic *propter quid* and *quia*, from Aristotle's *Posterior Analytics*. The first is Llull's celebrated demonstration *per aequiparantiam*, which he advocates throughout his career, and with special insistence in his later period. Several scholars have accepted the identification of Llull's demonstration *per aequiparantiam* as Averroes'

---

[5] 'Tres especies son de demostració. La primera es de equiparancia, so es assaber, con es feta demostració per coses eguals: axí con demostrar que Deus no pot peccar, cor son poder es una essencia metexa ab sa volentat qui no vol peccar, e la volentat es una essencia metexa ab la justicia qui es contra peccat, qui ab injuria se cové; e cor son eguals en essencia e en natura les dignitatz de Deu, per asò pot hom demostrar per equiparancia; e asò metex se seguex en les vertutz e proprietatz e entitatz de les creatures. Segona especia de demostració es con hom prova lefectu per la causa: axí con si es sol, cové que sia dia. Tersa especia es con per lefectu demostra hom la causa: axí con si es dia cové que sia sol.

Per estes .iij. especies de demostració decorre esta ART; e la primera especia es pus fortz que les altres con es de les dignitatz de DEU; e la segona especia es pus fortz que la tersa.' (*Obres Originals*, 16. 4.)

demonstratio propter quid et quia simul,[6] but there are several objections to this suggestion. First, Llull simply does not define his demonstration *per aequiparantiam* as a combination of *propter quid* and *quia*. Second, he does state that his new mode is stronger than the other two, implying a real material, and not simply formal, difference among their methods; he arranges them in a hierarchy, following his own moralizing predilection for telic order; the superior position of *propter quid* reflects Aristotle's assertion that scientific knowledge is properly knowledge of causes (*An. post.* 1. 2 71b11). Third, Llull stresses the function of equivalence in his demonstration *per aequiparantiam*, and this seems to be its most important feature by far.[7] This function is obvious in his example, where the conversion of the Divine Dignities becomes the universal paradigm of *aequiparantia* for all particular instances of it in the essences of creatures. This connection between *aequiparantia* and coessentiality is fundamental for understanding Llull's examples and arguments using his new mode. In this regard, it is probably not uncoincidental that in Scholastic doctrine the term *aequiparantia* designates one of the three species of the category of relation, which Peter of Spain explains as 'things called by the same name, such as *similis simili similis*, and *equalis equali equalis*, and *vicinus vicino vicinus*' (3. 18). These examples recall the terminology of Llull's own innate correlatives, which are the paradigmatic cases of coessentiality and appear frequently in his arguments *per aequiparantiam*.

Llull's examples of the three modes of demonstration from the *Compendium artis demonstrativae* clearly display their basis in relations of coessential equivalence and the priority of that equivalence over the Aristotelian relations of *propter quid* and *quia*:

Per aequiparantiam quidem miscendo dignitatem cum dignitate, ut tantum sit ipsa Magnitudo in existere et agere Bonitatis et in omnibus conditionibus ejus, quantum ipsamet Bonitas, et e converso . . . Propter quid vero, sicut propter suam Bonitatem oportet Deum esse bonum, et propter Magnitudinem suae Bonitatis oportet eum bonificare suum bonificatum, et sic de aliis. Secundum quia in eo, quod bonificativus et bonificabilis sunt in Deo, oportet in eo esse Bonitatem et sic de aliis. (p. 81)

---

[6] Platzeck summarizes the evidence for this claim in 'Raimund Lulls Auffassung von der Logik', p. 279 and *Raimund Lull*, 1. 424–5. See also Urvoy's suggestion that it derives from Avicenna's doctrines regarding conversion, *Penser l'islam*, pp. 376–7.

[7] Platzeck stresses it in 'La combinatoria luliana', p. 598 and his discussion in *Raimund Lull*, 1. 424–5, though perhaps without conceding its fundamentally non-formal conception.

Each example involves the coessential correlatives of the Divine Dignities and treats the relationships of cause to effect between them as a
reciprocal and necessary one. This necessity imparts a certain determinism to Llull's accounts of the Godhead and the emanation of
particular effects from the One Cause that is typical of his work. The
need to posit this reciprocity of Dignities in the Godhead as a paradigm for the interrelations of *Principia* in creatures leads to certain
difficulties regarding God's absolute simplicity. Where Aquinas states
that God's will really *is* His being and only separate in our way of
speaking about Him (1a. 19, 2), Llull goes on in this passage to argue
that they are 'equal':

> Propter quid et quia non sunt in Deo realiter, cum inter suas dignitates
> in existere et agere et in omnibus conditionibus sit aequalitas vel aequiparan-
> tia. . . . et sic affirmative ratione ipsius Dei et realitatis est in ipso Deo
> aequiparantia, ratione vero defectus nostri Recolere et Intelligere et Amare
> affirmamus et negamus in eo per propter quid et quia. (p. 81)

Thus Llull recognizes that there are real relations in God, as Aquinas
explains (1a. 28, 1–4), and posits equality or *aequiparantia* as such a
relation. By basing a mode of demonstration on this *aequiparantia*,
Llull attempts to establish, as it were, a 'logic of coessentiality'
grounded in the Godhead just as fully as the coessential *Principia* that
it manipulates. Yet Aquinas's objections to a real relation of equality in
God touch precisely on this coessentiality: it allows the potentially
infinite multiplication of further real relations (2a. 28, 4 ad 4; 42, 1 ad
3 and 4). As it happens, the trinitarian symbolism of Llull's correlatives
inhibits for him the multiplication of any further intermediary 'correlative' relations among them. Llull's demonstration *per aequiparantiam* in
fact functions chiefly in argumentation about the Divine nature, and
thus serves pre-eminently in his work as a kind of special theological
logic.[8]

None the less, in so far as this demonstration *per aequiparantiam*
operates among the innate and coessential correlatives, it necessarily
applies as well to all creatures, since they possess those correlatives.
This application is explicit in the passage quoted above from the *Art
demostrativa*, and is implicit in the following maxims from Chapter 140
of the *Proverbis de Ramon*, which nominally treat the 'solution' of

---

[8] Again, Platzeck rightly emphasizes this fact in 'La combinatoria luliana', p. 598 and
Raimund Lull, I. 425.

dialectical questions. Besides distinguishing demonstration *propter quid* and *quia*, Llull's aphorisms also propound that:

> Solution by *aequiparantia* is through equal reasons and acts.
>
> Whoever argues (*declara*) from *aequiparantia*, argues from the equality of active and passive properties.
>
> In the *aequiparantia* of *Bonitas* and *Magnitudo*, there can be no cause and effect.
>
> Equal necessity renders equal the agent, actable, and act of both.
>
> No demonstration is as necessary as *aequiparantia*.[9] (140. 4, 6, 14, 17, 20)

The last maxim assumes Aristotle's definition of demonstrative knowledge as that based on necessary premises that predicate attributes essential to a subject (*An. post.* 1. 6 74b5–12). The coessential aspects invoked in Llull's demonstration *per aequiparantiam* obviously fulfill this condition, but Aristotle also regards essence as properly the subject of definition rather than demonstration in the strict sense (*An. post.* 2. 10 94a11–14). Moreover, it is perhaps unnecessary to add that Llull's demonstration *per aequiparantiam* does not deal with causes at all, and hence is not demonstration at all, since demonstration always shows causes (*An. post.* 1. 2 71b9); as a consequence there will never be any middle or proximate causes in a Lullian demonstration *per aequiparantiam* (cf. *An. post.* 2. 2 98b38). This is simply another way of saying that demonstration *per aequiparantiam* relies on the participation that founds coessentiality and every other aspect of Llull's metaphysics. In so far as Llull associates his new method with Aristotelian demonstration, it is largely in order to subordinate the latter to Llull's use of his predilect theological and metaphysical values as the operative axioms of philosophical discourse, and thereby moralize logical practice as a means of expressing those values.

Necessary reasons

The passages examined thus far all identify aspects of demonstration that are in some ways peripheral to one of the most central features in all Llull's philosophy. This feature is the value and function of the

---

[9] 'Solució qui es per equiparancia, està per eguals raons e actus.
  'Qui declara ab equiparancia, declara ab egualtat de actives propietats e passives.
  'En equiparancia de bonea e granea, no pot estar causa e effectu.
  'Egual necessitat eguala agent agible e l actu damdós.
  'Neguna demostració es tant necessaria com de equiparancia.' (*Obres Originals*, 14. 146–7.)

necessary reasons that Llull so insistently claims to offer as proofs of Christian doctrine. These necessary reasons are one of the most studied aspects of his philosophy,[10] in part because they bear on several crucial issues: does Llull's claim to prove Christian doctrine make him a rationalist, as the fourteenth-century inquisitor Nicholas Eymerich maintained? Does such a claim contradict Llull's frequent appeals to the Anselmian dictum of *credo ut intelligam*? What kind of necessity do these reasons possess? Many helpful and some unhelpful contributions to answering these questions have appeared in modern scholarship on Llull and his work,[11] and the following remarks acknowledge these contributions in proposing a solution whose main theses are that Llull regards necessary reasons as any argument capable of rectifying the Intellect to participation with the truth that is God, and that he broadens the functional role of faith to include his first intention in general as desire for God, and his affirmation of possible true being in particular as the determined inclination of the Will towards God.

It is easiest to deal with the questions just mentioned by beginning with the last one concerning the character of Llull's necessary reasons. Immediate precedents for the term itself are easy to find: it appears in Anselm (e.g. *Monol.*, Prol.) and Richard of Saint Victor (e.g. *De trin.* 1. 4), who figure among Llull's favourite Prescholastic authorities. This suggests that one way of appreciating his use of the term might be to review their explanations of it: Anselm, for example, typically explicates necessity as a propositional mode through reference to the powers or 'possibilities' of the thing taken as the subject of the proposition,[12] and this approach is obviously consonant with

---

[10] J. E. Gracia summarizes the existing literature, though without adding any new insights, in 'The Structural Elements of Necessary Reasons in Anselm and Llull', *Diálogos*, 9 (1973), 105–29 and 'La doctrina luliana de las razones necesarias en el contexto de algunas de sus doctrinas epistemológicas y sicológicas', *Estudios Lulianos*, 19 (1975), 25–40.

[11] Besides the studies listed by Gracia (see n. 10), that of Leopoldo Eijo Garay, 'La luz divina en la gnoseología luliana', *Estudios Lulianos*, 15 (1971), 153–73 usefully reviews the relation of faith to reason, but attributes a very great role to *gratia cooperans*, which this study does not find warranted, as the analyses in Chapter 19 will show. Eijo Garay's article is not totally unfree from the tendency to polemicize this aspect of Llull's philosophy, attempting to mark him as either a fideist or rationalist, a solution that this study again finds untenable. Louis Sala-Molins illustrates this tendency in an especially unfortunate manner when he summarily rejects all of Llull's fideist claims in a single footnote, in order to sustain his own rationalist interpretation (*La Philosophie de l'amour chez Raymond Lulle*, pp. 185–95).

[12] See Desmond Paul Henry, *The Logic of Saint Anselm* (Oxford: Oxford University Press, 1967), pp. 138–40.

Llull's own physical and natural interpretation of the categories and other logical elements. However, this line of enquiry yields only very limited insight into Llull's notion of necessary reasons because these in fact have a much broader scope, which becomes obvious when one considers the other terms that he uses with or instead of it. The *Libre de contemplació*, for example, refers to the affirmation of possible true being as the basis of necessary reasons (217. 8); to syllogisms whose premisses and conclusions are proven by necessary reasons (291. 10–13, analysed above); to necessary reasons, syllogism demonstration [*sic*], and natural sense reasons (170. 22) or natural proofs and reasons, signified and demonstrated reasons, necessary reasons, logical arguments, syllogisms, and natural demonstrations (214. 22–4) as equivalent; and to 'true, syllogizing, demonstrating, signifying reasons' (170. 23) collectively. Similar examples of Llull's usage of these terms appear on virtually every page of his writings; taken as a whole, they clearly show that 'necessary reasons' and related terms have no determined technical sense, but embrace a wide range of argumentational elements, from lengthy arguments to single first principles. The *Libre de demostracions* illustrates this range very well: each chapter—which typically begins with some phrase such as 'It is a true (manifest, certain, acknowledged, natural, understood) thing that . . .'—is itself a necessary reason, according to Llull (1. Epil.). All these varieties of necessary reasons are functionally equivalent for Llull because, as various examples studied above have shown, they all serve to bring the mind to greater knowledge of truth, and thus serve to realize man's attainment of his Lullian first intention. Necessary demonstration is necessarily good, he avers, because it reveals truth to the Intellect (*LD* 2. 13. 1), and this is the chief criterion of necessity that Llull recognizes. Hence it seems unwarranted to distinguish Llull's use of syllogisms from his necessary reasons.[13] In the case of any argument or proof, Llull conceives the mind's reception of truth participationally, as indicated above with respect to the syllogism. All forms of demonstration are valid in so far as they function in this manner.

The rectifying function of necessary reasons and their participational foundation are implicit in Llull's first aphorisms regarding necessity and contingency in Chapter 154 of the *Proverbis de Ramon*:

The necessary is an image of the antecedent and consequent existing in agreement (*estants en concordana*) together from one species.

---

[13] As do the Carreras y Artau, *Historia de la filosofía española*, 1. 356.

Everything that *Veritas* places in the true is necessary.
The truth that the Intellect understands is necessary.
Since every being is, it is a necessary thing that it be.[14] (154. 1, 3–5)

The participation of all being and truth through the divinely caused
(and therefore necessary) hierarchy of creation establishes the causal
order that Llull's necessary reasons trace through relationships of
proportion, resemblance, congruence, or agreement. In this causal
order, the most important cause of any real or rational being is always
the final one, God. There is, then, no formal basis, in the common
sense, for Llull's necessary reasons; they are instead wholly material
because their demonstrative force depends entirely on their objective
content. Llull's constant elaboration throughout his work of these
necessary reasons as approximations to that objective gives them the
characteristically moralized appearance observed throughout this
study. This moralization constitutes, ultimately, the formal basis of all
demonstration in Llull's *Art* and of the version of Scholastic Logic that
he offers.

Faith and understanding

Having identified more exactly the character of Llull's necessary
reasons, it is now possible to examine in detail his conception of the
relationship between faith and reason (or, as Llull more commonly
says, understanding), and his alleged rationalism in maintaining his
ability to prove Christian doctrine. These are not strictly logical
problems, of course, but they are fundamentally important for understanding the demonstrative value of his whole *Art* and especially his
logical doctrine of affirming possible true being. Llull's conception of
the relationship between faith and understanding is perhaps the most
central of the basic theological values that his philosophy embraces.
Given its importance, it seems advisable to offer here a detailed
analysis of the various aspects of this relationship, which has con-
founded so many students of Llull's *Art*. The tendency to synthesize
Llull's treatments of this relationship into one fixed position has
produced some notable misrepresentations of his views. Llull certainly

---

[14] 'Necessari es ymage de antecedent e consequent estants en concordança amdós
de una especie.
  'Tot ço que veritat posa en ver, es necessari.
  'La veritat que lenteniment entén, es necessaria.
  'Tot ens pus que es, necessaria cosa es ell esser.' (*Obres Originals*, 14. 160–1.)

strove to establish a position that would allow rational proof of the articles of Faith, but it is one of the chief conclusions of this study that he never did—indeed could not—accomplish this. His ongoing attempts to do so, still frustrated at the end of his career, testify chiefly to the strength of his desire to justify philosophically his basic spiritual convictions, because these were fundamental and aboriginal to his life's project.

Faith and understanding are, for Llull, two different, but variously equal and unequal modes of knowledge; it is not true that he makes them 'perfectly equal'.[15] He commonly refers to them as two types of illumination: 'God has given to man two lights (*lums*), the light of faith and the light of understanding' (*DP* 52. 6). The objects of faith are spiritual things alone (*PR* 228. 17), following the traditional definition of Hebrews 11. 1; the understanding apprehends both corporeal and spiritual things (*LD* 1. 34). Llull identifies any knowledge of spiritual things, whether through faith or understanding, as a result of illumination: 'the soul is able to understand the articles using the light of understanding illuminated by the light of grace and necessary demonstrations . . . for the soul that believes the articles believes only with the light received from God, and the soul that understands the articles understands them with the light that receives from God the light of its understanding and with the demonstrations that creatures signify' (*LD* 1. 28).

Because of the diversity of men's minds, the two different lights are necessary: 'if someone lacks the light of understanding, he should have the light of faith, and believe what he does not understand. Hence, this light of faith is especially necessary to labourers and mechanicals and those of low Intellect' (*DP* 52. 6). Aquinas also recognizes this need for these diverse modes of knowledge (2a. 2ae. 2, 4 and *CG* 1. 4), but Llull emphasizes their unequal value much more vehemently: he asserts that understanding requires more effort than believing (*LD* 1. 45); faith results from defective co-ordination of the Senses and Intellect (*LC* 238. 18); it is more noble to desire to understand the articles of Faith than to desire to believe them (*LD* 1. 36); all men are 'obligated' to receive faith through grace, but not to receive understanding (*LD* 1. 6); and one believes precipitously, but understands with deliberation (*MP* 16. 6). Because faith can fully attain its spiritual belief in this life, it is more perfect in that respect than understanding, which can, according

[15] As the Carreras y Artau assert, *Historia de la filosofía española*, 1. 341.

to Saint Paul's dictum (1 Cor. 13. 9–12), only attain its spiritual knowledge fully in the next life (*LC* 239. 30; *DP* 52. 7; *LD* 1. 13). For example, the understanding cannot know God in Himself (*LD* 1. 45), or the full magnitude and nobility of the Trinity (*LD* 1. 35); however, faith is always capable of believing more than understanding comprehends (*LC* 239. 26) and therefore 'Faith exceeds understanding in this world because one can love God more through faith than remember Him through understanding, and faith believes immediately while understanding only rises to God through demonstrations from other things.' (*DP* 52. 7.) Llull repeatedly insists that faith and understanding seek the same object—God, the Highest Good—who is equally believable and intelligible and the most demonstrable being (*LD* 2. 35; 4. 6, 13). Here Llull stands in sharp contrast to Aquinas, who distinguishes the articles of Faith and similar theological truths as matters for belief alone (2a. 2ae. 1, 5). In part this single focus arises because Llull neglects the distinction between faith and belief, or rather tends to use the two terms synonymously, as Aquinas sometimes allows (2a. 2ae. 4, 2 ad 1). Only in the *Mil proverbis* does he note that 'there is one merit in believing corporeal, and another in believing spiritual things' (16. 18).

One of the most fundamental features of Llull's account of faith and understanding is its mechanistic psychological basis. Llull typically associates faith with the Will and understanding with the Intellect (*LD* 1. 10, 32; *LC* 244. 2), and prefers to focus on these two faculties because it allows him to combine the mind's desire for and belief in God much more closely, and thus attribute a degree of potential faith to non-believers (*LC* 238. 29). On the other hand, Aquinas also defines belief as 'assent moved by the Will', but distinguishes the Will's desire from belief, and thereby denies that the ideas of God held by non-believers are properly called 'faith' (2a. 2ae. 1, 8 and 2, 1–2). Llull also typically posits a broad equality among the powers, objects, and acts of the Intellect, Will, and Memory (*LD* 1. 2), a position that reflects the basis of his psychology in Augustine's trinitarian arguments concerning the soul. The *Libre de contemplació* (244) explains at length how faith and understanding each employ the three powers of the soul, and probably half of Llull's arguments in the first book of the *Libre de demostracions* appeal to the necessarily equal abilities of the Will in believing and of the Intellect in understanding Christian truth, claiming that if they were not equal, 'the Intellect could not use its nature as much as the Will, and would be demonstrated to be a lesser creature than the Will, and that God wished to be loved by the Will more than known by the Intellect, which is impossible' (*LD* 1. 10 and cf. 1. 1, 6, 26). Hence, the Will and Intellect agree (*convenen*) in desiring and understanding to an equal degree the theological and cardinal virtues and the articles of Faith (*LD* 1. 32). It is important to recognize that these claims regarding the psychology of faith serve in part Llull's missionological goals, by defining the level of the acts of belief and knowledge already realized by the infidels:

If God wills, the time and hour would be for us to know the Holy Trinity that is Our Lord God through necessary demonstrations; for the time is come in which the human Intellect is greatly exalted through the illumination of Faith, Holy Scripture, and philosophy, and the Will desires the Intellect to rise high so that it can be more fervent and pleasing to the Highest Good . . . and give knowledge of the Holy Trinity to the infidels who do not believe or know it.[16] (*LD* 3. Prol.)

This passage, especially in its final joint reference to belief and knowledge, broadly suggests how the manipulation of human psychology for evangelical purposes is the context of Llull's concern for the relationship between faith and understanding. Llull makes this psychology the basis for his analysis of the relative strength of belief among Christians, heretics, and infidels in the *Libre de contemplació* (242).

Despite the fact that the Intellect and Will share a common object, the Intellect is superior to the Will in various ways. For example, Llull claims that the Intellect tends to conserve the truths that it attains, while the Will can supplant desired truths with falsehood (*LD* 1. 12; *LC* 244. 19). If this capacity for falsehood in the Will extends to belief as well, then Llull apparently allows faith of the false (cf. *LC* 244. 3, 15), which Aquinas denies completely (2a. 2ae. 4, 5). Because of its weaknesses, Llull argues that faith be converted into stronger understanding (*LD* 1. 1, 12 and *LC* 242. 24). But by far the most important advantage of the Intellect is that it is the source of illumination of the Will:

---

[16] 'Si a Deu plaia, temps e ora seria que per necessaries demostracions aguessem conexensa de la santa trinitat qui es en nostre Sènyer Deus; cor vengut es lo temps en lo qual lumà enteniment es molt alt pujat per inluminament de fe e de la sacra escriptura e de philosofia, e la volentat vol que lenteniment pug mes a ensús per tal que ella sia pus fervent e pus agradable al subiran be, e . . . donen conexensa de la santa trinitat a los infeels qui la descreen e la innoren.' (*Obres Originals*, 15. 15.)

It is obvious that the Intellect illumines the Will to apprehend an object, loving or hating, accordingly as the object should be loved or hated and according to the degree (*quantitat*) appropriate to the Will in loving or hating that object. When it happens that the Will loves what it should hate or vice versa, then the Intellect illumines it with synderesis through which it converts the Will from the lesser thing, which is vice, to the greater thing, which is virtue and when it happens that the Will loves an object more or less than it should, then the Intellect illumines the Will demonstrating to it the degree in which the object agrees with greater or lesser nobility. But the Will is not thus sometimes . . . [and] because of this contrariety the understanding of the Intellect is converted to ignorance sometimes. Hence, since this is so, thus it is demonstrated that the Will agrees with the lesser, and the Intellect with the higher, nobility.[17] (*LD* 1. 39)

This passage contains one of Llull's very rare references to synderesis, the natural human disposition toward the good, which Aquinas does not recognize as an intellectual power (1a. 79, 12). Saint Thomas likewise grants to the Intellect a greater nobility than to the Will, in so far as its object, truth, is simpler and more absolute than the Will's, goodness, and he asserts that an object must be understood in order to be desired (1a. 82, 3). Aquinas also notes that the Will moves all the powers of the soul in general, and that in so far as understanding is itself the good object sought, then the Will is superior to the Intellect (1a. 82, 4). The comments cited above suggest that Llull does not acknowledge this latter possibility. Llull instead insists on the non-transitively relative nobility of the two powers, in order to construct his proportional argument. His mention of synderesis is almost certainly an effort to suggest the soul's natural attraction to the Supreme Good, which allows him to identify desire and belief, in the manner to be examined below.

Llull also organizes this process of illumination of the Will by the Intellect in a remarkable analogy that compares the sun's illumination

---

[17] 'Manifesta cosa es que lenteniment inlumina la volentat a pendre lobject, amant o desamant, segons ques cové lobject a esser amat o desamat e segons quantitat covinent a la volentat en amar o desamar lobject. On con sesdevé que la volentat ama so que deuria desamar e *e converso*, adoncs lenteniment inlumina aquella ab la sinderasis per tal ques convertesca la volentat de menor a major, lo qual menor es vici el qual major es vertut; e con sesdevé que la volentat ama mes o menys lobject que nos cové, adoncs lenteniment inlumina la volentat demostrant a ella la quantitat segons la qual se cové lobject ab major nobilitat o ab menor. Mas de la volentat no es enaxí alcunes vegades . . . per la qual contrarietat lentendre del enteniment se convertex en innorancia alcunes vegades. On, con assò sia enaxí, per assò es demostrat que la volentat se cové ab menor e lenteniment ab major en nobilitat.' (*Obres Originals*, 15. 38–9.)

of the moon or air (which then reflect and diffuse that light themselves) and their joint illumination of the wholly lightless earth, with God's illumination of the Intellect (which reflects or diffuses that illumination) and His illumination of the Will 'in shadows' without light of its own (*LD* 1. 29). The Intellect receives illumination more directly and fully from God because it is the part of the soul most created in His image (*LD* 1. 3, 43), according to traditional views recorded also in Aquinas (1a. 93, 2 and 6). The illumination of the Will by God and the Intellect together parallels the movement of the Will by any object and the Intellect; when that object is God, He 'moves the Intellect to understand and the Will to love the Articles of Faith' (*LD* 1. 44). Applied to faith, this scheme allows to understanding a role in fostering belief. In short, Llull acknowledges that God alone gives through grace the light of faith to those who only believe (*LD* 1. 1, 28 and *LC* 238. 16), but posits the Intellect's ability to receive illumination through grace and pass it on to the Will, thereby creating *both* infused understanding and infused faith. Such a view in itself obviously conflicts with Anselm's *credo*, so now it remains to be seen how Llull accommodates this famous doctrine.

Llull regularly invokes the traditional Augustinian tenet of the precedence of faith, and Gilson considered him one of its outstanding representatives in the Middle Ages.[18] Expressions of it appear in works from throughout his early period:

Through the light of faith the Intellect is exalted to understand, for just as a light goes ahead to show the way, so faith goes before understanding. (*DP* 52. 3)

The light of the faith that believes the Trinity sends down its influence to the Intellect so that it will be illuminated with that light through which necessary reasons demonstrate the Trinity to it. (*LD* 4. 13. 1)

You need to believe before you can understand.
Faith does not fear argument because it is its beginning.[19] (*PR* 228. 10, 18)

---

[18] *Reason and Revelation in the Middle Ages* (New York: Scribner's, 1938), p. 30.

[19] '[P]er lum de fe sexalsa lenteniment a entendre; car enaxí com lo lum va devant per demostrar les carreres, enaxí fe va devant al enteniment.' (*Obres Originals*, 1. 89.)

'[D]el lum de fe qui creu en trinitat, devalla influencia al enteniment con sia inluminat de tal lum per lo qual la subirana trinitat sia demostrada per necessaries rahons.' (*Obres Originals*, 15. 471.)

'Ans te cové creure, que pusques entendre.
'Fe no tem argument car ella es son començament.' (*Obres Originals*, 14. 251.)

The *Libre de contemplació*, with its long psychological account of faith and understanding, is notable for its lack of such pronouncements. Still, Llull obviously acknowledges that some act of faith is required in order to accept any argument about God. There would be no exercise of free will (and hence no virtue to reward) if understanding of God were through wholly self-evident principles (*LD* 4. Prol.; *LC* 244. 6). Aquinas notes that this applies only to acts of faith preceded and compelled by reasoning, and not to acts of faith simply followed by reasoning (2a. 2ae. 2, 10). Llull asserts, like Saint Thomas, that reasoning in the second case brings greater merit (*LD* 1. 45). Thus Llull does recognize that other considerations do attach to Anselm's *credo*, and most of the problems in understanding his relative conception of faith and understanding have arisen because scholars of Llull's work have mistakenly read his avowals of the precedence of faith as absolute or unqualified axioms, when in fact Llull constantly attempts to explain or reapply it, and in at least two critical ways.

The first of these is his view of faith and understanding as directly proportional processes: as he so often declares, 'Whoever believes more can understand more' (*PR* 228. 16); 'where you believe more, you can understand more; where you understand more, you can believe more' (*MP* 16. 8–9). This proportional view assures that neither member of Anselm's *credo* ever excludes the other completely. Llull posits degrees of faith and understanding, correlated to one another, a view perfectly consonant with his fundamentally Neoplatonic conception of the hierarchy of real and rational being; thus he speaks habitually of the understanding 'rising' to knowledge of the truth (for example *LD* 1. 45, 49). This proportional relation provides Llull with a basic argument in favour of the truth of Christian doctrine: if greater faith gives greater understanding, then the greatest faith gives the greatest understanding (*LD* 4. 13. 5). This greatness is not simply quantitative, but embraces a range of qualitative interpretations necessary as common terms in the analogous arguments that he proffers. Many of these seek to show that, for example, Christian doctrine induces the greatest effort of Will or Intellect, as in these instances:

A Saracen [who had killed a man] died despairing of God's pity; he could not have as great a hope as the Christian [who helped him kill the man] of God's pity, which every Christian can expect more than any man of any other religion. (*LM* 64)

Just as one earns more merit through faith when the faith is greater, so one earns more merit through understanding when one understands mediately rather than immediately: for just as faith requires more effort (*dona a hom major passió*) when one believes in the Trinity and Incarnation than in the unity of God only, so the Intellect that understands mediately requires more effort when it tries hardest to understand [i.e. through necessary reasons].[20] (*LD* 1. 45)

This determination of the greatest Faith is a foundation of Llull's method for disputing with the infidel, as Chapter 8 will show. Llull also claims that Christian doctrine allows a greater understanding of God; he does not argue for the truth of that doctrine itself, but rather 'demonstrates through necessary reasons that God in His great nobility has given to the Intellect the possibility of understanding the Catholic Articles of Faith' (*LD* 1. Epil.). The first book of the *Libre de demostracions* is devoted to showing not only that Christian doctrine is capable of demonstration through necessary reasons, but 'that the Intellect knows the honour and true light with which God has illuminated it because it can understand the articles through necessary reasons' (*LD* Prol.). This assumes, as he argues elsewhere, that Christian truth is the Intellect's highest object (*LD* 1. 30, 48).

A corollary of this proportional relationship between faith and understanding is Llull's metaphysical explanation of how understanding always exists potentially in faith, and vice versa:

The first mode, Lord, of potential understanding is in man when that understanding lacks actuality in the Memory, Intellect, and Will, while the soul does not remember, understand, or desire what it remembers, understands, or desires through faith without knowledge and necessary demonstration or arguments. (*LC* 239. 4)

As much as understanding extends through the Memory, Intellect, and Will of man, it creates faith potentially in the Memory, Intellect, and Will of man. (*LC* 238.8)

---

[20] '[Un] sarahí . . . morí desesperant-se de la misericòrdia de Déu; lo qual no poch haver ten gran sperança com lo crestià en la misericòrdia de Déu, en la qual pot tot crestià haver major esperance que negun hom d'altra ley.' (3. 116.)

'[E]naxí com hom guanya major mèrit per fe segons que la fe es major, que enaxí guanya hom major mèrit per entendre con entén ab mijà que con entén sens mijà: cor enaxí con la fe dona a hom major passió con hom creu trenitat e encarnació que no fa con hom creu en la unitat de Deu tan solament, enaxí lenteniment qui entén ab mijà dona a hom major passió hon pus fort sapodera a entendre.' (*Obres Originals*, 15. 44.)

Where understanding signifies and demonstrates more the things that are necessary, and faith more strongly takes those meanings from the Memory, Intellect, and Will, faith exists more strongly in absolute actuality. (*LC* 238. 11)

Just as the coldness in boiling water remains potentially, so the habit of faith remains potentially when you understand some truth of the articles or sacraments through necessary reasons.

If you sometimes do not know a truth that you understand, it remains habitually in your faith because you believe. (*PR* 228. 4–5)

The possibility that the Will actually has when it desires the articles signifies that the understanding has possibility when it has in potentiality the understanding with which it might understand the articles.[21] (*LD* 1. 40)

Explanations such as these establish a reciprocal relationship between faith and understanding based on a dialectic of actual and potential belief and understanding in which one always implies the other. None the less, Llull does recognize the positions, expounded by Aquinas (2a. 2ae. 1, 5 and 2, 10 ad 2), that the mind cannot both believe and understand the same thing, although it can simultaneously believe and understand different things (*LC* 238. 12; 239. 11, 29).

The real difficulty in Llull's account is explaining the inculcation of faith by reason, and therefore his second major qualification of the terms of Anselm's *credo* is his proposal of certain 'suppositions' as incipient acts of faith, which he describes in *exempla* such as this:

A layman . . . had few letters and knew little, and therefore when he tried to learn the articles and Scriptures of the Holy Page, he could not understand it

---

[21] 'La primera manera, Sènyer, de raó es potencialment en home, la qual raó priva de esser actual en la memoria e enteniment e voler dementre que la ànima no remembra ni entén ni vol so que remembra e entén e vol per creensa e per fe sens conexensa e demostració dargumentació necessaria.' (*Obres Originals*, 6. 118.)

'[A]itant com la raó sestén per lo remembrament e lenteniment e la volentat del home, aitant fa estar la fe potencialment en lo remembrament e lenteniment e la volentat del home.' (*Obres Originals*, 6. 111.)

'[On] pus rahó significa e demostra les coses qui son necessaries e fe pus fortment gita del remembrament e del enteniment e de la volentat aquells significats, pus fortment està la fe en la simple natura dactualitat.' (*Obres Originals*, 6. 112.)

'[E]naxí com la fredor de laygua escalfada roman en potencia, roman làbit de la fe en potencia con entens per necessaries raons alcuna veritat dels articles e dels sagraments.

'Si la veritat que entens alcuna vegada ignores, roman te en hàbit per la fe en quant la creus.' (*Obres Originals*, 14. 250.)

'[La] possibilitat que la volentat ha actual con ama los articles, significa que lenteniment ha possibilitat con aja en potencia entendre ab que entena los articles.' (*Obres Originals*, 15. 40.)

. . . But faith, by the virtue and grace of God, sustained him against disbelief, and made him suppose (*sotsposar*) what he did not understand, telling him and considering that Christian Faith and Scriptures are true, but he could not understand it, because there were many things that he did not understand, and Faith was one of them. Therefore that man so helped himself with faith against disbelief, that his understanding was exalted by the light of faith and he understood many things about the articles and other things that he did not understand before.[22] (*LM* 63)

The critical term here is 'supposition', which for Llull corresponds to his logical recourse of affirming possible true being, in a manner that is indistinctly creditive and intellective, as is evident from this passage:

The [gentile] philosophers did not suppose through faith anything about God, but rather followed necessary reasons; and therefore their Intellect could not reach God as high as the Intellect of the Catholic Christian theological philosophers, who supposed through faith the Trinity in God at the outset. And because faith is the light of the Intellect, the Intellect reaches higher to understand than the gentile philosophers can understand.[23] (*LM* 4)

This last passage is interesting especially for its suggestion that necessary reasons alone are not adequate means of attaining theological truth. It is very difficult to appreciate the fundamental role that Llull assumes for these suppositions apart from examples such as these, which is perhaps why their function has escaped previous notice. Yet they are present in nearly every argument where Llull claims to prove Christian doctrine through necessary reasons; they define an existing act of faith or right disposition of the soul. His suppositions are that act, in one way or another, and he develops it explicitly in his later

---

[22] '·I· hom lech volch jaquir totes les vanitats de aquest món, e donà's a conèxer e amar Deu. Aquell hom havia poques letres e sabia pau, e per açò con aquell hom volie entendre los articles e les scriptures de la santa Pàgina, no ho podia entendre; e adonchs descraença volie-lo induir e inclinar a descreure la fe romana. Mas la fe, per virtut e gràcia de Déu, lo sostenia contra descraença, e feïa-li sotsposar ço que no entenia, dient aquell hom e considerant que la fe e les Scriptures dels crestians són en via vera, mas que ell no ho podia entendre, car moltes coses són que ell no entenia, e fe era de aquelles coses que ell no entenia. . . . per ço com aquell hom enaxí se ajudava de fe contra descraenca, se exalçà son enteniment per lum de fe; e dels articles, de les altres coses, entès moltes coses que d'abans no entenia.' (3. 104–5.)

[23] '[L]os phisoloffs no sotsposaven per fe nulla cosa en Déu, mas que seguien rahos necessàries; e per ço lur enteniment no poch pujar tan alt a Déu, com l'enteniment dels phisoloffs crestians cathòlichs, theòlechs, qui per fe sotsposaven en lo començament esser trinitat en Déu. E car fe és luz d'enteniment, puja l'enteniment entendre pus altament que los phisoloffs gentils no pogren entendre.' (1. 65–6.)

period into a specifically logical procedure of contradictory suppositions, based on affirmation and negation of a truth. Louis Sala-
Molins rightly observes, then, that Llull makes faith depend on his
Regula B of *Utrum*, which posits the affirmation, negation, or doubt of a
proposition.[24] The *Libre de contemplació* notes that 'faith signifies the
possible' (238. 11) and 'affirmations of possibility or impossibility'—that is, the doubt that hesitates between accepting or denying a
position, as already explained— 'agree more closely with faith' (239.
23). This approach identifies supposition with the mind's natural
resistance to falsehood and attraction to truth, which makes heretics
and false believers naturally easy to defeat in disputation (*LC* 242.
18–21). This claim also illustrates how, in his early works, Llull
introduces this procedure by associating supposition with that identification of faith and desire in the Will that, as already noted, Aquinas
denies. It is interesting to note that Alexander of Hales distinguishes
precisely between 'suppositions' from natural law, 'principles' from the
articles of Faith, and 'consequences' deduced from those articles as
objects of faith (3. 1). Llull, in effect, elides all these.

These suppositions are the intellectual expressions for Llull of
man's natural orientation towards God, which he possesses in so far as
any creature enjoys a dynamic dependence upon the Creator. Llull
explicitly states his particular interest in exploiting this natural desire:

Because the Will wishes that the Intellect know its beloved so that it can love
Him more, therefore, Lord, I, who am recently made the procurer of the
desire (*apetit*) of the infidels, to which the glorious Incarnation of Our Lord
Jesus Christ is as desirable naturally in recreation as the Highest Good is to
the lower through creation and sustaining . . . strive as hard as I can to be able
to demonstrate with necessary reasons the Holy marvellous coming of the Son
of God.[25] (*LD* 4. Prol.)

The correct realization of this desire for God also corresponds to
Llull's first intention, as he indicates elsewhere (*LD* 1. 23). The fact
that for Llull all creatures possess this first intention—or in Anselmian

---

[24] *La Philosophie de l'amour chez Raymond Lulle*, pp. 192, 195.
[25] '[C]or la volentat vol que lenteniment aja conexensa de son amat per so que més lo
pusca amar, per assò, Sènyer, yo qui novellament son fet procurador del apetit dels
infeels, al qual la gloriosa encarnació de nostre Senyor Deus Jhesu Crist es apetible
enaxí naturalment per recreació, con es lo subiran be al jusà per creació e sustentació,
. . . mesfors aytant con es mon poder, con pogués per rahons necessaries demostrar lo
sant aveniment maravellós del Fill de Deu.' (*Obres Originals*, 15. 411.)

terms, ordination—towards God may perhaps explain why Llull does not attempt to distinguish belief and desire; 'reasoning about objects of belief obeys the desire coessential to reason' in man's nature.[26] This very loose conception of desire is obvious in his identification of the sense and intellectual appetites, which Aquinas distinguishes (1a. 80, 2), in this argument: man differs from beasts more through the Intellect, which man alone has, than through the Will, which they both have, and thus man becomes like the beasts when he desires what he does not understand (*LD* 1. 33). This ignores the fact that human acts of belief, which are presumably the kind of desire without understanding that Llull implies, use the intellectual appetite, Will, which animals lack completely as part of the rational soul. Aquinas argues that only rational creatures have an immediate order towards God (2a. 2ae. 2, 3), in any case, and thus he could never be the object of a 'beast-like' desire. This flawed argument none the less illustrates well the kind of rationalism that Llull offers. It is a rationalism based on desire for understanding as much as understanding itself. The most important consequence of this desire is that when realized as man's first intention, it finds expression in deliberate suppositions necessary for successful understanding. Thus Llull declares in his Prologue to the *Libre de demostracions* that the first two conditions for 'picking useful and virtuous fruit from this limb' are 'the intention of praising and serving God' and 'affirming the possibility of the Intellect to understand through necessary reasons these four books'. So, where Saint Thomas can allow only very limited results for natural theology, Llull with his necessary demonstrations and significations from creatures allows much wider natural powers of understanding the God of Christian revelation in his creation.

In the *Libre de meravelles* Llull illustrates very neatly how this desire founds the initial supposition of Christian truth. He gives the story of a Jew who did not believe necessary reasons proving the Trinity 'because he disliked the proof (*desamava la provança*) that the Christian made to him; for it is so difficult to prove the Trinity that no one can understand it unless he supposes first that one can prove it through necessary reasons' (4). The Will is free to desire or refuse its proper objects, as noted above, even though its basic nature is to desire them, as Aquinas explains (1a. 82, 1). Llull's suppositions allow the soul to attain potentially its proper objects. Thus Llull tells how a merchant,

---

[26] Sala-Molins, *La Philosophie de l'amour chez Raymond Lulle*, p. 193.

sick in body and spirit, doubted what he could not understand, and dying, wished that he had tried harder in his life to love and know God; 'because of the merchant's great desire to have served God, God inspired (*spirà*) into him the light of faith in his soul, so that he understood that he should not disbelieve what he did not understand' (4). It is relevant to note that Llull repeats the couplets 'love and know' or 'believe and understand' so often because they functionally express for him the directly proportional consequences of faith and understanding or Will and Intellect, as explained already. He recognizes that the light of faith received through grace is necessary for understanding, but insists no less on the ability of the light of understanding, also received through grace, to complete or actualize the potential faith created in a supposition.

Whether his suppositions constitute an act of belief sufficient to receive illumination through grace, whether they require a previous act of understanding in the Intellect that illuminates the Will in the manner suggested by Llull, and whether faith and understanding are directly proportional are theological judgements that this study can, happily, leave unanswered at this point, having explained the arguments presented by Llull. As for the three questions originally posed above, they can now be answered thus: Llull is not a rationalist, but rather an illuminationist and natural theologian of the soul's innate order towards God; he does posit an act of faith as a precedent to understanding theological truth, although this act is his curious doctrine of supposition; the value of these suppositions lies in their orientation of the creature to its Creator, which assumes the broadly Neoplatonic participation of being that also gives Llull's necessary reasons their force as means of assimilating (in the strong sense that this term bears in a metaphysics of resemblance) the mind to truth. The overall scheme of interrelations between faith and understanding proposed here thus stands as follows. The soul, recognizing its first intention, accepts a supposition that orients it toward its proper object, the true good that is God, and thus disposes it to receive illumination through his grace; in this respect the first intention and supposition constitute potential or incipient faith. The illumination enters with the understanding of necessary reasons based on the supposition, and from there moves the Will to a full act of belief commensurate with the understanding received. The directly proportional relationship of faith and understanding ensures that the former will always accompany the latter, as antecedent or consequent. There seems to be no place in

Llull's system for those persons incapable of understanding his necessary reasons; his *Art* cannot enlighten them, only God can.[27]

These answers already represent what is perhaps a too smooth synthesis of Llull's arguments in various texts from his early period, and therefore may admit the objection of creating a coherent (or worse, fabricating an illusory) theory from texts that in fact offer none. Indeed Llull himself seems never to resolve successfully the various competing elements in his view of faith and understanding. None the less, the interpretation of his efforts presented here can claim the advantage of explaining the apparent contradiction between his arguments for the force of necessary reasons and expressions of Anselm's *credo*, while allowing various problematic aspects to persist as still unreconciled. Obviously there is a need for continued close study of all of the questions and issues involved in this aspect of Llull's philosophy. As a conclusion to this analysis of it, it is important to emphasize the previously unrecognized role of Llull's first intention and suppositions in his theories. The function of the latter as a disposition to or incipient act of faith aids tremendously in understanding how he conceives the operation of necessary reasons. Supposition also summarizes the jointly ontological, theological, epistemological, and logical economy of Llull's entire *Art*: he broadly correlates basic notions of the Neoplatonic return of the many to the One, Anselm's doctrine of *rectitudo*, and Aristotelian views of the Intellect's natural pursuit of truth and the Will's of goodness as the basis for a system of argumentation that rectifies or 'induces', as he himself says in the Prologue to the *Libre de demostracions*, souls to knowledge of Christian doctrine. Llull's *Art* develops the natural demonstration that natural theology already includes, and which is necessary precisely by virtue of its basis in the nature of all created being. In his later works, it is this system of argumentation based on suppositions that Llull attempts to apply broadly to the structures of Aristotelian Logic. All his schemes for the manipulation of affirmation and negation in syllogistics and sophistics derive directly from these earlier attempts to develop a necessary and natural method of demonstration that will enable both faith and understanding. The use of supposition directly joins all Llull's later schemes of logical practice with his constant preoccupation to establish a common object for faith and reason.

---

[27] As J. E. Gracia rightly concludes in 'La doctrina luliana de las razones necesarias', p. 35.

8

Disputation

THE conception of Logic as an art and of particular logical doctrines as models of formally true discourse presented thus far in this study may well appear so idiosyncratic and so marginally concerned with techniques of verbal argument that it would be difficult to imagine their practical application. In part this difficulty arises from Llull's very attempt to remake Logic in the image of his Great Universal Art, and his notions of logical practice likewise reflect his views of the use and exercise of his *Art*. This is obvious in the general accounts of logical practice that he offers under the rubric of 'disputation'. Llull's disputation is not the academic exercise of the universities or *studia*, but the great debates between Christian and non-Christian apologists, such as the famous Barcelona contest of 1263. Many of Llull's own works—the *Liber de gentili et tribus sapientibus* (1277), *Disputatio fidelis et infidelis* (1288), *Liber de quinque sapientibus* (1295), *Disputatio eremitae et Raymundi* (1298), *Disputatio Raymundi christiani et Hamar saraceni* (1308), and *Disputatio Raymundi et Averroistae* (1311)—recall the practice of these debates and indicate their contribution to his conception of his own goals and work. This primarily evangelical application of disputation is explicit in the title of Chapter 187 of the *Libre de contemplació*, 'How one perceives and understands which is the best way and truest that one can hold forth in disputation about the Faith'. Since its doctrine is very similar to that of other chapters on disputation from other works, this selection will treat them all jointly, organizing their various claims and comments topically. The frankly incidental mention of received logical doctrine and preponderant focus on Llull's basic evangelizing goals in all these accounts of disputation offer an interesting glimpse of the concrete, practical application that Llull would have for his programme of argumentation, and recapitulate the relative importance of the various metaphysical, psychological, moral, theological, and even rhetorical principles that contribute to his accounts of Logic. In particular, they show Llull's confidence in the ability of his suppositions and necessary reasons to induce true belief in the non-believer. Recognizing those principles helps the modern student of Llull's *Art* to appreciate better how that confidence rests on real philosophical and theological doctrines.

Since Llull treats argumentation fundamentally as a means of rectifying the soul to awareness of truth, his accounts of disputation are predominantly psychological in orientation, an emphasis that they share, curiously, with Aristotle's account of rhetoric, even while owing nothing to the Philosopher's doctrines. This community of emphasis usefully recalls that medieval society perhaps perpetuated the rhetorical culture of antiquity in ways that are not necessarily dependent on the received tradition of rhetorical technique.[1] The title of Chapter 216 of the *Libre de contemplació*, 'How one apprehends the means acccording to which one sharpens, refines, and rectifies the Intellect and spirit of one's adversary in order that one might make him understand reason in the disputation', suggests a certain deterministic force, although Llull qualifies it in various instances, perhaps in order not to deny the role of free will in judgement, as explained by Aquinas (1a. 83, 1 and 4). In the *Libre de contemplació*, this psychology assumes that work's basic operative distinction between Senses and Intellect: Chapter 187 begins by asserting that the disputants must agree at the outset to move from sense to sense, sense to intellectual, and intellectual to intellectual objects (187. 2), while Chapter 216 states that the move to the higher level, which Llull likens to rising from individual to species to genera (216. 6), is necessary only when an adversary cannot understand the preceding one (216. 7). The *Proverbis de Ramon* state simply that 'disputation requires an artifical order that is an image of the natural order of the powers of the body and soul' (248. 2) and the *Libre de contemplació* also explains how the Intellect must sometimes use images of creatures from the Imagination in order to rise to consideration of the Divine Dignities in the Intellect alone (216. 22–3). The same chapter also begins by equating the refinement and rectification of an adversary's Intellect with its actualization from potentiality (216. 1–2), following the view of knowledge as a habit to be developed, as Aquinas explains (1a. 2ae. 52–3). In this same regard Llull remarks that heretics and others obstinate in error are 'long accustomed to receiving false meanings', and this custom requires

---

[1] On the possible non-Ciceronian contexts for medieval attitudes toward speaking, see Mark D. Johnston, 'The Treatment of Speech in Medieval Ethical and Courtesy Literature', *Rhetorica*, 4 (1986), 21–46.

long disputation to eradicate (236. 11–12); this comment recalls Aquinas's explanation that knowledge, as a disposition in part of the cognitive sense faculties, can decay, and that these faculties thus require repeated activation for improvement (1a. 2ae. 53, 1 and 54, 1). Elsewhere, however, Llull recommends not disputing at all with persons obstinate in error (*PR* 248. 10). The *Libre de contemplació* advises the disputants to know as well the parts of the soul (187. 4; 216. 11), since the disputant possessing truth must convince the one in error by rectifying his errant part, especially as it suffers from too much or too little fervour (*animositat*) (187. 5–6). Understanding and wit come when the Will, Memory, and Intellect agree (*LC* 216. 15), and it is better to demonstrate truth conclusively to the Intellect than simply to secure acquiescence to an argument from an adversary whose Intellect is not redressed or convinced of the truth (187. 22). Even an adversary who refuses to grant a demonstrated truth profits from hearing it demonstrated, because his conscience will actualize it (187. 24), exercising functions somewhat like those that Aquinas attributes to synderesis (1a. 79, 12). Finally, Llull recommends that a disputant speak of things pleasant to remember, since the Intellect understands most easily what the Will most desires to remember, and a man's Will and Intellect increase with this desire and understanding, making him more subtle in wit (*LC* 216. 13–14). The Will moves the Intellect and all the soul's powers, as Aquinas describes (1a. 82, 4), but the correlation posited by Llull is peculiarly reductive of this relationship.

All of the points mentioned thus far correlate closely with similar doctrines discussed in Chapter 7 on faith and understanding. Llull's accounts of disputation are notable for their sharp distinction between these two modes of knowledge, as regards the capacity of one's adversary in disputation. The *Libre de contemplació* presents them thus:

If one sees that [the adversary] is a man of thick wits (*gros enteniment*) and not quick, he can bring him from error much better with authorities and saints' miracles that make him believe, than he can with reasons and natural arguments; for a thick-witted man is nearer to faith than to reason. . . . When one quick man disputes with another . . . he should dispute with him through natural syllogizing reasons . . . for he leads a quick man to truth much better through reason than faith or authorities.[2] (187. 10–11)

---

[2] 'On, sil veu que sia home de gros enteniment e que no sia home subtil, molt mills lo porá trer de sa error ab auctoritats e ab miracles de sants que li fassa creure, que no fará ab raons ni ab arguments naturals; car home de gros enginy pus prop es de fe que de raó . . . Com home subtil disputa, Sènyer, ab altre home subtil, . . . cové que desput ab ell

Llull recommends that a disputant strive to reduce an opponent's active (non-Christian) faith into potentiality in order to free his Intellect from its prison (*LC* 216. 16–17). Since no authority is against reason, and vice versa, according to the *Proverbis de Ramon* (248. 4), and no authority contrary to the mind that loves truth and hates falsehood, according to the *Art demostrativa* (3. 13. 2), this latter work advises 'directing and reducing' authorities to reason, or rational arguments. Despite this apparent denigration of faith, Llull does posit authorities or reason as equal alternative methods of argument for the disputants to choose at the outset of their contest, although they must record this choice in writing in order to avoid subsequent disagreement (*LC* 187. 3). He also recalls that religion and Faith are intellectual, rather than sense, objects, and therefore require intellectual consideration (187. 27). None the less, Llull's enthusiasm for necessary reasons is unquestionable and his concern for illumination of the Intellect pre-eminent.

Llull also appeals to various elements of conventional logical doctrine in his accounts of disputation. He recommends arguments based on the predicables and categories because they bound all knowledge (*LC* 216. 10), continuous alternation between the subject and predicate (apparently in the manner of their 'conversion') in order to make an argument understood (216. 25), and using categorical, conditional, affirmative, negative, universal, or particular propositions according as one's adversary understands one type more easily (*LC* 216. 25), presumably with respect to the psychological distinctions noted already. Llull denounces any recourse to sophisms and fallacies (*LC* 187. 7, 216. 21) and elaborates Aristotle's definition of sophistics (*De soph. el.* 11 171b27), as apparent wisdom (*LC* 187. 23). The passage cited above (*LC* 187. 10) also mentions 'natural syllogizing reasons', but Llull nowhere discusses syllogistics. His maxim that 'he who disputes temptatively should consent to the truth that he finds' (*PR* 248. 15) alludes to Aristotle's examinational or 'temptative' disputation, which reasons from premisses accepted by the respondent (*De soph. el.* 2 165b5). Llull apparently applies conventional logical norms in denouncing such purely figurative statements as 'the man dies' or 'the wall wishes to fall' because of the discrepancy that they create

---

per raons silogitzans naturals en les coses sensuals e en les coses entellectuals, car molt mills endúu hom home subtil a veritat per raons que per fe ni per auctoritats.' (*Obres Originals*, 5. 172.)

between speech and understanding. According to Llull, neither of these statements is literally true: only man's body dies, while his soul is immortal, and walls lack the power of volition (*LC* 216. 12). In this respect, Llull rejects poetic and rhetorical practice in favour of a position like that advanced in the treatment of the supposition of terms from the *logica moderna*, where an authority such as Ockham considers the figurative use of a term an 'improper' application to be avoided by the logician (1. 62). More specifically, Llull's distinction here between the proper and improper senses of these phrases derives from the standard accounts of the fallacies—'The man dies' recalls examples from Peter of Spain (7. 120–9)—which Llull adapts in his new 'fallacy of contradiction' in his later period.

Despite this injunction against figurative language, all the texts under discussion here specifically recommend the use of comparisons, *exempla*, and metaphors. As a logician, Peter of Spain explicitly excludes induction, enthymemes, and *exempla* from the disputation as imperfect and deficient instruments of argumentation (7. 3). Albert the Great notes that induction is suitable for unlearned audiences (*Top.* 8. 3. 3), where Aristotle simply says that it best suits the 'crowd' (*Top.* 1. 12 105a17; 8. 2 157a21). Llull's use of these methods obviously fits the popularizing character of his *Art*, but they still function, for him, at a higher level than the authorities and saints' miracles used to instill mere faith in the simple-minded. His comments in the *Compendium artis demonstrativae* explain the value of similes and metaphors thus:

In faciendo iudicium recipiendae sunt in verbum phantasticum illae similitu-dines quae sunt in [actu Memoriae recolentis, Intellectus intelligentis, et Voluntatis diligentis vel odientis] . . . cavendum est, ne similitudines alterius improportionentur ascendendo plus vel minus quam oporteat, sunt etenim coaequandae, ne illarum nimia vel modica influentia particulare, quod quaeri-tur, faciat ignorari: et dandae sunt metaphorae, nam similitudo similitudinem attrahit, participante alia similitudine cum alia in verbo phantastico, et revela-bitur particulare per concordantiam principium et finem similitudinum, nec contradicens tantum repugnat similitudinibus et metaphoris, quantum objecto, quod odit, et sic respondens forte poterit transmutare opponentem ab [volun-tate odienti in voluntatem diligentem]. (p. 88, with abbreviations resolved)

In so far as all Llull's arguments from proportion, congruence, or agreement are metaphors or similes, a passage such as this describes the normative procedure of his entire *Art*. His comments here are surely one of the most concise and explicit statements from anywhere in his writings of how a metaphysics of participation, resemblance, and natural attraction sustains that procedure. Llull also avers that natural, proper, and substantial (i.e. essential) comparisons actualize the Intellect better than unnatural, improper, or accidental (i.e. non-essential) ones (*LC* 216. 8). Although the term 'comparison' commonly designates *exempla* or similes in the texts examined here, in this case it apparently refers to predication, as in the *Logica Algazelis*, which treats these Aristotelian distinctions. All demonstration requires essential predication (*An. post.* 1. 6 75a18–36) and Llull's arguments trace, he claims, the most real and natural connections between beings. According to the *Art demostrativa* (3. 13. 2), *exempla* and metaphors help lead one's opponent to acknowledge 'agreement or disagreement through possibility and impossibility', and the pre-eminent role of comparisons in these arguments is evident from his further remark that reasoning from the possible to the impossible most easily redresses the Intellect (*LC* 187. 30). These comments suggest a broad appeal to any kind of relationship as a sort of topical warrant, and in the *Libre de contemplació*, Llull recommends arguments in which the mind understands one contrary from another, act from potency or vice versa, natural (i.e. substantial) versus accidental forms, and dissimilar or similar comparisons and likenesses (216. 27). This broad use of so many relational constructs recalls the practice of contemporary rhetorical arts, especially the *ars praedicandi*. Sermon theorists such as Richard of Thetford (50), Francesc Eiximenis (3. 7. 1), or the *De faciebus* (19) attributed to William of Auvergne all recommend devising arguments based on commonplace logical, metaphysical, or physical relations. Llull's familiarity with the *ars praedicandi* is obvious from his own *Rethorica nova* of 1303 and *Liber de praedicatione* of 1304. Some of Llull's precepts clearly recall commonplaces of medieval rhetorical doctrine: his explanations of the ill effects of verbosity (*LC* 216. 19; *PR* 248. 18) parallel basic advice from Augustine (*Doc. christ.* 4. 8. 22–10. 25), as do his recommendations about offering material in segments and repeating it until understood (*LC* 216. 29). Llull's charge to choose the proper time and place restates fundamental Ciceronian doctrine (*De inv.* 1. 27. 40 and *De orat.* 3. 55. 210–11) largely in the simplified form known best from Isidore (2. 16. 1). It is curious that the last three paragraphs in Chapter 216 of the *Libre de contemplació* refer to the 'master and student' as well as to one's adversary; they perhaps reflect some knowledge of the precepts of the Pseudo-Boethian *De disciplina scholarium*.

The rhetorical contributions to Llull's accounts of disputation are especially interesting for their connections to the moral basis of these accounts: Llull's explicit recognition of the ethical considerations that bear on every use, and especially the persuasive use, of language is an important witness to the general medieval appreciation of the relationship between Rhetoric and Ethics.[3] This relationship was a primary concern of ancient authorities from Plato to Cicero, but often seems absent in the heavily technical doctrines of most medieval rhetorical theory. Medieval ethical and courtesy literature in fact kept awareness of this relationship very much alive. A noteworthy passage from the *Arbre de sciència* focuses on the ethical import of both Rhetoric and Logic, and in so doing, engages the long and complex tradition of distinctions between the two disciplines. Llull attributes a common deliberative and politico-civic function to both arts: 'The hermit asks if Rhetoric is as necessary as Logic? Solution: Through Rhetoric the prince is moved to piety and through Logic to justice.' (Quest. 5. 5. i. 178.) Llull's response recalls the Roman tradition of civil rhetoric, which early medieval encyclopaedists such as Isidore (2. 1. 1) and Cassiodorus (2. 2. 1) perpetuated from Quintilian's famous definition of Rhetoric as 'speaking well on civil issues' (2. 15. 38). Llull's response suggests the affinity between Rhetoric and Logic as arts of persuasive argument that Aristotle expounds in his *Rhetoric* (1. 1–2) and *Topics* (1. 1) and Boethius summarizes in his *De differentiis topicis* (4; 1205–7). None the less, Llull does not distinguish them as strictly demonstrative versus broadly persuasive proof, as does Aristotle, or as argument concerning theses versus argument concerning hypotheses, as does Boethius. This probably reflects the function of the Lullian *Art* as a system for reducing all persuasive and hypothetical arguments to the demonstrative proof of necessary reasons, which both Rhetoric and Logic could then employ.

As regards disputation, Llull states that it requires recognition of man's primary end or intention (*LC* 216. 11; *PR* 248. 16), which is love of God, one's fellow man, and the truth (*LC* 187. 1, 29; 216. 9; *PR* 248. 9, 11, 16). Llull emphasizes this need for mutual love between disputants or speaker and audience in the Prologue to his *Rethorica nova* as well, and extends it in precepts forbidding anger, indignation, ill will, vile language, or discourtesy (*LC* 187. 2, 7; *PR* 248. 19, 20).

---

[3] See James J. Murphy, *Rhetoric in the Middle Ages. A History of Rhetorical Theory from St. Augustine to the Renaissance* (Berkeley: University of California Press, 1974), pp. 97–100.

Many of these precepts are commonplaces from medieval ethical literature, especially treatments of the 'vices of the tongue', and courtesy or chivalry manuals, whose doctrines Llull specifically adapts in his own *Medicina de peccat* of 1300 and *Libre del orde de cavalleria* of 1276. They also appear in manuals of advice to Dominican preachers,[4] notably the *De eruditione praedicatorum* (2. 10; 3. 18–20) of the fifth Master-General, Humbert of Romans. These texts are the likely sources for Llull's warnings about prolix or turgid arguments, and the need to deliberate, if necessary, before responding to difficult issues (*LC* 218. 29; *CAD*, p. 88).

Llull treats the refusal to acknowledge truth and the use of sophistry or fallacies as consequences of bad intentions, especially the vainglory of appearing wise (*LC* 187. 7, 23), and this ethical perspective on specifically logical devices neatly illustrates the fundamentally moralizing (in a literal sense) import of his entire project. Its goal is not strictly scientific or academic, but proselytic: disputation serves not so much to 'persecute falsehood and acknowledge truth' (*PR* 248. 17) in any abstract or impersonal way, as it does to rectify immediately and personally another soul in knowledge of the truth. Thus the *Proverbis de Ramon* defines disputation as 'spiritual contrariety that manifests in speech the thought of one Intellect against another'; 'in disputation he who grants the truth is not vanquished, but learns', and 'is more praiseworthy than he that teaches, because he has more humility' (248. 1, 12, 14). It is difficult to overestimate the contribution of this spiritual perspective to Llull's conception of both the goals and method of his *Art* or logical programme.

These psychological, logical, rhetorical, and ethical considerations form the basis and context for the chief functional aspect of any disputation, which is the actual procedure of argumentation employed by the disputants. Llull repeatedly declares that the disputants must agree at the outset of their contest to a common protocol (*LC* 187. 1; *PR* 248. 7). This agreement should cover the ascent from sense to intellectual objects and use of authorities or reason already mentioned, as well as a common object or purpose (*CAD*, p. 86), avoiding the contrary significations of faith and reason or of speech and Intellect (*LC* 187. 9), appropriate vocabulary for the art or science in question (*LC* 216. 4), knowledge of the three religions under debate (*LC* 187.

---

[4] See R. F. Bennett, *The Early Dominicans. Studies in Thirteenth-Century Dominican History* (Cambridge: Cambridge University Press, 1937), pp. 75–127.

19), and acceptance of general rather than specific principles (*LC* 216. 5). The first of these is in fact Llull's first intention, the last the *Principia* of his *Art*. Hence the range of possible agreement is in fact much less generous than this protocol suggests. The *Art demostrativa* states that 'at the beginning of the disputation it should be arranged that the disputants follow the rule of this *Art*' (3. 3. 1). The *Proverbis de Ramon* aver that 'the first principles are those that most resemble God' (248. 8), that is, the Lullian *Principia*. The *Compendium artis demonstra-tivae* explains that 'if anyone denies the self-evident (*per se nota*) *Principia* of this *Art*, do not join battle with him; if he denies [only] those that are not self-evident, let them be proven to him through the mode of proof of this *Art*' (p. 86). Similarly, the *Libre de contemplació* maintains that each disputant must free his Intellect from all con-straints at the outset, in order then to rectify, sharpen, and prepare it in the various trees from the *Libre de contemplació* itself (187. 8). These initial agreements correspond, obviously, to the intentions and suppo-sitions necessary to establish belief potentially in the non-believer, and as such place an even greater burden of effective value on those doctrines as the grounds of Llull's entire programme.

Hence, Llull's disputation always pits Christian truth against infidel falsehood, in a contest to save the soul of the non-believer by guiding its natural attraction to Supreme Truth. The *a priori* determination of truth and error and of victory and defeat in the disputation makes several of Llull's precepts difficult to realize in practice. Even though he advocates giving each disputant equal time to speak (*LC* 187. 4), he none the less demands that

When a man who has truth contends with one who has falsehood, it is necessary that at the end of the disputation he conclude the truth to his adversary, so that the words end and terminate with that truth; and that the errant man not propose or respond, so that he thinks, imagines, remembers, and understands the end of the words, which conclude the truth to the adversary . . . he who has truth is more worthy of speaking the first and last words than he who has falsehood, for the beginning of the disputation ought to be the truth and not falsehood, and the end of the words ought to be the truth; and therefore he who has falsehood ought not to be at the end of the disputation nor arguing for falsehood at the beginning.[5] (*LC* 187. 25–6)

---

[5] 'Com lome qui es en veritat se contrasta ab aquell qui es en falsetat, necessaria cosa li es que a la fi de la disputació concloa a son aversari veritat, per tal que en aquella veritat sien afinades e termenades les paraules, e quel home errat no sia preposant ni responent per tal que sia cogitant e ymaginant e remembrant e entenent en la fi de les

Claims like these belie modern notions of Llull's sympathy or empathy for the integrity or sincerity of the beliefs of his infidel adversaries; Llull knew the doctrines of Muslims or Jews largely in so far as he knew them to be false.[6] More interestingly, part of Llull's basis for these claims seems to be a deliberately moralizing analogy between the various senses of his terms 'beginning' or 'principle' (*començament*) and 'purpose' or 'end' (*fin*), which allows him to correlate truth as a principle and purpose of argument with truth as the beginning and end of argument. He thus makes his first intention the beginning and end, in two senses, of disputation.

This discursive disposition of truth in the order of argumentation also figures prominently in Llull's detailed plan for a disputation. This plan shows explicitly how his first intention and suppositions function as a natural basis for belief and support the proof of Christianity as the greater Faith. Llull describes three stages in this plan. First, it is necessary to affirm and believe that God exists, and if either disputant doubts this, it must be proven to him (*LC* 187. 13). Second, it is necessary to find that God is perfect and complete, using significations from the Divine Dignities and from creatures (187. 14). This tenet establishes a telic model for Llull's proportional arguments, in a manner not unlike Aquinas's five ways (1a. 2, 3). Third, the disputants should accept and affirm all propositions that signify God's existence and perfection, and reject those that do not, and then write down those affirmative 'propositions through which the conclusion would be destroyed if they were denied' (*LC* 187. 15). Having completed these stages, the disputants are prepared to compare their respective beliefs, using this syllogistic argument as a general paradigm: the doctrine that best signifies God's being and perfection is most worthy of acceptance; doctrine X best signifies God's being and perfection; therefore doctrine X is most worthy of acceptance (*LC* 187. 16–19). Obviously this argument regarding the greater Faith relies almost entirely on proof of the minor premiss, which becomes the real ground of contention in the

---

paraules, les quals concloeŋ a son aversari veritat. . . . aquell qui es en veritat es pus digne que les primeres paraules sien sues e les derreres, que no es aquell qui es en falsetat, car lo comensament de la disputació deu esser en veritat e no en falsetat, e la fi de les paraules deu esser en veritat; e per assò so qui es en falsetat no deu esser en la fi de la disputació ni en lo comensament argumentador de falsetat.' (*Obres Originals*, 5. 176–7.)

[6] Urvoy calls Llull's attitude towards the Muslims 'contradictory' (*Penser l'islam*, pp. 158, 171).

disputations that Llull proposes. He presents this general syllogism, none the less, as a paradigmatic argument for the disputation because it more easily admits consideration according to the proportional conceptions of lesser and greater faith and understanding described in Chapter 7. Hence, Llull next claims that the Divine Dignities always agree (*convenen*) with true significations (*LC* 187. 2), which the Dignities thus measure like gold assayed to test its purity. This agreement is the participation of true statements with the Supreme Truth, as he explains in his *Compendium artis demonstrativae* with respect to arguments that appear contrary to truth:

Veruntamen argumenta, quae sunt verae conclusioni contraria, si non sunt alicujus efficaciae, interimantur; si vero habent aliquam efficaciam, hoc accidit ratione alicujus similitudinis vel concordantiae seu convenientiae, quam aliquod universale extraneum habet respectu ipsius particularis, de quo quaeritur, cum illo universali, cujus est ipsum particulare, ratione cujus similitudinis vel concordantiae eorum respective ad ipsum particulare latet vel latere videtur vera conclusio ipsius particularis, et falsa conclusio ratione indistinctionis apparet esse vera. (p. 81)

This kind of participational account of truth and falsity in things, which Aquinas rejects (1a. 16–17), is fundamental to Llull's entire philosophy, and explains the ultimate status of all real and rational beings as proportional analogues to truth. Thus he tells in the *Libre de contemplació* how two true propositions signify a true, and two false a false, conclusion, just as the Divine Dignities signify which things are true or false. This signification is not the conformity of things to the Divine Intellect that Aquinas recognizes, but rather the human Intellect's perception of the truth of the Divine Dignities in things. The Intellect may be more or less adequate to perceiving this truth: Llull observes that the ignorance created by sin may cause someone to believe something false, just as sophistry can cause false premises to give a true conclusion (*LC* 187. 21). The analogical connection 'just as' is in part causal for Llull: sophistry arises from the sinful vainglory of the bad intention of appearing wise. But this series of analogies to the syllogism also serves to moralize Aristotle's necessary causal relationship between premises and conclusion (*An. pr.* 1. 1 24b21). For Llull the truth of a proposition does not lie strictly in Aristotle's correct predication of an attribute about some subject (*An. post.* 1. 6 74b10), nor does the truth of a syllogism lie strictly in necessary demonstration of causes through a middle (*ibid.* 2. 11 94a20). Instead, Llull seeks the immediate correspondence of propositions with Supreme Truth, which effectively eliminates any need for syllogistic demonstration of causal connections at all. Llull's position is thus more extreme than that of Anselm, who distinguishes a truth in statements and thought, a truth in things that causes the truth in statements, and the Supreme Truth that causes the truth in things (*De ver.* 10). Only this Supreme Truth never perishes, as Anselm observes (13), and thus Llull concludes in the *Compendium artis demonstrativae* (p. 88) that error never befalls his *Art*, but only the mind of the Lullian artist, a claim with obvious pragmatic value for explaining the actual success or failure of a disputant employing Llull's method.

The value of Llull's various remarks on disputation from his earlier works lies precisely in the pragmatic perspective that they establish on the function and use of his necessary reasons and other logical recourses as modes of demonstration. In the absence of any known accounts by third parties of Llull's public practice as a disputant, his own comments offer the best insights available regarding the place of his activities within the actual practices of contemporary Scholastic life. Llull's accounts of disputation suggest that his early work up to 1303 remained largely and deliberately missionological in purpose, following the original conception of his evangelizing goals. For this reason alone it could never have found more than an awkward place in the universities and *studia* whose economic and social functions as professional training centres had come by 1300 to exclude such pastoral functions as evangelizing from the duties of most of their members outside the theology faculties. Indeed Llull's work attempts to bring the Scholastic learning of the university to the pastoral problems of the world at large, rather than vice versa, and this accounts in part for its popularizing character. It would be wrong to imagine, however, that all the peculiarities in logical doctrine or conception of demonstration found in Llull's accounts of disputation arise simply from this popularizing focus in his work. They are peculiarities of Llull's metaphysical, theological, or psychological doctrines themselves, and the following chapters of Part Two of this study will show how their continued application to logical doctrine generated the extraordinary technical innovations found in his later works. Just as his plan for disputation must have encountered a very unsympathetic response among his adversaries of other faiths, so the new plan of Logic developed in his final years must have encountered an equally negative reaction among his opponents in the schools. Both Llull's programme for disputation and for Logic undoubtedly found their greatest success when preaching to the converted.

PART TWO

Later Writings to 1316

9

Llull's Second Summa of Logic: the *Logica nova*

THE composition of the *Logica nova* at Genoa in 1303 marks a new epoch in the development of Ramon Llull's concern for, knowledge of, and attention to logical doctrine. Even though nearly all of Llull's basic values and assumptions remain constant, there are enough real changes after this date in his mode of presenting and interpreting their application to Logic to justify recognition of this new epoch as more than just an arbitrary division in his intellectual biography. Even granted that these are real changes, however, the choice of this date might still incur various circumstantial objections; for example, Llull's apparently increased knowledge of Scholastic doctrines is more likely the result of his earlier residence at Paris from 1296 to 1299 than his wanderings in the Mediterranean from Majorca to Cyprus and back during 1300 to 1302. The chronology of his writings strongly suggests, however, that the new directions and concerns in his intellectual activities begin in the years 1303 to 1305. The *Logica nova* is the first of several new applications of his *Art* to specific arts and sciences, according to the plan described in the *Liber de fine* (3. 1) of 1305. It also stands at the head of a multitude of shorter and longer treatises devoted to related topics of logical method, demonstration, and episte- mology and gnoseology; subsequent chapters will study their respec- tive concerns. Without attempting to enumerate here all of these, it is none the less possible to characterize them broadly, especially as they differ from his earlier works. First, Llull's later writings show an increased knowledge of technical Scholastic doctrines, as developed from the *logica vetus* and *logica nova*, but without any acknowledgement still of the terminist concerns of the *logica moderna*. Many of his accounts obviously depend on sources other than Algazel (as his *Logica Algazelis* already did in part), although the Arab's contribution to his conception of particular elements or doctrines is still clearly discern- ible from time to time. Second, Llull's later writings show a tremen- dous increase in the use of conventional Scholastic terminology; this probably reflects his increased activity in the schools themselves, and consequently his increased familiarity with standard texts and nomenclature; his success in the universities and *studia* would necessarily require from him a better command of those materials. In many cases it makes interpretation of his expressed positions much easier. The scholar's work also becomes lighter thanks to a third characteristic of Llull's later writings: many of them treat quite directly, and sometimes explicitly, specific questions of logical doctrine (such as the nature of fallacy), demonstration (in the function of his suppositions), or epistemology (as faith versus reason), and pose them in a fashion consonant with contemporary Scholastic debates regarding them. Even when employing his own idiosyncratic terminology, Llull's recognizable response to the same issues that exercised his contemporaries helps make his doctrinal positions more comprehensible. Thus his polemical anti-Averroist works, despite their distortions or simplifications of disputed tenets, none the less clearly define his own stance. His later works display less of the Prescholastic doctrine and philosophy so typical of his earlier writings. Moreover, his now occasional citations of or references to Biblical, Patristic, and even Scholastic authorities likewise serve to establish concrete points of reference for his views. All three of these broad characteristics were undoubtedly nourished by his labours in school centres such as Paris and Montpellier, and testify to the remarkable intellectual drive of an individual who never ceased to be an amateur schoolman himself, in the best sense of the term.

Taken in general as either cause or effect, these three characteristics combine to define a decidedly new technical orientation in nearly all of Llull's later writings on Logic and related issues, especially in their concern to develop new formal procedures of demonstration and proof. This new technical focus profoundly affects each of the three fundamental features of Llull's logical programme—its popular, natural, and moralizing qualities—that this study broadly traces. There are obvious alterations in each feature during his later period. The popularizing function of Llull's entire effort diminishes markedly. He writes very few works in Catalan after 1300, and the many Latin works that he does produce often deal with highly technical questions that, even when presented through the procedures of his *Art*, could not have been easily comprehensible to laymen outside the universities. This suggests a real shift in his audience, which becomes increasingly schoolish, as does Llull himself, in his attempts to combat theological and philosophical error at Paris and other universities. His use of genres such as the allegorical debate do, however, still testify to his own continued preference for popularizing presentations, and he never ceases to proclaim the value of his Great Universal Art as a facile method of mastering all knowledge.

The natural character of Llull's logical programme becomes overt and explicit with the *Logica nova*, which establishes it as perhaps the foremost virtue of his new plan. It appears in all subsequent descriptions of or references to its special strengths. He attempts to explain how the mind apprehends the natures of things necessary for this natural mode of logical discourse in various works with epistemological concerns, such as the *Liber de significatione* and *Liber de modo naturali intelligendi*. His efforts to explain how this natural Logic employs the nature of the mind itself generates the great number of works devoted to implementing his doctrine of supposition. Some of these propose new schemes of logical discourse that prove untenable, such as his 'new fallacy of contradiction'. Others prove more viable and become a regular feature of his method, such as the use of 'contrary suppositions'. These schemes for exploiting the heuristic and noetic value of supposition displace his demonstration *per aequiparantiam* as his predilect mode of argument, even though the latter always retains a sure pre-eminence because of its origin in the metaphysics of coessentiality of the Godhead.

The moralizing quality of Llull's programme appears to diminish as a result of his new technical focus, because he uses far fewer proportional arguments, necessary reasons, and *exempla*, while greatly increasing his use of propositional and syllogistic applications of contrary suppositions. Yet these new methods and general technical orientation are themselves more profoundly moralizing than the use of analogies or *exempla* because they propose formal procedures for making the ethical and theological ends or first intention that support this moralization the operative principles of logical discourse, usually in accounts of the metaphysics of intellection. Supposition becomes in his later writings the paradigmatic formal expression of *rectitudo*.

Finally, the sum of these changes and reorientations in Llull's interest in Logic causes a certain redistribution of the areas of logical doctrine that he treats. The detailed plans of disputation become less important than the reconstitution of specific formal constructs such as the fallacies; the slight attention to Logic as an art expands into more lengthy surveys of its chief divisions or doctrines. The somewhat different chapter headings of this second part reflect this redistribution; more specific analyses in each chapter will reveal the precise effects of this change.

The Logica nova *of 1303*

Not every one of the aspects just described appears in the *Logica nova*, written at Genoa in May of 1303, yet it clearly bears a comprehensive relationship to all of them. It is the second of Llull's two complete surveys of Logic, and like the first, the *Logica Algazelis*, it implicitly or explicitly presents nearly all the logical doctrines found in writings subsequent to it. Some of these it even repeats from the *Logica Algazelis* itself, but with a much more overt purpose than that aboriginal text offers. The *Logica nova* has seven distinctions devoted to these subjects:[1]

1. Natural and Logical Tree (Tree of Porphyry, expanded, and Llull's *Regulae*)
2. The Five Predicables
3. The Ten Categories
4. Catalogue of One Hundred Forms
5. Syllogistics (predication, definition, syllogistics, fallacies, and demonstration)
6. Application of the *Logica nova* (to Nature, Theology, Philosophy, Ethics, Law, and Medicine)
7. Catalogue of Questions (on each of the six distinctions).

In scope the *Logica nova* obviously does not exceed the *Logica Algazelis*, although its treatment of some areas is more detailed or complete, as later examination will show. Despite its more orderly structure, the *Logica nova* shows no attempt to imitate the organization of a Scholastic manual such as Peter of Spain's *Summule*. Instead, its sections on the hundred forms, application, and questions clearly mark the *Logica nova* as a version of Llull's *Art*. None the less, even though his *Principia* and *Regulae* appear throughout this work, there is no presentation or use of the combinatory mechanics of his *Art*; the *Logica nova* does not include

---

[1] The best existing account of the *Logica nova* is Platzeck's in *Raimund Lull* (1. 393–445), where it forms the basis for his entire review of Llull's specifically logical doctrines, although he of course treats them in various other works, already cited, as well. This study deals with the *Logica nova* and related texts in much more detail and for this reason a point-by-point comparison to Platzeck's conclusions would be both incongruous and unrewarding, since the main lines of difference between this study's perspective and Platzeck's have already been made clear. References to the relevant sections in *Raimund Lull* will appear below, with only actual points of conflict noted individually.

Llull's Figures or Tables. Thus, where the *Aplicació de l'Art General* of 1300 attempts to assimilate all logical practice to the methods of Llull's Great Universal Art, the *Logica nova* and all subsequent logical works either employ Aristotelian syllogistics or devise peculiar modifications of it. Llull thus accepts a basic difference between Scholastic Logic and his own *Art*, even while claiming that the former is somehow a particular derivation of the latter. His tremendous attention after 1303 to technical features of logical doctrine represents in large part an effort to validate that claim.

The Prologue to the *Logica nova* clearly presents the conflict between conventional doctrine and Llull's own interests. He begins by invoking the prolixity, proliferation of texts, and 'lability' of 'old and ancient' Logic. It is interesting to note that Ockham specifically condemns this 'vulgar' characterization of Logic as labile, which he attributes to those who 'neglect the pursuit of wisdom' (Proem). The defects of Logic, according to Llull, make it very difficult to learn and remember thoroughly, charges repeated in his *Ars generalis ultima* (10. 101). He proposes to remedy these defects by changing the methods and focus of Logic itself:

Verum quia logici consideratio circa intentiones versatur secundas, quas perfecte cognoscere nequit primis intentionibus ignoratis. Ideo in hoc nostro compendioso et opere novo ponentes, diffinientes et demonstrantes in aliquibus passibus naturaliter ac philosophice procedemus, ut primarum intentionum noticia naturaliter et logice a scientibus hunc librum plenarie ac clarissime habeatur. Istius quidem artis subiectum est veri et falsi inventio, cui cum modo principiis regulisque Generalis Artis auxiliabitur. (f. 58va; p. 1)

Perhaps the most immediately interesting feature of these remarks is that they define Logic as an art of invention, rather than of judgement also, as Cicero recognizes in his *Topica* (2. 6). This suggests at the outset the subordination of Logic to Llull's own inventive *Art*. But more obviously, these introductory lines also imply the epistemological processes that support Llull's natural programme for Logic. These involve redefining the roles of the first and second intentions, occasionally mentioned in earlier works, as noted above. Here Llull explicitly invokes Avicenna's dictum that the logician's primary concern is with second intentions (*Metaph.* 1. 2). These are natural mental signs for the first intentions, which are natural mental signs for extramental things. Because of this derivative relationship between them, Llull argues that the practice of Logic depends more on full knowledge of first intentions and what they signify, rather than on the second intentions. He makes the same claim in his *Ars generalis ultima* (10. 101) and in the *Liber de modo naturali intelligendi* (4. 1) he observes that his natural logician never abandons 'objects intelligible in themselves' for chimeras of the Imagination, as other logicians do. This emphasis on things themselves is not wholly untenable; it pertains to the long tradition of conceiving Logic as an *ars realis*, which the medievals never fully deny. Aquinas acknowledges the ultimately common concerns of Logic and Metaphysics when he argues that the subject of Logic is the same as that of Philosophy because second intentions are equivalent to natural things in so far as they derive from rational consideration of those things (*In 4 Metaph.* 4. 574).

Yet Llull's understanding of the first intentions is rather different from that of his Scholastic contemporaries, and certainly from the role attributed to it by the terminist *modernistae*, whose analyses of the supposition of terms obviously include terms of first intention. Where his peers are concerned to distinguish all possible functional modes of supposition as properties of terms themselves, Llull effectively recognizes only one broadly cognitive relationship between a term and what it signifies. All terms of first and second intention are tokens of things really existing in nature and this existence for Llull depends on their essences or natures. In this way he posits knowledge that is simultaneously natural and logical in using those terms. His definition of intention suggests both functions: 'the form with which a logician or mathematician abstracts likenesses from the resembled being (*a similato*) so that he might consider them outside their subject, and achieve a logical disposition' (*LN* 4. 30). Intentions are likenesses, as Aquinas explains (*CG* 1. 53), but for Llull this likeness is a participational relation. He defines it as an 'assimilated habit, so that the resembler and resembled (*assimilans et assimilatum*) can participate through likeness' (*LN* 4. 69). In the *Ars generalis ultima* of 1308 he defines it as 'the form with which the resembler assimilates the resembled' and gives as examples the humanity, shape, or colour that a father imparts to his son, the innate correlatives that all his *Principia* display, and all other 'higher, primary, and causal likenesses from which descend lower, sensible, and imaginable likenesses, just as many men who are similar in species and customs, and many luminous things in light' (10. 90). So, even while Llull now gives more attention to such specific logical doctrines as the first and second intentions, he none the less does so by bringing them within the embrace of the broadly conceived metaphysics of participational and proportional resemblance that is the foundation of his *Art*. As later analyses will show, his natural Logic relies on the status of intentions and other intelligible objects as members of the universal hierarchy of being. The final reference in the Prologue to Llull's own *Principia*, the master terms of all participation, imply the place of the intentions in that hierarchy and consequently their role in Llull's new logical programme.

The Prologue ends thus; the announcement of the text's divisions, a standard component of all Lullian *exordia*, follows immediately. Any further insights into his conception of Logic as an art must be gleaned from his treatments of specific doctrines, which subsequent chapters study. The Sixth Distinction on the application of the *Logica nova* does merit mention for its illustrative contrast of Llull's new with his old approach to Logic. At the outset of this distinction, he defines intrinsic (*intimus*) parts of application as the divisions of his programme and extrinsic parts as the actual use of his programme in other arts and sciences. In this way his logical programme is general to specific arts, and infuses its own divisions into them. The application of his programme becomes a search for the universal in the particular, which he achieves by moralizing logical doctrines as analogies to those of the various other arts and sciences, as in these comments on the role of syllogistics in Ethics, Law, and Medicine:

Sillogismus factus est de suis propriis principiis, et data est doctrina quomodo fit deceptio per fallacias et quomodo deceptio cognoscitur. Unde secundum quod sillogismus est discursus per b.c.d. et cetera, potest scientia moralis discurri cum b.c.d. et cetera in bono sive in malo. Et possunt cognosci deceptiones per vicia impetrate aut per malignum spiritum. (6. 9; f. 87$^{\text{ra–b}}$; p. 123)

This passage suggests that discourse through Llull's *Principia* makes both the syllogistic form and ethical analyses true, and implies that this truth is not a formal quality, but a result of individual *rectitudo*. Llull focuses more exactly on the necessary formal constitution of the syllogism in these analogies:

In quinta distinctione ostensum est de sillogismo per b.c.d. et cetera. Et illa ostensio est generalis scientia iuris et aliarum scienciarum. Quoniam ita ius ex propositionibus sibi coessentialibus et necessariis constitutum est, sicut sillogismus ex propriis et sibi coessentialibus propositionibus constituitur. Et ideo sillogismus ad ius applicari potest et maxime cum b.c.d. et cetera. (6. 10; f. 87ra; p. 125)

Sicut sillogismus indiget premissis necessariis ad conclusionem, eodem modo medicus indiget medicinis necessariis ad sanitatem, ex quibus medicinis potest habere noticiam cum b.c.d. et cetera. (6. 11; f. 87rb; p. 126)

Despite Llull's claim at the end of the second passage, none of these remarks define the use of syllogistic reasoning in Ethics, Law, or Medicine. Instead they posit analogies between some necessary, proper, or coessential formal aspect of syllogistics and relationships from these other arts, or they simply assert the common derivation of some logical principles and some principles from another field out of Llull's *Regulae*. These moralizations of syllogistics are especially clear examples of how the application of Llull's logical programme is an attempt to rectify other disciplines by analogically positing essential or necessary principles of truth in each one. Of course these principles all derive, for Llull, from his own *Principia*. The proof of this derivation lies in the resemblance that Llull describes between logical and other doctrines, and likewise the resemblance depends on the common term that Llull identifies as the basis of their similarity. Presented in this way, his programme is not a universal analytical method, like Aristotelian demonstration, but rather a universal paradigm for the right ordering of discrete elements from diverse bodies of knowledge as instances of demonstrative truth. It is precisely this application of an extrinsic paradigm that Llull seeks to supercede, or perhaps better to explain more fully, in his new concern for the specific technical procedures of argumentation and demonstration. The success of his efforts depends on the degree to which he mixes explanations from proportion or resemblance with analyses that accommodate the differences between his own *Art* and Aristotelian Logic. The development of these efforts is the subject of the chapters in this Second Part.

10

The Natural and Logical Tree

THE Prologue to the *Logica nova* already suggests how Llull will offer in it a programme for logical argumentation based on the true natures of things. The First Distinction attempts to survey those natures, as they appear in the hierarchy of being.[1] Hence Llull calls it the 'Natural and Logical Tree', and includes in it the Tree of Porphyry, as well as different modes of being and his own *Regulae*, whose questions concern the various ways in which any thing exists. Llull effectively accepts this order of being, but without truly 'logicalizing' it.[2] The terms being, substance, body, animal, man, and questions are nodes in the trunk of this tree, while the *Regulae* are its flowers (see Illustration 7). Llull claims that this tree renders his art of Logic more significative (1. Prol.) and this signification is the chief operative term in his epistemology and gnoseology. Its use in the *Logica nova* serves to embrace the whole art of Logic within the broad cognitive processes of interpretation and analysis that it names. A later portion of this chapter will deal in more detail with the functions of signification; here it is sufficient to note that the significative value attributed to the Natural and Logical Tree of the First Distinction derives from the increased knowledge that it allows of the substantial and accidental natures or essences of things, and this knowledge appears in logical discourse through the first intentions. Llull assumes that the fuller one's knowledge is (that is, the more significations or first intentions that one apprehends in the Tree), the truer one's logical discourse will be. Therefore Llull arranges the tree as he does 'so that the art will become more demonstrable and probable, and more necessary in its demonstration, by taking its beginning from being' (1. Prol.).

This Tree begins with an enumeration of various divisions of being,

---

[1] Platzeck's effort to interpret Llull's Tree in close relation to the doctrine expounded in Peter of Spain, especially the theories of supposition (*Raimund Lull*, 1. 404–10), seems at odds with the very disparate and non-logico-linguistic character of Llull's precepts, as analysed below.

[2] This observation of Platzeck's is very apt ('La combinatoria luliana', p. 153).

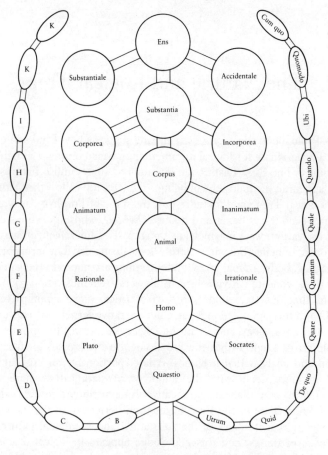

Arbor Naturalis et Logicalis

7. The Natural and Logical Tree from the *Logica nova* of 1303.

just as does Algazel's *Metaphysics* (1a. 1. 1–8), prefaced with this general characterization of being:

Ens commune substantie et accidenti est quoddam consideratum valde confusum innominatum. Dico autem valde confusam quia omnia sub se continet. Dico autem innominatum quia non est ei nomen impositum. Et istud tale confusum predicatur de substantia et accidente analogice. Et ideo quemadmodum confusum, predicatur de ente sic ens de substantia et accidente. Diffinitio ista utilis est et necessaria cum sit causa quare decem predicamenta que generalia sunt possint diffiniri. (1. 1; f. 58vb; p. 3)

Aristotle argues that the term 'being' is used analogically and variously, but not equivocally, in several passages from his *Metaphysics* (4. 2 1003a33–b11; 6. 2 1026a34–b2). Llull seems here to follow this received position and reject the univocity of being advocated by Duns Scotus and others. Because being is predicated analogously, it cannot be considered the genus of the ten categories according to Aristotle (*Metaph.* 3. 3 998b22), and Peter of Spain reiterates this view (2. 20). Still, Llull's last line here and later passages from the *Logica nova* clearly treat being as a *genus generalissimum*. There is a nameless general being corresponding to the term 'being'. Llull labels this term 'confused', rather than equivocal, because it has no 'specification or number' (1. 1). This designation thus reflects Avicenna's definition of universals as neither singular nor plural (*Metaph.* 5. 1). Llull probably uses 'specification' here in a broad sense to indicate that being is not peculiar to any single category of beings, just as Ockham asserts that a concept of being is common to all things (1. 38). In this respect, the genus of being is 'confused' in the sense that all the species of the genus exist indeterminately in it, as Aquinas explains (*In 7 Metaph.* 12. 1549), although Llull surely holds that the genus of being as a Real universal exists independently of its species, which Saint Thomas denies. Llull also refers here to his characterization of being as a definition, and cause of the categories' definitions, although the Scholastics usually treat the categories as *genera generalissima* and therefore indefinable, as Peter of Spain explains (2. 7, 13). Algazel argues that being cannot technically be defined or described (*Metaph.* 1a. 1. 1), but as in his earlier works, Llull's definitions do not always follow Algazel's exact prescriptions. The advantage to Llull of defining the categories is probably that it allows a more direct statement of their essences, whose identification as unique levels of ontic realization is the basis of his new method of definition, described in Chapter 14 below.

Llull examines being in detail, proposing first to consider it in three modes and eventually proceeding to enumerate five divisions, each with its various subdivisions: (1) potential and actual (entelechy, operation); (2) substantial and accidental; (3) singular (God absolutely, creatures compositely) and plural (combinations of substance and accident, individual and individual, and confused); (4) substantial (the Lullian *Subiecta*); (5) accidental (formal, actual, inseparable, separable, potential, actual, universal, particular, causal, occasional). The first part of Llull's list follows the conventional divisions of being into potential or actual, substantial or accidental, and singular or plural found in the deliberately comprehensive analyses of authorities such as Algazel (*Metaph.* 1a. 1–8) or encyclopaedists such as Vincent of Beauvais (*SD* 16. 60–2). The purpose of Llull's own divisions, apart from sheer comprehensiveness, is not immediately obvious. His remarks do not serve to establish a coherent basis for a metaphysical system, as in Algazel, but correspond more closely to the taxonomic methods of a compiler, as in Vincent, from whom his list of divisions may well derive.

Llull's second chapter in the First Distinction treats substance, whose conventional definition adapted from Aristotle (*Metaph.* 7. 1 1028a10) he deliberately revises: 'substance is being that exists by itself; and we do not put "properly" or "maximally" in its definition since these pertain (*se habeant*) to many definitions. And we do this in order to restrict the definition more' (1. 2). Llull thus overtly rejects the definition of substance found in Peter of Spain: 'what properly and principally and maximally is said to be' (3. 6). To Llull this is probably unacceptable because for him the essences of accidents are just as real as those of substances. Also, Aristotle asserts that only substance is strictly definable (*Metaph.* 7. 5 1031a1), but Llull's peculiar use of definition makes it unlikely that he is concerned with this more rigorous position and its ramifications. Llull divides substances into a hierarchy of real beings, corresponding to eight of his nine *Subiecta*, and groups them under the two headings of incorporeal (Divine, Angelic, Rational) and corporeal (Celestial, Elemental, Vegetable, Sensitive, Imaginative). The division of corporeal and incorporeal typically forms part of the Tree of Porphyry in authorities such as Peter of Spain (2. 11), but here serves Llull's natural, as opposed to strictly logical, perspective.

Chapter 3 of the First Distinction briefly defines body with an eclectic summary of distinctions: Avicenna's divisions of point, line, and circular, square or triangular figures (*Metaph.* 3. 6–9); Aristotle's three dimensions (*Phys.* 4. 1 209a4); and Porphyry's division of animate and inanimate (pp. 9–10). This very diverse collocation of senses for body offers an illuminating contrast with his remarks on being and substance; where the latter apparently develop a specific polemical position, the former follow Llull's typical unsynthesized aggregation of disparate notions, which he usually attempts to interrelate through moralizing comparisons or applications of his *Principia* or *Regulae*.

The account of animal in Chapter 4 includes the divisions of rational, irrational, mortal, and immortal pertinent to the Tree of Porphyry and defines animal as 'living substance'. Llull's etymology alludes to Isidore's explanation that 'the soul is so-called because it lives' (11. 1. 7), and Llull goes on to explain that 'animal is so-called from soul (*anima*) since just as form gives existence to matter, so the soul gives existence to the body with which it is conjoined' (1. 4). Llull's definition of the relationship between body and soul reflects his usual position, expounded more fully in the *Ars generalis ultima* (9. 44) and elsewhere: the soul is the substantial form of the body at the same time that the body and soul are two distinct, but conjoined essences. Llull's position is closer to that of Bonaventure (*Brevil.* 2. 9) than to the view of Aquinas (1a. 76, 1), which the Council of Vienne of 1311 endorsed.

In Chapter 5 Llull rejects the traditional definition of man— 'rational, mortal animal'—around which Porphyry constructs the example of his Tree. Llull proposes instead the definition '*animal homificans*' because it is 'more specific and convertible with the thing defined' (1. 5). Chapter 14 on definition will analyse Llull's reasons for this change more fully. The chapter concludes with three uses of the term 'man': as a primary substance; as species; and as an image in the Imagination or painted on a wall. All three recall distinctions from Aristotle's *Categories* (1 1a2; 5 2a13–15) and apparently define for Llull equivocal uses of a term, a concern of great importance for his new theory of fallacy, as later chapters will show.

The First Distinction of the *Logica nova* ends with eleven chapters describing Llull's *Regulae*. For several of these Llull specifies their utility for his Lullist or the logician. Thus his *Regula B, Utrum*, requires that one allow the possible truth of either the affirmation or negation of a proposition, before rejecting as impossible the position that one finds least able to recall, love, and understand. This obviously invokes his capital doctrine of supposition, which other works develop extensively in this period, although the *Logica nova* itself makes surprisingly little direct use of it. He adds that the investigation of truth must be directed by a 'healthy, functioning (*practicus*), and true Intellect', which is the only properly inventive faculty (1. 7). This recalls his doctrine of first intention broadly and his accounts of disputation in particular. His *Regula G, Quale*, teaches the logician how to make necessary demonstrations through proper qualities and proofs through appropriated qualities (1. 12). This parallels Aristotle's distinction between substantial and adjectival predication (*An. post.* 1. 22 83a19–35), although Llull's notion of necessary demonstration and proper qualities is not, of course, Aristotelian, and hence this claim is more of a moralizing analogy than explanation of basic principles.

In conclusion, the First Distinction of the *Logica nova* is largely taxonomic, and collects a miscellany of physical, metaphysical, and logical distinctions in order to illustrate the dual natural and logical character of its Tree of Being. This taxonomic and collective effort is, none the less, an advance over treatments of the same topics from his earlier period, since these rarely display any synthetic rationale other than 'derivation' from Llull's *Principia* or *Regulae*. Moreover, this First Distinction on being offers a rather wider range of distinctions and definitions. Most of these are unremarkable in themselves; indeed, they serve Llull's purpose largely in so far as they insinuate the operative principle of this natural and logical fusion—signification. Just as Aristotle observes that 'all substance appears to signify what is individual' (*Cat.* 5 3b10), so Llull implies that every being signifies the principles of its existence and his concern to explain this signification informs all redactions of his system, from the *Libre de contemplació* on.

Signification

A more detailed examination of what this signification is and how it functions is now necessary. In the *Logica nova* Llull defines signification in his list of one hundred forms as 'the being through which something secret is revealed, because signification attains to those things that enter and leave a subject' (4. 66). This definition clearly has little in common with the use of the term found in Peter of Spain, who calls it 'the conventional representation of a thing through a word' (6. 2). In the *Ars generalis ultima*, Llull explains that signification is the opposite of concealment (*occultatio*) and an implied principle whose definition is applicable to all the explicit *Principia* and *Regulae* (10. 50). It is the basic connection between any and all ontological and noetic categories; for example, *Bonitas* signifies to *Magnitudo* that a great good thing produces a great good thing as its effect. Some notion of its function can also be had from Llull's definitions of the other terms used in his definition cited above. For example, his statement regarding 'occultation' confirms, but does not clarify, the cognitive function of signification: 'the shadow of ignorance of the Intellect, which cannot function (*esse non potest praticus*) with ignorance because the Intellect can have no participation with ignorance' (4. 92). Intellection is participation of the Intellect with the intelligible. Signification makes intelligible what is hidden and decreases ignorance because it displays the accidents of things, as Llull's phrase 'enter and leave a subject' suggests. Porphyry defines accident as 'what is absent or present apart from the corruption of the subject' itself (p. 20); the subject is known through its accidents, as Aquinas explains (1a. 85, 3 ad 4) and Llull aphoristically asserts (*PR* 127. 15).

While these scattered comments give some notion of the basic epistemological import of signification, a fuller understanding of its exact function is available from Llull's *Liber de significatione*, composed at Montpellier in February of 1304. This work offers a sort of retrospective insight into the function of signification as developed in all Llull's works up to then, and illuminates the comments from the *Logica nova* on the role of first intentions and division of being. Through his account of signification in this text, Llull offers one of the clearest explanations of how his own *Principia* and many other conventional axioms that he employs are principles of both being and knowledge, and thus found his programme for a natural Logic. It shows especially well how this role depends on their use in arguments from proportion or resemblance that moralize them as terms of hermeneutic analysis devoted to finding the supreme theological or metaphysical truths of all real and rational existence.

The *Liber de significatione* begins with a definition of signification that asserts its epistemological import:

Significatio est ens cui proprie pertinet significare. Et quia significatio est principium cum quo, pro quo, et in quo incipit habitus scientiae, idcirco de ipsa dare notitiam proponimus investigando suas conditiones, et ipsam discurrere per principia et regulas *Artis generalis*, ad quam omnia sunt applicabilia explicite aut implicite; quoniam per talem cognitionem faciliter habitus scientiae haberi potest artificialiter. Subiectum vero huius libri est ut significatio materialiter et habitus scientiae formaliter sive finaliter habeatur. (Prol.; p. 14)

Llull introduces his work by identifying its material, formal, and final causes, in the fashion of contemporary Scholastic practice.[3] Llull's account of his method is somewhat cryptic, but still suggests that it depends upon the relationship of implicit to explicit associated with the union of universal to particular throughout his writings, and used in

---

[3] See A. J. Minnis, 'Discussions of "Authorial Role" and "Literary Form" in Late-Medieval Scriptural Exegesis', *Beiträge zur Geschichte der deutschen Sprache und Literatur*, 99 (1977), 37–65.

this work as the basis for its account of intellection, examined below. Since this is, in fact, but another realization of Llull's moralizing pursuit of the many in the one, it is difficult to see how it constitutes a 'method for obtaining precision of language through grammatical and speculative analysis of words' in which material content is of less interest than formal procedure.[4] Llull's designation of these modes of significations as 'conditions' is extremely important, because his usual notion of condition is something like 'necessary consequential relation', as in his definition of it from the *Logica nova*: 'the order set between antecedent and consequent, so that they pertain to each other (*se habeant*) relatively, since one cannot exist without the other' (4. 36). What Llull does in this work, then, is to recast each of these conditions of signification as a sort of necessary reason or inference warrant immediately evident to the mind.

In the First Distinction of the *Liber de significatione*—which, like that of the *Logica nova*, Llull calls a 'tree'—he explains how the relationship of implicit to explicit governs the ten conditions of signification, as well as his *Principia* and *Regulae*, in such a way that 'in it we speculatively apprehend (*speculemur*) it and transumptively (*transumptive*) collect from the implicit to the explicit those things that it signifies to our Intellect' (1. 1). The term 'collect' later designates the apprehension of universals from particulars, discussed below, and thus nominally serves to equate here this process with the move from implicit to explicit. The term 'transumptively' is rare in Llull's vocabulary, and its appearance here further serves to qualify his method, although its exact sense is not immediately obvious. There are various contexts for its use in traditional medieval authorities. Boethius, following Themistius, distinguishes several topics *a transumptione* (*De diff. top.* 3; 1201–2). Twelfth-century authorities use *transumptio* to designate the *translatio rationum* between corporeal and spiritual levels of being that Augustine denounces (*De trin.* 1. 1), but which eventually serves later Scholastic doctrines of the analogy of being.[5] In medieval grammar and the *ars poetriae*, *transumptio* is a synonym of *translatio* and metaphor, as Gervais of Melkley explains (1. B. b. a, b). In this sense it appears in Logic as one of the topics. When discussing its use, Peter of Spain distinguishes two varieties: the grammatical occurs 'when a noun is transumed for signifying something else through some like-

---

[4] So Louis Sala-Molins asserts in his introduction to the text (p. 4).

[5] On the development of this type of *transumptio*, see De Rijk, *Logica Modernorum*, vol. 1: *On the Twelfth Century Theories of Fallacy*, pp. 158–63.

ness' and properly pertains only to the sophist; another rightly pertains to dialectical argumentation, 'when one better-known noun is assumed for another not so well-known noun' (5. 35). The relationship of less-known to better-known may well explain Llull's transumption, perhaps as a name for the process that governs all production of demonstrative knowledge for Aristotle (*An. post.* 1. 2 71b32–72a5). The connections to both topical argument and the nature of demonstration in Llull's remarks here are indirect, but broadly emblematic of the relation to Aristotelian doctrine of his entire logical programme. Even if Llull has not employed the term 'transumptively' with any reference to any one of the senses mentioned, taken together they establish a rich context for his use of analogical and moralizing arguments to reduce the many to the one, particular to universal, or implicit to explicit, as their signification.

The Tree of the First Distinction in the *Liber de significatione* has as its members nine 'flowers' corresponding to the letters of Llull's Alphabet. These symbolize his *Principia* and *Regulae*, as well as the ten conditions of signification. These conditions comprise pairs of terms, each of which defines a well-known metaphysical or physical principle. Several of them are the same as the divisions of being listed in the Natural and Logical Tree of the *Logica nova*: simple, composite, general, specific, substantial, accidental, causal, occasional, real, and intentional. As he introduces them, Llull very briefly explains how their combinations further the pursuit of knowledge and his remarks form a very concise, though allusive, explanation of how his own Alphabet bears their significations and thus maintains natural values in logical discourse:

De conditionibus florum libri est, quod unus flos associetur cum alio ad investigandum significationem, sicut .b. cum .c. et .b. cum .d.; Et sic de aliis secundum quod competit ad materiam significationis, de qua quaeritur; quoniam significatio unam conditionem habet cum .b.c., aliam cum .b.d. . . . Combinatio autem florum multum utilis est ad habendum notitiam de significatione, quoniam subiectum est, in quo implicite sunt ea, quae per significationem cognosci possunt . . .

Per istas autem conditiones de significatione habere notitiam possumus, quoniam una est significatio simplex, alia composita; et sic de aliis. Et ideo significatio ex omnibus ista constituta, est obiectum sive subiectum, in quo omnia significata sunt. (1. 1, 2; pp. 15, 16)

Thus a letter of Llull's Alphabet may acquire different values in different combinations. In this respect, Llull's combinatory constructs rely on a principle such as the 'potential multiplicity' that Peter of Spain uses to explain the fallacies of composition and division: 'when the same word or statement signifies different things according to different ends (*perfectiones*)' (7. 57). But where Peter seeks a formal account of this multiplicity, Llull refers it to the subject-matter of signification under investigation, in which knowledge implicitly exists. His definition of signification as both object and subject suggests how this material has both an epistemological and ontological status, according to Scholastic usage of these terms to indicate mental objects and extra-mental objects, respectively. The jointly objective and subjective functions of signification thus serve to define each of the ten conditions as a real thing signified to the mind as a necessary principle or relationship, and object of intellection at the same time.

A typical example is Llull's account of causal signification. It appears paired with occasional signification and together they correspond broadly to Aristotle's distinction between the functions of the four causes and fortune or chance in nature (*Phys.* 2. 3–6). Llull summarizes his understanding of material, formal, efficient, and final causality thus: 'The cause (*efficiens*) signifies the effect, and the effect the cause, relatively; and form signifies matter, action, and completion, and matter signifies affection, form, and incompletion' (1. 2. 7). Llull seeks to cast the relationship of cause to effect as a necessary one, where Aristotle observes that every effect has a cause (*Phys.* 2. 3 195b25), but not every cause produces its effect (*Metaph.* 6. 3 1027a29-b16). Aquinas's commentary on the latter passage expounds the question of causal determinism raised here (*In 6 Metaph.* 3. 1191–1222), something that Llull's term 'relatively' leaves unresolved in its emphasis on the mutual necessity of cause and effect. Llull characterizes matter as potentiality and incompletion, and form as actuality and completion, just as Aristotle defines them (*Phys.* 1. 7–9). However, it is not clear what further mutual relationship Llull posits here when he states that each signifies the other, although as an advocate of universal hylemorphism he sees them joined in all beings. Aristotle argues that matter only exists when informed (*Metaph.* 8. 8 1050a15), while some forms can exist apart from matter (*ibid.* 12. 3 1070a15); matter exists 'for the sake of' form, in Aquinas's view (1a. 47, 1). Llull is not strictly interested, however, in arguing which of matter or form is the more determinative cause of being. He asserts the hylemorphic position against the more purely Aristotelian, while perhaps alluding to the mutual delimitation of matter and form, in the manner described by

Saint Thomas (1a. 7, 1), more as a topical warrant for the necessary consequential condition that the relationship of matter to form suggests. It is the necessity of relationships such as this that comprise the basis for Llull's necessary reasons in many cases. Llull also states that signification is diffused through the four causes, because a cause signifies itself to be a cause, as with accidental causes such as heat, which signifies 'to heat' (*calefacere*) as the cause of heating (*calefaciendi*) and hunger of eating; these are accidental formal and efficient causes, respectively. Llull typically describes the communication of a form without noting the enabling role of the subjects that possess it and this characteristic of his metaphysical arguments recalls the doctrines of Avicebron regarding the role of immaterial forms in causing all action (2. 9–10), and also indicates how Llull considers an active power as an innate correlative of all substantial and accidental essences. Here the specific example of accidental causes mitigates the more unconventional implication of innate accidental activity, since it assumes a substantial subject for the accident. The value of all his remarks in these accounts of signification is the way in which he uses the term 'signification' itself to define physical or metaphysical relationships as necessary conditions, in the sense already noted, and offers these conditions as intelligible objects, thereby giving them an intentional function as truths immediately available to the mind from things.

By bringing such signification within the system of logical discourse, Llull proposes to increase its natural character. He also deals with several specifically logical relationships, but in a way that illustrates how they too serve as necessary conditions that, as objects of intellection, signify their truth to the mind. The most obvious example is the first pair of significations, simple and composite; this is one of the fundamental metaphysical distinctions that Western medieval philosophy inherited from its ancient sources, and bears various senses, as Aquinas notes (1a. 3, 7). Many of these appear throughout Llull's work, but in this case he defines the simple and composite logico-linguistically as single or conjoined words or statements. Peter of Spain explains how among significant utterances, 'some are simple or non-complex, such as the noun or verb, others compound or complex, such as a statement' (1. 3). Peter's remarks appear in the first tractate of the *Summule*, which basically expounds the doctrine of Aristotle's *On Interpretation*, but in that work the Philosopher speaks not of simple and composite words, but of statements, or *enuntiationes* in Boethius's translation (*De interp.* 6 17a20). Peter's division matches the one that

Dominicus Gundissalinus takes from Alfarabi in his *De divisione philosophiae* (pp. 48–9), and which appears in other twelfth-century logical works, such as the anonymous *Tractatus de proprietatibus sermonum* (p. 708). The Pseudo-Augustinian *De dialectica* (1–3), which also figured among the texts of the *logica vetus*, describes both simple and composite words and statements. Llull's remarks apply the distinction to words first:

Significatio simplex est, sicut dictio; ut bonitas, quae significat bonum; et bonum, quod significat bonum agere; quoniam bonum sine bono agere non potest. Et bonum agere significat bonum agens et bonum agibile . . . et sicut dedimus exemplum super bonitatem, ita potest dari super alia abstracta. . . .

Significatio composita est, quando plures significationes componuntur per compositas dictiones. Sicut quando dicitur: Bonitas magna; quae significat, quod subiectum, in quo est, est bonum et magnum. Et subiectum bonum et magnum significat bonum et magnum agere. (1. 2. 1–2; pp. 16–17)

Llull effectively moralizes these conditions of signification as necessary perception of the innate correlatives of any being. As usual, he claims for his correlatives the function recognized for the category of relation, which Peter of Spain defines thus: 'it is characteristic of relatives that if one of the correlatives is definitely known, so is the other' (3. 20). Llull's claims constitute an argument from the topic of relative opposition, as described by Peter (5. 28), and indeed, all his conditions of signification become topics of relation by virtue of the necessary consequence that they attempt to define.

In his definition of composite signification Llull recognizes composite statements as well. The example that he gives implies a peculiarly organic explanation of formal logical relationships as necessary connections:

Et sic de aliis significationibus compositis. Sicut in syllogismo, in quo duae propositiones significant conclusionem. Sicut: Omne animal est substantia; omnis homo est animal; ergo significatum est, quod omnis homo est substantia. Et etiam omnis homo est substantia significat, quod inter animal et substantiam et inter hominem et animal est consanguinitas necessitata. Ex qua significatum est, quod necessitatum est, quod omnis homo sit substantia. (1. 2. 2; p. 17)

The type of naturalistic explanation that Llull offers here appears prominently in his treatments of 'finding the middle' in syllogistic argument, to be discussed below in Chapter 15. Neither the distinction between simple and composite utterances nor the organic explanation of composite logical statements figures in Llull's more extended treatment of simple and composite signification in the Second Part of the Second Distinction of the *Liber de significatione*. There he mentions only physical or metaphysical types of simplicity or composition. His limited concern with single or combined words and statements reflects the scope of the formal logical techniques of his own *Art*, whose combinatory mechanics deal only with terms and their predication in propositions. It is signally noteworthy that his treatment of these elements here in the *Liber de significatione* recognizes them as one more among many necessary relationships that signify their own truth directly to the mind. This is surely how he conceived the signification of the letters combined through his *Art*.

How the mind receives those significations is the explicit subject of the sections on real and intentional signification. Llull's remarks here make a major contribution to his natural logical programme by attempting to explain how the Intellect apprehends, as an object of intellection, the essential nature of any being, including its principles, relationships, or conditions. It does so in two ways: first, by arguing for the real existence of almost any distinction conceived by the mind; second, by describing a curious process of apprehending universal natures collectively and directly from several individuals.

The relationship between real being and its mental conception is obviously of fundamental importance in a system of philosophy that pretends to offer common principles of being and knowledge, and especially with respect to the status of the universals whose real existence Llull so insistently advocates. His awareness of the need to define that relationship is clear from his efforts in the *Liber de ente reali et rationis* of 1311, one of his many later writings that seems to represent his response to contemporary issues and polemics. In this work he tries to determine exactly which beings exist in reality and which only in the mind; his method for doing so assumes *a priori* the real existence of universals: 'because the concrete is known through the abstract, as the singular through the universal, we intend to maintain this procedure in this *Art* subjectively, keeping our mind objectively on the intelligible' (Prol.). Llull's explanation of cognition according to this principle is more or less unremarkable: 'the intentional or rational species is a likeness of the shape (*figura*) of the real species'; that is, from any real being 'the Intellect makes a conceptual being through the likeness that it collects from it' (2. 2, 4). Stated in this way, such a process evidently corresponds to Scholastic notions of the abstraction of intelligible species. Llull considers this abstractive relationship between thing and concept to be itself a necessary and therefore significative one, as he argues with regard to the mind's apprehension of the fundamental essence of *realitas* in the *Liber de significatione*:

Et supposito quod Intellectus non esset res, ipsa realitas esset res in suo esse per se sustentata; verumtamen, non significata, eo quia non esset, qui reciperet suam significationem, nec de ipsa notitiam habere posset. Et ideo realitas est illud ens, a quo intellectus primitive et principaliter fertur, et ab ipso abstrahit et multiplicat intentiones, quae sunt similitudines eius, ut habitus scientiae acquiratur. (2. 2. 9; p. 65)

The thing and its essence are what the mind first grasps, according to the well-known dictum of Avicenna (*Metaph.* 1. 5). The Intellect abstracts intelligible species from sense images, and these species are likenesses of the natures of the things sensed, according to the processes defined by Aristotle (*De an.* 3. 4–7). Although the Scholastics also speak of intentions of the external and internal senses, Llull uses the term here only with reference to the Intellect. Because he wishes to affirm that the essence called reality is a real being, and not just a conceptual one that would disappear with the Intellect that abstracts it, he claims that the essence called reality sustains itself in its own existence, and says nothing about its need to exist in concrete things. Llull also notes that although the essence called reality enjoys a real and subjective existence, it need not enjoy a significative—that is, intentional or cognitive—and objective existence as well. On the other hand, anything that exists significatively and objectively *must* have a real, subjective counterpart: this is the argument developed in most of Llull's remarks on real signification. Hence he argues for the reality of his *Principium* of *Differentia* thus: 'if *Differentia* were not a real being, beings would differ confusedly and intentionally through the Intellect; and thus if this Intellect did not exist, all beings would be one (*idem*), which is impossible' (2. 2. 9. 330). The caution in identifying mental with real distinctions that characterizes the moderate Realism of Aquinas (e.g. 1a. 76, 3 ad 4) or formal distinctions of Scotus (e.g. 1. 2. 2. 1–4) is wholly foreign to the super-Realist system of Llull's philosophy.

Now when Llull describes in detail the processes of cognition that produce the mental likeness of a real thing, these turn out to be not abstractive, but rather collective; moreover, they exploit the Intellect's own participation in the general principles to be conceived, either as means or object, in the manner noted in some of his earlier works. These passages adequately illustrate here this argument, which Llull also adduces in many other instances:

Magnitudo est ens, ratione cuius bonitas, duratio etc. sunt magnae. Et ideo, dum intellectus sic eam considerat, ipsam colligit de pluribus magnitudinibus et generalem facit, eo quia plures ipsam significant in communi.

Duratio est ens, ratione cuius bonitas, magnitudo etc. durant. Et ideo talem durationem intellectus colligit et in communitatem ponit intentionaliter, eo quia plures res eiusdem generis unum genus significant. Et sic de pluribus individuis eiusdem speciei, quae unam speciem significant in communi.

Virtus est origo unionis bonitatis, magnitudinis etc. Et quia plures sunt virtutes reales, sicut in corporibus supra caelestibus elementatis, et etiam in moralibus, ex omnibus istis intellectus colligit et multiplicat unam virtutem generalem, quae significant ei virtutes reales; sicut instrumentum instrumentatum, et effectus suam causam. (2. 2. 10. 340–2, 345; pp. 68–9)

Llull's scheme is neither the induction of universals from several individuals suggested by Aristotle (*An. post.* 2. 19 100a17) nor abstraction from a single individual described by Aquinas (1a. 85, 1), but rather a collective apprehension of the species directly from several individuals. The Intellect evidently apprehends their specific natures immediately, as it does for Scotus, but where Scotus allows this from one individual (2. 3. 2. 2), Llull requires several, and his use of the verb *colligere* to describe this recalls Boethius's famous definition of universal species as 'cogitatio collecta ex individuorum dissimilium numero substantiali similitudine' or of universal genera as 'cogitatio collecta ex specierum similitudine' (*In Isag.* 1. 11). Moreover, as the last passage quoted above suggests, this process is important to Llull because it allows the reverse procedure, that is, from universal to particular, as well. The real individuals cause the concept as their effect, and the latter serves therefore as an instrument for recognizing them in turn, as any effect gives knowledge of its cause. Thus, when Llull describes the same collective apprehension of universals in the *Liber de modo naturali intelligendi* of 1310, he claims that the Intellect, 'just as it ascends from the particular to the universal, also descends when it wishes to attain the particular' (4. 1. 1). The rejection of abstraction and advocacy of apprehending the individual with the universal is typical of many Augustinian thinkers after Bonaventure.[6]

---

[6] See Gordon Leff, *Medieval Thought*, p. 235.

This ascent from particulars to universals and descent to particulars again does parallel Aristotle's explanation of the application to particulars of universal knowledge inductively generalized from particulars (*Metaph.* I. I 981a15–24), but given Llull's extreme Realism, it is probably safe to say that he advocates this collective apprehension of universals from particulars largely because it extends to epistemology a procedure that he regards as fundamental to his entire *Art*.

There is also a participational aspect to this process, because the mind uses the Lullian *Principia* of *Concordantia* and *Differentia*, which are part of its own essential constitution, to compare or distinguish individuals, species, and genera. It is almost gratuitous to note here again that this represents the absolutely basic role of identity and difference as the types of all Lullian argument. In the *Liber de modo naturali intelligendi*, Llull explains that the logician 'considers many individuals different in number, such as this man and that and this ass and that, and so on for other things. And just as he distinguishes through *Differentia*, so through *Concordantia* he makes one man agree with another, and one ass with another, making and multiplying species.' (4. I. 3–4.) This use of *Differentia* and *Concordantia* fills the role of the collective generalizing anciently posited by Aristotle (*An. post.* 2. 19 100b1–3).

The vocabulary and analogies that Llull uses to describe these processes are themselves noteworthy for the wide-ranging sense of their conception that they imply. For example, his very broad notion of signification is clear from his references to the Intellect 'collecting', 'considering', 'multiplying', 'making', 'abstracting', or 'constructing' the universals and 'speculating', 'cogitating', 'reflecting', 'attaining', or 'understanding' the particulars that signify one another. In several instances he declares that the latter process occurs 'in a significative way (*significativo modo*)' (e.g. 2. 2. 10. 346, 356).[7] The phrase 'speculate in itself' that Llull sometimes uses is especially notable because it recalls a favourite image of Prescholastic authorities for describing the mind's recognition of the—usually divinely given—truth within itself.[8]

---

[7] Sala-Molins's reading of the abbreviations from the MSS as *significato modo* seems less likely; his conjecture of *specialiter excogitat* for *speculatur et cogitat* is clearly wrong, since the latter phrase (or variations of it) appear on the same page (69); all this does not arouse great confidence in his editing of the text.

[8] The locus classicus is Hugh of Saint Victor, *De sacramentis* 1. 10. 9; on the mirror metaphor of the Prescholastics, see Robert Javelet, *Image et ressemblance au douzième siècle de Saint Anselme à Alain de Lille*, 2 vols. (Strasbourg: University of Strasbourg, 1967), 1. 376–90.

Llull uses such mirror images frequently in his early *Libre de contempla-ció* and declares in one passage here that 'the Intellect speculates and attains the real *Gloria*, just as vision does, and much more he who represents his face with a mirror' (2. 2. 10. 347). All these terms designate Llull's signification as the immediate perception of the universal in the particular or vice versa and as a necessary relational or causal connection, received in the mind as a first intention of the natures of things. Thus he renders his logic more natural, as he suggests at the outset of his remarks on intentional signification: 'intentions are likenesses of real beings, from which the Intellect multiplies predicables and other general principles, such as genus, species, etc. And these intentions through significations joined to the first [intentions?] we wish to exemplify with the *Principia* of this *Art*.' (2. 2. 10. 338.)

One interesting analogy employed by Llull suggests an attempt to explain the broadly conceived apprehension of conditions of signifi-cation with the intellective processes recognized in Scholastic faculty psychology. Llull claims that the Intellect uses its intentional universal to attain or speculate the real universal, just as colour is attained with light, Taste uses bitterness to speculate the tastable, or the body uses Touch to speculate what is felt (2. 2. 10. 349–50). He thus posits the following scheme of correspondences:

Power	Object	Instrument
Intellectus	reale	intentionale
[Visus]	color	lumen
Gustus	gustabile	amaritudo
Corpus	sensatum	sentire

The value of this analogy for Llull assumes the doctrine, explained by Aquinas (1a. 77, 3), that the powers of the soul are distinguished by their acts and objects. Llull proposes that the Intellect apprehends the real universal just as immediately and properly as the senses do their sense objects. There are various problems with this analogy, not the least of which is the disparate character of the instruments named for each power. However, the basic analogy between the Senses and the Intellect has the authority of Aristotle (*De an.* 3. 5, 7 430a10–17, 431a14–17), although Aquinas frequently qualifies it precisely because of the difficulties that it creates if extended too far (1a. 75, 2 ad 3 and 3 ad 2; 84, 4 ad 2). Llull's choice of vision, taste, and touch as the three senses that he compares to the Intellect may be completely fortuitous,

but it does suggest a certain natural hierarchy that adds strength to his
overall analogy. This hierarchy derives from the fact that all Senses
have an immaterial element, the 'intention of a sensible form' as
Aquinas calls it (1a. 78, 3), but not all of them have a material element
as well. Sight has no material element, and is deemed the noblest of
the external Senses for that reason. Taste does, but the tongue none
the less does not undergo any physical change from contact with its
object, the sweet and bitter. In the case of Touch, however, the flesh
does undergo physical change and therefore Touch is deemed the
least noble of the external Senses. Aquinas summarizes their relationship in this manner (1a. 78, 3 ad 3–4), following principally Aristotle's
remarks in his *On the Soul* (2. 10–11). Llull's analogy effectively
arranges the faculties of perception and cognition in order from the
least material and most noble (the Intellect) to the most material and
least noble (Touch).

Llull's identifications of respective objects and instruments reveal
the non-technical, moralizing quality of this analogy in their imperfect
correlation. Colour is the object of Vision and is rendered visible by
light, according to Aristotle (*De an.* 2. 7 418a26–419b2). Flavour
(called *humor* in the medieval Latin *versio antiqua* of the *On the Soul*), is
Taste's object (termed the tastable or *gustabile* in the *versio antiqua*),
while sweet and bitter are species of flavour (*De an.* 2. 10). The objects
of Touch are the differentiating qualities—hot or cold, hard or soft,
etc.—of a body as body, and the sense of Touch is some internal part
of the human body that is potentially receptive of those qualities (*De
an.* 2. 11). Compared to these elements of received Aristotelian lore,
Llull's analogy between the real, colour, the tastable, and the touched
is adequate, but that between the intentional, light, bitterness, and
sensing obviously is not. Llull does, however, seem to regard them as
parallel, or at least ignores the discrepancy because the most important
comparison for him, the chief moral (as it were) of his analogy, is that
between the Intellect and Vision. Because light is required to make
colours visible, Aristotle compares light to the active Intellect (*De an.* 3.
5 430a15), and from this remark some Averroists therefore likened
sight to the passive Intellect, light to the active Intellect, and colour to
the sense-image, an argument that Aquinas is concerned to refute in
various instances (e.g. 1a. 76, 1; 79, 3 ad 2–3; 85, 1 ad 3–4). More
traditional authorities, such as Bonaventure, also employ this analogy
in relating the active Intellect to divine illumination, and their arguments are the likely source for Llull's application of it here. In Llull's

case the possible identification of illumination with the influence of his *Principia*, either as universals in the mind or as essential constituents of it, makes this analogy especially attractive.

As a general conclusion to this review of Llull's account of signification, it is most useful to recall simply that the *Liber de significatione* explains the rather eclectic divisions of being from the First Distinction of the *Logica nova*. It interprets them as necessary relations or connections between things—'conditions'—whose necessity the Intellect immediately apprehends in those things as essential constituents of their nature. These ten conditions thus establish a range of relations useful as topical inference warrants that is much greater than the several class relationships defined by the original Tree of Porphyry that underlies the scheme of the First Distinction. At the same time, however, Llull abandons the formal logical structures recognized by Porphyry in favour of a material discourse of truth in which every term already bears a natural and immutable value. In this respect, he seeks a *rapprochement* between being and consciousness which is 'praeterlogical' in the sense that it posits a simple material, rather than complex formal, correspondence between real and conceptual entities. The *adequatio rei et intellectus* thus admits only one non-metaphysical element, which therefore determines by itself the attainment of truth or falsehood. This element is the first intention of orientation towards God. If Llull did in fact achieve a material system of inviolable truth, then all formal recourses—including perhaps the combinatory mechanics and other devices of his own *Art*—would become superfluous. The significance of all beings would be immediately obvious to the mind, guided unerringly by that proper first intention. The *Liber de significatione* and First Distinction of the *Logica nova* thus become a sort of 'reader's guide to the *liber naturae*', in which one seeks the uncreated and universal from the created and particular. At the same time, Llull's exposition of these guidelines in a survey of Logic and treatise on signification represents an attempt to postulate their formally logico–linguistic value. These texts too serve Llull's new concern in his later writings to incorporate his basic theological and metaphysical concepts into a programme of Logic for demonstrating their truth.

11

Predicables

THE review of Llull's accounts of the predicables in his earlier works has already shown how they occupy a fundamental position in his philosophy as nearly self-evident modes of transcendence among the particular and universal,[1] and as counterparts to the basic elements manipulated in his own *ars combinatoria*. They are one of the few components of received logical lore regularly treated in his early writings. They occupy a no less important position in his later works as well, and if anything Llull devotes even more attention to them, in part as a means of defining his new natural Logic as a *scientia realis*, and in part as a response to the more problematic aspects involving his extreme Realist conception of them. Their importance in the *Logica nova* is clear from his mention of this text in the *Liber de fine* as a work 'that teaches how to contract the most general *Principia* of the General Art to the five predicables and ten categories' (3. 2. 13). Such a claim suggests his awareness of the difficulty of deriving the predicables from his *Principia*, which the *Aplicació de l'Art General* certainly reveals, even though it implies no recognition of the reasons for this difficulty.

Now, in the *Logica nova*, he de-emphasizes that applicational explanation in favour of expounding their real existence as universals, using not only metaphysical, but physical arguments as well, based on cosmology and the four elements. Thus it imitates the account of the predicables in the early *Liber chaos*, but now focuses on the question of their real existence almost exclusively and as an issue in itself. He devotes a short treatise to it, the *Liber de quinque praedicabilibus et decem praedicamentis* of 1313. This text employs Llull's new method of argument from contrary suppositions (discussed in Chapter 17) in order to present many of the same arguments found in the *Logica nova*, but reiterates two above all others. This emphasis suggests that the views expounded in these arguments may themselves be the justifi-

[1] Platzeck rightly stresses this aspect of their treatment in the *Logica nova* (*Raimund Lull*, 1. 412), but the following remarks will stress the method by which Llull asserts this function.

cation for Llull's extreme Realism, which they sustain, rather than vice versa. The first is the necessarily hierarchical procession of less universal from more universal beings. For example, he posits a general difference from which particular differences spring 'because otherwise a rupture and void would result between the universal and particular, which is incongruous and contrary to philosophy' (1. 3). These arguments provide superlative expressions of the Neoplatonic axioms underlying Llull's system. The second type of argument favoured in the *Liber de quinque praedicabilibus et decem praedicamentis* is the natural determinism of divine activity, and draws Llull directly into the field of contemporary disputes over God's power. He argues, for example, that genera must be real beings, because otherwise 'Divine *Aeternitas* would not cause the duration of the world as much, nor would Divine *Potestas* be as great', and so on for the other Dignities. Therefore genus is a real being in order for the world to be a greater creature and the motion of nature to be more 'successive' (1. 1). Such arguments involve many well-known difficulties concerning the function and nature of Divine Will, Power, and Knowledge, most of which Aquinas examines at one point or another in the disputed questions *De potentia Dei* or in various articles of the *Summa theologiae* (1a. 19, 4; 25, 5–6; 104, 3–2). Llull's repeated use of these arguments indicates how far removed his views were from those of his contemporaries, such as Scotus, who were coming to stress God's freedom and omnipotence. Aquinas speaks directly to the most basic assumptions of Llull's system in two particular texts. In determining the disputed question 'Whether things proceed from God by necessity or free will', he considers two arguments for natural necessity that explicitly appeal to the need for God to communicate completely his goodness (*De pot. Dei* 3. 15 ad 12, 14). His reply, which argues that God's goodness loses nothing for not being communicated, effectively denies one of the most basic tenets of Llull's *Art*: the necessary propagation of real beings and relationships from *Bonitas* and the other Divine Dignities. Furthermore, Aquinas notes that nothing that acts from natural necessity determines its own ends, which is obviously untrue of God. The basic error of those who argue as Llull does is, according to Saint Thomas, 'that they judged the order of created beings to be somehow commensurate to Divine Goodness in such a way that without them it could not exist' (*De pot. Dei*. 1. 5). In responding to the question 'Whether something should be judged possible or impossible according to lower or higher causes' (*De pot. Dei* 1. 4), Saint Thomas specifically denies that higher causes such as the Divine Attributes, which are Llull's *Principia*, should be applicable to effects of lower causes. Llull rarely recognizes a chain of successive causes and effects in creation, since all creatures exist for him participationally as particulars from universals. Aquinas's objections usefully serve to identify the precise theological and metaphysical values that are central to Llull's philosophy, and to his logical programme. Recognizing these values helps appreciate the degree to which that programme is both an expression and justification of them, rather than an independent investigation of the pre-eminent medieval *scientia sermocinalis*. Llull's defence of real universal predicables and categories through arguments from the necessary hierarchy of being and natural determinism of divine activity underscore the profoundly spiritual character of his entire logical programme.

The more diverse arguments regarding the predicables in the *Logica nova* also invite this same conclusion because they rely so heavily on Llull's predilect metaphysical values. Review of these arguments is most worth while as an insight into his capacity to moralize for his own broadly spiritual ends such basic doctrines as the precedence of essence over existence, the plurality of substantial forms, and the origin in essence of both substantial actuality and accidental activity (which Llull does not sharply distinguish in all cases), all of which support together the peculiar definitions of essences that he offers. His conception of the procession of the world form, matter, and body explain his presentation of the Tree of Porphyry and its divisions as a cosmological scheme of the hierarchy of real being. Equally fundamental is his undeviating explanation of all class relationships between genera, species, and individuals as participation through resemblance and as an organic union of parts in a whole; while this notion does appear in the notorious passage from Porphyry (p. 14), Llull extends it much further than any ancient authority. Taken together, all these doctrines comprise Llull's most complete exposition of the real object of logical science and most emphatically moralize the terms of logical discourse to conformity with the truth in things.

Genus

Llull's account of the predicable genus in the *Logica nova* opens with the question posed by his *Regula B*, 'Whether genus be a real being', which he proposes to answer affirmatively with five reasons. His first reason invokes the Tree of Porphyry: 'since body is prior in nature to animal, as is signified in the logical tree, it is necessary that body be a real genus. Otherwise body would not be naturally divisible between animate and inanimate body, but conceptually (*rationaliter*), which is impossible.' (2. 1. 1.) This argument involves two assumptions that Llull must introduce in order to make his conclusion tenable. First, that the Tree of Porphyry in fact represents a hierarchy of real, natural beings. Llull habitually takes this for granted. Second, that things that differ specifically must belong to a common genus, as Aristotle explains (*Metaph*. 10. 8 1057b37). Then, Llull can argue that if the differences animate and inanimate exist in reality, and not just in the mind, then the genus body must also be a real being itself. That is, in order to be real, these differences must divide a real being. Llull's first assumption is clearly necessary in order to counter the objection that the conceptual distinction necessarily derives from the real distinction, as Ockham insists (1. 16).

Llull's second reason for the real existence of genera is the most frequent from all his arguments regarding universals:

Quia natura universi vacuitatem pati non potest, quam pati posset si genus non esset ens reale. Videlicet, quia esset aliqua unitas generalis indivisibilis, et sic esset genus illa unitas et non genus, quod est contradictio. Unde sequitur quod genus est ens reale et hoc quia unum est in numero de quo plures species differentes predicari possunt. Tamen genus invisibile et [in]ymaginabile est, verumtamen extra ipsam animam genus ens est, ut probatum est. (2. 2. 2; f. 62^{ra-b}; p. 18)

The principle of the necessary plenitude of being undoubtedly finds a more cogent expression in other medieval thinkers such as Aquinas (1a. 21, 1 ad 3; 23, 5 ad 3; 47, 1–3) than in Llull, but it is certainly no less fundamental to his philosophy. Indeed, since Llull's metaphysics relies so heavily on participation and so lightly on causality, this plenitude must be a basic metaphysical value in his system. His argument here makes again a tacit assumption, in this case that unity can be a genus, something that Aristotle denies (*Metaph*. 10. 2 1053b23). From this assumption Llull argues that to admit a general indivisible unity and to deny that it is a genus is a contradiction. He also offers a definition of genus that drastically revises the conventional one found in Peter of Spain: 'what is predicated of many things differing in species with respect to their essence (*in eo quod quid*)' (2. 2). Llull's version makes species predicable of their genus, apparently as the participated source of their own existence; the universal always bears in itself the particulars derived from it. Finally, he notes that genus is a real being, although it cannot be perceived by the Senses or

Imagination. He thus counters the common objection regarding the reality of universals, stated by Aristotle (*Metaph.* 7. 4 1039b1), that no single being can be found that corresponds to a subsistent universal, and implicitly makes the comprehension of universals—like his 'collection' in the *Liber de significatione*—a higher, more wholly intellectual, mode of knowledge.

Llull's third reason for the real existence of genera draws on cosmological and physical doctrines:

> Tria entia sunt generalior et integriora, scilicet substantia celi, elementorum et individuorum. Et ex istis substantia mundi constituta est, que constitutio esset impossibilis si genus non esset ens reale, quoniam hec tria predicta generaliora essent distincta per discretas quantitates, non participantes per continuam quantitatem, quod est impossibile cum mundus sit ex ipsis compositus. (2. 1. 3; f. 62rb; pp. 18–19)

This division of being into three types of substance derives from Avicebron (2. 1–10). Llull argues that these three general substances must be parts of a more general substance with continuous quantity, in the Aristotelian sense that they have a common boundary, as do the parts of time or space (*Cat.* 6 5a6–14). Llull thus makes the composition of the world's substance from the three other substances equivalent to the composition of a genus from its species in a typically organic analogy. Aristotle, however distinguishes division in quantity from division in species (*Metaph.* 5. 25 1023b12–18). Llull follows Porphyry's more basic Neoplatonic correlation of part to whole with species to genus (p. 14) in order to stress the continuity in the hierarchy of being. Llull's account of nature and corporeal substance in his *Liber novus physicorum* (1. 4–2. 2) describes fully the procession of first matter, first form, and first body in the universe, drawing largely on Avicebron (1. 17; 2. 24; 3. 27, 45, 56). The latter's Neoplatonic cosmology is much more congenial to Llull's Realist arguments than Aristotelian physics.

Llull's fourth reason is also cosmological, and implies a view of the celestial bodies as strongly active in sublunary affairs:

> Si genus non esset ens reale, ut puta corpus significatum per B, inferiora, scilicet individua specierum, non susciperent influentiam a corporibus supercelestibus. Et hoc quia deficerent subiectum et medium influentie superveninientis, que accidens est. Sequitur ergo quod genus ens reale est in quo influentia superveniens sustentata est. (2. 1. 4; f. 62rb; p. 19)

The genus body must really exist in all bodies in order to mediate the influences of the celestial bodies to individual bodies in this world. It thus plays a role similar to Llull's own *Principia*, which must be present in every individual in order to communicate their influence. This does not necessarily require that the genus body exist independently, which is what Llull seeks to prove. He obviously correlates the relation of genus to species with that of higher heavenly to lower sublunar bodies and regards both relations as participational. The doctrines of Avicebron provide, as noted, the general basis for Llull's account. Llull states in his *Metaphysica nova* that 'heaven is a very great body, containing all other bodies, moving all mobile beings, and existing in the greatest motion' (2. 2. 11). This characterization of heaven is basically Aristotelian (*De caelo* 1. 9 279a7–17; *De gen. et corr.* 2.11 338a17–b6). The supervening influences are the movements and changes in sublunary beings, which the motions of the heavens cause. Thus Llull notes in the *Liber novus physicorum* (3. 2) that 'the motion of heaven, since it is superior, is the cause of inferior motions'. Aquinas expounds the same general principle, but with certain qualifications (1a. 115, 3, 4, 6). Llull here refers to the influence of the heavenly bodies as 'accidental', where Aquinas refers to it as direct, substantial, and *per se* with regard to other bodies (1a. 115, 4). Llull does posit a substantial and accidental motion among his innate *Principia* that compose the heavens. The latter motion is the instrument of the former, and is signified in the mixture of contrary qualities in the four sublunar elements (*LN P* 3. 2). Llull's somewhat oblique explanation of the relationship between the behaviour of the contrary qualities and elements and the motion of the heavens perhaps corresponds to an objection noted by Aquinas, that the behaviour of contrary qualities and the elements is not found in the heavens, and therefore cannot be caused by them (1a. 115, 3 ad 3). Aristotle attributes the transformation of the elements to the sun's annual movement (*De gen. et corr.* 2. 10 337a1–15); Aquinas responds that 'whatever is brought into being in lower things is precontained in the heavenly bodies by reason of their universal power' (1a. 115, 3 ad 3). Llull takes the relation of the general to the specific broadly as a necessary and natural one of participation, and this is sufficient for him to explain the connections between any higher and lower, or heavenly and sublunar, beings.

In his fifth reason for the real existence of genera Llull appeals to potentiality in a manner reminiscent of the Augustinian doctrine of seminal reasons:

Supposito quod omnia animalia destruerentur; adhuc habitus animalitatis sic remaneret in potentia in primis principiis et in natura eorum, sicut habitus frigiditatis in aqua calida sustentatur. Qui sustentatus non esset si aqua non esset ens reale. Subiectum habitus illius animalitatis dicimus esse reale ens quod genus vocamus. Et hoc per regulam de B indicatum est. (2. 1. 5; f. 62rb; p. 19)

Llull attempts to solve the standard question of whether a universal would continue to exist if all its individual instances were destroyed. Aristotle rejects, of course, this as impossible (*Metaph.* 7. 13 1038b33). Llull proposes that the universal essence animality exists as a habit in the manner that coldness exists in hot water. He generally conceives of habit broadly as a type of potentiality. The example of water and coldness involves some notable difficulties, however, in the context of Aristotelian doctrine. It assumes that animality is essential to some subject in the way that coldness is to water. Coldness is, after all, the defining quality of water; the complete loss of coldness would result in the transformation of water into the element air (*De gen. et corr.* 2. 3 331a5; 2. 7 334b25). Moreover, none of the four elements exists in a pure state on earth (ibid. 2. 8 334b32), and this mitigates further the value of Llull's analogy. The relationship between the quality of coldness and water hardly seems parallel to that between the habit of animality and Llull's innate *Principia*, since animality does not exist in the *Principia* actually, nor is it a constitutive element of their existence. Finally, the last sentence in this fifth reason requires that the *Principia* already mentioned be equated with some genus as the subject of the habit animality. It could be objected that whatever this genus might be, it cannot exist apart from its species, even though it is said to contain them potentially, as Aquinas explains (*In 7 Metaph.* 12. 1545–50). Moreover, it is not clear what agent, other than God, would bring the potential animality into actual existence as particular animals if all particular animals had already been destroyed. The question of the natural determinism of divine creativity thus arises implicitly. Llull's analogy in this passage simply cannot bear even a limited interrogation of its argument, and its difficulties are illustrative of the problems that many of his other claims also incur, though less obviously.

After giving these five reasons for the real existence of genera as understood through *Regula B*, Llull continues with other arguments based on the remaining *Regulae*. Some of these simply reiterate the constitution of genera from Llull's innate *Principia* or their function in the Tree of Porphyry. Some explicate the nature of genera as real beings; for instance a genus has real constituent parts, just as the real genus body has general corporeal form and matter, presumably in the manner explained in the *Liber novus physicorum*. Some of Llull's other remarks repeat his special understanding of conventional logical doctrine, as when he states that a genus is 'diffused' in its species, as a whole in its parts. Aristotle maintains that species are said to be parts of the whole that is their genus, not in a quantitative sense, but rather as constituent elements, or as a class of objects includes them as a whole (*Metaph.* 5. 25, 26 1023b18–24, 28–32). Llull's term 'diffused' does not clearly indicate whether species pertain to their genus essentially or by participation. Aristotle accepts only the former explanation (*Metaph.* 7. 4 1030a11–14). Llull also associates quantity with genera, claiming that they are diffused in their species through discrete and continuous quantities. Since Llull considers genera to be substances, they of course have quantity; he takes the relationship of species within a genus to exemplify Aristotle's division of quantity according to which each part of the whole has a relative position to the others (*Cat.* 6 4b21). This substantial understanding of quantity further illuminates the argument already cited, in which Llull posits the substance of the heavens, elements, and individuals as constituents of the substance of the world. Overall, his further remarks on genera using the other *Regulae* serve to underscore his organic conception of the hierarchy of being as concentric levels of existence.

Species

Llull's views on the logical status and functions of genera become clearer in the second chapter of the Second Distinction from his *Logica nova*, which treats species, and chiefly in relation to genus. He begins, as before, with five reasons drawn from his *Regula B* (2. 2). The first four are the four elementary syllogisms used to illustrate the first four modes of the first figure of the syllogism, as in Peter of Spain (4. 6). Llull uses them more or less analogically as *exempla*, and offers his own peculiarly naturalistic interpretations of these modes. With the first he argues thus:

Omne animal est substantia. Omnis homo est animal. Ergo omnis homo est substantia. Unde sequitur quod si animal non esset species realis et ultra animam, predictus silogismus non esset verus naturaliter, eo quod substantia et homo non possent participare naturaliter, quod est impossibile. Unde sequitur quod species est ens reale. (2. 2; f. 62vb; p. 21)

As noted already, Aristotle argues that species possess their genus essentially, rather than participationally. Llull espouses the latter view, which Aristotle attributes to the Platonists. The type of natural participation that Llull advocates combines the principles of the plenitude and gradation of being, but effectively begs the question that it seeks to answer: it assumes in advance that the genus of substance and species of man are real, and therefore need another real being, the species of animal, to serve as a medium for the communication of their natures.

Llull explains the second syllogism in a similar manner: 'No animal is a stone. Every man is an animal. Therefore no man is a stone. From whence it follows that species is a real being. Because if not, the two aforesaid general negatives would not have a subject through which they would be true, which is impossible.' (2. 2. 2.) One of the consequences of Llull's more exact attention to specific logical doctrines and structures in his later writings is a clearer understanding of his very unconventional conception of them. The propositional terms 'negative', 'affirmative', 'particular', and 'universal' are signal examples of this. Llull uses the label 'general negative' to describe the two premisses that Peter of Spain calls 'universal negative' (4. 6). The term 'general' serves to intimate etymologically the relation of genera to species, while the term 'subject' indicates the stone that must be a real species in order for the syllogism to be true. Llull uses 'subject' and 'predicate' to name general or specific levels of being, or their essences, rather than terms in a proposition itself.

His interpretation of the third syllogism illustrates even more clearly this conception:

Omne animal est substantia. Quidam homo est animal. Ergo quidam homo est substantia. Unde sequitur quod species est ens reale. Quia si non, universalis affirmativa cum duobus particularibus affirmativis participare non posset naturaliter. Nec per consequens particulare cum universali, quod est impossibile. (2. 2. 3; f. 63ra; pp. 21–2)

The truth of the syllogism justifies or insures the real existence and real participation of the universal and particular beings joined in predication. Llull in effect appeals to this truth in order to moralize the syllogism with his own naturalistic interpretation. This is one of many instances where Llull accepts the validity of received doctrine, but attempts to rectify its apprehension according to his own system. Here the example patently shows that Llull conceives of universals and particulars entirely ontologically, and without reference to their function as quantifying terms in propositions. Thus he simply subordinates the affirmative particular terms 'some man' to the affirmative universal 'every animal' participationally, explaining this connection only very implicitly as common possession of the universal nature called substance.

Llull's explication of the fourth and last syllogism drawn from his *Regula B* is somewhat terse: 'No animal is a stone. A certain man is an animal. Therefore a certain man is not a stone. From whence it follows that species is a real being. Because if not, the conclusion could not be from its premisses naturally, which is impossible.' (2. 2. 4.) The real and natural truth of the syllogism requires the real and natural existence of the beings and relations predicated in its premisses. The appearance of a negative syncategorematic term, as Peter of Spain (1. 5) and other *modernistae* call it, does not affect Llull's appeal to the homology of ontological and logical elements.

Llull's fifth reason according to his *Regula B* is not a syllogism, but an extraordinary appeal to the telic character of his doctrine of supposition: 'this *Regula* would be destroyed and its contrary true if the Intellect were necessarily compelled to understand species not to be a real entity' (2. 2. 5). That is, the question *Utrum* designated by *Regula B* would be useless if species did not exist, because one could not ask whether they do or not; of course, the same claim is possible if species do exist. Llull's reference to a nonsensical 'contrary' of the question *Utrum* reveals his unexpressed assumption: *Utrum*, like his suppositions, always serves to oppose the true affirmation and false negation of the quantified terms used in predication. For Llull, one side of a question is always determinately true, and it is the mind's task to discover how this is so; there is never the possibility that one side *or the other* is true. Subsequent developments in his treatment of contradiction show this conception more clearly.

In his analyses of species according to the *Regulae C* to *K*, Llull offers some very illustrative indications of the participational relationships that he would posit among individuals, species, and genera. In his answer to the *Regula C* he repeats his peculiar definition of species as 'the being from which many numerically different individuals are predicated' and adds that a species 'is in that genus under which it is receiving existence and it is existing and flowing (*influens*) into its individuals' (2. 2. C3). This explanation obviously appeals to the actual procession of individuals from species in the hierarchy of being, and the primacy of this relationship in Llull's system effectively justifies his rejection of the standard definition of species as, in Peter of Spain's words, 'what is predicated of many things differing in number as regards their essence' (2. 8). Llull's treatment of species as the 'being from which' or 'beneath which' many individuals are predicated conflates the very functions of 'being in' and 'being predicated of' that Peter deliberately introduces in order to distinguish real universals from logical predicables (2. 1). Llull also claims that a species is 'constituted from', 'predicable by virtue of', and 'has' its individuals as its parts. This again remits to the Neoplatonic axioms of Porphyry's seminal treatment of the predicables, where he states that a whole is in its parts, and takes a genus always to be a whole, an individual a part, and a species either a whole or a part (p. 14). Peter of Spain also notes, in this regard that universals such as genera or species are the form of those beneath them, while individuals are the matter for that form (12. 7). Llull extends his previous explanations of how a genus exists in its species, and describes how a species exists in its individuals, observing that 'species exist by reason of their ends, hence man is so that Sortes and Plato might be' (2. 2. E2). In this procession of being, the end of all generation is individuals, just as in the non-universalist ontology of Aristotle (*Metaph.* 7. 8 1033b18). In this procession, species occupy a middle position between a genus as beginning and individuals as ends. Llull asserts that this beginning, middle, and end are mutually dependent, but then adds that 'if all animals were to die in one moment, the species would still remain in its genus habitually and naturally situated' (2. 2. H). The dependence of beginning, middle, and end is not totally reciprocal: the beginnings are prior to ends in nature, and genera are prior to species or individuals in the natural procession of being, regardless of their mutual participation.

Many of Llull's other remarks on species represent no significant departure from received Aristotelian doctrine, and hence need no comment in themselves. Their presence amidst an account that is so thoroughly Realist and so completely founded on participation raises the question of how well Llull could even acknowledge non-Realist and non-participational explanations of the received doctrines that he interprets. Yet he does recognize his opponents' positions, at least broadly, and if he rejects them it is because of his own profound conviction of the truth of his position. This conviction is spiritual, not philosophical, and Llull's more astonishing or idiosyncratic explanations are best understood as testimony to that crucial difference. It is also important to recall that all his remarks examined thus far pertain to natural species that are real entities. He also mentions in several passages the 'logical' species, as he understands them, that are *entia rationis*. Llull's logical species are in fact the intelligible species of cognition:

Per modum autem logici, species est quia intellectus ut agens in suo proprio intelligibili habet modum imprimendi, carat[er]izandi species peregrinas, quas intelligibiles facit adiuvante sensu et ymaginatione. Ut puta species hominis, leonis et rose, quas intellectus facit esse intelligibiles, ponendo in ipsis suam similitudinem. (2. 2. K2; f. 63va; pp. 24–5)

The Intellect does not perform any functions of abstraction of species from individuals, as is clear from the *Liber de significatione*. Instead, the universal species that it comprehends corresponds directly to, and is the likeness of the real universal species existing as such in the individuals in nature. It is perhaps impossible to determine whether this conflation of logical and cognitive species is deliberate or not, but it is a corner-stone of Llull's new programme for a natural Logic.

Difference

Where Llull's accounts of genus and species focus primarily on the question of their real existence, his remarks on the three remaining predicables concern more their role as varieties of essences and the mind's apprehension of them. His treatment of difference only initially deals with its role in dividing genera into species and thereby establishing the terms of a species' definition, probably because Llull rejects this conventional mode of formulating definitions. He begins his remarks by proposing to answer the *Regula B* through a syllogism of the second figure. He offers his own variation on the example that Peter of Spain (4. 8) gives for the first mode of that figure. According to Llull, 'No animal is a stone. Every pearl is a stone. Therefore no pearl is an animal. From whence it follows that difference is a real and general principle, without which animal and stone cannot naturally differ.' (2. 3. B.) All things of course differ either in genus or in species according to Aristotle (*Metaph.* 10. 3 1054b27). In this case the difference between animate and inanimate divides the genus body and establishes the species that include animal and stone. Llull does not, however, treat difference as a logical, but rather as a 'real and general' principle. He proceeds immediately to define difference with the definition of his own *Principium* of *Differentia*. Almost all his subsequent remarks deal with the nature and functions of difference as a *Principium* of the

Lullian *Art*, where it certainly does constitute, along with identity, one of the poles that orient all his arguments.

For example, Llull avers that 'difference has its existence and operation in the subject in which it is'; difference is the part through which the subject has 'the many different parts of which it is constituted'; it also serves the subject instrumentally 'just as a man's hand, since as the subject acts with difference, which is its part, in making distinctions, so man does with his hand in writing' (2. 3. D3). Here Llull's conception of the contribution of his *Principia* as constituent elements in all beings achieves a sharper definition as a substantial instrumental form of difference. He also distinguishes between proper or substantial differences and appropriated or accidental differences, calling the latter likenesses of the former. Llull's doctrine is remarkable for the relationship that it implies between difference and the parts of a thing's essence. For Aristotle, essence is expressed in a definition combining a genus and specific difference (*Metaph.* 7. 4 1030a2–18), but Llull, as noted already, ignores this role of specific difference. The parts of that definition or formula (*ratio*) of a thing correspond to the parts of a thing's form alone, rather than those of its matter as well (*Metaph.* 7. 10 1035b32). For an animal, this form is the soul, and not the parts or functions derived from it or the body (1035b10–28). Aristotelian doctrine suggests a single substantial form, but Llull posits many, and admits many definitions as well, as in the example of man from his *Ars generalis ultima* (9. 44). Here he explains that the proper substantial difference of a lion distinguishes its substantial parts of elemental matter, and vegetative, sensitive, and imaginative souls. Llull's appropriated difference is an accidental instrument of the subject man by which this subject performs those derived functions with distinct bodily parts such as the hand. Llull's example recalls a similar one used for the opposite conclusion by Aristotle, when he argues that man's hands or other body parts are not truly such unless disposed to functioning, something that depends on the soul's power for sensation, motion, and so forth. Hence the soul is the source of their true existence as body parts and most properly belongs in the definition of man (*Metaph.* 7. 11 1036b29–33). Llull's *Differentia* apparently enables the functions that Aristotle attributes to the soul, by distinguishing their corresponding spiritual or corporeal activities. The latter are accidents of the whole, the former of the soul alone, for Aquinas (1a. 77, 5). Llull's reference to *Differentia* as a substantial part through which a subject has other substantial parts especially confuses these relationships in attempting to define them all as varieties of participated substantial or accidental qualities. The subject of proper accidents is their cause, according to Aristotle (*Metaph.* 7. 4 1029b28–1030a16), and Aquinas remarks that any accidental form serves to complete its subject (1a. 77, 6), a principle that Llull repeatedly invokes and extends. He attempts to account for these same relationships and functions by claiming that appropriated differences are likenesses of the proper differences, a notion that does have a parallel in Aquinas's observation that accidental differences are 'signs' of essential differences (*In 7 Metaph.* 12. 1552). For Llull, this relationship of resemblance or signification realizes the participation between similar beings.

In this chapter Llull again distinguishes real difference from a logical difference that is in fact epistemological: 'physically in so far as one considers difference naturally existing and acting; logically in so far as one considers it intentionally and as a likeness' (2. 3. I). He also refers to an internal psychological function, saying that 'difference is thus a light (*lumen*) for the Intellect to know things, as light (*lux*) for sight to attain visible beings' (ibid.). Since the *Principia* are the Divine Dignities, this function of *Differentia* parallels that of the intelligible form with which God illumines things known, according to Albert the Great in his *Summa de creaturis* (2a. 56, 1 ad 5).[2] None the less, Llull's analogy seems to imply that *Differentia* renders objects intelligibly distinct as light renders them visible, although whether this applies to singular material objects or to intelligible species is not clear, given Llull's non-abstractive explanation of the apprehension of species. It ultimately may even refer to the distinction of one universal essence from another. Llull's *Differentia* probably serves a function like the 'individual difference' advocated by Duns Scotus (1. 2. 2. 1–4, 398), but rejected by Ockham (1. 17) as superfluous to mere difference in number. Llull's attempt to explain many differential and distinguishing functions through the direct action of his *Principium* of *Differentia* confuses, in any case, the exact definition of his explanation of all those functions. His attempt to explain them as separate functions represents a popularizing effort to acknowledge and account for the various divisions and tenets of received Scholastic theories in one simplistic way.

---

[2] On Albert's views as expressed in this passage, see R. Z. Lauer, 'St. Albert and the Theory of Abstraction', *Thomist*, 17 (1954), 68–83.

Property

Where Llull's account of difference in the *Logica nova* probably has the least debt to received doctrine, and the greatest dependence on his own *Art*, his account of property in the fourth chapter of the Second Distinction reveals a much more obvious effort to reinterpret received doctrine. Peter of Spain summarizes Porphyry's teaching on property and accident in this manner: property belongs always and only to every member of one species, as the capacity to laugh belongs to man; it differs from an inseparable accident, such as the blackness of a crow or an Ethiopian or the whiteness of a swan, because these accidents appear always and in every member of other species as well (2. 14–16). Llull's awareness of these conventional definitions is evident in the example that he employs to illustrate his account of property: 'Property has its actuality in the subject in which it is, just as the ability to laugh has in man its actuality, which is laughing'; 'another property is quantitative (*quanta*) in relation to discrete quantities, as in the crow, whose proper colour is black, and the swan, whose proper colour is white'; 'one special property is in one subject, another indeed in another, just as laughing in man, barking in dogs' (2. 4. C4, F2, I). Peter of Spain also quotes Aristotle's statement that 'Property belongs to one species alone and is predicated convertibly of a thing, but does not indicate its essence.' (*Top.* 1. 5 102a18.) Llull's comments indicate his familiarity with all these distinctions, and his expression of them here in largely unaltered form parallels the equally conventional summaries of property and accident in the *Logica Algazelis*. Llull's willingness to repeat these views without drastic revision probably reflects their facile revision according to his own more idiosyncratic notions. For example, Llull also posits a substantial property, which corresponds broadly to those attributes of a subject called always true, essential, and universal by Aristotle (*An. post.* 1. 4 73a26). In the Latin version of Avicebron, 'proper accidents' pertain essentially to their subject (3. 10. 54), while Aquinas suggests that properties stand somewhere between essence and accident (1a. 77, 1 ad 5). Thus the already diverse Scholastic understanding of property easily allows Llull to regularly associate property with a thing's essential forms or essences. He explains the exemplary syllogism 'every animal is a substance, every man is an animal, therefore every man is a substance' by observing that this is true 'properly and substantially, since animal properly and substantially is the middle between man and substance, which would not be if every property were an accident' (2. 4. B1).

Animal is thus a substantial property or form or essence of man in Llull's view.

He goes on to explain his view of this substantial property very concisely:

Adhuc quicquid habet esse, habet esse per suam propriam essentiam. Sed homo habet esse. Ergo habet esse per suam propriam essentiam, videlicet humanitatem. Unde sequitur quod homo habet esse per suam substantialem proprietatem, non per proprietatem accidentalem. Sicut ignis qui non habet esse substantiale per suam propriam caliditatem, set per suam substantialem proprietatem, que est ignitas. (2. 4. B2; f. 64vb; p. 29)

Llull's definition of the relationship between essence and existence is the opposite of that recognized by Aquinas, who came to advocate that 'existence is the actualization of every form or nature, for actual goodness or humanity is not signified except as we signify it existing' (1a. 3, 4). Llull claims on the other hand, that 'property, in as much as it is an essence, exists formally by itself, that it might have its proper concrete, that is, proper existence, through its proper essence' (2. 4. E1). Llull's position presupposes Avicenna's famous declaration that 'everything that exists has an essence by which it is what it is and by which its necessity is and by which its being (*esse*) is' (*Log.* 1. 4). Aquinas considered this position in his early *De ente et essentia* (1), but abandoned it, while Llull extends it to the extreme point of creating a wholly essentialist ontology. Where Avicenna still recognizes a limited definition of property as 'what is predicated of individuals of one species with respect to qualities, not substance' (*Log.* 1. 11). Llull's essentialism dismisses such restrictions. This extension of essentiality becomes an especially acute problem in Llull's treatment of the predicable of accident.

As he often does, Llull introduces the four elemental qualities as accidental properties of the four elements, in which they exist either 'properly' as heat in fire, or 'appropriatedly' as heat in air. Except for his use of the term property, he simply expresses Aristotelian doctrine (*De gen. et corr.* 2. 3) and in fact he employs the elements as an *exemplum* of a specifically logical problem regarding the contingent predication of property. His remarks appeal to the elemental qualities in order to resolve this question:

Proprietas vero propria est causativa, videlicet, causa proprietatis appropriate. Et est necessaria tendens ad unum suum possibile sive impossibile: ad impossibile sicut aquam non esse frigidam naturaliter; ad possibile sicut ad aquam cui possibile est esse calida per ignem. Proprietas vero appropriata est occasionativa et non necessaria. Sicut caliditas aeris que est occasio caliditatis aque, infundente ipso aere suam humiditatem calefactam in ipsam aquam. Et ista proprietas tendit ad duo: videlicet ad possibile quod sic et possibile quod non. Aquam enim esse calidam et non esse calidam possibile est. Et de istis duobus terminis sequitur contingentia. (2. 4. G1–2; f. 65ra; p. 31)

This conforms to the received doctrine summarized by Peter of Spain: the matter of a proposition is contingent if the predicate either may or may not be in the subject; contingency is convertible therefore with possibility (1. 13, 24). Ockham, when discussing the predicable of property, uses the example of heat in fire, and observes that any simple affirmative proposition in which a property is predicated should be considered equivalent to a contingent formulation of the same proposition, since God could cause a true proposition such as 'man laughs' to be false, by changing the real circumstances to which it refers; the proposition 'it is possible that man laughs' is, on the other hand, necessarily true since it adequately recognizes that contingency (1. 24). Llull describes the same function of necessary contingency, but his first example posits an instance of natural determinism opposed to Ockham's emphasis on divine omnipotence; it is impossible, according to Llull, for water not to be naturally cold. So, although Llull's comments evidently acknowledge the issue of contingency, he does not recast the verbal form of the proposition to reflect this, and his focus on the affirmation or negation of possibility best corresponds to the function of his suppositions, where one side of a question is determinately true. In this respect, it is difficult to say whether Llull's concern for the problem of contingency shows his awareness of contemporary disputes, or simply a convergence between his own peculiar doctrines and certain aspects of those debates.

Another important feature of Llull's account of property is his explanation of how accidental property contributes to a subject's unity or 'numerically individual form'. He avers that 'property is the form because of which a being consists in its proper number' as a conclusion consists in its proper number from its premises, and 'property in a subject appropriates number, as proper heat *per accidens* appropriates to fire its number' (2. 4). His use of 'to appropriate' suggests a sort of natural contraction in the manner of the natural attraction or sympathy that so many of his doctrines assume. The claim just quoted specifically suggests a view of the numerical unity, as opposed to non-numerical commonality, of universals. The comparison to a syllogism echoes Aristotle's characterization of premisses as the cause of a conclusion (*An. post.* 1. 2 71b19), apparently as a sort of acknowledged truth with exemplary value for Llull's own argument, Llull concludes his comments on property and number by arguing that 'no being can have its absolute unity (*numerum simplicem*) without property. However because difference diffuses itself in all entities, so also property diffusing itself draws forth (*deducit*) unity in every entity different from another. There is one specific property in one subject, another indeed in another, just as laughter in man, barking in dogs.' (2. 4. I.) Llull thus identifies property as a specific difference that divides each species from the *genus generalissimum* of being. Thus the property of heat found in fire sets fire apart from all other species, and similarly the property of being able to laugh in man or being able to bark in dogs sets them apart as species. On the one hand, Llull's 'specific properties' ignore the connections of coordinate and subordinate genera; on the other, his claims ignore the difference between the unity of an individual and that of a species, that is, of first and second substances. Aristotle notes that 'things that are primarily called one are those whose substance is one either in continuity or in form or in definition', and 'things that are one in number are also one in species, while things that are one in species are not all one in number' (*Metaph.* 5. 6 1016b36–1017a1). As usual, Llull emphasizes the common factor, rather than the differences, among these types of unity. His advocacy of substantial as well as accidental property correlates unity of continuity, form, definition, being, and species. His arguments also imply, of course, a real distinction between a being and its unity, a position denied by Aquinas (1a. 11, 1) as well as Ockham (1. 44). Others, following Avicenna (*Metaph.* 3.3), would make unity an accident like number, and this seems to be Llull's view as well.

In general, Llull's remarks on property are especially valuable because they directly impose his essentialist interpretation on recognizable tenets of conventional doctrine. They illustrate clearly the very broad conception of essence that he maintains, and how it serves his view of the hierarchy of being as a scale of discrete essential realizations, each perfected and constituted in its own proper nature.

Accident

Llull's account of the fifth predicable, accident, in the fifth chapter of the Second Distinction of the *Logica nova* is not especially heterodox or remarkable in its doctrine. Most of the responses to his *Regulae* simply reiterate the main features from Porphyry's characterization of accident: that which comes into being or passes away apart from the destruction of the subject, may be either separable or inseparable, and always exists in a subject (p. 20). Hence Llull declares that 'an accident exists because its subject exists, without which the accident cannot exist, just as an effect that exists through its cause' (2. 5. E1). Aquinas also notes that some (chiefly proper) accidents are caused by the nature of their subject (1a. 3, 6). Llull avers that accidents are innumerable, just as Aristotle observes (*Metaph.* 6. 2 1026b7), and also mentions the nine predicamental accidents or categories. In Scholastic literature, such as the Pseudo-Aquinas's *De natura accidentis*, these are called 'natural accidents' derived from the nature of things and distinguished from the 'logical accidents' derived from the Intellect's operations with respect to the predicable of accident. Llull's exclusive attention to the former in his *Logica nova* obviously serves his programme for a natural Logic, and it is possible to wonder whether he in fact recognized the other type.

Most of Llull's remarks on accident deal with two principles often invoked by Aquinas: accidents constitute a means for a subject to achieve actuality (e.g. 1a. 3, 6) and all things act through their forms (e.g. 1a. 3, 2). Llull's expressions of these principles reflect his ambivalent distinction between substantial and accidental forms or essences and participational conception of their relationship. This is evident in his claim that 'accident exists from the influence of the substance as a likeness from an exemplar (*similato*), just as heat from fire, and heating which is a likeness of the actuality of the fire; and action, which is a likeness of the form of the substance, and affection of the matter of the substance' (2. 5. D2). Llull thus applies the principle that 'every agent does something similar to itself' to the cause and effect relationship that he sees between substance and accident by virtue of their participation and procession of the latter from the former as its 'influence'.

Perhaps the most surprising feature in Llull's analysis of accident is his denial of the existence of a real universal accident. He advocates this uncharacteristic position using a characteristic argument:

Omne animal est substantia. Omnis homo est animal. Ergo nullus homo est substantia. Unde sicut ista ultima propositio non participat in aliqua veritate cum duabus premissis supradictis, sic veritas et falsitas, malum et bonum, caliditas et frigiditas et sic de aliis accidentibus inmediate contrariis de uno accidente generali et reali et simplici per suum numerum procedere non possunt. Quia si ab eo procedere possent, 'omnis homo est substantia' [et] 'nullus homo est substantia' vere ab ipsis premissis predictis et invicem procederent, quod est impossibile et contradictio. Et talis impossibilitas per regulam de B concessa est. (2. 5. B; f. 65^{rb-va}; p. 32)

Stated more simply, Llull's argument is, like so many of his logical ratiocinations, a moralization employing an *exemplum*: contrary accidents are no more likely to proceed from one general accident than are contrary conclusions from the same pair of premises. Llull's treatment of contrarity does not strictly observe Aristotelian teaching: contrarity is one type of opposition, while truth and falsehood are another, which only exists in word combinations such as propositions (*Cat.* 10 13b1–35). Llull's broad conception of contrarity becomes one of the enabling principles of his new 'fallacy of contradiction', discussed in Chapter 18. Here Llull's comparison of contradictory premises or conclusions from a syllogism with contrary qualities such as good or bad and cold or hot is irremediably incongruous. The most basic difficulty in his argument is that it must refuse the fundamental doctrine that contrary species belong to the same genus (*Metaph.* 10. 8 1058a17–27), although Llull's neglect of the relationships between coordinate and subordinate species facilitates this refusal. His habitual explanation of all physical and metaphysical relationships according to participation or procession of being requires resemblance, not disparity or contrarity, among beings that participate in the same source. Difference or contrarity functions in Llull's system largely as it is necessary in order to separate the many likenesses that constantly tend toward identity.

The necessity of participation and procession in fact leads Llull to argue in the *Liber de quinque praedicabilibus et decem praedicamentis* (1. 5) that there is a real universal accident from which all particular accidents derive. He claims that if there were no real universal accident, then the predicamental categories and other accidents 'would not have agreement in genus or in species, and likewise individuals; and the world would be deprived of the real commonality (*communitas*) of accidents; and the Dignities of God would not be creative or causes in an orderly manner'. Even where the Scholastics recognize no *genus generalissimum* beyond the ten categories, Llull must treat every general principle of being, such as his *Principia* or the predicable of accident, as such a genus by virtue of its originary role in the orderly procession of particular from universal and necessary derivation of the many from the one. It is Llull's insistence on this transcendent procession and derivation that ultimately makes it impossible for him to accommodate the class logic of Aristotle.

As a conclusion to this review of Llull's account of the predicables in the *Logica nova*, one general observation suggests itself: from his earliest works, Llull argues for the real existence of universals and explains their ontological functions participationally, while almost completely ignoring the functions of the predicables in logical predication. Now, in the *Logica nova*, he transfers that metaphysical conception of the predicables to Logic, and attempts to explain the formal demonstrative value of the syllogistic figures according to relationships of participation and resemblance among universals and particulars, in arguments that he has often developed many times before in other non-logical writings. Some of these arguments do approximate Aristotelian class relationships through curiously organic appeals to connections of part to whole, but without ever recognizing the divisions of coordinate or subordinate classes. Llull's universals contract through procession and emanation, rather than specific differentiation. These arguments and others are certainly notable examples of how Llull's moralization of received doctrine relies on metaphysical, as well as theological, ends. Yet in so far as they establish no coherent doctrine of predicative classes, they remain largely a show of Lullian curiosities and wonders in the idiosyncratic revision of conventional theory. Thus one might ask if a logical programme based on universal predicables of this type can ever be a plan of formal logic at all. The answer is evidently no, but with the qualification that Lull does offer the basis for a programme of persuasive argument based on his fundamental theological and metaphysical values. The larger discursive applications of this programme, Llull's spiritual Logic, become clearer in his accounts of syllogistics and sophistics. In so far as those applications also moralize the five predicables according to principles of participation, resemblance, or proportion, Llull's treatment of the predicables in the *Logica nova* clearly indicates that the technical rules that he confects in his subsequent writings concerning his spiritual Logic will not be bound by Aristotelian rules of predication.

12

Categories

WHERE Llull's account of the five predicables in the Second Distinction of the *Logica nova* focuses on their real existence as universals, his review of the ten categories in the Third Distinction is devoted to demonstrating a substantial as well as accidental mode for each of the predicamental accidents. This emphasis apparently generalizes the view, encountered in his earlier works, of a being's substantial actuality and accidental activity as two modes of a common action. His curious doctrine supports his assumption of a participational connection between a subject and its accidents and also implies a basis for explaining apprehension of a being's essential natures. Individual examples examined below will illustrate both aspects.[1]

Llull's use of his *Regulae* as an inventional scheme of analysis for interpreting the categories serves chiefly to introduce a mass of metaphysical and physical considerations regarding each one. Some of his comments are also unusually idiosyncratic or obviously distort received doctrines in attempting to respond to the particular question posed by each *Regula*. All these responses contribute, however, to establishing the natural character of Llull's programme for Logic, and he concludes his analysis of each category with the claim that it offers doctrine for the 'natural philosopher and logician alike'. In many cases, he begins each analysis with a question that obviously refers to contemporary disputes regarding a particular characteristic of the category in question. While these allusions are thus more explicit than those found in his account of the predicables, they just as typically serve to introduce very tangential or moralized explanations of a category's features. Still, they do show Llull's effort to join in the Scholastic debates of his time, and to challenge the positions of his contemporaries in their own terms.

[1] Platzeck dismisses Llull's treatment of the categories in the *Logica nova* with a few words about their obvious interest (*Raimund Lull*, 1. 412), and rarely discusses them in depth in his other works, perhaps because Llull's handling of the categories almost always displays very obviously his moralization of material doctrine, rather than manipulation of formal structures that interests Platzeck most.

Substance

Llull's analysis of substance in the *Logica nova* begins with the question 'Whether a created substance stripped of all accidents can exist outside the soul?' (3. 1. B1.) He answers affirmatively, arguing that, just as a syllogism 'would remain potentially and habitually in its premisses, though stripped from the last proposition, so a substance stripped of its accidents would remain in its first substantial principles, namely its form and matter, in which substance the removed accidents would remain potentially'. Aquinas reaches the same conclusion through different arguments (*In 7 Metaph.* 1. 1257). Llull's response offers one of his frequent appeals to the truth or necessity of syllogistic structure as an analogy for true or necessary metaphysical relationships. This is an obliquely moralizing way of introducing logical elements into his decidedly non-logical account of the categories, and is thus parallel to similar arguments applying Logic to other arts in the Sixth Distinction of the *Logica nova*. Such a moralization ultimately reflects Llull's conception of the syllogism itself as an intelligible object, as explained below in Chapter 17. The next lines in the *Logica nova* give the standard definition of substance:

Substantia est ens quod per se existit. Substantia etiam est illud ens considera-tum, innominatum, insensibile, inymaginabile et cognitum extra genus accidentium. Quoniam sicut iste silogismus logice est habituatus et cognitus—'Omne animal est substantia, omnis homo est animal'—eo quod ultima propositio est considerata, non ore prolata, sic essentia sive esse substantie est illud ens consideratum quod de genere accidentis non predi-catur. Quod ens est insensibile et inymaginabile. Sicut enim visus non attingit substantiam, sed colorem et figuram, ita gustus amaritudinem et dulcedinem, et sic de aliis. Et ideo substantiam ymaginatio non attingit. (3. 1 C1; ff. 66^{rb–va}; p. 36)

Aristotle distinguishes between sensible and insensible substances (*Metaph.* 12. 1 1069a30–6), but Llull seems to regard all substances as insensible in so far as they are not perceived, but known wholly apart from accidents. Aquinas claims in this regard that substantial forms are unknowable *per se*, and that substances are often known only through their incidental features (1a. 85, 3 ad 4). Just as in the earlier *Libre de contemplació* (219), this unknowability of substance apparently offers primarily a moral lesson regarding the status of the Intellect: it is wholly spiritual and therefore knows substance spiritually without reference to its material accidents.

Several of Llull's other remarks on substance in this chapter expound his innate correlatives and reiterate his familiar axioms, such as 'substance has dominion over its accidents because it causes them and the actuality of them' and 'substance acts with its accidents just as an agent with its instruments'. Other passages reiterate conventional doctrine, such as the Tree of Porphyry's division of substance into corporeal or incorporeal and of accidents into separable and inseparable, as well as Aristotle's divisions of primary and secondary substances (*Cat.* 5 2a11–3a5). Where Aristotle states that separate substances must be immaterial (*Metaph.* 12. 6 1071b21), Llull follows his usual hylemorphic position and simply states that all substance includes matter and form.

Finally, Llull asserts that 'substance exists for the sake of individuals, without which there could be no number . . . in the individuals from which number is constituted, as one, two, three etc. men, lions, etc.' (3. 1. E2). He also avers that second substances, such as genera and species, exist in order that individuals exist, in the same way that body and soul exist for man, and two premisses for a conclusion. This analogy to a syllogism assumes a relation of cause and effect that functions through participation, especially since genera do not divide into individuals directly. The comparison to man involves Llull's view of the body and soul as distinct essences, and in this case as distinct substantial forms. The mixture here of logical, metaphysical, and physical relationships in a sort of imprecise analogy is one of the most typical features of Llull's moralizations in the *Logica nova*, where he often seeks to establish its logical import through comparative references to the relationship of premisses to conclusion in a syllogism.

Quantity

Llull begins his treatment of the second category, quantity, in the *Logica nova* by inquiring whether it can be defined (3. 2. B). Several passages already examined have raised this same question, which, as noted above, receives a negative response from many authorities, because all the categories are *genera generalissima*. Llull argues however that such a definition must be possible in order for quantity truly to be called 'divisible, namely discrete and continuous quantity, since without some real or mental universal, no division can be made'. This argument is, of course, irrelevant, because the division of the universal quantity that it invokes does not define quantity itself, but rather its species of discrete and continuous. Llull's reference to universals perhaps recalls Aristotle's dictum that definition necessarily concerns universals (*Metaph.* 7. 11 1036a28).

The rest of Llull's remarks all concern, in one manner or another, the nature of the relationship between a substance and its quantity, which was a problem that exercised most of his Scholastic contemporaries. Some of the difficulties in this relationship already appear in the work of Boethius (*In Cat.* 2; 202C) and gave rise to several controverted questions, as the discussions of Ockham (1. 43–8) or Aquinas (*In 5 Metaph.* 15. 978–86) indicate. Llull's treatment of this relationship appears in the claims that he makes about two elements of received Aristotelian teaching from the *Categories* (6 4b23–5a13) concerning continuous and discrete quantity: the former is 'a measure in the subject limiting it through existence and agency', while the latter 'imposes its proper number'. Llull's usual characterization of all forms as principles of both existence and activity leads him to call quantity a power or potentiality with which 'a substance quantifies quantified entities; and we give this definition because a power is known through actuality and actuality through its object' (3. 2. C1). This relationship of potentiality, actuality, and their object parallels closely that recognized by Aquinas (1a. 77, 3). Llull tends to associate these with the general principle that a substance acts through its accidents, and thus explains that quantity is in its subject 'through the mode of existence, because with this quantity the subject is habituated and bound (*terminatus*)' and 'through the mode of acting because it does how much (*quantum*) it does with quantity' (3. 2. I). Llull probably indicates by quantity only number, and his view of quantity as the power of imparting number remits to the difficult issue of the sources and principles of individuation, which he does not mention further.

With regard to the real distinction of a substance and its quantity, Ockham concludes that 'quantity of length, width, or depth is not something distinct from the substance and quality' (1. 44). For Llull they are distinct, but very closely related, according to his usual view of accidental forms as deriving from substantial ones. Thus he remarks that quantity 'has its existence in the essence of substance', is 'from the likenesses of substance accidentally', and 'exists through the mode of influence of its subject, and this through its mode of disposition, its habit and situation and natural power and impotence' (3. 2. K1). This last remark evidently reflects Aristotle's doctrine that all accidents are only quantitative by virtue of their inherence in a quantified subject (*Metaph.* 5. 13 1020a14–31), although Llull certainly conceives this connection participationally. Still, since Llull emphasizes the agency of quantity, an ambiguity remains regarding just how quantity achieves this activity. Quantity, as an accident, certainly exists in its subject, but it only acts in so far as the subject employs it. The syntax of Llull's remarks imply this, although he does not explicitly state it. It is tempting to regard this ambiguity as yet another instance of Llull's equivocal views regarding the respective functions of accidental and substantial forms and as proof of his participational conception of the inherence of the former in the latter. Llull's explanation here of how a subject acts through its accidents is itself unclear: he recognizes a cause of the accident's potential existence, and states that it exists through the mode of flowing from its subject, which draws it out of potentiality into actuality and activity. In part this simply expresses how substances stand in potentiality to receiving accidents and can be their efficient, material, and final cause, according to a process of 'emanation' or 'resultance', in Aquinas's words (1a. 77, 7 ad 2–3). However, Llull also observes that 'quantity exists with its cause, which puts it in potentiality, for the quantity is sustained in that potentiality that is drawn into actuality (*reducitur ad actum*), just as a sprout from a seed and the heated from the heatable, and moving from the mobile' (3. 2. K2). While Llull may only suggest the dependence of accidents on their substance, his examples of innate or natural dispositions, and terms such as 'influence', more obviously recall some function like that of the Augustinian seminal reasons.

Quality

Llull's account of quality in the *Logica nova* is notable chiefly for one or two unusual elements of terminology that illustrate well his capacity for idiosyncratic elaboration of conventional doctrine. He begins by asking whether quality more properly indicates a property than a disposition (which is, strictly speaking, a sub-type of quality). He answers affirmatively, because 'property denotes the existence and agency of beings, and disposition denotes the possibility and proportion of being' (3. 3. B). Properties are, as already noted above, predicated with respect to the quality (*in quale*) of a thing, as Ockham notes (1. 24), and he also argues that any predication of a property affirms a possibility, so that the proposition 'man laughs' should be understood to mean 'it is possible for man to laugh' (3–3. 20). This view of property as related to possibility apparently underlies Llull's question and answer regarding quality. His distinction between property and disposition parallels the one that Aristotle makes between essential permanent and relative temporary properties (*Top.* 5. 1 128b16). Thus Llull also distinguishes between proper and appropriated qualities: 'a natural and proper quality always exists, just as the motion of the heavens, which is inseparable from its subject; however an appropriated quality exists in temporal succession, just as the heat of water, which is sometimes in time, sometimes not, and a man is sometimes good, sometimes bad.' These remarks evidently derive from the basic doctrine outlined by Porphyry (p. 31) regarding property and inseparable accidents. Llull offers good and bad character as examples of an appropriated quality or disposition; Aristotle considers these characteristics and the other virtues as habits, because they are relatively stable, and cites such characteristics as hot or cold as dispositions or affective qualities, because they are easily changeable (*Cat.* 8 8b29–39, 9a30).

Llull lists sub-types of quality, following in part Aristotle's account, which explicitly recognizes four types: habits or dispositions, natural power or impotence, affective qualities or affections, and form or figure (*Cat.* 8 8b27, 9a16, 10a11). Llull only mentions the first two pairs, and calls them the four species of quality. He also offers a somewhat idiosyncratic definition of quality itself: 'Quality is a form indicative of the states (*statuum*) of beings, as when one asks "How (*qualis*) is Sortes?" and one should respond good or bad, healthy or sick, etc.' By 'indicative', Llull seemingly refers to the predication of accidental forms of a substance, but he characteristically does not distinguish the logical, metaphysical, or physical signification, as he so often calls it, of the substance–accident relationship. Llull also refers several times to the natural qualities of hot, cold, dry, and moist and their primary proper or secondary appropriated presence in each of the four elements, as defined in Aristotelian physics (*De gen. et corr.* 2. 3). Overall, his comments on quality display his typically eclectic and selective compilation of received lore, partly as a taxonomic exercise, and partly as a statement of the kind of knowledge of the natures of things that his natural Logic offers. This knowledge comprises Llull's basic metaphysical values, which the logical doctrine under consideration may not always reveal without some moralization of its doctrine.

Relation

Llull's remarks on the next predicamental accident, relation, constitute one of the more important passages from his treatment of the categories in the *Logica nova*, because they remit directly to contemporary polemics over the nature of relation, as well as to the fundamental role played by his correlatives and other relational distinctions in his *Art*. The requirements of his *Art* perhaps ultimately determine the orientation of most of his remarks, but the need to distinguish his position from those of his contemporaries also clearly influences some of his claims. Llull begins by asking whether any relation can be substantial, a question that he does not in effect distinguish from that of whether any relation is real. Aristotle hesitates in his *Categories* to deny completely that substances can be related *qua* substances (7 8a12–b24), although in the *Metaphysics* he excludes this possibility entirely, and states that relations possess the least being and least substance of any category (14. 1 1088a23–b5). Aquinas and Ockham express divergent interpretations of Aristotle's doctrines, and provide a context for Llull's own rather unorthodox views. Saint Thomas declares that although the relations among the Persons of the Trinity must be substantial, they can never be so in creatures, and notes that relation alone among the categories refers to conceptual as well as real beings (1a. 28, 1–2). The Venerable Inceptor argues, of course, that only terms are relative, not beings, and that relation is not anything really distinct from the subject of which it is predicated (1. 49). Llull's consideration of these issues is extremely important to the whole system of his *Art*, because it depends so heavily on the recognition and elaboration of relational connections between beings. Llull begins his own remarks with an answer that alludes to the theological, physical, and logical difficulties that the nature of relation poses:

Et dicimus quod sic, sicut in deo in quo relatio est substantialis in patre et filio et spiritu sancto, et in suo intellectu et sic de aliis suis rationibus, in quo intellectu se habent substantialiter intellectivus, intelligibilis, et intelligere. Et sic in rebus creatis, sicut in substantia ignis in quo se habent relative substantialiter forma et materia, et in intellectu intelligere, intelligibile et intelligere. (3. 4. B; f. 68va; p. 45)

The parallel that Llull asserts between the substantial relation among the Persons of the Trinity and the substantial interrelation of his correlatives in creatures expresses the fundamental and pervasive trinitarian exemplarism of his metaphysics. The claim of a real relation in the union of form and matter is rejected by the disciple of Ockham responsible for Chapter 51 from Part 1 of the Inceptor's *Summa logicae*. Llull suggests it several times more, as when he states that 'relation is in the subject indicating the existence of the subject and its agency, just as in fire, in which it indicates the essence through form and through matter, and indicates its operation through ignition and calefaction' (3. 4. D3). Here the function of indication is again the natural signification expounded in the *Liber de significatione*. The disciple of Ockham observes that this real relation must be either a basic principle like form and matter, or result from another union, which implies an infinite regress. Llull does in fact regard his correlatives as basic principles, and he calls relation a *principium primitivum*. Relation in turn is composed of its own primary coessential principles of activity and passivity, greatness and smallness, halfness, and equality, which are all examples of relations given by Aristotle in the *Categories* (7 6b8, 20, 7b16) and *Metaphysics* (5. 15 1020b29). As a genus, relation also possesses its own specific differences and properties, according to Llull.

Llull's correlatives serve above all to define an innate activist nature in any being, since they are essential to it. He explains the essential correlatives by analogy: 'just as a word exists with its syllables, and a proposition with its words, and a syllogism with its propositions, so relation exists with its subjective parts, namely father and son, heater, heatable, and heating' (3. 4. K2). This passage is remarkable not only for its moralizing assertion that the part to whole relation of syllable to word parallels that of father to son, but also for the successively inclusive levels of syllable, word, proposition, and syllogism that it posits, as though relations were also organized in similarly successive and inclusive schemes, which obviously mirror the Neoplatonic hierarchy of being that Llull conceives. Such a view is completely non-Aristotelian, since the *Categories* state flatly that neither the wholes nor the parts of primary substances are relative (7 8a16).

Because Llull regards his correlatives and other distinctions as essential and substantial, rather than accidental, aspects of beings, he explicitly recognizes a distinction between substantial and accidental relations in various passages. The latter are subordinate to the former as effect to cause: 'relation exists because its cause exists, as day exists because the sun exists, and so that substantial action and affection might be causes of accidental action and affection' (3. 4. E1). Llull's position ultimately implies the separate existence of accidents, which is one of the chief reasons why Aristotle rejects it (*De gen. et corr.* 1. 3–4). His comments on relation thus combine some acknowledgement of contemporary controversy regarding its nature with his own insistence on his fundamental metaphysical conceptions, with the result that the divergence between Llull's views and current concerns is especially

obvious. His comments on relation also show very well how his
moralizing comparisons and analogies reinterpret conventional distinctions for his own ends, with a notable decrease in the value of those
distinctions outside Llull's own metaphysical programme.

Action

Where Llull's remarks on relation offer a fairly clear view of
its importance for his own metaphysics and of its deviation from
contemporary doctrines, his treatment of action sets forth even more
precisely its fundamental role in his ontology, his fusion of logical and
metaphysical categories, and his position with respect to other late
thirteenth-century opinions. He begins by explicitly distinguishing
between the substantial and accidental activity of a being (3. 5. B).
Llull's primary activity is substantial form, which gives actuality, as
Aristotelian doctrine suggests (*Metaph*. 8. 2 1043a28). Since he
typically assumes the plurality of substantial forms, one should not
immediately imagine that Llull here allows only one. As in many other
passages already cited, he does not distinguish between the terms *actio*
and *actus* as differentiating activity from actuality. Hence he posits that
substantial and accidental forms are 'convertible' with their *actio*,
where Aquinas says *actus* (1a. 77, 6). Llull, like Saint Thomas (1a. 45,
8 ad 2), recognizes that accidental forms act in virtue of the substantial
form that precedes them, and subsequent remarks define accidental
activity as the 'form with which the agent acts in the subject', a notion
that recalls the dictum 'every agent acts in virtue of its form', often
cited by Aquinas (e.g. 1a, 3, 2; 47, 1 ad 1; 115, 1). The accidental is
therefore a likeness of the substantial activity. Llull also calls accidental
activity the instrument of a distinct substantial activity, where Aquinas
argues that the whole substance, and not any of its constituent parts,
acts (1a. 75, 2). Llull concludes his entire treatment of action by noting
that it offers sufficient instruction to the logician or natural scientist,
who may thus understand the nature of the related category of affection, which he does not discuss. Llull's remarks in this section on the
category of action reveal clearly the innate activism that he consistently
ascribes to all substances, and which is a corner-stone of his exemplarist metaphysics as a justification for the propagation of likenesses that
realize participation. The relationship of similitude that he posits
between substantial and accidental types of action is one especially
important instance of the active resemblance that his *Art* ultimately
assumes among all beings, and which his own system of Logic would

trace in its consequential conditions of signification and moralized analogies.

Habit

Llull's account of habit is one that exploits its diverse and sometimes obscure description in received authorities, which Aquinas labours to harmonize (1a. 2ae. 49–54). Llull gives habit a major role in his metaphysics by characterizing it broadly as power or potency, according to one of its functions as identified by Aristotle in his treatment of habits and dispositions (*Metaph.* 9. 1 1046a13). Llull begins his analysis by asking whether vegetativity is a corporeal habit in a rose. Aquinas treats the vegetative, sensitive, and rational powers of any being as three types of soul; these are not merely corporeal, but intrinsic spiritual principles of self-change (1a. 78, 1). Llull's reply eschews this analysis of the thing's own constitution in favour of analysis of its participation in different classes or levels from the hierarchy of being, each of which has its corresponding essence:

Et dicimus quod sic, quoniam rosa est substantia composita de forma et materia elementorum. Et est per vegetativam sibi coniunctam deductam in speciem vegetati. Et per hoc dicitur quod rosa est sic substantia vegetata, sicut leo est substantia sensata. Hoc autem fieri non posset si vegetativa non essent habitus corporeus in suo subiecto non occupans locum, eo quod non est habitus lineatus secundum suum genus, sicut natura que in suo naturato quo ad se lineata nec figurata est. (3. 6. B; f. 70ra; p. 51)

The conclusion of this passage is only a corollary to, not an explanation of, Llull's initial response. It justifies that first position by moralizing it with a putatatively indisputable analogy. It asserts simply that habit, like nature, exists undelineated and unshaped in itself and in its subject; this is because, as a form, it is not a body possessing dimensions. Llull's definition of vegetativity as a corporeal habit reflects his usual view of the body and soul as discrete essences. Aquinas regards the vegetative and sensitive souls as deriving from the rational soul in man, because the rational soul is the substantial form that founds man's entire being (1a. 76, 3). In a plant, which possesses only the vegetative form, this must be part of the plant's substantial form. Llull regards the plant as a substance already constituted from matter and an essence of substantiality, and the vegetative power as a habit added to this substance; it is probably a further substantial form, and not merely an accidental one. Once added, this vegetative power or habit draws the substance of the plant into the species of vegetable life. The vegetative habit thus plays the role of a specifying form: Llull defines a rose as 'vegetable substance' and a lion as 'sensate substance', using formulas that combine the *genus generalissimum* of substance with a specific difference indicating their highest type of soul. These definitions fulfill in a broad way the requirements postulated by Aristotle: they include a material potential element and a formal actual element involving a specific difference (*Metaph.* 8. 2 1043a2–20). It seems clear, though, that the vegetative habit is not a plant's only substantial form. Moreover, vegetable substance and sensate substance define the proximate genera for rose and lion (that is, plant and animal), but certainly not the rose or lion itself. They thus violate the basic rules of definition through genus and difference, as described by Aristotle (*Top.* 6. 5–6). The consideration of Llull's peculiar new method of definition in Chapter 14 of this study will show how he eventually posits the direct contraction of the essence proper in every species to being in general. Although Llull's definitions here seem especially impractical, he certainly regards the recognition of habitual natures as another contribution to the significative character of his natural Logic: 'habit exists by reason of an end, so that through the habit the substance might be manifested (*indicata*) and known' (3. 6. E2).

Where Aristotle observes that all dispositions and affections arise naturally from their subjects (*Top.* 6. 6 145a35), Llull posits his usual exemplarist relationship of similitude between the accident of habit (and its correlatives) and the substance (and its correlatives) in which the habit exists. Thus, habit 'has a likeness to the subject, as heat to the hot thing, chastity to the chaste person, or the hood to the monk' (3. 6. C4); similarly, he notes that habit 'is a likeness of its subject infused (*influxa*) *per accidens* from the subject, as the habit of heat is diffused in the heater, heatable, and heating sustained in the ignitive, ignitable, and igniting [of fire]' (3. 6. D2). The reference to a monk's hood displays the same confusion between habit and having already noted in Llull's earlier works, and derived from the post-predicamental category of having. He develops it analogically here when he observes that a habit has its correlatives and discrete quantities just as a piece of cloth can be divided into a tunic, cloak, or hood, and these are also the material cause of a habit in the sense of clothing, such as a tunic. Finally, Llull acknowledges, as in his earlier works, the conventional classification of knowledge and virtue as habits (*Cat.* 8 8b28), but offers some peculiar difficulties in describing how the disciplines of Logic and Grammar function as habits:

Habitus est quando suum subiectum est. Et est in tempore tribus modis: sicut habitus logicalis qui est in potentia in grammatica. Secundus est quando est theoricus, sicut homo grammaticus et logicus in quo habitus grammaticus est theoricus quando docet logicam. Tertius est quando est praticus, sicut logicus docens logicam. (3. 6. H; ff. 70^{rb–va})

The 1744 edition of the *Logica nova* gives a rather different version of this passage: 'for one habit is potential, as the habit of dialectic, which is potential in the grammarians; another however is actual, namely when the logician teaches dialectic, which habit is rightly called practical; another habit is theoretical, namely when that dialectician reads theory' (pp. 52–3). Both versions appeal to Aristotle's dichotomies of potential and actual existence (*Metaph.* 9. 1 1045b35), and speculative (or theoretical) and practical thought (*De an.* 3. 10 433a14). Llull identifies the actual with the practical as simply the active realization of knowledge. He distinguishes the potential from the theoretical habit of knowledge as unacquired (but capable of being acquired) from unused (but already acquired), where Aristotle simply calls both of these 'potential' (*Phys* 8. 4 255a30–b4). In the context of his discussion of habit, Llull's remarks display his usual uncritical application of one accidental category, time, to another, habit. His suggestion of theoretical, practical, and potential as types of time probably serves a merely taxonomic function, even while deriving from Aristotelian discussions of how actual is prior in time to potential knowledge (*Metaph.* 9. 3 1046b28–47a9; 9. 8 1049b29–50a38). However, Llull rarely considers related questions that Aristotle raises regarding potential or actual knowledge, such as the status of pre-existent knowledge (*An. post.* 1. 1).

Llull also attempts to make the arts and sciences, as habits, serve the spiritual mode of knowledge that is proper to man. He distinguishes external from internal habits, noting that the former are subordinated to the latter 'just as the habit of Logic is subordinated to the natural habit of the Intellect'. This apparently means that Logic concerns cognitive objects, and he extends this suggestion to all the arts and sciences when he distinguishes the natural and proper habit of the Intellect from the appropriated habits of imagining and sensing that the Intellect takes on 'when it understands imaginable and sensible things and makes them intelligible in its proper coessential and substantial habit, just as fire multiplies appropriated habits in its ignible habit, and these are *per accidens* from the genus heat because they are from a hot subject, and likewise for the mechanical and liberal arts' (3.

B. G2). Llull's distinction between extrinsic and intrinsic and proper and appropriated habits of the Intellect serves to valorize the processes of cognition and intellection according to their corporeal or spiritual objects. Aristotle suggests (*Eth.* 6. 3 1139b16), as does Aquinas after him (1a. 2ae. 50, 4), that the arts, science, prudence, wisdom, and intellection are natural habits of the soul. Aquinas also argues that internal Senses such as the Imagination have habits because the Intellect directs them to different activities, but the external Senses do not need habits because they are determined to only one activity each (1a. 2ae. 50, 3 ad 3). Llull assumes that the Senses and Imagination have habits and objects proper to them that the Intellect appropriates in cognition, while possessing as well its own proper habits and objects. Thus he maintains distinct and unequal, yet parallel, habitual stages in the knowledge of material beings by the spiritual soul. His analogy to fire, which appropriates accidental habits of heat into its substantial habit of igneity, indicates how he seeks to correlate any accident with a similar substantial nature. This correlated appropriation thus exceeds the merely instrumental use that a substance makes of its accidents, and implies a more direct relationship to the substance's essence. The substance man makes use of the liberal and mechanical arts, which figure among the accidental habits of his soul, in order to complete the operations of his substantial nature, which apparently possesses other, higher modes of knowledge as its own substantial habits. This dichotomy between sensory and intellectual knowledge becomes a basic tenet in Llull's later accounts of faith and understanding, and he especially relies on the habitual character of faith in defining its role.

In general, Llull's diverse elaborations of the functions of habit reflect its importance for him as a metaphysical explanation of the potential or innate or natural tendencies that he must posit in beings in order to explain their various active features. Llull never appeals explicitly to the Augustinian doctrine of seminal reasons, yet his comments on habit suggest a similar conception of the natural dispositions latent in beings and emanating from their essences.

Position

As in his earlier works, Llull's account of position in the *Logica nova* relies chiefly on the *Liber sex principiorum* (60–8), whose doctrines he does not, however, develop very extensively. Most of what he says simply illustrates, in a somewhat analogical and moralizing manner, how the accident of position functions in various substances. He does mention in passing certain commonplace aspects of the relationship of position as an accident to its subject: position indicates the situation of its subject, without which it could not exist; position is an instrument for its subject and enables the subject to act; the mode of position 'follows the mode of the subject' (3. 7. K1). Many of Llull's other allusions or references to position are difficult to reconcile with its role as an accident of substance, and reflect his rather loose and simplistic interpretation of this category, in the absence of any extensive received doctrines concerning it. Among the most notable examples is the following:

Situs habet in se per accidens situationem, situabile, et situare in quantum de se induit ista tria, in quibus essentia eorum est assituata. Et ipsa in ipsis, sicut substantia in suis coessentialibus concretis. Adhuc situs est in subiecto, assituante ipsum de se ipso, sicut color in colorato in quo assituatus est. (3. 7. C2–3; f. 70vb; p. 54)

This passage explains that position only possesses its essential correlatives *per accidens*, from its subject, as Llull also notes with reference to the category of action and its correlatives. Thus Llull states that position is properly situated in the manner of *Bonitas* or nature in their correlatives, or appropriatedly in the manner of man in his position, heat in water, knowledge in the Intellect, or time in motion. His distinction here between proper and appropriated position corresponds fairly evidently to that between substantial and accidental forms: the appropriated positions listed are all accidents of the substances named, while Llull's correlatives pertain to the essence of a substance. On the other hand, Llull makes the relationship between a substance and its essential correlatives parallel to that between the accident of position and its essential correlatives. As explained already, Llull does not differentiate between the kind of essence that accidents have and that in substances, despite Aristotle's insistence on this distinction (*Metaph.* 7. 4 1030a18–b12). Similarly, Llull asserts here that position exists in its subject just as colour is positioned in a coloured subject; he thus ascribes one predicamental accident (position) to another (the quality of colour), but without explicitly observing the kind of *per accidens* or derivative relation that this assertion involves, according to Aristotle (*Cat.* 6 5a37–b10). Llull's treatment of position is another that shows the incompatibility of his basic metaphysical values with the received doctrine that he seeks to reinterpret as an expression of them.

Time

Llull's remarks in the *Logica nova* on the category of time again parallel his earlier treatments in ignoring the *Liber sex principiorum* in favour of Aristotle's account in his *Physics* (4. 10–14). Llull defines time as 'the being with which movement participates more than with any other accident' (3. 8. C1). Llull clearly regards time as an accident of substance, as when he states that 'time exists in that mode in which it has its being in a subject, and through which the subject is temporalized by time' (3. 8. K1). None the less, his use of the term 'to participate' in defining the relationship between accident and substance again signals the idiosyncracy of the views that he proceeds to set forth in several subsequent passages. He observes that time exists in a subject 'as the disposition or medium by which it is mobile, since a subject cannot be mobile without time' (3. 8. C3). This treats time as a pre-condition, rather than a concomitant, of motion, although Aristotle very clearly asserts the latter role (*Phys*. 4. 12 220b15–31). In another passage he explains the correlation of time and movement in their subject through an analogy: time moves with its subject as a sailor sleeping or sitting in a ship. This analogy is perhaps slightly inexact, but does recall one used by Aristotle (*Phys*. 6. 10 240b11–20) and is closer to conventional doctrine than Llull's suggestion that time is a disposition of a subject for movement. Llull's explanation of time as a disposition of the subject seems a strange way of indicating the relation of time to motion, but perhaps recalls some characterization of time such as the 'certain habitual number of motion' offered by Albert the Great (*4 Phys*. 3. 16).

Most of the rest of Llull's remarks directly or indirectly recall Aristotelian tenets regarding the physics of time and movement, but he also adds comments on the astronomical basis of time, not found in his earlier works, and evidently taken from some traditional compilations. For example, Llull observes that the motion and time of the eighth sphere of the heavens is 'instantaneous and continuous'. The notion of instantaneous time appears in Boethius's definition of eternity as an instantaneous whole (*tota simul*) in his *De consolatione philosophiae* (5. 6) and this definition figures prominently in Aquinas's account of eternity (1a. 10, 1). The eighth sphere is the highest of those found in the sidereal heaven and contains the fixed stars, according to the scheme often repeated from the *Glossa ordinaria super Genesim* (1, 1). Virtually all of Llull's astronomical lore derives from basic notions such as this, probably through encyclopaedists. Thus where Llull claims that the motion of the stars is 'instantaneous and continuous', Isidore calls it 'perpetual' (3. 62) and Bartholomaeus Anglicus 'eternal and continuous' (8. 33), following Aristotle's terms (*De caelo* 2. 4 287a23–7). Llull presumably uses the term 'instantaneous' here to indicate eternity, although Aquinas notes that, properly speaking, eternity belongs to God alone, and any other eternal beings merely share in his (1a. 10, 4). Finally, Llull observes that 'the sun by its presence propagates days and by its absence night'. This is a common definition of the sun's functions, as in Isidore (3. 51. 1), and again suggests that both the content and scope of Llull's account of time depends on some encyclopaedic treatment of the topic, which he perhaps consulted in order to improve his previous accounts. This new material may represent part of his effort to increase the natural basis of his new programme for Logic.

Place

Place is the last predicamental accident that Llull treats in his survey of the categories in the Third Distinction of the *Logica nova*. Just as he does with the category time, he continues to base his exposition on Aristotle's account in the *Physics* (4. 1–5), where the Philosopher defines it as 'the boundary of the containing body at which it is in contact with the contained body' and 'the innermost motionless boundary of what contains' (4. 4 212a7, 20). This received definition of place is now much more obviously the authority for several of Llull's statements. He argues that place must be a common entity between the container and contained, because it is the 'general principle for the sake of which all entities are collocable' and as a general principle it is necessarily a common entity (3. 9. B). Thus because of place, one body can be placed in another or a part in a body, and the specific places of container and contained participate in the same genus. None the less, these claims still offer patent examples of Llull's characteristic explanations of all logico-metaphysical and physical principles according to participation. Aristotle views the relationship between the container, the contained, and their location as expressly material, and as an effect of their physical existence. Llull considers that this, like any relationship between two separate things, necessarily requires a metaphysical explanation according to the participation of the many in the one. Thus Llull refers to special places for the container and for the contained, as well as to the common universal place in which they participate as their genus.

Llull departs even more drastically from received Aristotelian doctrine regarding place in various passages that attempt to describe it solely as the inherence of an accident in a subject. He asserts that place has its correlatives from the essence of the subject 'in which place is sustained, and the ·subject is collocated in place' (3. 9. C2). Place is subordinated to its subject, 'which with place collocates itself and its parts just as it vests itself with habit' (3. 9. D3). Place exists with all the other accidents in the subject without which they could not exist. The most immediately obvious feature of Llull's remarks is the lack of any reference to place as a relationship between container and contained. Less obvious, but more important, is his focus on the relation of the accident of place to the located or contained subject. Aristotle explicitly recognizes that place can be said to be 'in' a subject as one of its accidents (*Phys.* 4. 3 210b23), but this is a derivative and non-locative sense of 'being in'. He defines place as a function of the container or locater rather than of the contained or located thing (4. 4 210b35, 212a2–29); hence Aquinas notes in his commentary that place exists 'as an accident is in a subject, in so far as place is the terminus of what contains' (*In 4 Phys.* 4. 443). With regard to the thing contained or located in place, Aristotle observes that 'place is coincident with the thing, for boundaries are coincident with the bounded' (*Phys.* 4. 4 212a30) and that place is somewhere, 'as the limit is in the limited' (4. 5 212b28). For Llull, these derivative definitions of place that Aristotle treats as secondary are just as important as those that the Philosopher regards as primary and based on the relationship of container to contained. Stated most simply, Llull does not rigorously distinguish the various modes according to which one thing is in another or in place. Llull's claim that a subject collocates itself with place, just as it clothes itself with habit, recalls his typical emphasis on the role of accidents as subordinate instruments of their subject's activity.

Llull extends this explanation of place as an inhering accident through his references to motion, which necessarily involves place because, according to Aristotle, local motion is the primary kind of motion (*Phys.* 4. 3 211a11). Llull asserts that place has its power (*virtutem*) and actuality in a subject, which through place is 'collocable and mutable from one place into another' (3. 9. C4). This claim is almost the inverse of Aristotle's observation that place is unthinkable without motion. Avicenna mentions and rejects the notion that place is somehow the form of motion or the mobile, and explains that place may be prior to motion in nature, but not in causality (*Suff.* 2. 5, 9).

Llull also avers that 'place is mobile when its subject is mobile from one place into another, as a man from a chamber into a hall . . . and the place in which man is man is one place in one time when he is in the chamber and in another when in the hall' (3. 9. H). This account heavily qualifies Aristotle's conclusions that place in itself is immobile (*Phys.* 4. 4 212a18), that every body has a place, and every place a body (4. 2 209a26). What happens, as Aquinas explains, is that different bodies succeed each other in a place, which gives them 'the same order and site in comparison to the whole world' (*In 4 Phys.* 6. 463). There is nothing to prevent a body in one place from serving as the container and thereby giving place to some other body. A body changes place, then, in the sense that it comes to be located in another place, not in the sense that it carries around one and the same place, which thus undergoes change (ibid. 5. 446). Place is, of course, an accident and cannot in itself be the subject of further accidents. Thus, when Llull explains that, because a subject moves or changes from one place into another, 'place is mobile', this phrase must be understood to mean that 'the specific place occupied by the individual subject is capable of changing'. Llull's remarks include or allow this sense, but it is not obviously primary, given his focus on place as a function of the inherence of an accident in a substance. Llull's account of place is certainly the most idiosyncratic in his review of the categories and it is difficult to know how much his unusual interpretations result from the too literal application of his *Regulae*, the zealous insistence on finding his own predilect metaphysical values in Aristotelian doctrine, the sheer misunderstanding of received doctrine, or all of these factors together.

Llull insists that his exposition of the categories in the Third Distinction of the *Logica nova* offers valuable knowledge to the natural scientist and logician alike, and this claim is broadly consistent with his effort to establish common principles of being and knowledge. Yet it seems clear that Llull does not maintain this dual focus, but rather substitutes a natural for logical conception of the categories, and thus renders his logical programme as fundamentally material in character as possible. This substitution is certainly facilitated by the metaphysical and even physical nature of the doctrines in Aristotle's own *Categories*, and to modern eyes Llull's account may look no less logical than the Philosopher's. None the less, Llull does introduce an important and clearly non-Aristotelian element into his account. This is the participation between a substance and its accidents, which he invokes through occasional references to the influence or likeness of the former in the latter. This participation explains very simply the production of a being's accidental features from its essence, which Aquinas regards as a causal relationship (1a. 3, 6; 9, 2). It also provides an implicit basis for the cognitive processes necessary to Llull's natural Logic. Llull suggests in his remarks on substance quoted above that the Senses apprehend only the accidents of a thing, but also notes when treating quality, relation, and habit that accidents give knowledge of, or 'indicate', as he says, their substance; both positions have Aristotelian authority (*De an.* 1. 1 402a22; 2. 12 424a22). Aquinas recognizes accidents as an incidental way of knowing a substance, whose nature the mind can abstract (1a. 85, 1 and 3 ad 4). Llull does not have a theory of abstraction nor does he rigorously distinguish between a being's substantial form and its essence, as Saint Thomas does (1a. 29, 2 ad 3). For Llull a being comprises multiple substantial as well as accidental essences, which participation orders as proper to that being. This order through participation validates apprehension of any one of those essences as insight into the being's true nature, which, as a sort of master essence corresponding to the being's species, controls the collection of other essential forms as derivations from itself. This is in fact the basis for Llull's new method of definition. As applied to Logic in general, Llull's notion of the participation between substantial and accidental essences in a being renders non-problematic the inherence of accidents or properties in a subject, and therefore most questions of predication as well. The following chapter will show how this affects his treatment of propositional logic, which becomes in his hands not the formal association of predicative classes or much less the realization of suppositional modes for terms, but the identification of participational relations among beings.

13

Llull's Programme for Logical Discourse

THE interpretation of predicative relations and their expression in propositional form are among the fundamental aspects of formal logical doctrine that especially concern Llull in his later writings. In the *Logica nova*, he treats them together with syllogistics, sophistics, and demonstration in that work's Fifth Distinction, which thus offers in itself a comprehensive plan for logical discourse. Because each of the areas covered in the Fifth Distinction merits special attention in itself, subsequent chapters will deal with them individually. This chapter will merely present an overview of the Fifth Distinction, discussing its scope, arrangement, and method as a prelude to those further analyses. The Fifth Distinction of the *Logica nova* deserves this attention in part because it is, among all Llull's writings from his entire career, the one text that comes closest to offering a complete programme for logical discourse as Llull would conceive it.

Even though the fields of propositions, syllogistics, sophistics, and demonstration are those where Llull displays his greatest technical innovations, many sections of the Fifth Distinction are notable as the least original portions of that treatise, and thus belie his continued reliance on received doctrine as a model for his own programme. Many passages have evident parallels in the *Summule* of Peter of Spain, and others apparently still rely directly on Algazel as well. Table 3 summarizes the doctrines expounded and gives the corresponding passages from Peter or Algazel, or ultimate Aristotelian basis for each section of Llull's Fifth Distinction.

The phrases or labels quoted in the table suggest few truly functional changes in the principles and tenets of received doctrine; Llull's exposition does frequently misrepresent or misinterpret them, usually because he simplifies and summarizes so severely. Some lines, such as his definition of a proposition as composed of true words, introduce his peculiar interest. For the most part, however, the Fifth Distinction attempts to present comprehensively the Scholastic *logica nova*; the topics appear explicitly for the first time in Llull's work, even if only in

TABLE 3. *Contents of the Fifth Distinction of the* Logica nova

The first column gives the chapter titles from manuscript P, along with their number in the 1744 edition (which rearranges some of them); next comes a summary of the technical terms or distinctions described by the chapter. Finally, in parentheses appear the page numbers from the 1744 edition and folio numbers of manuscript P for that chapter. The second column gives the parallels, using these abbreviations: *SL*, Peter of Spain's *Summule logicales; LA*, Algazel's *Logic;* Aristotelian references use standard forms.

Chapter titles and numbers, doctrine, and page and folio numbers	Parallel texts
De quinta distinccione: 'Argumentum ex tribus veris et necessariis propositionibus constitutur'; 'semper verus est'; partes extra in potentia, partes intra in actu (p. 77; f. 76rb).	*SL* 5. 1–3; *LA* Proem. 65–73 and 4. 7–25, 495–505
De propositione (1): 'Est materia syllogismi de pluribus veris diccionibus constituta'; omnino necessaria, partim necessaria et partim non, nullo modo necessaria; in potentia, in actu; brevis et clara, longa et obscura; convertibilis et non convertibilis; coniunctiva, disiunctiva; universalis affirmativa, particularis affirmativa, universalis negativa, particularis negativa; conversio per accidens, mutare subiectum in predicatum et predicatum in subiectum; per oppositionem modi propositionum: (1) 'magis est totum quam sua pars', (2) per sensibilitatem, (3) 'quando subiectum continet in se ea per que cognitum est', (4) per experientiam, (5) per communem conceptionem, (6) per opinionem, (7) de publico, (8) de suppositione, (9) de consensu, (10) de similitudine, (11) publica fama, (12) de existimatione, (13) de infecta ymaginatione; maior (antecedens), minor (consequens); per se nota, dubitativa; modi propositionum in quibus videtur esse contradictio: (1) per equivocationem, (2) quando mutatur subiectum in predicatum, (3) per universale et particulare, (4) per potentiam et actum, (5) de relatione, (6) de loco, (7) de statu, (8) de tempore; conversio: universalis negativa, affirmativa particularis, affirmativa universalis, particularis negativa (pp. 77–81; ff. 76rb–77rb).	*LA* 4. 495–505 *SL* 1. 19–25; *LA* 3. 125–47 *SL* 7. 12 *SL* 1. 15–18 *SL* 1. 16 *LA* 3. 69–123; *SL* 1. 12 *SL* 1. 15; *LA* 3. 188–210 *LA* 4. 531–675 *SL* 4. 2; *LA* 4. 45–60 and 3. 39–46 *LA* 5. 141; *SL* 5. 4 *LA* 3. 149–86 *SL* 1. 15
De diffinitione (2): Per quatuor causas; per actum proprium et necessarium potentie sive subiecti sibi coessentialis (pp. 81–2; ff. 77^{rb-va}).	cf. *An. post.* 2. 10–11

Chapter titles and numbers, doctrine, and page and folio numbers	Parallel texts
De demonstratione (3):	
Propter quid et quia, per equiparantiam (pp. 82–3; f. 77^{va-b}).	*LA* 5. 37–65; cf. *An. post.* 1. 1 71a11–17
De locis (5):	
De maiori ad minorem.	*SL* 5. 32–3
De loco minori ad maiorem (6):	
De loco equali ad equalem (7): (pp. 84–5; ff. 77vb–78rb).	
Quomodo fit sillogismus (10):	
'Coniungendo suas coessentiales dicciones ut ex ipsis sint propositiones et ut ex propositionibus sit sillogismus' ponendo suas proprias dicciones in genere, specie, individuo, differentia et proprietate; per universalem affirmativam et negativam, de particulari affirmativa et negativa; per quatuor modos: integre (sillogismus integrus), particulariter (entimema), per inductionem, per exemplum (pp. 87–8; ff. 78^{rb-va}).	cf. *LA* 4. 14–51, *An. post.* 2. 13–14 and *SL* 4. 1–2 *LA* 2. 90–139; *SL* 5. 1 *LA* 4. 64–70; *SL* 5. 2 *SL* 5. 3
De comparatione sillogismi (11):	
Tres gradus: (1) verus, de aliqua propositione necessaria et de aliqua non necessaria, (2) verior, de una diccione sensuali et de alia spirituali, ex propositionibus necessariis simpliciter, (3) verissimus, de propositionibus spiritualibus simpliciter gratia essentie spiritualis; alius gradus: altioris expressus gratia essentie divine, de infinitis propositionibus (pp. 88–9; f. 78^{va-b}).	
De impossibili (8):	
Per contradictionem, per defectionem cause ad effectum, per perfectionem potentie.	*Metaph.* 5. 12 and 9. 3–4
De possibili (9):	
Per causam et occasionem, per actum infinite potestatis (pp. 85–6; ff. 78vb–79ra).	.
De conditione [syllogismi] (12):	
Novem conditiones (pp. 89–90; f. 79ra).	*SL* 4. 1–4
De probatione (4):	
Quando probatio convertitur cum sillogismo; quando una propositio est necessaria et alia non necessaria; per contingentiam; quando probatio fit per autoritates, aut in iure per testes est possibile (pp. 83–4; f. 79^{ra-b}).	cf. *SL* 5. 2 and 7. 5 *SL* 1. 19–25; *LA* 3. 125–47

Chapter titles and numbers, doctrine, and page and folio numbers	Parallel texts
De sillogismo in questione posito [deducto per regulas] (13): (pp. 90–2; ff. 79rb–80ra).	
De tribus figuris sillogismi et primo de prima (14):	
	LA 4. 53–110; cf. *SL* 4
De secunda figura (15):	
De tertia figura (16): (pp. 92–4 f. 80^{ra-b}).	
De paralogismis (17): conditiones: (1) nulla dictio impertinens nec desideretur necessario pertinens, (2) nullum medium inaequale, (3) nullus terminus superfluus additus, (4) aequivocatio, (5) amphibologia, (6) propositio absoluta, (7) deliberationis absentia, (8) conclusio secundum terminos improprios, (9) a sensu secretiori propositionis, (10) a propositione publica (pp. 94–6; ff. 80^{rb-vb}).	*LA* 4. 742–807
De fallaciis (18–32): Tredecim fallaciae Aristotelis (pp. 96–111; ff. 80vb–84vb).	*SL* 7. 22–178
De fallacia contradictionis (33): 'Videtur contradictionem concludit, cum non concludat' (pp. 111–13; ff. 84rb–84vb).	*LA* 3. 149–86

one type. It is interesting that Llull includes, just as he did in his compendium of Algazel, both the Arab's summary of the fallacies (under the heading 'On paralogisms') and an account of the thirteen Aristotelian fallacies as defined by Peter of Spain. This testifies to Llull's continued dependence on the basic authorities of his early studies, and gives some idea of the unchanging content of his most basic knowledge. Despite the comprehensive scope of the survey of Scholastic doctrine in the Fifth Distinction, Llull's account lacks any clear rationale for its structure; he occasionally treats the same area, such as the varieties of propositions, in several ways; many of the specific doctrines or precepts that it includes appear largely for the sake of taxonomic completeness alone, since he never employs them in his own practice. For these reasons, not even the most careful analysis of the Fifth Distinction would reveal fully the quantity or quality of the revisions that Llull makes in received doctrine in subsequent writings. The less ambitious scope of the changes suggested in the Fifth Distinction probably reflects both Llull's continued desire to engage conventional Scholastic doctrine in its own terms, and this doctrine's resistance to Llull's efforts at revision, which never cover the entire field of Scholastic logical doctrine, but only reformulate several particular aspects. In sum, the Fifth Distinction confirms the function of the *Logica nova* as a prospectus for Llull's logical reforms, a sort of road-map of the routes to be followed, without any definite itinerary clearly marked. In retrospect, it is easy to see how such critical areas as affirmation and negation or the fallacy of contradiction are already marked in the *Logica nova* for future exploration; others, such as the use of contrary suppositions, do not even appear.

Llull's real achievements in his reform of propositions, syllogistics, sophistics, and demonstration generally appear in subsequent special treatises devoted to them. The following chapters will consider each of these areas in turn, taking the relevant remarks (if any) from the Fifth Distinction of the *Logica nova* as a point of departure, and examining in detail the special treatises concerning it. Taken together with the analysis of Llull's exposition of the predicables and categories from the Second and Third Distinction, this survey of the formal logical structures treated in the Fifth Distinction provides the most comprehensive account possible of Llull's logical programme, as he left it at the end of his career.

Before moving on to these areas, it is appropriate to recall that they concern only the recognizable and deliberate changes that Llull offers in specific areas of Scholastic logical doctrine, such as definition or fallacy. Llull's writings also include, however, a multitude of other references to elements of Logic that do not contribute directly to those changes, but instead serve a broadly instrumental function as recourses of invention in his own argumentational discourse; they are logical *exempla* or *auctoritates*, in a rhetorical sense. His analogies to the syllogism noted in several passages of the Third Distinction are typical of this function. These analogical references to elements of logical doctrine can be extremely important to understanding Llull's own conception and methods of reforming Logic because they often comprise the moralizing kernels that he nurtures into full-grown schemes for rectifying logical practice. It would be impossible here to consider all the possible examples from his later writings, but one satisfactorily illustrative instance of such an uncultivated kernel is the distinction between antecedent and consequent in hypothetical propositions.

Antecedent and consequent as a logical auctoritas

In Chapter 1 of the Fifth Distinction of the *Logica nova*, Llull describes hypothetical propositions, without commenting or even identifying them as such: 'Proposition has two species, namely conjunctive and disjunctive. Conjunctive such as "Peter and William eat". Disjunctive has two species: the first, such as saying, "Peter is good or bad"; the second is conditional, such as saying, "If you give me money I will give you bread".' (5. 1.) The definition of conditionals as a sub-type of disjunctive propositions obviously does not follow the standard account found in Peter of Spain (1. 16), and apparently is a very garbled condensation of Algazel's prescriptions (3. 21–67). None the less, in the *Liber de praedicatione* of 1304, Llull specifically names hypothetical and categorical propositions among the methods of dividing a sermon's theme (Scriptural citation) for exposition; this is a common technique, recommended by authorities such as Robert of Basevorn in his *Forma praedicandi* (31, 33–4). Llull's explanation shows, however, little dependence on the strictly logical conception of hypothetical or categorical propositions:

Primus modus, qui est per propositionem hypotheticam, est colligere plures propositiones, et de illis facere unum sermonem; sicut diceremus sic: In principio erat Verbum; et Verbum erat apud Deum; et Deus erat Verbum . . .

Secundus modus est dividere propositionem categoricam, sicut dividere istam: In principium erat Verbum, in quattuor partes . . .

Tertius modus est per divisionem, sicut dividere per prius et posterius partes propositionis categoricae . . . (2. A. 1–3; p. 399)

The first verse of the Gospel of John illustrates what Peter of Spain calls a copulative hypothetical proposition (1. 16); the distinction of prior and posterior is a basic Aristotelian one (*Metaph.* 5. 11 1018b8–19a14) that Llull frequently invokes, sometimes as a functional metaphysical distinction and sometimes as a sheerly inventional device, in the manner suggested here. Likewise, in his *Ars brevis, quae est de inventione iuris* of 1308, Llull names the antecedents and consequents of hypothetical propositions as one of five modes of expounding a legal text:

Antecedens et consequens venabimur videlicet per prius et per posterius et per aequale. Et primo per prius et posterius et hoc sic: [si] creatura est, Deus est;

et non convertuntur, eo quia Deus est per prius, creatura autem per posterius
... per aequalitatem ostendo sic: nam si pater est, et filius est, et e converso ...
Et ideo iurista, quando facit consequentias, debet respicere, si sint de genere
aequalitatis et si ipsa aequalitas est necessaria in causis, debet ipsa uti, alias
quidem iniuriosus est. (6. 1. d; p. 198)

This analysis of equality according to prior and posterior illustrates
very well Llull's direct reference of propositional terms to levels in the
hierarchy of being, which his theory of the natural medium explicitly
develops. It is instructive to note how much Llull's hierarchical analysis differs from the more strictly verbal analysis of the equipollence of
hypotheticals in Peter of Spain (1. 18). It is even more instructive to
compare Llull's analysis to Ockham's claim that this consequence
from prior to posterior—'no substance exists, therefore no accident
exists'—is not absolute because God could create an accident alone
(3–3. 5). It is precisely the unrestricted necessity of such relationships,
which Llull so often invokes as necessary reasons, that his contemporaries no longer accepted as such. They seek to incorporate this
limited necessity into their terminist analyses of propositions *de consequentibus*,[1] which developed doctrines from Aristotle's *Topics* and
Boethius's *De syllogismo hypothetico* into some of the most advanced
formal theories of Scholastic Logic.[2] Scholastic interest in consequences may have fostered Llull's own awareness of them, but his
understanding of them is wholly non-technical, as his varying references to them suggest, and wholly concerned with their material value
or *rectitudo*. Most of his references to them are, in fact, merely nominal
acknowledgements of their existence as elements of logical method. In
a passage such as that from the *Ars brevis de iure*, his moralizing
interpretation takes the first step towards the kind of wholesale explanation of its value and function that would have produced a Lullian
novus modus consequentiae. These mentions of hypothetical propositions
illustrate thus the kernel of moralization that typically sustains each of
Llull's more developed revisions of doctrine regarding propositions,
syllogism, fallacy, or demonstration. This original moralizing conception of any element of logical doctrine must be acknowledged as a
necessary component in all of the Lullian arguments now to be
considered.

[1] See Gordon Leff, *The Dissolution of the Medieval Outlook*, pp. 79–80.
[2] This brief survey of Llull's remarks on consequence should show that he is not an
exponent of these theories, as Julius Weinberg implies when he quotes one of Llull's
definitions second-hand in *A Short History of Medieval Philosophy* (Princeton: Princeton
University Press, 1964), p. 180.

14

Definition

DEFINITION is one of the few conventional aspects of predication that Llull explicitly reformulates in his own terms in the Fifth Distinction of the *Logica nova*.[1] As summarized in the *Liber de diffinitione* of the fourth-century writer Marius Victorinus (attributed to Boethius), definition was a component of the early medieval *logica vetus*. It figures as well in the Scholastic *logica nova* thanks to Aristotle's treatment of it in the *Posterior Analytics* (2. 3–10) and *Topics* (Bks. 6–7). Various passages from Llull's earlier works and from elsewhere in the *Logica nova* have revealed Llull's dissatisfaction with the received teaching regarding definition and his proposal to offer an alternative form of definition. His short comments on definition in the Fifth Distinction of the *Logica nova* assume the basic Aristotelian function of definition as statement of a thing's essence or nature, consisting of a genus and difference (*Top.* 1. 4 101b21 and 1.8 103b16); Aristotle also describes another type of definition as the formula showing the cause of a thing's existence (*An. post.* 2. 10). Llull mentions the latter first, giving examples of material, formal, final, and efficient causes, just as he does in the *Lògica del Gatzel* (lines 140–53), which adapts Algazel (2. 141–84). Then he turns to essential definition, explaining it thus:

> Diffinitio est etiam per actum proprium et necessarium potentie sive subiecti sibi coessentialis, sicut quererer 'Intellectus divinus, quid est?' Et respondendum est quod intellectus divinus est ens habens intelligere. Et sic de caliditate que est ens habens calefacere. Et homo est ens habens ridere. Et essentia est ens habens esse et sic de consimilibus. (5. 2; f. 77va; p. 82)

Llull ignores definition through genus and difference in favour of predications that better express his metaphysics of coessentiality, especially the activity that every being more properly possesses than mere existence alone, as Llull often declares. Thus his definitions serve his doctrine of innate correlatives and reflect his usual indistinction between substantial and accidental forms. This passage also

---

[1] Pascual offers various important insights into Llull's conception of definition, 'De las definiciones', pp. 52–5.

displays his related indistinction between property, inseparable accidents, and difference in his definition of man as 'the being who has
laughing', since according to Porphyry (p. 20) laughing is a property
and therefore not part of a being's essence. Similarly, Llull declares in
Chapter 5 of the First Distinction of the *Logica nova* that such definitions as 'homo est animal homificans', 'leo [est animal] leonans',
'planta [est ens] plantificans', and 'homo [est] faber fabricans' are
'more proper since they are of a greater property immediately of the
subject' (1. 5).

In Chapter 5 of the First Distinction of the *Logica nova*, Llull also
directly criticizes the standard definition of man as a 'rational, mortal
animal', but his argument involves an obvious logical difficulty:

Homo est animal homificans. Hec definitio est magis specifica et magis
convertitur cum definitione, quam ista: homo est animal rationale, et mortale;
quia Angelus etiam est de genere et natura rationalitatis, et Leo de genere
mortalitatis. (1. 5; f. 60ᵛᵃ; p. 10)

Llull's reference to being more specific (i.e. more essential) and
convertible alludes to the function that Peter of Spain (2. 14), following Aristotle (*Top.* 1. 5 101b38–102a19), assigns to definition: 'definition is convertibly predicated of a thing and indicates its essence'.
However, Llull's criticism of the terms 'rational' and 'mortal' taken
separately as inconvertible with 'man' is in this instance a fallacy from
composition and division, even though such critiques form part of
Aristotle's teaching on correct definition (*Top.* 6. 13). His criticism is
especially interesting, none the less, because it illustrates the difficulties that Porphyry creates when trying to explain subordinate and
coordinate genera.[2] Peter of Spain omits any mention of these difficulties when treating the Tree of Porphyry (2. 9–13), and Llull's
explanation of them in this passage reflects his general view of
Porphyry's scheme as a hierarchy of inclusive classes of beings, rather
than of divisions of predicative classes. Llull's definition thus serves, as
Platzeck has rightly noted, to define the place of each being in that
hierarchy.[3]

When Llull criticizes the same definition of man in his *Ars mystica*,
he offers what he calls a more 'explicit' formula—'man is composed of
a rational soul and body' (4. 4. 2. 243–4). This is more explicit because

---

[2] On these difficulties, see the comments of Edward W. Warren in his translation of
the *Isagoge* (Toronto: Pontifical Institute of Medieval Studies, 1975), p. 37.
[3] 'La combinatoria luliana', pp. 149, 601.

it literally expresses the composition of body and rational soul 'in which nothing naturally participates except man. But beasts naturally participate with man in animal for they are mortal animals like man. Moreover man and the angels participate with God in rational.' (Ibid.) This expression need not be so literal, however: Llull claims that the definition 'homo est animal homificans' is 'clearer' than the definition 'leo est animal leonans' because a lion naturally produces another lion, but man only the human body (since God gives the soul). Similarly, 'man is a writing animal' is 'clearer' than 'a bee is a honey-comb making animal' because man employs more powers of the soul (4. 4. 2. 246–7). Llull's criteria of explicitness and clarity are thus moralizing, in the regular exegetical sense, and wholly extensional in their consideration of the value of terms of predication. Indeed, this is not a logic of terms at all, but of whole propositions. His treatment of definition has little to do with the analysis of the signification and supposition of terms that occupied his contemporaries. If Logic is an *ars sermocinalis* for Llull, its principles of discourse correspond better to the rhetorical ones of clarity, brevity, and plausibility recommended by Cicero (*De inv.* 1. 20. 28), though these criteria depend entirely on their moralizing application according to Llull's first intention. Understanding predication becomes a hermeneutic exercise devoted to weighing a proposition's *rectitudo*.

The *Ars mystica* also suggests the broadly dialectical function of Llull's approach in one passage that speaks not of definitions, but of descriptions. He claims that Porphyry's formula 'homo est risibilis' is not as clear a 'description' as his own 'homo est ridens' because the former merely signifies a substance disposed to laughing while the latter signifies a substance actively laughing (4. 4. 2. 245). According to a dictum from John of Damascus's *Logic* (8; 554B) that Scholastic authorities often repeat, a description rightly states a thing's properties, which do not pertain to its essence, for Aristotle (*Top.* 1. 4 101b19–23). Llull's account of property in the Second Distinction of the *Logica nova* has already shown how he posits substantial or essential properties, and his apparently interchangeable use of 'description' and 'definition' further testifies to that view, perhaps as its consequence.

Finally, in his *Ars generalis ultima* (9. 45) of 1308, Llull suggests how this type of definition also realizes his correlation of affirmative predication with truth and being: 'predicating a predicate of a subject affirmatively is to define the subject about which the predicate is predicated, a nature existing between the subject and predicate' because 'affirmation posits the true things that are in the subject'; Llull offers thirty definitions of man, such as 'the animal who uses virtues and vices' and 'the animal with which all corporeal things serve God'. The *rectitudo* of these propositions is obvious. More than one definition of a thing's essence is impossible for Aristotle (*Top.* 6. 5 143b35), but Llull's multiple definitions naturally express his conception of multiple essential attributes and plural substantial forms.[4] Llull's definitions of a thing through its correlatives may appear tautological, but for him best express the fully active nature of the thing and thus help the mind to apprehend more fully its truth. In this regard, they contribute to making his Logic more significative of nature, that is, more natural.

[4] See Platzeck's suggestions in 'La combinatoria luliana', pp. 148, 602; he does not stress the consequences of Llull's metaphysical theories for his notion of definition in *Raimund Lull* (1. 423).

15

Natural Middle

MUCH of Llull's attention to predication focuses, as several passages have already intimated, on his doctrine regarding the discovery of the 'natural middle' of predication. Although some of his earlier works attest to this interest, the *Logica nova* only mentions this natural middle in passing in its very last chapter (7. 27), and his most extensive treatments of this doctrine appear in several works from his last years. The natural middle is, none the less, a keystone of Llull's edifice of natural Logic, and its importance is evident from the attention that it attracted among sixteenth-century Lullists.[1] As occasionally happens in Llull's work, his natural middle seems to depend on the conflation of two related terms from Aristotelian doctrine: one is simply the middle term necessary for attributing one thing to another in any syllogism (*An. pr.* 1. 23 41a3); the other is the middle, or causal connection between a thing and an attribute that demonstration exhibits (*An. post.* 2. 2 89b37). Llull's natural middle most clearly corresponds to this second type, but in so far as it typically explains the union of subject and predicate in a conclusion, it also serves the first.

Subject and predicate are always related as real and diverse beings from the hierarchy of creation, whose participation the natural medium explains, as is evident from examples in works written before the special treatises devoted to it. For example, in his *Ars brevis*, Llull declares that

In qualibet camera [of Llull's Third Figure] sunt duae litterae in ea contentae, et ipsae significant subjectum, et praedicatum, in quibus Artista inquirit medium, cum quo subjectum, et praedicatum conjunguntur: sicut bonitas, et magnitudo, quae conjunguntur per Concordantiam; et huiusmodi: cum quo medio Artista intendit concludere, et propositionem declarare. (1. 4; p. 14)

The processes described here serve broadly to correlate logical predication with the combinatory mechanics of Llull's own *Art*. They

---

[1] See Mark D. Johnston, 'The Reception of the Lullian *Art*, 1450–1530', *Sixteenth Century Journal*, 12 (1981), 31–48.

include two aspects, which Llull describes more exactly in his instructions for 'evacuating' the Third Figure by forming all the possible combinations of meanings for each pair of letters. On the one hand, the Absolute and Relative *Principia* signified by each pair allow 'twelve propositions, changing the subject into the predicate and conversely' (6. 2). Examples are '*Bonitas* est magna, *Magnitudo* est bona, *Magnitudo* est concordans, *Concordantia* est magna' and so forth. These propositions are wholly the result of combinatory mechanics, and require no interpretative work from the Lullian artist in order to generate them. On the other hand, Llull advises evacuating the Third Figure with

duodecim mediis: et dicuntur media, eo quia consistunt inter subjectum et praedicatum, cum quibus conveniunt genere, aut specie; et cum istis mediis, intellectus facit se disputativum, et determinativum, ut cum dicitur: omne id, quod magnificatur a magnitudine, est magnum; sed Bonitas magnificatur a magnitudine: ergo bonitas est magna. (6. 3; p. 35)

This process is, presumably, more 'disputative and determinative' because it creates a syllogism, which is the act of disputation for Peter of Spain (7. 1), that determines or limits some general thing with a specific qualification. Llull, however, states that these middles 'agree' generally or specifically with the subject and predicate, which is not so much a restrictive class relationship as one of likeness and participation. The middle term here, 'Everything magnified by *Magnitudo*', explains that participation metaphysically as a kind of contraction, and the syllogism really serves only to define '*Bonitas* magna' as a specific instance of general *Bonitas* in the manner already described by Llull's earlier *Aplicació de l'Art General* (lines 432–3). The innovation here is the attempt to define a causal 'middle' for this contraction of one level or category of being to another.

A very clear illustration of the participational nature of Llull's natural middle appears in his *Ars brevis, quae est de inventione iuris*. There he explains how one can determine if any predication about law (*ius*) involves natural law because 'just as animal is a natural medium existing between man and substance, because man cannot be a substance without (*praeter*) animal, so nature is a natural medium between the subject and predicate when no instance befalls the predication' (4. 3. c). The analogue of animal suggests that Llull's natural middle simply concerns 'mediation' between classes of being from the Tree of Porphyry. However, Llull does not define any similarly well-ordered hierarchy of classes of law (cf. 4. Prol.), but instead takes nature as the defining characteristic of, and therefore natural middle in any predication about, natural law. Naturalness becomes, as it were, the homology in any Lullian analogy regarding types of law, and requires interpretation of what is or is not natural in the rule under consideration. Llull determines the presence or absence of naturalness in any predication by accepting or rejecting contrary instances, which depend wholly on specific material circumstances, rather than any general formal class relationships. Thus he rejects the predication 'every law is durable' because 'when injury is introduced into the subject, justice and law are corrupted' (4. 3. a). This predication may not be necessary, as Llull says, recalling Aristotle's definition of demonstrative premisses (*An. post.* 1. 3 73a23), but it is not clear why it lacks nature, except in so far as Llull rejects it, assumes that all acceptable predications about natural law possess nature by participation, and thus attributes the validity of the predication to this nature as the causal middle relating subject to predicate. This determination of nature as a participated middle present in all acceptable predications about natural law, where that acceptability is not itself a formal consequence of that presence, exemplifies again how Llull moralizes Aristotelian logical doctrine according to his own Neoplatonic metaphysics and axioms of moral theology. The interpretation that discovers this participation is in fact the kind of inventional exercise described in Classical accounts of forensic rhetoric, such as Cicero (*De inv.* 2. 4. 12–15. 154).

Llull's use of his *Principia* in predications displaying a natural middle intimates already that this element, like so many in his *Art*, depends heavily for its efficacy on the metaphysics of the Godhead, and this dependence is obvious in Llull's first complete treatise on the middle, the *Liber de conversione subiecti et praedicati et medii*, composed at Paris in July of 1310. In the Prologue to this work, Llull asserts that it, like so many of his other writings, offers a doctrine by which the mind might be 'habituated with demonstrative arguments and thereby attain knowledge rather than opinion'. Llull proposes to do this by discoursing on his nine *Subiecta* through four 'modes': predication, conversion, opinion, and demonstration. The collocation of these modes evidently comprises Llull's attempt to correlate his peculiar conception of the former two with the Aristotelian distinctions (*An. post.* 1. 33 88b30) embodied in the latter two. Thus, Llull offers various propositions and syllogisms regarding each Subject, and some of these employ convertible predications that make them 'demonstrative', in Llull's view, while others do not, making them merely 'opinative' as a result. This distinction depends on the kind of middle involved in each predication, since, as he avers in his *Ars generalis*

ultima of 1308, 'Logic is the art with which the logician finds a natural
conjunction between subject and predicate, which is the medium with
which he knows how to make necessary conclusions.' (10. 101.) None
the less, Llull's necessary demonstration is not that of received Aristotelian theory, as he declares in the *Liber de divina voluntate infinita et
ordinata* of 1314:

> Facere scientiam sive scientias per syllogismum demonstrativum, tenendo
> modum philosophorum antiquorum, valde est difficile. Ratio huius est, quia
> medium naturale existens inter subiectum et praedicatum intellectui valde
> secretum est. Et ignorato tali medio oriuntur opiniones, confusiones et errores;
> et de hoc experientiam habemus, quando disputamus. Et ideo bonum est,
> quod inveniatur novus modus ad faciendum scientiam sive scientias. (Prol.; p.
> 462)

As part of his new method, Llull's natural middle will serve that
rectification of the soul from error and confusion, especially in the
practice of disputation with an unbelieving Intellect. It is difficult to
read Llull's mention here of things 'secret' to the Intellect, and not
imagine that this discovery of the natural middle is in fact another
expression of the pursuit of the significations hidden in real things, as
described in the Prologue to his *Liber de significatione*.

Llull begins his account of this natural middle in the *Liber de
conversione* by defining it according to the participation of particulars in
their universal:

> Est autem unum medium omnino generale, quod est origo omnium mediorum
> existentium inter subiectum et praedicatum; ut puta quando terminus omnino
> universalis trahitur ad terminum non omnino particularem, ut puta quando
> bonitas omnino generalis contrahitur ad magnitudinem, et dicitur bonitas
> magna; quae bonitas magna non est omnino generalis neque omnino
> particularis.
> Sed quando contrahitur et dicitur: Bonitas Petri est magna, tunc est omnino
> specialis; et ideo bonitas magna est medium existens inter omnino generale et
> particulare. (1; p. 262)

Llull extends the notions of middle from the nature of the relationship
between a subject and a predicate to the relationship between the
successively more restricted realizations or contractions of a universal
form, which in this example are *Bonitas*, '*Bonitas* magna', and '*Bonitas*
Petri magna'. Llull's designation of these successive restrictions as
completely or incompletely universal, general, specific, and particular
deviates obviously from Scholastic practice: Peter of Spain defines
'man' and 'Sortes' as 'common' and 'singular' terms, but refers to 'all'

and 'some' as 'universal' and 'particular' signs (1. 8). As seen in many passages examined already, Llull usually ignores the qualifications introduced by universal or particular signs in a proposition in favour of the real classes denoted by common and singular terms, since this view best represents them as levels in the hierarchy of participated being. Llull's examples do illustrate very well the functions of restriction as described by Peter of Spain (11. 1–13), although of course he interprets them from a sheerly metaphysical, rather than a formal logical, perspective at all times. Hence his explanations of the proposition '*Bonitas* Petri est magna' define the connection between an attribute and its subject, but not as expressed in the relationship of predicate to subject. In this respect, Llull's account of his middle displays some of the same difficulties as the doctrines upon which it ultimately depends: Aristotle's accounts of the middle term (*An. post.* 1. 6 74b26–75a37) and causal connection in demonstration (2. 2 89b37–90a2) never successfully align the structure of the proposition with the inherence of attributes in a subject. Llull is much less concerned than the Philosopher, however, to reconcile the metaphysical and physical status of causes with their representation in the form of syllogistic argument.

Llull goes on to describe three types of middle and defines each of them thus:

Medium mensurationis est, quando existit aequaliter inter extremitates, ut puta intelligere naturale, quod existit aequaliter inter intelligentem et intelligibile. A tali medio oritur relatio et conversio inter subiectum et praedicatum.

Medium coniunctionis est causa, quare extremitates connectuntur, et sequitur unio.

Medium extremitatum est respectu continui subiecti, sicut linea inter duo puncta. (1; p. 263)

Llull confects his characterizations of each type of middle by collating, in his typically moralizing fashion, various basic Aristotelian doctrines. The first mensurational middle links the reckoning of the mid-point of continuous motion (*Phys.* 8. 8) to the existence of intermediaries between relative terms (*Metaph.* 10. 7), and from these derives the convertible relations of subject and predicate (*An. pr.* 1. 2–3). The continuity between extremities or relative terms is an important common factor in all three of Llull's definitions of middle because it defines the participated nature common to them in an organic way as a real connection of proximity. The second conjunctive middle refers to the definition of continuity as a union of extremities (*Phys.* 5. 3 227a13) and may also extend to the connection between extreme terms in a syllogism (*An. pr.* 1. 4 25b31–26a1). The third middle of extremities derives from the definition of individual beings as continuous (*Metaph.* 5. 6 1015b30–1016a16), especially in the example of a line (*Phys.* 5. 3 227a30). Llull appeals to these types of middle, and develops their definitions more widely, in order to distinguish among the demonstrative and opinative syllogisms that he offers for the nine *Subiecta*, as a few representative examples will show below.

Llull also sets forth several other somewhat disparate preliminary considerations in the First Distinction of the *Liber de conversione*. He notes that there are many types of predication, although he maintains only the division between the convertible and non-convertible. He defines the former as demonstrative, and exemplifies it by predicating one Divine Dignity of another: '*Bonitas* is *Magnitudo*'. He defines the latter as opinative, and exemplifies it with the Scholastic commonplace 'every man is an animal' as well as his own formula '*Bonitas* is great', in which the middle is, he claims, a 'copulative accident'. Llull's own combinatory pairs of letters have no copula, and he may believe that this enhances the substantial character of the union expressed by those pairs. However, he notes in the *Logica nova* (5. 1) that 'animal substance' is a potential proposition and 'every animal is a substance' an actual one; Peter of Spain offers this same distinction (7. 12). However, Llull's denomination of the copula as a 'middle' reflects his participational understanding of the relationship that it creates, and his examples explicitly reverse the classification of Aristotle, who asserts that reciprocal predication lacks demonstrative force (*An. post.* 1. 19 82a15 and 1. 22 83a36–b12), while the 'natural' predication of essential or categorical attributes, as in 'every man is an animal' or '*Bonitas* is great', is the only type of predication that does have demonstrative force (*An. post.* 1. 22 83a21). In the *Liber de conversione* (1) Llull goes on to state that when the Intellect discourses, 'recurring to its own nature and mode of understanding, seeking the middle between subject and predicate, it knows that demonstration is made from such a middle, and if not, an opinative syllogism'. The mind's reflection on its own nature is a Prescholastic commonplace[2] with axiomatic force in Llull's gnoseology, as the subsequent chapter on demonstration will show. Llull's substantial medium presumably refers to Aristotle's natural predication of an essential attribute, and is thus entirely conventional in conception. Llull adds that when the Intellect discourses

---

[2] See Javelet, *Image et ressemblance*, 1. 368–408.

by means of 'philosophical opinions', rather than its own nature, it has only a contingent, opinative, and creditive habit of knowledge. Knowledge of the nature of the middle between subject and predicate allows the Intellect to understand with certainty and to avoid sophistical reasonings. This simply restates Llull's usual view of the opposition between his own necessary, because real, Logic, and the opinative, because intentional, ratiocinations of his Scholastic adversaries. Opinative and sophistical knowledge would correspond technically in this view to predications based on accidental (as opposed to substantial) middles, a view consistent with Aristotelian doctrine. Llull concludes his theoretical introduction by reasserting that demonstration requires the reciprocal conversion of the subject, and predicate, and middle in a syllogism using 'true, necessary, and primary principles'; any syllogism lacking this conversion is merely opinative. The principles mentioned are, of course, Llull's own *Principia* and the examples to be discussed will show how his entire doctrine of the middle and conversion of subject and predicate assumes the relational characteristics of those *Principia*. As a conclusion to this review of his theoretical presentation of the natural middle in the *Liber de conversione*, it is worth noting how many of his pronouncements, terms, or distinctions bear a conventional Aristotelian sense; only his explicit claims for conversion of subject and predicate and examples from his *Principia* confirm his very different conception of the predicational middle. This revalorization of conventional terminology or doctrine is, of course, a signal instrument of his moralizing method.

The first Subject that Llull treats according to his doctrine of the natural middle is God. He first proves the existence of God, using an argument from supposition that could be said to apply a kind of Neoplatonic account of cause and effect to Anselm's ontological argument. God must be the most perfect perfection, glorious glory, and so on because if he were not, Llull argues, 'the Intellect would have a higher force (*virtutem*) in conceiving God and His attributes, than God and His attributes are, which is impossible, since it would not be caused from the first cause, since it would be conceptually superior' (2. 1). Llull makes the relevant application of his doctrine of middle, giving this demonstrative syllogism based on true, necessary, and primary principles, and explaining it as follows:

Quidquid est Deus, est bonitas optima. Sed magnitudo maxima est Deus; ergo magnitudo maxima est bonitas optima. . . .

Probatum est, quod optimitas et maximitas convertuntur. Converti autem non possunt sine medio conversivo, quod sit purus actus, scilicet optimare, maximare, cum quibus rationes sunt in superlativo gradu existentes, habentes naturam ab omni otiositate prolongatam. Tale autem medium non potest esse sine extremitatibus, ut ita loquar, cum sit purus actus; quas extremitates vocamus maximans, maximatum. Medium autem coniunctionis coniungit, quod optimans maximans sint unum suppositum et optimatum maximatum aliud suppositum; et sic oritur relatio et per consequens distinctio trium suppositorum. Medium autem extremitatum, ut ita loquar, ponit, quod omnia tria supposita divina in suo numero remanentia sint una essentia divina. Unde cum ita sit, ostensum est, per quem modum intellectus humanus de divina trinitate potest habere notitiam. (2. 1; p. 264)

Based on this passage, it is entirely legitimate to conclude what will be evident later: that Llull's doctrine of the natural middle applies his doctrine of correlatives and demonstration *per aequiparantiam* to the Aristotelian model of predication, especially as a means of proving demonstratively the Trinity. Like his demonstration *per aequiparantiam*, Llull's doctrine of the middle is an attempt to extend the kind of relationships found in the Godhead to created beings, to uncover yet another *vestigium Trinitatis* in created beings, in this case the *entia rationis* of Logic. God is, according to Llull's *Liber de deo et de mundo*, 'divine conversion' (3. 17). Llull's middle is not Aristotle's syllogistic middle term or causal connection of demonstration, although his use of the term is almost certainly intended to recall them. Llull's middle is instead a general label for any reciprocal, convertible, or mutually determined elements joined in any metaphysical or physical relationship—such as form and matter or substance and accident—that he invokes in his arguments. In so far as the introduction of these arguments is in fact an inventional use of *exempla* from Scholastic philosophy, Llull's doctrine of the middle is an attempt to justify metaphysically the enormous number of relational arguments, most of which manipulate the poles of identity and difference or contrarity and concordance in reducing the many to the one, that comprise the bulk of his moralizing procedures.

Llull's further examples concerning God show the other types of causal connections that he would recognize or reinterpret as middles. The predication 'God is good' is invalid and unsuitable for a demonstrative syllogism, according to Llull, because it lacks the mensurational middle of convertibility between the terms 'good' and 'God'. This is so because God is not the sole—although he is the supreme —good. It is especially noteworthy that this example does not appeal to the distinction between abstract common and concrete particular terms (such as 'goodness' and 'good') recognized in Scholastic logico-linguistic analyses since Anselm's *De grammatico*. Most of Llull's examples serve to introduce similar moral or theological values indirectly as reasons for the function of some middle in the example offered. As with most of his logical structures, Llull's formal relationships of middle are highly 'material-specific'. He explains the predication 'God is the highest cause' by arguing that 'God cannot be the greatest cause without a greatest effect, which we call Christ, since they exist relationally. But the middle of conversion cannot convert cause and effect, and thus for the middle of extremes, naturally speaking.' (2. 5.) The purpose of this argument, evidently, is to assert the real distinction of Father and Son in the Trinity, although this seems almost irrelevant to the original predication. Llull's definition of the specifically natural character of the middle of predication cited here becomes the focus of his second treatise on the conversion of subject and predicate, discussed below.

As an attempted revision of formal structures of argument, Llull's doctrine of the middle is most remarkable for its restriction of demonstration to syllogisms employing convertible propositions. Since this conversion is only possible fully among Llull's *Principia*, the only demonstrative knowledge that Llull recognizes is knowledge of God and his attributes. Thus the effective purpose of his remarks on the other eight *Subiecta* in the *Liber de conversione* is to show that the 'middle of conversion exists in no substance but God' (5. 4). In created being, the middle of extremities serves to explain their unity as continuous subjects, while the conjunctive middle serves to explain the contraction of species to individual, superior to inferior, substance to accident, or form to matter. None of these contractions admits conversion among its terms. Thus the middle of conversion does not hold between action and affection or any relative term (7. 4). This claim clarifies the non-relative nature of Llull's innate correlatives, which do admit a kind of conversion, and qualifies his use of the term 'relative' in regard to them (as in his remarks on God from the First Distinction of the treatise). Similarly, the middle of conversion does not hold between actuality and potentiality, but rather serves to 'proportion' the latter to the former. This proportion of potency to act explains how the 'principles' and terms of a syllogism are 'disposed' to being linked by the middle of conjunction and extremities (9. 1–5). It is not clear here whether the 'principles' of a syllogism are the same as its terms, or if

Llull means the union of premisses to produce a conclusion. Most importantly, Llull's survey of non-convertible relations clearly invokes the fundamental value of both proportion and natural disposition in his metaphysics, as means of joining beings in non-causal relationships. Even the relationship of cause to effect itself is,thus moralized as a 'proportional' one of participation. Finally, Llull ends his treatise by explaining that his remarks on each Subject exemplify the function of the real, natural middle from which the soul apprehends a conceptual middle. He gives examples of how the logician, jurist, moral philosopher, and physician recognize the real middle through the conceptual middle, which thus fulfills a purely cognitive function (10. 5), in the manner set forth in the epistemological model of the *Liber de significatione*.

One of Llull's very last works, the *Liber de medio naturali* composed at Messina in 1313, patently displays the derivation of his doctrine of middle from that of his innate correlatives and general trinitarian apologetic. The theoretical content of the work is cryptically brief. Llull begins with what is in effect an *exemplum* based on his correlatives: *intelligere* constitutes the health of the Intellect because it is a 'natural middle' between *intelligens* and *intelligibile*; hence this work will treat the 'permanent natural middle' between subject and predicate that the Intellect requires for knowledge. Llull scarcely recognizes the logical nature of this middle, which is here simply a metaphysical relation. His comments also imply his usual view of the Intellect's proper natural acts and objects, which figure prominently in his accounts of demonstrative knowledge, examined in Chapter 19. He also defines predication, noting that it occurs in many ways, of which he offers only one example: 'Man is an animal; Peter is a man; therefore Peter is an animal.' This syllogism displays, he declares, 'necessary predication', a 'natural middle', and a 'necessary conclusion'. This is entirely consistent with Aristotelian teaching, but the criteria of Llull's judgements here are in fact theological. He argues, for example, that in the proposition 'the world is created', there is no natural middle between subject and predicate, because the world was not created naturally, and therefore this proposition is merely opinative. The recognition of a 'natural middle' that Llull demands here exemplifies the use of equivocation that he develops in his new fallacy of contradiction. As in the *Liber de conversione*, the label 'middle' effectively designates any association of physical or metaphysical elements necessary for the elaboration of Llull's argument. The body of the *Liber de medio naturali* is merely a list of syllogisms about the Godhead based on permutations of Llull's Absolute and Relative *Principia*. The treatise concludes with one of the purest expressions of Llull's 'trinitarian world-picture'—'The Holy Spirit is relatively the exemplar of all other natural middles'—which Llull then identifies with the verbal infinitives that designate his innate correlative act. This treatise is, he ultimately declares, 'an art for generating knowledge with the natural middle' (17). Whether this refers to theological knowledge alone, or to the role of the Holy Spirit in attaining any knowledge, is probably irrelevant to Llull's purposes. The *Liber de medio naturali* clearly shows how the nature in Llull's natural middle is the nature of being as defined through his *Principia*; this doctrine, like so many others, pursues as far as possible his moralization of Logic according to divine ontology and moral theology.

Llull's doctrine of the middle represents therefore his most ambitious effort to recast predication and propositional structure, considered as far as possible apart from their use in syllogistic argument, as expressions of the participation, proportion, and coessentiality that organize his metaphysics. The distinction between the convertibility of predications about God and the proportionality and disposition of all predications about created beings is especially critical because it represents Llull's attempt to introduce a dynamic force into the middle that will order predication to active pursuit of its Lullian first intention. Proportion and disposition necessarily draw the created particulars of the world towards the one universal Creator. The middle thus serves the activist character of his metaphysics, and attempts to impart its activation of the proportional disposition and participation of being to predicative statements about individual beings, while referring or reducing that activity to its source in the active conversion and coessentiality of the Godhead.

16

Affirmation and Negation

EVEN though Llull's doctrine of the natural middle displays his attention to the functions of predication, something scarcely noticed in his early writings, his handling of logical discourse in general relies on a technique for manipulating propositions that has little to do with the mechanics of predication. This is his use of affirmation and negation, which he develops from the earliest years of his career, and which always overshadows all other aspects of logical predication in importance.[1] His works from before 1303 have shown how he correlates affirmation and negation with possibility, impossibility, good, evil, truth, and falsehood, and associates them with the resolution of doubt and postulation of suppositions regarding any subject. He continues these developments in his later works, and takes them as the basis for his attempted reforms of Aristotelian logical discourse. The two outstanding results of this effort are his method of argument from 'contrary suppositions' and the so-called fallacy of contradiction. These new methods are the special subjects of Chapters 17 and 18. This chapter will focus exclusively on Llull's final refinements in his correlations of affirmation and negation, emphasizing the aspects that bear most directly on their contribution to those new methods of argument.

The treatment of affirmation and negation and their correlated distinctions in the *Logica nova* is limited and scarcely suggests their importance in Llull's logical programme from his later period. He does no more than mention affirmative and negative propositions when enumerating the propositional modes (5. 1), and his remarks concerning possibility and impossibility (5. 8–9) simply review basic Aristotelian distinctions in the physical and metaphysical senses of potency, power, and possibility. This focus obviously supports the pretended

[1] Platzeck's relative indifference to the function of affirmation and negation, which this study regards as fundamental, is one of the chief divergences in their perspectives. In *Raimund Lull*, he notes it mainly as it appears in the catalogue of one hundred forms from the *Logica nova* (1. 415), yet in other studies he clearly recognizes its contribution to Llull's method: 'Descubrimiento y esencia', p. 152; 'La combinatoria luliana', p. 131.

natural character of Llull's new logical programme, and the explication of logical possibility according to physical potency does have a well-known precedent in Anselm. As for the metaphysical and physical doctrines themselves, Aquinas's commentary on Aristotle (*In 9 Metaph.* 3–4) covers most of the distinctions suggested by Llull. This more or less unrevised incorporation of conventional doctrine suggests again that Llull possibly drew on more new sources of information in an effort to fortify the contribution of 'natural' doctrine in the *Logica nova*.

On the other hand, it is important to recognize that Aristotelian doctrine regarding contradiction or the predication of possibility (*De interp.* 11–13) has only minimal import for the type of impossibility 'through contradiction' that Llull describes thus:

sicut dicere Petrus fuit; Petrus non fuit; Petrus est bonus; Petrus non est bonus; veritas est falsitas; falsitas est veritas; et sic de aliis. Et ista impossibilitas dicitur contradictio quia denudat subiectum et praedicatum ab omni convenientia et in ipsis simpliciter contrarietate ponit. (1. 8; f. 78vb; p. 86)

Llull's examples combine one illustrating contradiction in the conventional sense of opposed affirmative and negative propositions with another illustrating the 'remote matter', as Peter of Spain calls it (1. 13), that creates the variety of sophistical disputation called simply 'false' (7. 15). As typically happens, however, Llull has no regard for the formal differences between true or false propositions, but rather seeks the real differences between true and false values. Thus he adduces his *Principium* of *Contrarietas* to explain the lack of participational agreement between the subject and predicate 'truth' and 'falsehood' from his second example, although this explanation is inapplicable to the first example. For Llull, the explanation is adequate to both, however, in so far as these are both instances of contrarity or opposition, whose heuristic value is paramount for Llull, and which he understands in a much broader sense than logically formal contrarity or contradiction in propositions. This value is the mutual reference of contrary or opposing terms, which Aristotle attributes especially to relative terms (*Cat.* 7 8a35; 10 11b24) and which Llull asserts throughout his later writings, as in the opening lines of his *Liber de concordantia et contrarietate* of 1313 or *Liber facilis scientiae* of 1311, which declare that 'one opposite is known from another'. Possibility and impossibility or affirmation and negation are such opposites, and their presence in the discourse of Llull's arguments serves to organize the corollary oppositions of true and false or being and non-being and thereby make available the knowledge of one from the other. This function is evident in Llull's use of these terms in the two special treatises devoted to them, where they moralize the questions expounded by aligning the answers to these with the affirmation of true, possible good being or the denial of false, impossible, evil non-being, as needed for proof of Llull's position on each issue.

The first of these treatises is the *Liber de possibili et impossibili*, composed at Paris in 1310. The work's argument is nominally theological: Llull seeks to prove 'from the nature of possibility and impossibility that God can produce what is incomparably more noble than what nature can', in order to refute those 'modern philosophers' who assert that God cannot work above nature and that they cannot comprehend anything higher than the work of nature (Prol.). Llull does not pursue this argument through a demonstration of the necessary and contingent nature of being, in the manner of Avicenna's *Metaphysics* (1. 6), but rather through a comparative analysis of various doctrines that moralizes them through proportional arguments as analogues to possibility and impossibility. The treatise is largely a compendium of Lullian teaching regarding each level of created and uncreated being (analysed through his *Subiecta*), or a sort of Lullian *ars brevis* in which the titular dichotomy of possibility and impossibility fills the role of the combinatory mechanics of the *Ars magna*. Hence it is difficult to see the treatise as a specific response to the Aristotelian and Averroist views of John of Jandun (d. 1328), as its modern editor has suggested.[2] The work's Second Distinction on God does fulfil Llull's announced purpose by discussing his absolute and ordained power and claiming to offer a 'higher mode' of understanding to the Intellect; the Third Distinction on the 'Order of the Universe' explains the individuation of beings from each Subject as composition from likenesses of the Divine Dignities; the Fourth Distinction offers one hundred maxims concerning possibility and impossibility and 304 questions regarding the doctrines of the Second and Third Distinctions.

The brief First Distinction on possibility and impossibility themselves is notable for its very oblique relevance to the arguments from possibility and impossibility that Llull actually employs in the treatise. Like the *Logica nova*, it reviews the metaphysical and physical senses of

---

[2] In the introduction to the text (p. 384). On John of Jandun, see Stuart MacClintock, *Perversity and Error: Studies on the "Averroist" John of Jandun* (Bloomington: Indiana University Press, 1956).

power, potency, and potentiality, dividing them exhaustively (Llull claims) into three species of possibility: (1) when neither possibility nor impossibility belongs to a subject as its essence or parts, but are instead its effect; (2) when both are parts of a subject, with which it acts, is affected, and exists; (3) when one or the other exists in a subject (1. Prol.). The first type defines God. The second type includes a thing's potentiality to existence, as defined by Aristotle (*Metaph.* 9. 8 1049b18–29), which Llull calls its 'coessential possibility'; the powers of living creatures, again in Aristotle's sense (9. 5 1047b30–48a24); and the impossibility of a thing possessing and not possessing a quality at the same time—as in 'Peter is unjust while he is just'—which founds contradiction in the *On Interpretation*, although Llull in no way acknowledges this logical function, despite its importance for his own fallacy of contradiction. The third type defines necessary and contingent existence.

While some of these specific senses of possibility and impossibility from the First Distinction do appear attributed to some of the beings discussed in Llull's arguments, they do not define the functional relationships that the arguments themselves employ. These relationships are much broader in scope, and appear throughout the treatise, as in this passage from the Prologue: 'The subject of this book is necessity, since it is the genus of possibility and impossibility, because what is possible is necessarily possible; and thus for the impossible; otherwise it would imply contradiction.' This relationship between necessity and possibility evidently recalls Aristotelian doctrine, but ignores the qualifications introduced by the Philosopher (*Cat.* 9 18b10–19b4; 13 22a37–b18) in order to make possibility and impossibility mutually exclusive positions. This mutual exclusion sustains many of the arguments by reduction to impossibility that Llull offers, as when he asks 'Whether it is possible that a philosophy existing in opposition to Theology be knowledge or a figment?' and responds, 'I say it would be a figment, otherwise the Intellect would cause it *per se*, not by receiving the influence from the general possibility constituted from the Divine Dignities, which is impossible.' (4. 2. 112.) Of course, this deduction is invalid, since the premiss is not singular, as Aristotle requires (*De interp.* 11 20b15–31). Llull's argument is enthymematic in so far as it assumes several unexpressed premisses defining knowledge as the opposite of figment. Yet its validity for Llull more likely depends on the correlation of that opposition with those of truth and falsehood and possibility and impossibility, so that his reasoning in fact seeks to join the terms philosophy and figment through the middle term of impossibility, and Theology and knowledge through possibility. These are, obviously, two separate syllogistic deductions.

The axiomatic value of these correlated oppositions appears in many of the maxims from the Fourth Distinction:

Possibile et impossibile, contrariando super unum, implicant contradictionem.
Bonitas et malitia opponuntur per possibile et impossibile.
Quia possibile dicit esse, et impossibile non esse, plus potest potestas cum possibili, quam cum impossibili.
Impossibile est, quod intellectus appetat magis credere, quam intelligere.
Voluntas cum velle ponit possibile et cum nolle impossibile.
Veritas, quae ponit possibilitatem, ponit ipsum, ut possit ponere possibile.
Concordantia ponit possibile et contrarietas impossibile.
Plus potest altitudo per possibile, quam per impossibile.
Omne possibile appetit quietem. (4. 1. 4, 12, 27, 34, 37, 50, 74, 95, 98; pp. 428–33)

Possibility and impossibility organize these correlations as general principles of knowledge because they are general principles of existence (4. 2. 114) caused by God (1. 1) and sustaining the specific possibilities and impossibilities that sustain in turn all the likenesses of him that constitute creation (3. 1. 1). Their function in his metaphysics of participation and resemblance could not be clearer. These maxims, and not the doctrine of the treatise's First Distinction, define the status of possibility and impossibility as a master dichotomy beneath which Llull arrays all other relationships of being and knowledge. Once their status is thus understood, it becomes easy to appreciate their function in arguments such as these:

Dignum et iustum est, quod ens optimum sit causa optima. Impossibile autem ponit, quod non possit esse causa optima, nisi causet effectum optimatum. Possibile quidem ponit, quod dignum et iustum sit, quod talis effectus sit in causa optima optimatus, cum ipsa coniunctus et in ipsa sustentatus. Et talem effectum vocamus Iesum Christum, Filium Dei. (2. 1. 3. 3; p. 390)

Possibility and impossibility embrace the proportional values of nobility and worth that order the hierarchy of being:

Sensitiva est substantia generalis ad omnia sensibilia. Et est una pars universi, composita ex principiis innatis, ad ipsam contractis et appropriatis, sine qua universum esset vacuum . . . De qua descendunt plures substantiae particulares, per quas animalia individuata sunt sensata. Et ideo possibilitas ponit per

talem modum suam individuationem generalem, et ponit plures individua-
tiones particulares ab ipsa tamquam rivuli ab una fonte.

Sensitiva autem sic individuata, ab ipsa descendunt sex fontes, per quos
principia sensitiva transeunt ad causandum sensibilitates peregrinas, ut puta
potentia visiva, auditiva, gustativa, olfactiva, tactiva et affativa.[3] Et ideo omnia
ista ponit possibile. Impossibile autem non impedit, quia cum possibile con-
venit in serviendo primo principio. (3. 2. 5. 1–2; pp. 420–1)

Even impossibility serves the Lullian first intention, as the last line
suggests. Llull's quasi-allegorical terms of 'possibility' and 'impossibility' analogically moralize the doctrines presented as correlations of
either truth or falsehood, being or non-being, good or evil, and so
forth. However arbitrary these correlations may appear in some cases,
and however incompatible with the senses of power, potency, and
potentiality enumerated in the work's First Distinction, it is necessary
to recall finally that for Llull they assert the participation of real and
rational truths, falsehoods, goods, evils, beings, and non-beings as a
means of rectifying the soul always to accept the possible and reject the
impossible.

This rectification through possibility and impossibility takes the
form of a disputation in Llull's other work devoted to them, the *Liber
contradictionis* composed at Paris in 1311. It is one of his polemical and
anti-Averroist writings, and like many of his works of this type employs
the literary artifice of a debate format: a Lullist (*Raimundista*) and an
Averroist are engaged in disputation at Paris. They both have good
intentions—Llull's natural desire for God or supposition of his truth
—but cannot agree. The Averroist maintains the double truth of faith
and reason, while the Lullist responds that this incurs a contradiction.
They retire to a meadow outside Paris where, alongside a beautiful
tree and fountain (symbols of the procession and participation of all
truths in one truth), the allegorical figure of Contradiction appears to
them. She suggests that they seek the truth by syllogizing opposing
positions based on the one hundred maxims of possibility and impossibility listed in the Fourth Distinction of Llull's *Liber de possibili et
impossibili*. The 'greater, more durable, more powerful, more virtuous,
and truer' syllogism thus formed will clearly give the truth of the

---

[3] This is Llull's sixth sense of speech, called *affatus*. For the text of the treatise in
which Llull advances this theory, see Josep Perarnau i Espelt, 'Lo sisè seny, lo qual
apel·lam affatus, de Ramon Llull', *Arxiu de Textos Catalans Antics*, 2 (1983), 23–103. For
an explanation of how this theory arises from Llull's moralization of Scholastic physiolo-
gical and ethical doctrines regarding language, see Mark D. Johnston, 'Ramon Llull's
Proposal of Speech as a Sixth Sense', Paper delivered at Twentieth International
Congress on Medieval Studies, Kalamazoo, Mich., 11 May 1985.

question in dispute. The text in fact only gives the Lullist's positions, and ends with a challenge to the Averroist to counter these with opposing statements, if he can.

These syllogisms necessarily expound the maxims of possibility and impossibility because these are the two species of contradiction,

unam intensam per impossibile, aliam extensam per possibile. Per impossibile, quia circa idem non sum ens reale, ut puta: Per impossibile est, quod illud, quod est, non sit, dum est; et quod fuit, non fuerit; et quod album est, dum est album, sit nigrum et e converso; et huiusmodi.

Alia autem species est per possibile; et oritur a prima per accidens. Quae causat entia contraria, sicut est contrarietas inter calidum et frigidum, inter verum et falsum, et huiusmodi. (Prol.; p. 139)

All disagreement arises, Contradiction continues, from confusion of these two species. The principle of non-contradiction is obviously as fundamental for Llull as it is for Aristotle (*Metaph.* 4. 3–4), and he derives contrary from it *per accidens*, perhaps following the Philosopher's explanation (10. 4 1055a33–b17). Llull makes contradiction the source of all the other types of logical opposition that Aristotle defines, but does not rank with respect to one another (*Cat.* 10 11b34–12a25, 12b33–41 and *De interp.* 9 18a28–19b4). Where these types come to form the scheme of the Scholastic square of oppositions, for Llull they form a scale of homologous levels. As noted already, Llull takes possibility and impossibility as the paradigmatic terms of opposition, and employs them to order a hierarchy of ontologically and gnoscologically equivalent elements. And, as also noted earlier, Llull regards any opposition as a union of correlative terms in which one necessarily implies the other. The fact that Llull does not, in effect, distinguish correlation, contradiction, and contrarity as modes of opposition exhibiting different modes of interdependence among their terms constitutes a very broadly moralizing synthesis of all these modes into one great proportional relation.

In the examples cited from the *Liber de possibili et impossibili*, the phrases 'possibility posits' or 'impossibility posits' also correlate with the formulas 'it should be affirmed' and 'it should be denied', following the sequence of correlations that distinguish denying impossible, false, and evil non-being from affirming possible, true, and good being. Affirmation and negation offer the most clearly logical (because most discursive) contributions to these correlations, and this preeminently logical character is evident from this passage in the *Ars generalis ultima* of 1308, where Llull explains that praedicari praedicatum de subjecto affirmando est diffinire subjectum de quo praedicatum praedicatur, existente natura inter subjectum et praedicatum: ut cum dicitur, homo est animal rationale. Quando autem praedicatum praedicatur de homine negative, nulla quidem certitudo sive notitia de homine habetur, ut cum dicitur, homo non est lapis: homo non est planta. Affirmatio enim vera ponit ea quae sunt in subjecto: negatio autem semper removet a subjecto. Falsa quidem similiter habet modum removendi a subjecto. Adhuc quoniam affirmatio praecedit ad negationem, sicut antecedens praecedit ad suum consequens: quare patet quod magis est homo cognoscibilis per affirmationem quam per negationem. (9. 45; p. 419)

This passage is exemplary in its obvious shift from conventional to Lullian doctrine. Llull begins with appeals to Aristotle's precepts that affirmation asserts, while negation denies, one thing of another (*De interp.* 6 17a25), that definitions should not use negations (*Top.* 6. 6 143b36), and that definitions are basic premisses of demonstration (*An. post.* 2. 3 90b23). He then adduces his usual correlations, until he arrives at the claim that affirmation allows more knowledge than negation, a view that fuses its participation in the truth with its role as the necessary positive premiss of understanding. In so far as Llull's doctrine of supposition relies on affirmation, it is a variety of the *via affirmativa*. Llull's careful extrapolation here of Aristotelian precepts into his own positions testifies to the deliberate, as opposed to merely coincidental or nominal, reinterpretations of received doctrine that he is capable of pursuing.

Llull very neatly summarizes all the correlated values of affirmation and negation in his *Liber de affirmatione et negatione*, composed at Messina in 1314. Like so many of his last writings, it is extremely succinct in its exposition of his views. The work has five distinctions whose respective purposes are (1) to prove God's existence, (2) to prove the Trinity, (3) to prove the Incarnation, (4) to prove the Trinity and Incarnation through contradictory syllogisms, and (5) to pose and solve questions regarding these doctrines. The first four distinctions consist entirely in a sort of dialogue between the quasi-allegorical figures of Affirmation and Negation, in which each rather artlessly pronounces its arguments in turn. In the Prologue, Llull calls them 'absolute principles', just as he calls possibility and impossibility 'general principles' in the treatise devoted to them. He describes the two contradictory positions thus:

Verumtamen affirmatio est magis principium absolutum quam negatio. Ratio huius est, quia affirmatio non respicit aliquid super se, quia superius natat, sicut quando dicitur: Homo est animal. Negatio autem respicit super se aliquid, et per hoc inferius natat, sicut quando dicitur: Lapis non est homo. Et dicitur, quod non est homo, per hoc quia homo est animal, et lapis non. (Prol.; p. 21)

It should be noted immediately that Llull's examples are inconsistent with the divisions of the Tree of Porphyry precisely because he is not speaking of higher and lower genera and species, but rather of discrete essential natures from the hierarchy of being. He none the less attempts to equate the former with the latter. Thus, affirmation or negation defines the relative hierarchical position of the being designated by the subject term in a proposition. Llull thus assumes that the opposition of superior to inferior is similar to that of affirmation to negation, although Aristotle distinguishes them (*Cat.* 10 13b1–35).

In the course of the treatise, Llull goes on to adduce various other opposing characteristics for affirmation and negation, as indicated in Table 4. Thus Llull identifies affirmation with being, knowledge,

TABLE 4. *Characteristics of Affirmation and Negation in the* Liber de Affirmatione et Negatione

Affirmatio	Negatio	
Non respicit aliquid super se.	Respicit aliquid super se.	(Prol.)
Superius natat.	Inferius natat.	(Prol.)
Ponit bonum infinitum esse (bonum convenit cum esse).	Ponit nullum bonum infinitum esse (malum convenit cum non esse).	(1. 2)
Est de genere positionis.	Est de genere privationis.	(2. 4)
Positio convenit cum esse.	Privatio convenit cum non esse.	(2. 5)
Principium absolutum positivum.	Principium consecutivum.	(2. 5)
	Est simpliciter contraria affirmationi.	(2. 6)
Velle convenit cum esse.	Nolle convenit cum non esse.	(2. 7)
Principia contraria non possunt esse superius.		(2. 9)
	Est de genere impossibilitatis.	(2. 10)
Habet modum arguendi et generat scientiam.	Non habet modum arguendi et non generat scientiam.	(4.1)
Probat affirmando.	Dicit negando.	(4. 1)
Probat.	Nihil concludit.	(4. 3)

good, proof, and the primacy of the simple highest one over the contingency of the diverse (because contrary) and lower many. One of the striking features of this list is the absence of a strong correlation with possibility and impossibility, which Llull had recognized long before in such early works as the *Lògica del Gatzel* (lines 644–65) and *Proverbis de Ramon* (173. 1). This may be because the subject of this treatise is God, who is in no way possible, but necessary. Also, there is no explicit correlation with truth and falsehood, perhaps because the correlation with superior and inferior levels of being necessarily defines superior truth and inferior error, as Llull suggests (2. 9). Knowledge of what is is the truth, following the Augustinian dictum that the true is that which is. The participational necessity of affirmation and negation in their correlated elements is assumed, and this is why the answer to every one of the questions posed in the Fifth Distinction is simply that Affirmation affirms and Negation denies the question, thereby invoking the entire range of correlated elements.

As in the *Liber de possibili et impossibili*, Llull's dichotomous master terms order the positions presented in each argument. In the First Distinction, for example, Llull describes how 'Affirmation says an infinite Intellect exists. Negation says an infinite Intellect does not exist. And thus Negation posits that ignorance is higher, and knowledge lower; which is false. Therefore it is proven that an infinite Intellect exists, and that God exists.' (1. 6.) One might object to this argument that it extends the category of relation from accidents, such as knowledge or ignorance, to a primary substance, infinite Mind, and that this extended application contradicts Aristotle (*Cat.* 7 8a12–33), although in God all relations are substantial, even if they are not in creatures, as Aquinas explains (1a. 28, 2). Llull's valoration of affirmation and negation not only moralizes these as structures of predication, but also asserts the primacy of the *via affirmativa* over the *via negativa* in theological inquiry. This primacy is broadly the conviction that Llull expresses in his claims to prove the Articles of Faith. Affirmative propositions best serve the announced purpose of his treatise, 'to make knowledge of God' (Prol.), and thereby rectify the soul towards its first intention of knowing, loving, and remembering the Creator. Llull's conception of the positive value of affirmation motivates his efforts to extend that value functionally into all the larger syllogistic and sophistic structures, as the following chapters will show.

17

Syllogistics

SYLLOGISTICS occupies a much more prominent place in the logical programme of Llull's later writings than in that of his earlier works. This increased prominence corresponds to a decreased emphasis on the value of necessary reasons, or rather, more accurately, to an increased identification of syllogistics with necessary reasons; in the same manner Llull increasingly identifies demonstration in the Aristotelian sense with his own conceptions of demonstration. One measure of his new attention to syllogistics is the several works whose titles announce syllogistic arguments: *Liber ad probandum aliquos articulos fidei per syllogisticas rationes* (Genoa, 1304), *Liber de duodecim syllogismis concludentibus duos actus finales, unum intrinsecum, alium extrinsecum* (Montpellier, 1308), *Liber de centum syllogismis* (*Liber contradictionis*) (Paris, 1311), and *Liber de syllogismis contradictionis* (Paris, 1311). This new explicit reference to syllogistics displays well Llull's desire, suggested in Chapter 9, to accommodate his work more to the methods of his Scholastic contemporaries, in the hope of attracting their interest and acceptance. It also creates a new impetus for developing his conceptions, already evident in earlier works, of the syllogism as participated truth and of its use according to his dichotomies of affirmation and negation or possibility and impossibility.

The *Logica nova* testifies to Llull's developments in the first aspects in its various modifications of conventional syllogistic doctrine.[1] As noted in Chapter 13, the Prologue of the Fifth Distinction announces that the subject of the entire distinction will be syllogistics, and five subsequent chapters offer a complete, if somewhat condensed, review of Aristotelian precepts regarding the syllogism: 'On the Constitution

---

[1] In *Raimund Lull* (1. 438–45), Platzeck extrapolates an entire scheme of syllogistic modes from the application to its figures of a *lex luliana* founded on Llull's new fallacy of contradiction (discussed in Chapter 18 below), although Llull nowhere suggests such a scheme himself. While this extrapolation is an interesting exercise, the fact that Llull himself does not pursue it suggests, arguably, that his concerns lie not with formal schemes, but with other problems in the correct use of syllogistic argument.

of the Syllogism', 'On the Comparison of the Syllogism', 'On the Condition of the Syllogism', 'On Deduction of the Syllogism through the *Regulae*', and 'On the Figures of the Syllogism' are the titles of Chapters Ten to Fourteen in the edition of 1744. These correspond in part to similar sections of Llull's early *Logica Algazelis*. Unlike that first 'compendium', however, the *Logica nova* creates a much more heterogeneous mix of peculiarly Lullian and conventional doctrine in its attempt to introduce the former within the system of the latter.

An example of the received theory in the *Logica nova* is Llull's short enumeration of the three syllogistic figures, which is completely orthodox, as in the *Lògica del Gatzel* (lines 1259–1376). In fact, he justifies its brevity by concluding that 'the ancients have treated it at length'. In presenting another aspect of conventional doctrine, however, Llull is less faithful to standard terminology: he identifies the four types of argument as 'integral, particular, inductive, and exemplary' in his chapter on constitution of the syllogism (5. 10). Since the integral is the perfect syllogism, and the inductive and exemplary are obviously induction and *exemplum*, the particular should be the enthymeme, in order to complete the scheme described by Peter of Spain (5. 3). However, it is induction, not the enthymeme, that argues from particulars, and Llull's example of 'some man runs, therefore Peter runs', is apparently a truncated version of the example of induction from the *Summule*. Llull also modifies the received divisions of argument in the Prologue to the Fifth Distinction, where he calls it a genus with true and false species; since he identifies the syllogism as the true species, the other three types presumably comprise the false. Peter of Spain, however, merely calls them 'deficient' instruments of disputation (7. 3), and Algazel describes them as instruments of persuasion, but not strictly false, in his *Logic* (4. 334–67). Llull's division of the false perhaps recalls Algazel's distinction between correct (true) and incorrect (false) syllogisms, which he mentions when defining argumentation (Proem. 65–8).

In other passages, Llull somewhat abruptly collocates his own precepts with conventional doctrine. In the short chapter on syllogistic conditions (5. 12), he reiterates the sections of his *Lògica del Gatzel* (lines 505–16, 436–67) regarding correct construction of a syllogism, but begins the chapter by defining condition as the 'form because of which many things consist conditioned necessarily all at once (*simul et semel*)', and prefaces the second section with the rule that 'the Intellect should rest in [the syllogism] by understanding'. The latter comment expresses Llull's identification of the syllogism as a true object sought by the mind, and the former represents his attempt to define the syllogism metaphysically as an *ens rationis* that realizes knowledge participationally in the mind.

This metaphysical definition is the explicit concern of several precepts that appear in Chapter One 'On the Proposition', which begins by defining propositions composed of true words as the matter of the syllogism, according to Aristotle's famous analogy (*Phys.* 2. 3 195a18). After enumerating the thirteen modes of propositions defined by Algazel (*Log.* 4. 532–675) and repeated in his *Lògica del Gatzel* (lines 358-99), Llull adds:

Propositionum alia maior, alia minor in sillogismo: Maior sicut 'omne animal est substantia', minor 'omnis homo est animal'. Et dicitur maior quia causat minorem, cum maior sit antecedens et minor consequens in conclusione, scilicet, 'omnis homo est substantia'. Propositionum alia per se nota, alia dubitativa: per se nota est 'Omne animal est substantia', dubitativa ut 'curritne Petrus?' Prima est materia solutionis questionis, secunda est materia questionis. In sillogismo maior propositio causat minorem. Et in simul causant conclusionem. Conclusio vero causat premissas formaliter eo quod ipsas deducit in formam sillogismi sive in essentiam, quoniam sine conclusione non essent in sillogismo. In sillogismo propositiones differunt invicem, eo quod una propositio est una ratio in ipso et alia propositio est una ratio et in simul sunt essentia sillogismi. (1. 1. 17–19; f. 77ra; p. 80)

In this passage, Llull distinguishes 'materially' between a proposition as premiss and as question, where Peter of Spain simply says that a proposition, conclusion, and question are the same 'substantially', but different in principle (*ratio*) or definition (5. 4); there is no basis for Llull's distinction in Algazel's *Logic* (cf. 4. 45–50 and 5. 141–3) and it does not appear in the *Lògica del Gatzel*. On the other hand, the notion of the simultaneous union of the premisses in the conclusion is an Aristotelian axiom (*An. pr.* 1. 1 24b16–26) and thus appears in Algazel (ibid.) or Peter of Spain (4. 2) and in Llull's own *Lògica del Gatzel* (lines 452–7), but without any reference to the essence of the syllogism. The view of the conclusion as the formal cause of the premisses appears in Averroes' commentary on the *Physics*.[2] Llull's treatment thus reflects somewhat disjointedly his increasingly metaphysical conception of the syllogism as an intelligible object governed by the same laws of being as other *entia rationis*.

---

[2] Cited in Ockham, *Summa logicae*, p. 531.

In describing the metaphysical constituents of the syllogism, Llull simply attempts to develop Aristotle's own suggestion, just as do Aquinas (*In 2 Phys.* 5. 184–5) and Ockham (3–2. 15). But where Llull's Scholastic contemporaries seek to interpret the material, formal, or final causes involved in the constitution of a syllogism as contributions to its function as a verbal construct, Llull adduces participational causes in order to explain its validity. This is obvious in his reference to the 'major antecedent' that causes the 'minor consequent', just as he explains in Chapter 10 that the inductive syllogism 'man, lion, and other animals entered Noah's Art, therefore all animals entered Noah's Ark', functions because of the 'great agreement (*convenientiam*) that exists between the antecedent and consequent' (5. 10. 5). It is tempting to regard this agreement as the same sort of collective apprehension of a universal from particulars described in the *Liber de significatione*. These examples also illustrate, it is worth noting, how Llull uses 'antecedent' and 'consequent' in a broadly relational sense, rather than as names of the parts of a hypothetical proposition, although his usage here perhaps reflects Aristotle's references to the conclusion as 'consequence' of the premises (*An. pr.* 1. 1 24b21). Llull's participational conception of the relationship between propositions is patent in his example of a syllogism based on *exemplum*: 'just as finite act pertains to every finite being, so infinite act pertains to every infinite being and this syllogism is made through the great likeness between one proposition and the other' (5. 10. 6). The example chosen describes itself the analogical relationships that realize the participation by likeness suggested in Llull's explanation. In his *Liber de praedicatione* of 1304, Llull offers an especially remarkable trinitarian analogy regarding the metaphysical constitution of the syllogism: 'Supposed that the syllogism were a substance and an eternal, infinite being, it would rightly be compared to the Trinity; because in it the minor is from the major, and the conclusion issues from the major and minor' (2. A. 6). This analogy is especially valuable because it describes the syllogistic entity by direct reference to the Divine essence that is the paradigm of Llull's entire metaphysics of coessentiality. Like any being, the syllogism must repeat the metaphysical structure of the Godhead in its own and participate in the Absolute and Relative *Principia* as its constitutive principles. In the chapter of the *Logica nova* devoted to deducing the syllogism from Llull's *Regulae*, many of the precepts attempt to define the syllogistic essence: it exists from itself and formally from the premisses and conclusion that are its coessential

principles; from itself it has continuous quantity, and from its propositions discrete quantity; it is either potential or actual; it exists in the
mode of its parts, which are words and propositions (5. 13. C2, F1, H,
K1). The view that the syllogism does not function only through causal
relations between its terms, but rather through an essence that it
realizes actively in its complete existence seems to refuse Aristotle's
precept that the definition of a syllogism's form is not a premiss of
syllogizing itself (*An. post.* 2. 6 92a12-19). Llull's conception of a
syllogism's essence is partly possible, however, precisely because he
does not understand the relationship between terms causally, as this
passage suggests:

Sillogismus fit coniungendo suas coessentiales dicciones ut ex ipsis sint
propositiones et ut ex propositionibus sit sillogismus, dicendo sic: substantia,
animal, homo. Sunt dicciones sillogismi, et quando coniunguntur, est ex ipsis
propositio, sicut 'omnis homo est substantia'. Et quando propositiones coniunguntur invicem sequitur sillogismus, dicendo sic 'Omne animal est substantia;
omnis homo est animal; ergo omnis homo est substantia.' Adhuc fit sillogismus
ponendo suas proprias dicciones in tribus gradibus in arbore significatis,
scilicet in genere, specie et individuo, distinguendo genus cum differentia ut
genus sub se plures species habeat. Et sic de specie, ut species per differen-
tiam et proprietatem habeat sub se plura individua. (5. 10. 1–2; f. 78rb; p. 87)

The noteworthy terms here are 'coessential' and 'proper', which
describe for Llull not only the relationship between subject and
predicate, but also the essential and proper truth of the syllogism as an
expression of that relationship. Llull's references to placing the terms
of a syllogism in the three levels of being from the 'tree' and to the
plural divisions of genera and species suggest that for Llull the syllogism functions primarily as a means of relating the many to the one or
particulars to universals, and thereby serves the structure of his entire
Art. It also seems to ignore Aristotle's rejection of an infinite series of
substantial (and causal) predications (*An. post.* 1. 22 83b2) in favour of
predication that traces participation through likenesses in the infinite
plenitude of the hierarchy of being. Llull's hierarchical conception of
the divisions of subaltern genera and species is implicit in the chapter
on Logic from his *Ars generalis ultima*, where he refers to them as
'making a predicate of the superior from the inferior' (10. 101).

Llull clearly defines the status of the entire syllogism hierarchically,
and thereby reinforces his conception of it as an *ens rationis* participating truth, in the first paragraph of his chapter on deducing the
syllogism from his *Regulae*. He declares that some syllogisms are truer

and more necessary than others, a view that is patently non-Aristotelian (*Top.* 1. 1), in so far as it applies to demonstrative syllogisms. The less true he illustrates with the standard example of 'Every animal is a substance, etc.' and the truer with 'Whenever there is infinite *Potestas*, there is infinite act of *Potestas*; but in God there is infinite *Potestas*, therefore in God there is infinite act of *Potestas*.' (5. 13. B.) The latter is truer because its subject is infinite, the former less true because its subject finite. This claim displays very well the material character of Llull's Logic, in which the formal value of terms results from their participation in the truth and necessity of the Absolute *Principia*. This participation ultimately renders formal structures superfluous, as Llull in fact suggests in the *Ars generalis ultima*, when he claims that his artist mixes *Principia* and *Regulae*, instead of joining two premisses like a logician, in order to reach a conclusion (10. 101). Llull's example of a true syllogism illustrates the syllogizing practice that his theories of syllogistic essence seek to justify. Much better than they, however, it shows very clearly how Llull mitigates the syllogism's function as an instrument of ratiocination by emphasizing its objective status as an *ens rationis* defined, like any being, through the metaphysics of Llull's own *Art*.

Degrees of the syllogism

Llull's examples of truer and less true syllogisms also provide the basis for a wholly moralizing account of syllogistics in his Chapter 11, 'On the Comparison of Syllogisms'. He proposes that, just as the grammarian recognizes three degrees of comparison for the genus 'good', so the logician should recognize three degrees in the genus 'true', and compare the corresponding true syllogisms:

Sillogismus verus est quando fit de aliqua propositione necessaria et de aliqua non necessaria sicut 'Omne animal est substantia; omnis scriptor est animal; ergo omnis scriptor est substantia.'

Secundus gradus est quando fit propositio de una diccione sensuali et de alia spirituali sicut quando dicitur 'Ubicumque corpus et anima rationalis coniunguntur est homo; sed in specie humana corpus et anima rationalis coniunguntur ad invicem; ergo in specie humana est homo.' Et iste sillogismus est verior quam primus eo quod est ex propositionibus necessariis simpliciter. Sillogismus autem primus non simpliciter sed secundum quid.

Tertius gradus est quando fit sillogismus de propositionibus spiritualibus simpliciter dicendo sic 'In omni essentia in qua est intelligere est intellectivum et intelligibile; in essentia angeli est intelligere; ergo in essentia angelis est intellectivum et intelligibile.' Iste sillogismus est verissimus et est in superlativo gradu gratia essentie spiritualis in qua plus de veritate consistit quam in essentia corporali. (5. 11; f. 78va; pp. 88–9)

The triad of positive, comparative, and superlative degrees is one of Llull's favourite hierarchical patterns,[3] and he employs it in other works to organize schemes of proportional elements. Here he adds a fourth, higher degree of syllogism composed of 'infinite' propositions: 'In every essence in which there is infinite *Potestas*, there is infinite act of *Potestas*, or *possificare*; in God's essence is infinite *Potestas*; therefore in God is infinite *possificare*.' (Ibid.) The degree of truth in each syllogism from this scheme depends on the rank in the hierarchy of being of the thing signified by its terms or propositions, which participate the truth of that being as their cause. Llull's varying references to both corporeal and spiritual terms and necessary, spiritual, and infinite propositions is symptomatic of the conflict between a conventional conception of the syllogism as a composite instrument and Llull's treatment of it as a whole participated truth. That Llull imagines a hierarchy and participation of terms rather than of propositions is evident in his explanation that 'comparison' is only valid among beings 'that agree (*se conveniant*) in some common thing, as when one says "water is colder than earth" but cannot say "water is colder than white" ' (5. 11. 5). In this respect, Llull's comparison probably recalls the logical comparison or analysis of subject-predicate relations described by Algazel (*Log.* 2. 5–11) or Peter of Spain (6. 11; 7. 107; 12. 6), and invoked by Llull in various other works.

Llull elaborates a somewhat more motley version of this same scheme in his *Liber de modo naturali intelligendi* (94. 3) of 1310. There he divides the positive degree into an opinative mode based on supposition or belief and non-necessary propositions extraneous to true understanding, and a non-convertible mode where the subject and predicate are relatively superior or inferior, as in 'Every animal is a substance; every man is an animal; every man is a substance.' These opinative and non-convertible modes apparently separate out the non-necessary and necessary propositions employed in the positive degree of the scheme from the *Logica nova*. The comparative degree is 'more

---

[3] Llull's frequent application of this scheme for ordering various logical elements suggests that it is not the foundation of a particular theory of demonstration, as Platzeck seems to regard it: 'La combinatoria luliana', pp. 598–600. Platzeck's argument that Llull's three degrees derive from the Scholastic *grammatica speculativa* has little basis in its doctrines; on these see Geoffrey Bursill-Hall, *Speculative Grammars of the Middle Ages* (Paris & The Hague: Mouton, 1971).

assertive' and uses inferior things as very disparate (*separatae*) extreme terms, as in 'No man is a stone; everything capable of laughter is a man; nothing capable of laughter is a stone.' Why this is more assertive than the first degree is not clear, except in so far as its conclusion asserts a more disparate attribution or comparison of subject and predicate. The superlative degree employs convertible subjects and predicates, which Llull illustrates with the Divine Dignities, and these provide 'infinitely distant' extreme terms. This example usefully reminds us that for Llull the paradigm of conversion of subject and predicate is always the coessential interchangeability of the Divine Dignities.

Finally, Llull applies his scheme of degrees to enthymemes as well as syllogisms in the *Ars mystica* of 1309. Here he distinguishes the positive degree when subjects of the one premiss and the conclusion are not convertible, the comparative degree when they do, and the superlative when the subjects are superlative and convertible; an example of the latter is 'si creator creatissimus est, creatura creatissima est' (3. 3. Intro.). He illustrates the positive degree with an example, 'If Socrates runs, man runs', that recalls those found in Peter of Spain (5. 13), but is in fact a fallacy from consequent for Peter (7. 154). Llull explains the faulty reasoning as lack of convertibility, which again suggests how he opposes the inferior exclusive class relationships among individuals, species, and genera to the superior inclusive relationships among the Divine Dignities.

The reference to corporeal and spiritual propositions in the example of Llull's scheme of degrees from the *Logica nova* also suggests how Llull's hierarchical classifications of syllogisms assume his basic distinction between an inferior, external mode of knowledge through the Senses, and a superior, internal mode through the Intellect alone. The value of the latter mode necessarily depends on Llull's conception of the illumination of the Intellect and the mind's participation in truth. He applies this more basic distinction to the syllogism in the Prologue to his *Liber de vita divina*, composed at Messina in 1314. There he proposes 'Since the syllogism is a brief speech and invention (*brevis oratio et inventio*), we intend to find the Divine Trinity syllogizing. And because from those things that are inferior, demonstrative syllogisms can be made, much more so can they be made from those things that are superior.' (Prol.) This argument, which is in fact an example of the topic from lesser to greater (discussed below), establishes the proportional character of his scheme, which he continues to develop thus:

Syllogismus, qui est ab inferius, ostenditur sic: Ubicumque sunt sex, sunt quattuor et duo. Sed in quinque et uno sunt sex; ergo in quinque et uno sunt quattuor et duo. Syllogismus iste est demonstrativus et necessarius, per hoc quia quattuor et duo convertuntur cum quinque et uno, et nihil superius et nihil inferius, sed per aequale . . .

Syllogismus, qui est a superius demonstrativus, sic ostenditur: Omne ens infinitum vivens vivit cum infinito vivere. Deus est ens infinitum vivens; ergo Deus vivit cum infinito vivere. Iste syllogismus est demonstrativus et necessarius, per hoc quia nihil est superius neque inferius, sed per aequale. (Prol.; pp. 75–6)

Llull's definition of the syllogism as a 'brief speech and invention' is highly idiosyncratic and perhaps reflects his attribution to it of the inventional and compendious qualities of his own *Art*. Llull's use of numbers as an example distantly recalls a model of fallacy from division in Peter of Spain (7. 75). It apparently alludes to the Aristotelian view of mathematical principles such as unit and magnitude as indemonstrable basic truths (*An. post.* I. 10 76a35).

Hence, Llull's superior syllogism about divine life becomes more demonstrative than the indemonstrable. In the *Liber de fide sancta catholica* he declares that God is more necessary and demonstrable than any mathematical demonstration (Prol.), which relies on the Senses and Imagination, according to the *Liber de modo naturali intelligendi* (6. Prol.). Llull chooses numbers, however, chiefly in order to argue the demonstrability of conversion in the superior Godhead by analogy with the demonstrability of conversion among inferior equal units. God is most demonstrable for Llull, as he argues in his early *Libre de demostracions* (4. 6, 13), and the formal value of any syllogism depends for him on the hierarchically defined degree of demonstrability enjoyed by the subjects in its premisses.

Topics

Before leaving the aspects of syllogistics treated in the Fifth Distinction of the *Logica nova*, it would be a great oversight not to mention that it includes one of Llull's very rare references to the topics, which were a major component of Scholastic Logic,[4] but do not typically appear in his programme. Chapter 5 is entitled 'On the topics', but treats only the topic 'from greater to lesser'; Chapter 6 treats 'from lesser to greater', and Chapter 7 'from equal to equal'. Since the first

---

[4] See Otto Bird, 'The Tradition of the Logical Topics: Aristotle to Ockham', *Journal of the History of Ideas*, 23 (1962), 307–23.

two correspond to the topics of the same name in Peter of Spain (5. 32), the third probably corresponds to his topic 'from similarity', which follows immediately in the *Summule* (5. 33). The first two concern the relative power or force (*in potentia vel in virtute*) of things, according to Peter of Spain, and Llull follows this interpretation for all three topics, in order to apply them to questions concerning God's absolute power: if God can act infinitely, so also he can finitely; if man is naturally great, so God must be naturally greater; if man can equally love and know God, so his Will and Intellect must be equal. Llull offers other, more natural examples based on the four elements and on those used by Peter of Spain: whatever can conquer a great army can also a smaller one; if a soldier can give a horse, so can a king. In his brief *Liber de minori loco ad maiorem* (Messina, 1313), Llull correlates this topic with the first two degrees in his favoured scheme of positive, comparative, and superlative degrees. He cites there the example of the soldier, horse, and king as 'true, necessary, and primary', arguing that it must be so because otherwise the hierarchical order of inferior and superior would be destroyed (Prol.). The import of this appeal to proportion in the natural order of the universe scarcely requires comment. In the body of the work, however, he proves the Trinity and Incarnation with arguments using these two schemes:

Si durans minus durans agit minus duratum, magis durans agit magis duratum. Et si magis durans agit magis duratum, multo magis aeternans magis aeternatum; et hoc sine tempore. Hoc autem esse non potest sine aeternare. Et ista tria correlativa singularia divinam trinitatem vocamus. . . .

Si anima rationalis, quae est nova potest recipere corpus humanum, natura divina, quae est aeterna, potest assumere corpus humanum aeternatum. (1. 4 and 2. 4; pp. 271, 274)

The deduction of Llull's correlatives from the topic of lesser to greater in the proof of the Trinity is an excellent example of how he conflates relational arguments as mutually supportive necessary reasons that each effectively moralizes the other as its validation or proof. Llull incorporates the topic of 'lesser to greater' in a similar manner in his *Liber de accidente et substantia* of 1313 as well.

The echoes of standard examples in both the *Logica nova* and *Liber de minori loco ad maiorem* imply that Llull knew some standard account of the topics, and his inclusion of them in the *Logica nova* shows that he recognized their logical function. Still, he never offers any systematic survey of them, and this oversight in the work of a writer so diligently compendious is puzzling. Their absence in Algazels' *Logic* perhaps influenced Llull, and there remains, of course, the undeniable coincidence between many of the topics and Llull's favourite necessary reasons based on proportion, resemblance, or analogy, but it is impossible to know whether he himself recognized this affinity or with what response.

This concludes the survey of syllogistic doctrine presented in the Fifth Distinction of the *Logica nova*. In general, it offers a hybrid collection of conventional precepts and Lullian revisions or moralizations that are chiefly notable for their expression of his view of the syllogism as participated truth. His comments do not develop a fully adequate account of how this participation functions in the syllogism's essence, but they perhaps represent the most sophisticated explanation that Llull was able or willing to offer. His scheme of degrees evidently represents an effort to discriminate between the value of Aristotelian syllogistics and his own superior modes of demonstration, although the mere hierarchical ranking of various modes still seems incapable of adequately relating his own forms of argument to the Peripatetic doctrines followed by his Scholastic contemporaries. In any case, none of his later works discuss syllogistics in equal detail, in part because their focus of attention shifts after 1310 to Llull's use of 'contradictory syllogisms', which he proclaims as a new mode of demonstration.

Contradictory syllogisms

This new method involves no special modifications of syllogistic structure (which is not to say that Llull always constructs formally perfect syllogisms), but rather extends to the entire syllogism as one statement the oppositions between propositions that affirm possible, true, good being or deny impossible, false, evil, non-being. The genesis of Llull's new method in this opposition is explicit in his *Liber contradictionis* of 1311, where the allegorical figure of Contradiction defines her two species as possibility and impossibility (Prol.), and asks the contending Lullist and Averroist to syllogize opposing positions from the hundred maxims in the *Liber de possibili et impossibili*. Since the real importance of Llull's procedure lies in the relationship that it assumes between the use of opposing positions and the psychological mechanisms of demonstration, it will be discussed more fully in Chapter 19. Here it is pertinent to note that most of Llull's works after 1311 employ his new method and to consider some examples of its use.

In the *Liber de syllogismis contradictoriis* (1311), a sequel to the *Liber contradictionis* that specifically proposes to illustrate his new method,

Llull offers his most illuminating comments on and examples of the logical validity of his procedure. The work consists in three distinctions: in the first Llull makes 'proposition against proposition, syllogism against syllogism, consequence against consequence, predicating in the superlative degree, affirming and denying through the ten Divine Dignities' (Prol.). In the second distinction, Llull applies the consequences of these syllogisms to forty-four 'Averroist' positions. A brief Third Distinction offers combinations of the first syllogism with each of the other nine. Thus the syllogisms themselves, most of which are completely valid from a formal standpoint, comprise the smaller part of Llull's overall argumentation in the treatise, and it is indeed the application of their 'positions' and 'consequences' in the Second Distinction that presents the most problematic aspects of Llull's arguments.

The First Distinction presents the ten predications about the Divine Dignities—such as 'Divine *Bonitas* is optimal', 'Divine *Magnitudo* is maximal', and so forth—that are 'primary, true, and necessary' if one assumes that God exists with all his due powers. Not even God can 'impede or destroy' these propositions, because that would be contrary to his end. The latter claim obviously raises important claims regarding God's freedom that are, for Llull, non-problematic, and the conditions of the certainity of this knowledge do not preoccupy him, either. He is instead concerned to argue, analogically, that since God cannot destroy these propositions, no one or thing else can either:

Et hoc patet per istos duos syllogismos demonstrativos primitivos, veros et necessarios.

Omne ens magis agens agit propter maiorem finem. Deus est ens magis agens; ergo Deus agit propter maiorem finem.

Omne ens magis bonum potest magis agere bonum, quam ens minus bonum recipere. Forma est ens magis bonum quam materia; ergo forma potest magis agere bonum, quam materia recipere. Isti syllogismi sunt impugnabiles, eo quia primitivi, veri et necessarii. (1. Prol.; p. 173)

The second syllogism assumes the reality of subsistent forms as beings in its minor premiss, which obviously requires no little further proof itself. Llull concludes from these syllogisms the 'consequence' that God can do more in creation than creation can naturally receive, which proves his original claim that since God cannot destroy the ten predications about his Dignities, no creature can either. Thus Llull offers his predications about the perfection of the Divine Dignities—in themselves probably indisputable, as Aquinas would allow (1a. 4, 2; 6,

2; 11, 4)— within the context of other claims that his contemporaries would certainly challenge vigorously. Whether Llull recognizes such claims as disputable, or disputable in the same degree as the 'Averroist' propositions that he himself attacks, is probably impossible to determine, in part because his arguments for some—such as the real existence of the predicables and categories—inevitably invoke others —such as universal hylemorphism—as their first principles. This inseparable matrix of values may well have comprised in its apparently self-evident mutual proof the grounds for Llull's conviction of its truth.

None the less, despite the fact that this complex of disputable tenets surrounds Llull's ten predications in the First Distinction, the opposing syllogisms that he constructs from them are largely indisputable in themselves. They all follow an identical format, exemplified in the first, which concerns *Bonitas*:

Divina bonitas est optima. Omne ens, existens bonitas optima, existit et agit optime. Deus est bonitas optima; ergo Deus existit et agit optime. Ad consequentiam istius syllogismi sequitur, quod non est aliquod ens, quod possit resistere Deo, quin sit ens optime existens et agens . . .

In oppositum arguitur sic:

Divina bonitas non est optima. Quodcumque non est bonitas optima, non potest optime existere et agere. Deus non est bonitas optima; ergo Deus non potest optime existere et agere. Ad consequentiam istius syllogismi sequitur, quod sit, aliquod ens impediens, quod Deus non possit existere et agere optime . . . Cum autem iste syllogismus sit falsus et erroneus, necessarie sequitur, quod syllogismus in oppositum sit verus et necessarium. (1. 1; p. 173)

For each syllogism, the predication about a Divine Dignity evidently appears first as simply an introduction; otherwise its restatement as a premiss of the syllogism would be superfluous. The purpose of these syllogisms is not entirely clear. Llull has, after all, already proven that the predication underlying the first syllogism could not be impeded or destroyed, even by God. What then is the reason for constructing syllogisms based on that predication or its opposite? One answer is that Llull's presentation of these predications in syllogisms gives them the trappings or appearance of demonstrated truth—in these cases, something like Aristotle's reduction to impossibility (*An. pr.* 1. 29 45a23)—that Llull's contemporaries commonly employed. In this respect, Llull's use of 'contradictory syllogisms' is simply a means of restating demonstratively the tenets that he previously proved through his necessary reasons. Another answer, though, lies in his application of these syllogisms to the forty-four 'Averroist' positions presented in the Second Distinction.

This application is extremely diverse in character and rarely involves a strictly logical deduction from, or reduction to, the ten syllogisms presented in the First Distinction. These ten and their opposites instead stand as paradigms of the opposition between affirming possibility and denying impossibility, to which Llull refers each Averroist position by moralizing it as a psychological, ethical, logical, or metaphysical correlate of denying impossibility. Thus he rejects the first position, that God does not have infinite power (*vigor*), because any quick, well-founded, wise and pure Intellect that discourses through the ten syllogisms knows that God has infinite power, and any that judges otherwise is perverse and unwise (2. 1). This is moralization in a literal ethico-theological sense, and it is patent that the operative assumption of this argument is the *rectitudo* that founds the affirmation of possibility in Llull's views. Likewise, he rejects the second position, that God is not triune, by arguing that just as primary matter is potentially receptive of all forms, so if God is not triune, his *Bonitas* is only potentially optimal, optimalized, and optimalizing (its three Lullian correlatives), which contradicts the first syllogism given above (2. 2). The operative assumptions here are obviously the very disputable, and imperfect, analogy between primary matter and form and God and his goodness, and the distinction between his goodness and its co-essential optimal realization. It would be tedious to enumerate all the analogies that Llull employs in moralizing the Averroist positions as correlates of his impossible syllogisms. In some cases, he refers only indirectly to the syllogisms (e.g. 2. 13, 38, 42); in many others, he merely states that an argument agrees with the ten true syllogisms or ten false syllogisms (e.g. 2. 5, 8, 12, 15).

More interesting are the instances where he refers to the role of the Intellect that is 'well-considering' (2. 2), 'benevolent' (2. 3), functioning 'according to the mode of understanding' (2. 5), 'reasonable' (2. 16, 29), or 'sinful and perverse' (2. 32), 'base' (2. 33), and so forth. These qualifications obviously testify to the identification of good will and true understanding that founds Llull's entire opposition between affirming possibility and denying impossibility, and the 'contradictory syllogisms' derived from it. Taken broadly, they all comprise applications of his doctrine of supposition. Llull accuses the Averroist of using only inferior possibilities and impossibilities, while he uses superior ones (2. 42–4), a claim that implies the universal role of the

Principia as participated foundations of Llull's arguments. He also asserts in the treatise's epilogue that no religion can posit syllogisms as true, primary, and necessary, as those of Christian doctrine. Any claim to the contrary uses the term 'understanding' equivocally, Llull declares, because it fails to distinguish between an inferior, external mode of understanding, and a superior, internal mode. The former is, of course, the Averroist's, and the latter, Llull's. Thus Llull's new mode of demonstration through contradictory syllogisms relies directly on the psychological and gnoseological tenets of his conception of the relationship between faith and reason. It is thus not surprising to see Llull conclude this treatise with the same arguments regarding the 'greater benefits' of the Christian religion that he employed in earlier treatments of the faith and understanding made possible by affirmation (e.g. *Libre de demostracions*, 1. 45). The interest of this new mode in Llull's overall logical programme is the real effort that it suggests on his part to accommodate his own use of necessary reasons, and notions regarding the affirmation of possibility as a basis for faith, to conventional syllogistic argument. This accommodation serves to restate Llull's doctrines in syllogistic form, but also offers, in a moralizing fashion, the use of syllogistic argument as a sort of *exemplum* of demonstrative truth that buttresses the truths of Llull's own philosophy.

18

Sophistics

JUST as Llull gives more attention to syllogistics in his later period, so he does to the fallacies, and with similar results: references to them appear in the titles of various works, and he eventually proposes a new mode of fallacy from contradiction. But where his attention to syllogistics only affects its formal principles in his attempt to define syllogistic structure metaphysically as an essence participating truth, his accounts of the fallacies come to include very detailed and exhaustive considerations of their specific formal features. These considerations ultimately attempt to assimilate Aristotelian teaching on the function of contradiction in refutation to Llull's own opposition between affirming possibility and denying impossibility, which he never applies to the composition of a syllogism from its premisses. Llull's application of his basic dichotomy to the fallacies represents an effort to impose the *rectitudo* that sustains it upon Scholastic modes of argument, and thereby render them incapable of serving as vehicles for propounding false doctrines. Llull's new fallacy of contradiction in fact argues that the assertion of separate philosophical and theological truths is itself a fallacy, because it allows contradiction. Llull's attempt to remedy the misuse of Logic by his contemporaries develops in stages from a simple reiteration of conventional doctrine to full-fledged exposition of his new fallacy of contradiction. This chapter attempts to trace those stages.

The point of departure for this development is Llull's treatment of the fallacies in Chapters 17 to 32 of the Fifth Distinction of the *Logica nova*, which are remarkable as one of the least original portions of that treatise. As in his *Lògica del Gatzel*, Llull includes a summary of both Algazel's ten conditions of sophistic syllogizing and some Latin authority's account of the thirteen Aristotelian fallacies. The summary of Algazel (*Log.* 4. 744–804) in Chapter 17 does display a dubious sort of originality in its further deviations from the Arab's precepts, probably by adapting Llull's previous treatment in the *Lògica del Gatzel* (lines 1177–1258). For example, Algazel's third mode warns against diversity in the extreme terms of a syllogism (4. 765); the *Lògica del Gatzel* says not to add a term to the major and minor (lines 1195–6); the *Logica nova* cautions against an unequal middle term (17. 3). Or, Algazel's eighth mode proscribes using a question as a premiss (4. 794); the *Lògica del Gatzel* advises not to use a conclusion as a premiss (lines 1235–6); the *Logica nova* warns against a conclusion composed of improper terms (17. 9). There is no apparent rationale or purpose underlying these further departures from Algazel's precepts, and they offer a signal example of the mutations that received doctrine can undergo in Llull's hands. The best explanation for most of these changes is that they mix parts among the ten precepts, perhaps because of Llull's inadequate perception of their individual concerns. Conversely, his remarks in Chapters 18 to 32 offer a very close, though condensed, version of the same doctrine found in Peter of Spain (7. 22–178). A few differences in terminology and classification suggest that Llull has followed some text other than Peter's. For example, Llull notes that the second mode of the fallacy of equivocation relies on a term used *metaphorice sive transumptive*, where Peter says *per prius et posterius* and *transumptive* (7. 57, 73, 78). Llull's classification agrees in these cases with that of Vincent of Beauvais (*SD* 3. 93), whose remarks are none the less far too abbreviated to have served as Llull's immediate source. Llull illustrates each fallacy with adequate examples, usually the standard Aristotelian ones employed by Peter of Spain, but does not imitate Peter's lengthy digressions on the relative classification of certain fallacies and their reliance on various *modi significandi*. Llull's use of the latter term in his remarks on fallacy from form of expression (5. 24) is notable as one of the very few acknowledgements of modistic or terminist doctrine in his work. His more or less faithful summary of received doctrine regarding the thirteen fallacies is important, then, as a standard of comparison for his later more unusual interpretations of them.

Fallacy of contradiction

In the last chapter of the Fifth Distinction of the *Logica nova*, Llull introduces one of his most remarkable and idiosyncratic doctrines, his new 'fallacy of contradiction'. He claims that this new fallacy depends on the eight modes of apparent contradiction that he repeats from Algazel (*Logic* 3. 149–86) in his first chapter on propositions. This is indeed true in some cases, while in others Llull in fact seems to adapt types of fallacy described in Aristotle's *Topics* and *Sophistical Refu-*

tations. Thus, from its very inception, Llull's new fallacy has an obvious basis in received doctrine. While Llull offers fairly conventional examples for each mode of his new fallacy, he does so in the single unusual form to be commented below. First, it is desirable to examine each mode in detail, in order to see how Llull treats it as fundamentally a problem of equivocation, whose opposing senses he dubs a contradiction.

The first mode is equivocation itself, as in the syllogism 'Every ram is edible; some ram is not edible; therefore some ram is edible and not edible.' The equivocation arises because 'the ram eating grass is edible, the constellation Ram is not' (5. 33. 2). This example adapts one used to illustrate equivocation in both Peter of Spain (7. 30) and Algazel's *Logic* (3. 155–8), but relies on a wholly implicit reference to the zodiacal ram, just as Algazel's example does; this use of implicit multivocity further suggests Llull's debt to the Arab's 'apparent contradictions'.

The second mode occurs through intrinsic and extrinsic habits, as in the syllogism 'No stone is visible; some stone is visible; therefore some stone is visible and not visible.' Llull explains that 'a stone in itself is not visible . . . but is visible through the visual sense, which in its proper, coessential visible imprints and shapes the visibility of the stone anew' (5. 33. 3). A similar type of situation appears in examples given by Aristotle (*Top.* 5. 8 138b27–139a8; 6. 6 145a35–b11) and by Peter of Spain when he treats fallacy from form of expression (7. 86).

The third mode results from the presence or absence of the Senses, as indicated in the syllogism 'Every man is imaginable; some man is not imaginable; therefore some man is imaginable and not imaginable.' This is because 'all men are imaginable in the absence of the sense of sight, but not in its presence, because that which is perceived in the present by the eyes is not then apprehended in the Imagination' (5. 33. 4). This reflects Aristotle's teaching in his *On the Soul* (3. 3 428a4–429a8) and a parallel example appears in the *Topics* (5. 8 138b27–139a8).

The fourth mode combines equivocation and the fallacy *secundum quid et simpliciter* (terms applied in a qualified and absolute sense), as in the syllogism 'No man is visible; some man is visible; therefore some man is visible and not visible.' (5. 33. 5.) According to Llull, 'the true man is not visible just as a dead man is not dead, since just as man does not die except bodily, so the true man is not seen except in shape and colour. The man however painted on a wall is put in the species man equivocally, absolutely because of shape and colour, but not essentially.' The latter example of equivocation comes from Aristotle's *Categories* (1 1a3) and has a parallel (along with the example of the dead man) in Peter of Spain's illustration of fallacy *secundum quid et simpliciter* (7. 120, 122, 126). Llull also cites it in his remarks on the Subject of man in the First Distinction (1. 5), discussed above. Aristotle also notes in the *Topics* (4. 5 126a22–5) that only the body, not the soul, of an animal is visible.

The fifth mode of Llull's new fallacy involves existence and agency, as in the syllogism 'All honey is sweet; some honey is not sweet; therefore it is and is not sweet.' (5. 33. 6.) Llull simply observes that 'honey is essentially sweet, but seems bitter to the taste of one who is ill'. This explanation comes from Aristotle's *On the Soul* (2. 10 422b8), and the Philosopher discusses the unreliability of the senses in the *Topics* (5. 3 131b19–37). Llull's use of an example involving honey perhaps echoes one of the syllogisms typically used to illustrate a mode of fallacy from the consequent, as in Peter of Spain (7. 157).

Llull's sixth and last mode involves potentiality and actuality, which he illustrates thus: 'Every understanding (*intellectus*) is true; some understanding is not true; therefore some understanding is true and not true.' He explains that 'as a faculty the understanding is true, because it is a creature, and created to understand the true; but when it is in ignorance, it judges what is false to be true, and what is true to be false'. This mode corresponds to one of Algazel's (*Log.* 3. 168–72), and has parallels in Aristotle (*Top.* 5. 2 129b30–130a28) as well as Peter of Spain (7. 86). Llull's explanation displays his paramount concern with the spiritual well-being of the mind, which motivates his attention to contradiction as a deviation of the Intellect from its proper object, truth.

The labels and commonplace examples that Llull gives to each of his six modes in the *Logica nova* make them easily comprehensible as derivations from received Aristotelian doctrine, through Algazel for the most part. It is important to note Llull's explicit reference to equivocation as the basis of several of his modes, because his later works appeal to principles of equivocation in order to explain the one unusual form used in all his examples of fallacy from contradiction. This form is the distinguishing feature of Llull's new fallacy and his chief contribution to its creation. This form is not original, but corresponds to the fallacy from ignorance of refutation described by Peter of Spain (7. 132–40). Ignorance of refutation relies on contradiction, and

Llull's new fallacy is, like his argument from contradictory syllogisms, simply an application of the law of contradictory propositions—if one is true, the other must be false, as explained in Peter of Spain (1. 12–14). Llull joins two contradictory propositions, the major a negative universal and the minor an affirmative particular, about the same subject and predicate (i.e. 'No A is B', 'Some A is B'). Since they produce a false, because internally contradictory, conclusion ('Some A is B and not B'), Llull declares that the major premiss is false, and its contradictory (which happens to be the minor premiss), true. Of course an argument formed in this fashion violates the formal laws of Aristotelian syllogistics (*An. pr.* 2. 15–16), and is therefore simply a fallacy from ignorance of refutation. Llull, however, attempts to justify it as a merely apparent paralogism by recognizing equivocation in its two terms, thereby producing the three terms necessary for a properly deductive conclusion. Even if one grants the validity of this explanation—which is formally impossible, as subsequent consideration will show—Llull's procedure still depends on the correct predication of contraries, which Llull often ignores, and especially on the choice of a major premiss, which is necessarily determined by his fundamental dichotomy of affirmative possibility and negative impossibility: Llull always takes the universal negative as the major premiss, in order to prove its contradictory affirmative particular to be true. In effect, he gives a true counter-example. In his final comments on his new fallacy in the *Logica nova*, Llull claims that it combines a 'natural and logical habit', and this phrase not only emphasizes the putatively natural character of his whole logical programme, but may also foreshadow his later attempts to explain the new fallacy according to the natural disposition towards truth formalized in his dichotomy of affirming possibility and denying impossibility. He says nothing more, and Chapter 19 of this study, on demonstration, will deal in detail with developments in Llull's conception of that fundamental dichotomy and its relationship to the natural activity of the Intellect. The remainder of this chapter will study in depth Llull's attempts to offer a formal explanation of his new procedure.

It is probable that Llull appreciated the special value of the fallacy from ignorance of refutation because it can include all the others, according to Aristotle (*De soph. el.* 6 169a16–21), in so far as its two causes—apparent contradiction and imperfect syllogizing—correspond to the broad divisions of the fallacies into verbal and non-verbal errors. Peter of Spain explains in detail this 'reduction' of all the fallacies to ignorance of refutation (7. 179–90), and Llull's concluding remarks in the *Logica nova* do in fact refer to his new fallacy as a means of finding many other fallacies. It is thus general, just as Llull's own *Art* is, a not unappreciable advantage in Llull's eyes. The specific procedural principles of his new fallacy all depend, none the less, on received doctrine regarding equivocation, ignorance of refutation, and contradiction, which he attempts to fuse and harmonize in subsequent works, under the rule of his dichotomy of affirmation and negation.

Llull's major exposition of the rationale for his new fallacy of contradiction appears in the lengthy *Liber de novis fallaciis*, composed at Montpellier in 1308. This work is a compendious application of his fallacy of contradiction to numerous topics invented through the *Principia*, *Subiecta*, and *Regulae* of his *Art*. This broad application may represent some kind of test by Llull of his new fallacy's universal value. The work includes long sections of arguments employing contradictory syllogisms and suppositions, suggesting their common dependence on his dichotomy of affirmation and negation. The work comprises five distinctions: the first and second give examples of fallacies concerning each Lullian *Regula* and Subject (including the virtues and vices); the third explains each of Aristotle's thirteen fallacies and nineteen syllogistic modes as instances of the fallacy of contradiction; the fourth offers contradictory syllogisms concerning the Divine Dignities and ten credible suppositions; the fifth is a catalogue of questions, including forty-four with full answers, an unusual feature in such lists.

This mass of examples of the fallacy of contradiction certainly illustrates very well Llull's conception of its universal applicability, but his explanations of its principles are rather more difficult to understand. The Prologue to the work offers various general claims regarding its function and value, beginning thus:

Quoniam intellectus humanus est valde gravatus, per hoc quia opiniones philosophantium, et iuristarum, et etiam medicorum in eorum scientia sunt dispersae; idcirco dictus intellectus potest difficiliter invenire et per consequens concludere veritates, cum ad unam rem sequuntur plures voces, et sub eadem voce multae res continentur. Qua de causa opiniones inter scientificos oriuntur. Quare intendimus Novas Fallacias compilare sub una generali fallacia existentes. (Prol.; p. 12)

Llull's reference to the multiplicity of words and of things probably echoes Aristotle's explanation of the cause of equivocation in the first chapter of the *Sophistical Refutations* (165a11) and thus recalls the fundamental role of equivocation in Llull's new fallacy. This is, like his *Art*, compendious and universally general to the 'new fallacies', which are the philosophical and theological positions that he casts as errors, using the form of his new fallacy. He attempts to define it more exactly thus:

Quam fallaciam 'apparentem contradictionem' appellamus, eo quia videtur contradicere, et nihil realiter contradicit. Et per hoc ab aliis antiquis fallaciis est diversa, quia antiquae verum significant, et verum tamen non concludunt. Differt in hoc etiam ab antiquis, quia generalior est, quam sit per se quaelibet antiquarum. Quapropter antiquae ad istam fallaciam reducuntur, et sic de syllogismis omnibus ut patebit. (Prol.; p. 12)

This short paragraph recalls several basic Aristotelian and Scholastic doctrines regarding the fallacies. First, there is the general status of the fallacy from ignorance of refutation, as explained already. Second, the phrase 'apparent contradiction' explicitly recalls his debt to Algazel's presentation of these. It is also a term that appears in Peter of Spain's treatment of the fallacies of *secundum quid et simpliciter* and ignorance of refutation, which create apparent contradictions in their premisses and true contradictions in their conclusions (7. 127, 139). Third, Aristotle defines refutation in general as 'syllogism involving the contradictory of a given conclusion' or position (*De soph. el.* 1 165a3); hence Peter of Spain explains that every syllogism produces its refutation through contradiction (7. 181). The sum of these doctrines provides Llull with a broad basis for imagining a general fallacy based itself on contradiction and presented as the contradictory of a given thesis. None the less, it must be observed that there is a difference between a syllogism that contradicts another as its refutation, as in Llull's 'contradictory syllogisms', and a syllogism that suffers itself the fallacy of *secundum quid et simpliciter* or ignorance of refutation. This difference tends to disappear in Llull's distinction of his new fallacy from those of the ancients. From Aristotle's definition of sophistry as 'apparent wisdom' (*De soph. el.* 1 165a11), Llull evidently confects the view that the ancient fallacies 'signify the truth, but do not conclude it', and even extends this to Aristotelian syllogistics, whose nineteen modes he applies to his new fallacy in the Third Distinction of the *Liber de novis fallaciis*. His new fallacy, on the other hand, 'seems to contradict, but really contradicts nothing'. Thus, Llull's new fallacy broadly serves the polemical and moral function of further distinguishing his *Art*, which seems false but is not, from Scholastic Logic, which seems true but is not. Or stated in another way, Llull opposes his false (i.e. only apparent) fallacies to the true (i.e. really so) fallacies of his contemporaries. Or in yet another manner, Llull offers one omnivalent refutation for the manifold syllogistic errors of his opponents.

It is not clear from the Prologue in what respect this new fallacy 'exists by itself', but Llull immediately adds that

Ratio, quare ista fallacia est generalissima, stat in hoc, quia est composita ex universali negativa et particulari affirmativa, et ex subiecto et ex obiecto, et ex syllogismo et paralogismo. Et quia sub eadem forma semper generaliter haec concludit, ut declarabitur in progressu, fallaciae antiquae differunt per formam, sed novae fallaciae sunt per materiam differentes. Et de hoc exemplum dabimus in prima distinctione, et etiam in secunda. (Prol.; p. 12)

It is obvious that Llull's new fallacy incorporates universal negative and particular affirmative premisses; the combination of syllogism and paralogism expresses Llull's claim that his fallacy is only apparent and thus reveals or includes its true contradictory syllogism within itself. The orientation of this new fallacy towards truth probably explains the composition from subject and object, understood as truth of the subject of predication, which is sought or objectified in the contradictory syllogism generated. Llull apparently regards the single form of his new fallacy as an important improvement over the multiple forms of the thirteen Aristotelian fallacies. None the less, he uses the ten *Regulae* and nine Subjects to define nineteen types of new fallacy; he claims that these include all the old fallacies (2. 9. 16. 2) and are 'subaltern' to the new fallacy of contradiction, which he thus counts as the twentieth (not because it completes the nineteen syllogistic figures[1]).

He concludes his explanation here of the new fallacy with this reference to its psychological function:

Quia intellectus habet duos actus, scilicet credere et intelligere, et in generando scientiam ante credat, quam intelligat, ut sit finaliter successivus, igitur, in primo actu fallaciae habent ortum, et per consequens opiniones. Et sic in maiori propositione ipsius paralogismi causa apparentiae apparebit; et causa defectus ipsius apparentiae in minori, concludendo realiter veritatem. (Prol.; pp. 12–13)

The psychological basis for Llull's new fallacy includes the distinction between faith and understanding, and the association with the former of opinion, doubt, and supposition, as in his earlier works; there this

---

[1] As the editor of the text erroneously suggests (p. 5).

psychology supports, of course, his opposition between affirming possibility and denying impossibility, but he does not explicitly introduce this opposition until the Fourth Distinction of this work, to be discussed below. It is not clear whether he associates belief with the ancient fallacies, and would thus define them as 'truth that only appears so', or with his new fallacy, defined thus as 'falsehood that only appears so'; his final references to 'concluding the truth really' suggest the latter. Llull's phrases 'cause of the appearance' and 'cause of the defect' directly recall Peter of Spain's use of similar expressions. However, where Peter typically sees these as formal linguistic relationships—such as the 'agreement' or 'diversity' of two terms taken *secundum quid et simpliciter* in ignorance of refutation (7. 134)—Llull typically explains them physically or metaphysically by reference to the beings signified by the terms, in keeping with the natural orientation of his logical programme.

Llull concludes the Prologue to the *Liber de novis fallaciis* with his usual claims for the superior utility and facility of his own *Art*:

Ars ipsa, sive scientia contenta in hoc libro, propter modum altum, quem habet in faciendo fallacias istas novas, utilis multum erit; eo quia docebit cognoscere syllogismos distinguendo inter sophisticum, dialecticum et demonstrativum; etiam syllogismum et antiquas fallacias in quo peccant; et similiter precavere a punctis variis et casibus defectivis in opinionibus et auctoritatibus, glossulis, aphorismis,[2] et deinde in quaestionibus litigiis et libellis.

Scientia ista, quantum est de se, est difficilis et prolixa, sed quia per *Artem Generalem* ipsam tractabimus, erit facilis et sub compendio comprehensa. (Prol.; p. 13)

Aristotle's distinction between sophistical, dialectical, and demonstrative argument (*De soph. el.* 2 165a37–b12) plays little role in Llull's scheme, which really recognizes only two species of argument, the true and the false. It is a peculiar ambiguity of Llull's account of the fallacies that their derivation from his 'new fallacy' makes them modes of true argumentation, while his analyses of them still serve to explain their error. Since the treatise's five distinctions offer an exhaustive survey of all the philosophical and theological issues that Llull attacks or defends, the *Liber de novis fallaciis* fulfils the same purpose as Llull's other works of applied Logic, such as the *Liber de syllogismis contradictoriis*: it surveys and rectifies the errors of the infidels and heterodox philosophers. Close analysis of several arguments from each distinc-

---

[2] The printed text gives the meaningless 'amphorisinis', against all MSS.

tion will show how Llull proposes to use his new fallacy for this purpose, and what formal procedures it entails.

The First Distinction uses Llull's *Regulae* to list various relationships—such as definition to thing defined, being and non-being, prior and posterior, antecedent and consequent, and so forth—whose confusion or misunderstanding can cause fallacies. In this regard, these relationships serve a more or less topical function as inference warrants that Llull rarely acknowledges explicitly, since he more typically conceives of them as necessary reasons. Here he presents them as objects of belief, so that the fallacy made from his *Regula B, Utrum*, based on possibility and impossibility, consists in 'believing first that either part of a contradiction is possible. And it arises because one believes that any (*quaelibet*) part of a contradiction is possible, and this possibility in the other (*altera*) part is impossible.' (1. 1.) Llull thus simplifies tremendously Aristotle's pragmatic conclusion that 'Everything must either be or not be, whether in the present or in the future, but it is not always possible to distinguish and state determinately which of these alternatives must necessarily come about.' (*De interp.* 1. 9 19a27–9.) For Llull, on the other hand, one of two contradictory propositions is always determinately possible, and the other impossible, thanks to his doctrine of suppositions, and the place of this fallacy as the first of all in the long *Liber de novis fallaciis* clearly establishes the primacy in his conception of fallacy of his dichotomy between affirming possibility and denying impossibility. He goes on to distinguish three species based on this dichotomy—question or doubt (*dubitatio*), affirmation, and negation—and offers a fallacy concerning each one, beginning with doubt:

Nullum dubium est affirmabile. Quoddam dubium est affirmabile; ergo quoddam dubium est affirmabile et non affirmabile.

Maior est duplex, eo quia est ex sensibus contrariis, quia uno modo nullum dubium, in quantum dubium, est affirmabile, eo quia dubium non est de genere affirmationis. Alio modo est affirmabile, propter hoc quod dubium est actu, cum quidquid est actu, sit affirmabile. Minor simpliciter est vera, eo quia ponendo secundum sensum maioris, privat primum. Et sic, propter duplicitatem maioris, argumentum est paralogismus, et per veritatem minoris est syllogismus. (1. 1. 1; pp. 14–15)

Llull's example recalls Peter of Spain's for the first mode of fallacy *secundum quid et simpliciter*: 'a chimera is possible, therefore a chimera exists' (7. 122). The distinction illustrated comes from Aristotle ultimately (*De soph. el.* 5 167a1).

More importantly, Llull introduces here, without prior explanation, his assumption of equivocation or double sense in the major premiss, which is the means of generating truth in his new fallacy. Peter of Spain makes frequent references to the double sense or function of premisses in his accounts of the verbal fallacies, and this feature is certainly not peculiar to major premisses (e.g. 7. 45, 46, 75, 76). In order to understand Llull's procedure, it is helpful to note that where Peter simply ascribes double sense to one or another or both of the premisses, it would be more exact to say that each premiss uses one of the two or more possible senses borne by their common term. For example, where he says of the standard example 'Every dog barks; some marine animal is a dog; therefore some marine animal barks' that both premisses have a triple sense, it would be more exact and useful to distinguish the sense of the subject in the major premiss as 'canine quadruped' and in the minor as 'seal' (or 'dogfish'). This distinction creates four terms, eliminates the repeated middle term, destroys the syllogism, and is therefore the means of recognizing this conjunction of propositions as fallacious. Llull faces a related problem: he must distinguish different senses for one of his two terms in order to create the three necessary for a valid syllogism, and thus eliminate the fallacy from ignorance of refutation. However, he can only acknowledge one sense as true, since he seeks to distinguish one premiss as true and the other as false; and therefore he attempts to ascribe that one sense to both predications of the same term, which again creates a contradiction between the premisses. *Llull's new fallacy can never work successfully in the manner that he proposes because he attempts to conflate equivocation and contradiction as modes of opposition.* It is possible to summarize the steps that he proposes schematically in the following manner; first, he creates a paralogism in the form

> No A is B;
> Some A is B;
> Therefore some A is B and not B.

Llull distinguishes separate senses A′ and A″ for term A. If, as suggested above, he assigns different senses to each premiss, the result is one of these syllogisms:

No A′ is B;	No A″ is B;
Some A″ is B;	Some A′ is B;
Therefore some A″ is no A′	Therefore some A′ is no A″

which correspond to the second mode of the second syllogistic figure (*Festino*). But in these syllogisms the two premisses are not contradictory nor do they imply a contradiction, which frustrates Llull's purpose. Similarly, Llull glosses his major premiss 'no question is affirmable' as 'no question is an affirmation', and thereby revises the terms of predication, producing an argument of the form

> No A is B;
> Some A is C;
> Therefore some C is not B.

which corresponds to the sixth figure of the third mode (*Ferison*), and again frustrates Llull's attempt to infer a contradiction from the major premiss.

What Llull instead does is to attribute one sense to the minor premiss and two to the major premiss, and then 'remove', as he says, the sense from the major that does not match that of the minor. Yet, unless Llull also changes the quantifying signs 'no' and 'some', this univocal removal simply creates one of these paralogisms:

No A′ is B;	No A″ is B;
Some A′ is B′;	Some A″ is B;
Therefore some A′ is B and not B.	Therefore some A″ is B and not B.

These again are fallacies from ignorance of refutation. Thus the only recourse left for Llull is to change both the terms and their quantifiers, and create

Some A′ is B;	Some A″ is B;
Some A′ is B;	Some A″ is B;
Therefore some A′ is B.	Therefore some A″ is B.

Thus he tautologically excludes the contradiction. This is literally what Llull describes when he argues that question 'in another way is affirmable, as an actual [existing] question', since it reinterprets and replaces the original major premiss with the minor, which is the contradictory of the major. This rejects the major premiss as a false proposition, which is precisely what Llull pretends to show, but which makes it unacceptable in Aristotelian demonstration (*An. post.* 1. 2 71b21). Similarly, in his examples for affirmation and negation, Llull offers the minor premisses as the second sense of the major, thereby rendering the latter false and unsuitable for demonstration. These methods of reinterpreting the premisses, and the resulting argument, are needless to say, not formally Aristotelian.[3] They are none the less perhaps valid for Llull as somehow akin to his demonstration *per aequiparantiam* and other quasi-circular schemes of coessential predication. In short, Llull insists on maintaining a paralogistic form, but proposes to recognize a syllogistic truth in it. Thus he claims that his examples combine paralogism and syllogism, even though the latter is in no way formally possible, as the preceding analysis has just shown. The reason for Llull's peculiar position is probably best found in his basic claim, noted in the Prologue to the *Liber de novis fallaciis*, to offer a mode of reasoning that contrasts to that of his Scholastic contemporaries as true paralogism to false syllogism, a distinction that both formally and spiritually expresses the contradiction between Llull's and his opponents' arguments. Understanding Llull's true paralogism and false syllogism is formally impossible from Aristotelian principles of argumentation, but spiritually possible from Lullian ones, although this is not always easy to accept. His examples concerning doubt, affirmation, and negation show very well that Llull is not concerned with affirmation and negation as formal verbal modes, however, but rather with the 'affirmable' and 'deniable' as material, or better, spiritual truth and error.

Llull's new fallacy and Aristotelian argument

Further insight into the rationale of Llull's new fallacy of contradiction is available from the Third Distinction of the *Liber de novis fallaciis*, where he proposes to reformulate both syllogistics and sophistics through his new fallacy. His method in each case is the same. For the standard syllogistic mode or fallacy, he creates a new fallacy whose major premiss reformulates the major premiss from the standard example, but using a negative universal predication, regardless of whether this is actually the contradictory of the original major premiss. The minor premiss in the new fallacy is the affirmative particular contradictory of the new major one. From these Llull concludes paralogistically that a subject both does and does not possess its predicate. Since Llull adapts his new fallacy in each case entirely from the major premiss of the standard example, his new syllogism often bears little resemblance to the complete form of that original deduc-

---

[3] Platzeck comes to the same conclusion after a similar review of the formal mechanics of Llull's new fallacy: *Raimund Lull*, I. 435–6.

tion. More importantly, this procedure produces a minor premiss in Llull's new fallacy that is not the same as the major of the original standard example, with the result that Llull's peculiar appeal to a double sense and the law of contradictories does not always apply. His new fallacies merely 'declare', as he says, the error in the old, in a sort of indirect explanation that is most interesting when it implies the operative principles of his own method, rather than any correct recognition of the explanation offered by an authority such as Peter of Spain.

Sometimes Llull's declaration does match the conventional explanation, as with the double sense created by fallacy *secundum quid et simpliciter*. In other cases, he recognizes the cause of the fallacy in his own formulation: thus he argues that the contradictory conclusions of his new fallacies for equivocation and amphiboly are 'absolutely true because said of different things', while the original paralogistic conclusion is absolutely false because said 'of the same thing'. Llull apparently means that his new conclusions recognize, in their own contradictory form, the double sense necessary to understand the error in the original argument. It is their function of realizing this recognition that makes his new fallacies true. They serve a heuristic, rather than eristic, purpose. His explanation is adequate in the cases of equivocation and amphiboly because these concern the double sense that he seeks in all fallacies. In his conclusion for a new fallacy based on composition he must introduce significant formal changes in order to reveal this double sense: he adds temporal adverbs and produces the conclusion 'therefore something possibly white is possible [so] *in one time* and not possibly white *in another*' (3. 1. 3; italics added). In this instance Llull uses fallacious composition, as well as additional syncategorematic terms, in order to obtain a true conclusion from one false (Nothing possibly white . . . etc.') and one true premiss ('Something possibly white . . . etc.'), thereby creating the true paralogism that he seeks.

In other cases from the Third Distinction, Llull's explanations ignore received doctrine, as when he claims that his new fallacy regarding division 'declares' the standard example because their premisses and conclusions are all contrary, even though formally this is obviously not true. Llull's minor premiss 'Some animal is rational or irrational' is not the contrary of the standard example's minor premiss 'Not every animal is rational'. As subsequent analyses will show, Llull's use of the labels 'contradictory' and 'contrary' does not follow the technical distinctions of Scholastic doctrine.

In other cases, Llull must drastically extend the sense of a predication, as when he improbably argues in his example for ignorance from refutation that his minor premiss 'Something which is the double of one is the double of three' means that 'two triples are the double of one triple, as two units are of one unit' (3. 1. 9). Finally, in those instances where any explanation escapes him, he simply states that his new fallacy 'declares' the old and nothing more.

When analysing fallacy from pronunciation, Llull explains that the minor premiss removes one of the two senses from the major premiss because 'the power (*virtus*) of the minor arises from the power of the major in some way' (3. 1. 5). This obscure claim seeks the difficult formal relation between equivocation and contradiction that Llull assumes in any fallacious predication. He systematically applies it to each of the nineteen syllogistic modes in Part Two of the Third Distinction. His treatment of the third mode of the first figure (*Darii*) is typical:

Omne animal est substantia. Quidam homo est animal; ergo quidam homo est substantia.

Nullum animal est substantia. Quoddam animal est substantia; ergo quoddam animal est substantia et non est substantia.

Maior est duplex, quoniam quod est inferius, non est quod est superius. Verumtamen hoc animal potest esse haec substantia. Minor simpliciter est vera, quoniam ponendo secundum sensum maioris, privat primum. (3. 2. 3; p. 53)

For every one of the nineteen syllogistic modes, Llull posits some double sense in the subject of its major premiss, which makes the syllogism sophistical and which his new fallacy 'declares' (3. 2. 1). In this case, the double sense corresponds to Peter of Spain's basic distinction between common and personal supposition (6. 4–9), although it is obvious that Llull does not understand these as properties of terms. The practical advantage of introducing this double sense into every major premiss is not clear, and the preceding analyses have shown that it is formally untenable. Some idea of its value as a spiritual proof for Llull appears in his concluding remarks on application of the nineteen syllogistic modes to his new fallacy: 'this doctrine is highly useful in recognizing the sophistications of syllogisms in disputation, and especially with respect to the fallacy of equivocation' (3. 2. 19). Despite its technical elaboration in paralogistic form, Llull's new procedure is fundamentally an expression of the differences in philosophical and theological perspective—what he calls 'equivocation'

—between Llull and his adversaries, and in this regard represents an effort to moralize their views formally as expressions of truth or error.

Part One of the Fourth Distinction of the *Liber de novis fallaciis* offers one of Llull's major deviations from the formal rules of Aristotelian Logic in his broad application of the term 'contradiction', which appears frequently and prominently in the thirty syllogisms regarding the Divine Dignities. He calls each syllogism 'true, demonstrative, and necessary', and proposes to 'contend' each one with a new fallacy. He presumably means contend in the Aristotelian sense of contentious disputation, which 'reasons or appears to reason to a conclusion from premises that appear to be generally accepted but are not so' (*De soph. el.* 2. 165b7). None the less, the universal negative propositions that he sets as major premises rarely express generally acceptable philosophical or theological axioms, and in this respect his arguments show that the difference between philosophical or theological truth and error is rarely the simple moralized conflict of contradictories that he conceives. All his arguments are identical in form to this, the first:

Omnis bonitas est ratio bono, quod agat bonum. Sed omne ens est bonum naturaliter per bonitatem; ergo omne ens naturaliter agit bonum.

Nulla bonitas est ratio bono, quod agat bonum. Sed quaedam bonitas est ratio bono, quod agat bonum; ergo quaedam bonitas est ratio bono, quod agat bonum et non est ratio bono, quod agat bonum.

Maior simpliciter est falsa, cuius oppositum dicit maior primi syllogismi; quare primus simpliciter est verus et necessarius et demonstrativus. (4. 1. 1. 1; p. 57)

Llull's propositions do not offer the correct predication of contradictories, since 'No *Bonitas* . . .' is not the contradictory of 'Every *Bonitas* . . .' but rather its contrary, and thus there can be no refutation through contradiction of a given position. Llull's use of the term 'opposite' shows, however, that he deliberately extends the law of contradictories to cover all oppositions, including contrarity, where Aristotle only allows this for contraries that have no intermediate, and cites goodness and badness as examples (*Cat.* 10 12a9–19). The minor premise of the new fallacy, 'Some *Bonitas* . . .' is the true contradictory of 'No *Bonitas* . . .' but expresses the limited or intermediate view regarding diffusion of the good that Llull wishes to reject. In all these examples, Llull allows only a single sense for the major premise, which insures that the complete argument will be a genuine paralogism, and thus its contradictory, the major premise of the first syllogism, must be true. It should be noted that Llull does not prove the truth of the conclusion of the first syllogism, but since he conceives the complete syllogism as an essence and participated truth, as explained in Chapter 17 of this study, he undoubtedly assumes that he has proven the entire syllogism. In many of Llull's examples from the Fifth Distinction, he constructs arguments in which the conclusion to be refuted does correspond to a premiss in his new fallacy that contradicts a supposed truth.

This presentation in the Fourth Distinction of his new fallacy as a genuine paralogism incurs at least two problems related to the formal rules already discussed: first, since he denies that there are two senses, it cannot function as a paralogism (i.e. apparently true syllogism); second, the denial of two senses leaves only two univocal terms in the major and minor premisses, and therefore no possibility of syllogistic deduction. These considerations are completely absent in the set of negative syllogisms with negative paralogisms that Llull offers next, as in this example:

Nulla substantia est visibilis. Sed omnis lapis est substantia; ergo nullus lapis est visibilis.

Nulla substantia est visibilis. Sed quaedam substantia est visibilis; ergo quaedam substantia est visibilis et non visibilis.

Maiores simpliciter sunt verae, quia nullum abstractum est visibile. Sed quia minor paralogismi contradicit maioribus, erit falsa; et sic minor syllogismi erit vera. (4. 1. 2. 6; p. 63)

The same argument about visibility that Llull here calls absolutely true appears twice as an example of equivocation in the account of his new fallacies from the *Logica nova* (5. 33. 3, 5). This shift suggests how for Llull all contradictions depend upon equivocation, as though all the fallacies were only verbal; his natural Logic avoids these, of course, by discoursing with the natures of things alone. Establishing this univocal sense in Llull's new fallacy creates, however, the formal problems already noted. Llull's broad conception of the law of contradictories and disregard for both the identity and quantity of terms in predication is obvious from his inference that the syllogistic minor premiss 'Every stone is a substance' is true because it somehow does not oppose the major premiss 'No substance is visible', while the paralogistic minor 'Some substance is visible' does.

Llull's new fallacy and supposition

The Second Part of the Fourth Distinction in the *Liber de novis fallaciis* deals with 'demonstrative syllogisms from hypothesis [i.e. supposition] with true faith' and makes patent how Llull's procedure in constructing his new fallacy rests securely on his dichotomy of affirmation and negation. Using the *Principia* and *Regulae*, he constructs ten true suppositions or hypotheses that 'all nations concede', such as the existence of the Divine Dignities, God's unity, the identity of his essence and existence, the real distinction of the Divine Dignities, and so forth. The truth of the syllogisms based on these suppositions will signify the specifically Christian doctrines of the Trinity, Incarnation, and so on. Llull's first syllogism regarding his first supposition, 'I firmly believe and have true faith that God is a being more active' through the Divine Dignities, offers a paradigmatic example of his procedure:

Omne ens magis agens per bonitatem agit per totam bonitatem, et de tota essentia bonitatis. Sed Deus est ens magis agens per bonitatem; ergo Deus agit per totam bonitatem, et de tota essentia bonitatis.

Nullum ens magis agens per bonitatem agit per totam bonitatem et de tota essentia bonitatis. Sed quoddam ens magis agens per bonitatem agit per totam bonitatem et de tota essentia bonitatis; ergo quoddam ens magis agens per bonitatem agit et non agit per totam bonitatem et de tota essentia bonitatis.

Maior paralogismi est simpliciter falsa, eo quia est contraria maioris syllogismi, quae simpliciter est vera per veram hypothesim sive fidem. Sed minor paralogismi est vera simpliciter, cum sit contradictoria suae maiori. Quare conclusio syllogismi, cum sit ei aequivalens, necessarie erit vera. (4. 2. 1. 1. 1; p. 66)

There is a staggering problem here. Llull asserts that the major premiss of the syllogism is true by true 'hypothesis or faith', when in fact it is the minor premiss of the syllogism that asserts the true supposition. He argues, none the less, in this same manner throughout this part of the Fourth Distinction, because his method for presenting his new fallacy requires a negative universal in its major premiss, in order to serve as the contradictory of the major premiss of a true syllogism. Llull's explanation of this example is itself an argument: he claims that the paralogism's minor premiss 'Some being more active through *Bonitas* acts through all *Bonitas* and all essence of *Bonitas*' is 'equivalent' to the syllogism's conclusion that 'God acts through all *Bonitas* and all essence of *Bonitas*.' This equivalence forms an enthymeme reducible to the true syllogism itself through the predication 'God is the being more active through *Bonitas*', which is of course already the syllogism's minor premiss. This suggests that Llull's argument might conform to Aristotle's rules for circular proof (*An. pr.* 2.

5–7), but there are two major differences: the second syllogism (found in the enthymeme just described) does not use or create a converted premiss from the first, but simply changes quantity in the subject 'All being . . .' to 'Some being'; the second syllogism does not use a premiss from the first as its conclusion. The coincidence of conclusions suggests again a procedure more like Llull's demonstration *per aequiparantiam*.

Llull's confusion regarding the supposition of his major and minor premisses shows how in fact they both require supposition as true propositions in order to reject their contradictories as false. Neither proposition by itself can prove its truth or falsehood, but only that it is not its own contradiction. For Llull, however, contradiction always depends upon determinate truth and falsehood. The sequence of predications presented in the example above expresses this dependence by alternately affirming and denying a position, comparing it to the truth, as described by Llull in his earlier works. The doctrine of supposition affirms the truth in question, while the 'new fallacy' denies the falsehood. It is interesting and perhaps supremely indicative of the basic consistency of all Llull's methods of argumentation that in one passage from this section he compares his completed proof through the new fallacy to his demonstration *per aequiparantiam* (4. 2. 2. 2. 1. 3).

The arguments from supposition in the latter half of the Fourth Distinction establish an interesting trajectory for the *Liber de novis fallaciis* (the Fifth Distinction simply recapitulates the scope of the first four). On the one hand, it applies the new fallacy to yet another subject-matter, and its method should remain unchanged. Of course, the change in subject does occasion a change in method, as Llull acknowledges when he declares that the arguments from the first half of the Fourth Distinction are undeniable according to the Intellect's 'nature of understanding', while those of the second half are demonstrative 'under the disposition of faith' (4. 1; 4. 2). Llull thus implies some distinction between a lower and a higher mode of knowledge. Llull recognizes the contribution of his suppositions to the latter, but not to the former, or to any of the arguments from the first three distinctions of the work. He does acknowledge this contribution in the short fragment *De conversione syllogismi opinativi in demonstrativum cum vicesima fallacia* (Montpellier, 1308–9). There he defines as 'dialectical or opinative' a syllogism such as 'Every man is an animal; Peter is a man; therefore Peter is an animal' because its major premiss is a hypothesis and allows a double sense. Application of Llull's new fallacy eliminates the double sense and thus makes the dialectical syllogism demonstrative. Obviously this explanation relies on Llull's own peculiarly moralizing use of the terms 'dialectical' and 'demonstrative', rather than consideration of their formal or material distinctions according to Aristotelian doctrine, but its greatest interest lies in its application of equivocation to hypothesis or supposition as creditive acts. In arriving finally at this explicit use of suppositions in the Fourth Distinction, Llull in fact retraces the derivation of his entire procedure of new fallacies from his basic principles of affirmation, negation, supposition, and first intentions. What is truly noteworthy about the *Liber de novis fallaciis* is that this retracing begins so far from the elements of Llull's own *Art*, amidst the complex technical rules of Scholastic doctrine concerning the fallacies. This shows how far Llull had penetrated into the dense mass of Scholastic logical doctrine, and represents his usual effort to embrace it compendiously within his own programme. His special attention to sophistics also suggests a real conviction on his part that he had found the motor of all error and heresy in contradiction. Rectifying this general principle of fallacy would, in a very direct sense, make error impossible.

Fallacy and error

Preceding analyses have described the formal problems in Llull's new fallacy. Whether he ever recognized these or not is difficult to say, but it is apparent that after 1310 he ceases to proclaim his new fallacy as a master sophism embracing all others, and relegates it to a somewhat incidental role as a special addition to the standard Aristotelian fallacies. He uses it little after 1310, preferring instead his method of contradictory syllogisms, whose contrastive procedure obviously relies as well on the opposition of truth and error. The limited success of his efforts or perceived difficulties with his new fallacy perhaps motivated his other major writing on the fallacies, in which he applies his dichotomy of affirmation and negation very directly to the thirteen fallacies and to his own new one. This work is his *Liber de fallaciis quas non credunt facere aliqui qui credunt esse philosophantes, contra purissimum actum Dei verissimum et perfectissimum* composed at Paris shortly after 1310. Its title expresses wonderfully Llull's spiritual concern with problems of formal logic. The modern editors of the text profess satisfaction with its received state,[4] but some problems still seem

---

[4] See the introduction to the text (p. 473).

apparent: the text begins very abruptly and lacks the dated colophon customary in Llull's later works; it treats the fallacy of accident twice, once at the very beginning of the treatise (where he exemplifies it with a form of fallacy by division) and again in its usual position as the first of the non-verbal fallacies. Llull also refers in the second chapter to a non-existent 'First Distinction'. Evidently there are still some portions of the text missing or never completed.

The *Liber de fallaciis* is as much concerned with combating theological and philosophical error as it is with reforming logical doctrine regarding the fallacies, and in this regard suggests very well how Llull equates the two tasks. He pursues this polemical function of the work mainly by illustrating each fallacy with arguments that recall Averroist positions such as the unity of the Intellect (15); errors of unbelievers such as denying the Trinity or Incarnation (9–12); or rejection of his own tenets such as the innate correlatives. Llull effectively makes each position an analogue of the standard example of each fallacy that he includes (except in the case of fallacy from equivocation). Llull attempts to define, just as Peter of Spain does, the cause of each fallacy, and his remarks represent again a very technical consideration of received doctrine. Where these causes are various in Peter, Llull attempts to restate every fallacy's basis according to his dichotomy of possibility and impossibility. Where Peter seeks to define the fallacies through reference to modes of signifying, Llull adduces physical or metaphysical principles that explain the error in each example as ignorance of the nature of things. His interpretation is thus more material in every case. It also moralizes the Aristotelian fallacies as correlates of impossibility, just as does his treatment of the forty-four Averroist positions in the *Liber de syllogismis contradictoriis*. Peter of Spain's explanation of the 'productive' and 'destructive' principle of each fallacy provides a ready dichotomy for Llull to equate with his own of possibility and impossibility. This equation creates, however, some predictable distortions of each example, and difficulties in explaining them, as the following representative instances show.

Llull's syllogism illlustrating fallacy in the form of expression (7), appears in Peter of Spain (7. 96) as an example of that fallacy's second mode: 'Whatever you saw yesterday, you see today; you saw white yesterday; therefore you see white today.' The productive cause of this fallacy for Peter is the 'likeness of one word with another in an accidental mode of signifying', while the destructive cause is the 'incompletion or diminuition of that likeness'. In the syllogism quoted,

' "white" expresses quality (*quale*), even when taken as existing by itself; but since it is taken in a middle term expressing quiddity, from this mode of taking it beneath the middle, it appears to signify quiddity, and thus "white" enfolds in itself different modes of signifying, one truly, another apparently, and thus quiddity is changed into quality' (7. 91, 96). Llull's explanation completely ignores the distinction between substance and quality: 'Possibility posits that if you saw white yesterday, today you can see white; impossibility however posits that if today you see black, you do not now see in the same thing the white that you saw yesterday.' Since Llull advocates the real existence of universals, a distinction between true and apparent modes of signifying is irrelevant to him in considering the signification of a term indicating a quality. His assertion of the 'possibility of seeing white today' does, of course, alter the strictly necessary consequence concluded in the original syllogism. It is interesting that Llull's approach converges with arguments of Ockham, who suggests that every predication of a property affirms a possibility, especially given the power of God to forbid the possible or create the impossible (1. 24; 3–3. 20). The latter option rarely preoccupies Llull, however.

Llull illustrates fallacy from the consequent with this syllogism: 'An ass is an animal; you are an animal; therefore you are an ass.' (12.) This is not a fallacy from consequent, but of accident, as Peter of Spain notes (7. 163); it corresponds to this example that Peter gives for the first mode of fallacy of accident: 'An ass is an animal; man is an animal; therefore man is an ass.' (7. 109.) The productive principle of this fallacy, according to Peter, is the 'identity in part (*secundum partem*) of the middle term as repeated in the premisses' while the destructive principle is the 'difference in nature (*secundum rationem*) of the repeated middle' (7. 106). Hence Llull explains quite correctly that 'possibility posits that animal is a genus, but man and ass differ in species'. The difference between man and ass is perhaps the 'cause from impossibility', although Llull does not identify it as such. He confuses this fallacy of accident with that from the consequent because, as Peter explains, the former may involve the subject's relationship to an accident that appears as an antecedent, consequent, or convertible term (7. 108). Aristotle also classifies fallacy from consequent as a branch of fallacy from accident (*De soph. el.* 6 168b28). However, given Llull's frequent, but broad and simplistic, appeals to these distinctions, his confusion here is not exceptional.

Finally, Llull illustrates fallacy from false cause with this argument:

'The soul and life are the same; death and life are contrary; generation and corruption are contrary; but death is corruption; therefore life is generation, and to live is to be generated.' (13.) Llull's example is an imperfect rendering of the argument that Peter of Spain presents in this manner:

> Suntne anima et vita idem?;
> quo concessu, contra:
>> mors et vita sunt contraria;
>> generatio et corruptio sunt contraria;
>> sed mors est corruptio;
>> ergo vita est generatio;
>> quare vivere est generari;
>> hoc autem est impossibile, quia qui vivit
>> non generatur, sed generatus est;
>> non ergo anima et vita sunt idem.

(7. 167; p. 175)

Peter explains that the productive principle of this fallacy is the 'agreement (*convenientia*) of what appears to be a cause but is not, with what is a cause, and this results from some agreement through some term signifying the same thing'; the destructive principle is the 'difference of the proposition that is not a cause from the cause of the conclusion' (7. 166–7). In the argument that Peter gives as an example, the original question is only apparently resolved through the premisses introduced, because these also use the term 'life' from the original question. These premisses in fact only prove that death and life are contrary. Peter adds that death is not, strictly speaking, contrary to life, but is either a process that occurs in beings while they are still alive, or the complete privation achieved at the end of that process; death is, then, equivalent to corruption in the first sense, but not in the second (7. 169–70).

Llull's explanation recalls some of the observations that Peter makes regarding the natural processes of death, but chiefly appeals to the oppositional relationships defined by his dichotomy of possibility and impossibility. His explanation must in any case be different, since he cites the original example in a different form. According to Llull,

possibile ponit, quod anima et vita sint distincta diversimode, anima existente se ipsa, ipsa existente vita corporis, cum quo est coniuncta; et impossibile ponit, quod mors et vita non sunt contraria, et possibile ponit, quod mors et corruptio sunt diversa, cum corruptio sit superius et mors inferius, ut puta

lapis qui corrumpitur et non moritur. Et sic dicendum est de vita et generatione, ut puta anima, quae vivificat corpus, sed non generat ipsum; et sic potest
dici de vivere et generari; etiam de impossibili suo modo. (13; p. 484)

The impossibility in the last line indicates the denial of contrarity,
while possibility indicates the assertion of diversity. Here Llull applies
contrarity and diversity more or less according to their established
Aristotelian sense (*Metaph.* 10. 3–5). He thus argues that death and
corruption cannot be contrary because they are not species of the same
genus; they are instead simply diverse, and death is a species of the
genus corruption. Thus a rock is said, using the general term, to
corrupt, but man is said, using the specific term, to die. Llull extends
this distinction to the terms 'generation' and 'life' and 'to live' and 'to
generate'. In this manner he recognizes, as Peter does, a contradiction
in the conclusion that life is generation, hence to live is to be generated. However, where Peter shows that this conclusion is irrelevant to
the question, 'Is the soul the same as life?' Llull has already taken that
question as the first premiss in his argument, and thus attempts to
establish its relevance by noting that 'the soul vivifies, but does not
generate, the body'. In a sense, Llull himself incurs a fallacy from false
cause here: first, to vivify is not the same as to live; second, the soul
does not both vivify and generate in the same way that rock does not
both die and corrupt, or that man does both die and corrupt. What
Llull produces is a series of imperfect analogies as a causal
explanation.

This is perhaps the most extreme deviation from received doctrine
in Llull's treatment of the fallacies from the *Liber de fallaciis*. In
general, he identifies and defines them in a manner that is broadly
consistent with the reasons suggested by Peter of Spain. The examples
quoted are, none the less, real testimony to Llull's typically oblique
understanding and practical revision of conventional Scholastic teaching. They show well the fundamental gap that exists between his own
appreciation of its technical elements and his contemporaries'. Llull
does accept and appeal to the validity of that received doctrine,
however, in so far as he tries to identify the Averroist and other false
positions as instances of the thirteen known fallacies. He achieves this
identification by moralizing both those positions and the fallacies as
instances of his own principle of impossibility. Seen in this regard, the
Liber de fallaciis is one long analogical argument, that takes all sophistics as one *exemplum* in support of his anti-Averroist campaign.

At the end of the *Liber de fallaciis*, Llull also treats his own new fallacy of contradiction, and his comments are an especially concise statement of its operative principles and value, as he had evidently come to conceive them. They are most interesting for their neglect of its presumed general status as a master fallacy, and for allusions to some of the formal aspects analysed in detail above. He introduces this 'Fallacy of Ramon' as based on contradiction 'and separate from the mode of the other fallacies, because the middle enters the conclusion, and the other fallacies signify that what is false is true, and this fallacy signifies that what is true is false, and the major proposition of this fallacy is always double, causing a disjunction' (15). In fact there is no true middle in Llull's new fallacy and this creates the disjunctive conclusion, but the advantage of this is not clear, except in so far as it helps Llull separate truth from falsehood explicitly in the same argument. His basic concern for this task is evident in his claim that the Aristotelian fallacies make falsehood appear true, while his own does the opposite. In his conclusion he notes that his new fallacy is truly a fallacy because the sophist requires two opposed species of fallacy, which Llull thus posits as a genus to be divided, although this creates a very unusual meaning for both 'sophist' and 'fallacy' as somehow comprehending both the true and the false.

All Llull's examples of his seven types of new fallacy concern philosophical and theological errors that he explicitly attributes to his contemporaries. He illustrates the first type with the example of 'No stone is visible . . .' used occasionally elsewhere, and applies it here to the question of God's really and substantially infinite power. He concludes that this fallacy is applicable to all, as explained in the *Liber de novis fallaciis*; this is the only passage in this text that claims any supremely general status for the new fallacy. All the other examples of its types offer major premises that state the doctrine disputed by Llull: no being creates something from nothing; no being acts beyond the limits of nature; no created being (e.g. the soul) can be everlasting; no being can be a first principle without moving and changing; no Intellect is limited in a body (i.e. there is one Intellect for all men); no (individual) Intellect is capable of understanding universals. In these examples of his new fallacy's modes, Llull's identification of fallacious argument with philosophical and theological error is obvious.

Pursuing this joint rectification of logical method and philosophical or theological doctrine, Llull concludes that his procedure of distinguishing two senses, and removing one, will allow masters in the Theology and Arts Faculties (*catholici et artistae*) to agree, 'because logicians coming to natural philosophy will not be disposed to habituating themselves with the errors of philosophers against the Holy Catholic Faith'. This reference to the disposition of the Intellect reaffirms that Llull's attention to the fallacies serves as always his pursuit of *rectitudo*: paralogisms are damnable because they create disparity between the Intellect and the intelligible. They subvert the mind's natural disposition to receiving truth.

As a conclusion to this chapter on sophistics, two related and broad aspects of Llull's treatments of the fallacies merit comment. First, this treatment is perhaps Llull's most technical formal analysis of any part of Scholastic logical doctrine. His summaries of the fallacies show a close knowledge of received precept. For this reason, his deviations from or simple silence regarding various general or specific formal rules appear all the more extraordinary. Llull's loose handling of predication and contradiction when constructing paralogisms may simply show that he had digested doctrine concerning the fallacies more thoroughly than the rules of syllogistics or propositions. However, the imputation of simple ignorance or inadequate training (even if true), do not explain his procedure as fully or convincingly as the postulation of a broadly different purpose or design of his own. For this reason it seems legitimate to emphasize Llull's own basic distinction between the false old fallacies and his own true new fallacy, because it recalls the basic polemical thrust of his logical programme as part of his overall project for universal moral and intellectual rectification. The impact, as it were, of this thrust on the general mass of received doctrine produces the peculiar distortions and even fractures found in Llull's account of specific precepts and rules. Sometimes, the results of the impact are immediately apparent, and his treatment of fallacy is one such instance. In the *Liber de syllogismis contradictoriis*, the Lullist says to the Averroist, 'You and I are in equivocation, not in contradiction.' (2. 41.) This remark summarizes the effect of Llull's association of equivocation and contradiction in his new fallacy: he declares that talking about the same thing in different ways produces disagreement. In the *Sermones contra errores Averrois* of 1311, Llull asserts that the 'Averroists create equivocation in philosophy by implying contradiction according to the mode of believing and of understanding' (Prol.). In the *Liber de novo modo demonstrandi* he argues that the proposition 'Faith is not provable' suffers the *fallacy secundum quid et simpliciter* because it is only true in one sense (Prol.). For Llull, the only real differences are in things, and knowledge of them allows more or less perfect participations in their truth, which are thus equivocal in their relative likeness. Recognizing this likeness or equivocation resolves the disagreement, and this recognition is thus a rectification of the Intellect to fuller grasp of its objects. Moreover, since Llull's *Art* is pre-eminently a scheme for reducing the many verbal and conceptual likenesses of reality back to the one truth in things, equivocation and contradiction also name the fundamental poles of identity and difference that serve as means of achieving that reduction, according as Llull manipulates them in his characteristically proportional analogies. In this respect, equivocation and contradiction are principles of moralization, understood in the special sense employed throughout this study, and Llull's explicit appeal to those two principles in his treatment of the fallacies therefore represents his most explicit recognition of their importance as technical foundations of his moralizing methods.

19
Demonstration

THE previous chapters in this second part have analysed in considerable detail Llull's accounts of the fundamental structures of propositions, syllogistics, and sophistics in his writings after the *Logica nova*.
These analyses have necessarily encountered already many of Llull's
references to the general nature and function of demonstration, as well
as to the handful of fundamental concerns that support his conception
of it. These are his doctrines of supposition, dual sense and intellectual
knowledge, and habituation of the Intellect by faith. Just as Llull
addresses much more directly the specific formal aspects of Aristotelian Logic in attempting to reform them, so he addresses much more
directly these special concerns in several treatises devoted to them. He
attempts to justify and explain them much more fully than in his earlier
period, with diverse results. His handling of these concerns therefore
evolves, and not always uniformly, during the years from 1303 to 1316.
This chapter will treat each one in turn, following where necessary
their chronological development. After reviewing the contribution of
supposition, the division of sense and intellectual knowledge, and
habituation of the Intellect by faith to Llull's overall logical programme, this chapter will conclude by examining his explicit treatment
of demonstrative argument itself, and especially the capital role that he
assigns to his method of demonstration *per aequiparantiam*.

Supposition

Llull's doctrine of supposition is first in importance to all his logical
works after 1303 because it gives the dichotomy of true, good, possible
being and false, evil, impossible non-being its formal expression in
logical affirmation and negation. In this way it founds all his new
schemes for methods of demonstration in this later period. It contributes to his new fallacy of contradiction, as it tries to explain the
opposition between a supposition and counter-supposition as equivocation. The apparent failure of this effort leaves Llull simply with the
use of contradictory suppositions as the basis for opposing syllogisms,

which he baptizes 'a new mode of demonstration', even while elaborating the basic dichotomy of affirmation and negation itself in works such as the *Liber de possibili et impossibili* of 1310 or *Liber de affirmatione et negatione* of 1314. All his schemes, no matter what their formal evolutions, rely on the value of a supposition as the necessary affirmation of true, good, possible being. The critical question then becomes, what is the gnoseological value of supposition that sustains its logical function in Llull's various schemes? His earlier works have already revealed that it apparently consists in the mind's natural attraction to the truth as its proper object, but Llull now makes this much clearer, and tries to establish a complete epistemology and gnoseology around such a conception.

The introductory remarks that comprise the brief First Distinction of Llull's *Liber de novo modo demonstrandi* provide a very succinct statement of supposition's value in formalizing the dichotomy of elements opposed through affirmation and negation:

Ista Distinctio est de Contradictoriis Suppositionibus sive de Impossibili; et suum Subjectum est Magnitudo, super quam fundatur iste Liber sive Ars Praedicativa Magnitudinis.

Ens autem bonum, magnum, verum intelligibile et amabile sunt uniformiter quinque termini hujus Artis; oppositum vero horum terminorum est magnum malum, magnum falsum, ignorabile et odibile.

Suppositio, quando est vera, est de genere Bonitatis, et quando est bona, est de genere Veritatis; ratio hujus est, quia bonum et verum conveniunt cum esse. Et quando Suppositio est falsa, est de genere malitiae; et quando est mala, est de genere falsitatis; ratio hujus est, quia malitia et falsitas conveniunt cum non esse.

Et ideo intendimus syllogizare faciendo Contradictorias Suppositiones, et Propositiones bonas et veras declaratas reducere ad Affirmationem, et oppositas ad Negationem, et hoc cum magna intelligibilitate et amabilitate, bonitate et veritate uniformiter. Talis Modus autem demonstrandi est Novus, et extra modum et figuram antiquorum Syllogismorum. (1; p. 2)

This last line is notable as an expression of Llull's recognition that his methods do not integrate easily into conventional practice; thus the failure of earlier attempts to do so, as in the *Liber de possibili et impossibili* and *Liber de fallaciis* of 1310, may have motivated his proclamation now in 1312 of this entirely new mode of argument, which is still general to all conventional modes as a higher to lower truth. This passage from the *Liber de novo modo demonstrandi* very effectively organizes all the correlated oppositions of Llull's basic dichotomy of affirmation and negation, encountered in so many other works, into this unitary correlation:

Affirmatio—Verum—Esse—Intelligibile—Bonum—Amabile
Negatio—Falsum—Non-Esse—Ignorabile—Malum—Odibile

This scheme defines, as it were, the vocabulary and parts of speech of supposition, but not its syntactic rules. These come from the ancient pre-Aristotelian axiom that likeness between knower and known is the condition of cognition. Llull argues from this tenet in many ways in many works, and from these the following epistemological process can be synthesized.

The mind first considers its own spiritual nature and determines that its proper object, the intelligible, must be spiritual as well (*LFSC* 1. 2). The likeness between the mind and its objects is not absolute, but gradated: the closer they are to it in nature, the more the mind understands (*ABI* 4. 3. e). Yet, because understanding is the primary, true, and necessary act of the mind, it is infallible when actually and fully possessing its object (*DRA* 1), and therefore the intelligible is the true (*LPER* Prol.; *LLP* Prol.). Now, this likeness exists specifically through the common participation of the mind and all its objects in the eighteen Absolute and Relative *Principia*, so that the mind 'understands a good object with *Bonitas*, a great one with *Magnitudo*', and so forth (*LMNI* 5). Moreover, 'everything through which one *Principium* participates with another is intelligible' (*DRA* 5). Thus Llull's *Principia* are truly principles of knowledge as both its means and its object, and the arguments in support of Christian doctrine based on the Divine Dignities are so necessary that they are undeniable (*LFSC* Prol.). Whatever the mind encounters with the *Principia*, it affirms, and whatever it does not, it denies (*LMNI* 5). That is, whatever makes the mind more understanding is to be affirmed, and its opposite, denied, since the greater intelligibility must be true and the 'lesser or its opposite' false (*LEE* 2. Prol.). In this way the mind best realizes its own nature and natural activity. At this point, the line of reasoning synthesized into these stages comes to involve logical discourse in two ways that Llull recognizes. First, when the mind strays from its proper object, the intelligible likenesses of the *Principia* and their interrelations, it strays from the truth; thus Llull regards his logical programme as more natural because it deals only with the properly intelligible natures of things constituted through his *Principia*, which he considers first intentions, while other logicians abandon these for mere figments of the mind, which he identifies with logical disputation *ad nomen*

(*LMNI* 4. 1. 5). By *ad nomen*, Llull apparently refers to disputation frustrated by lack of agreement over terminology, as explained by Ockham (3–2. 28). Second, 'the Intellect by its nature with a self-evident (*per se*) proposition naturally knows the thing defined' in the proposition, and either affirms the proposition as true or denies it as false (*LMNI* 3). The Intellect can also consider a hypothesis, denying it if contrary instances should prove it false. From these propositions or hypotheses it constitutes syllogisms, always recognizing that affirming the true is natural and affirming the false unnatural to its own spiritual being (ibid.).

This, in short, is the gnoseological model that supports Llull's schemes for affirming and denying any proposition or supposition. Llull's model is a fairly unremarkable construct using widely diffused Neoplatonic tenets, most of them known from Augustine or the Prescholastics, and Llull's own *Principia* in the role of transcendentals. Were his schemes for deploying affirmation and negation in logical discourse *only* derived from this gnoseological model, they would constitute something like a purely Neoplatonic Logic, and be a remarkable accomplishment, but very different in character from the Lullian *Art*. What Llull can and does accomplish is something else altogether: he attempts to reform the Aristotelian logical doctrine received by both medieval Christian and Islamic culture, in order to rectify that doctrine as a surer means of attaining theological truth. The results of his efforts are the volumes of theoretical and practical treatments of Logic analysed in this study, in all their complexity and diversity. Their greatest interest is not simply that they elaborate Llull's gnoseology of supposition or dichotomy of affirmation and negation, but rather the manifold arguments that he produces in attempting to reinterpret or moralize Aristotelian logical doctrine according to his own basic axioms.

The modern editor of Llull's *Liber de novis fallaciis* has observed that his doctrine of supposition represents a 'deliberate abandonment of a theory of truth as the adequation of the intellect with things in favour of a theory of truth as the Intellect's experience of itself as the place where truth takes place'.[1] This is true in so far as the things in question are material, but Llull does insist on the correspondence between the Intellect and its own spiritual objects, which are the most proper to it. Llull needs these separate spiritual objects in order to explain the infallibility of supposition, but he thereby must reject a

---

[1] In the introduction to the text (pp. 6–7).

prime tenet of Aristotelian psychology, the sufficiency of sensory cognition, and posit a radically dual scheme of sense and intellectual knowing. This scheme is the second major tenet of Llull's theory of demonstration in his later writings.

Sense and intellectual knowledge

Llull's new insistence on the separation of sense from intellectual knowledge contrasts with the coexistence of Aristotelian faculty psychology and the division of sense and intellectual understanding in his early *Libre de contemplació*. Even the *Lògica del Gatzel* describes both modes, but independently. Llull's rejection of Aristotle's theories of knowledge from sense perception and vehement arguments for its subordination to spiritual or intellectual understanding is one more measure of the highly polemical character of so many of his later concerns. In arguing these issues, he joins in the long series of debates engendered by the introduction of Aristotle's *On the Soul* into the West in the twelfth century.[2] Llull in fact advocates one of the particular doctrines, the *sensus agens*, that most inflamed contemporary debates on human psychology.[3] His interest in this theory seems to reflect its easy reconciliation with his own explanations of perception and cognition through his innate correlatives. In many other respects his theories are more traditional, however. The Augustinian divisions of Will, Memory, and Intellect always constitute the core of his psychology, by virtue of their function as the trinitarian *vestigium par excellence*. This is true even in those works, such as the *Arbre de sciència*, where he most fully develops an Aristotelian account of sensation and intellection. His earlier works also include many references to illumination of the Intellect, but only one of his later accounts explicitly attempts to make it a basis for the relationship of faith to understanding. This neglect perhaps reflects Llull's assent to the general abandonment of illuminationist theories among the Franciscans after Scotus rejected it.[4]

On the other hand, Llull also replaces illumination with his new view of a pre-eminent spiritual knowledge, which he explicitly sets against the Aristotelian doctrine of sensory cognition. The latter is one of several basic Aristotelian positions that Llull typically labels 'Aver-

---

[2] David Knowles calls 1275–85 years of 'acute controversy' in this debate: *The Evolution of Medieval Thought* (New York: Random House, 1962), pp. 292–6.

[3] See Stuart MacClintock, *Perversity and Error: Studies on the 'Averroist' John of Jandun* (Bloomington: Indiana University Press, 1956), pp. 10–50.

[4] See Gordon Leff, *The Dissolution of the Medieval Outlook*, p. 39.

roist', and thus shows the degree to which he applies that label broadly, without regard to particular nuances of theory. His opposition to these positions hardened as a result of his stay in Paris from 1309 to 1311, but he had long opposed most of them. The *Lògica del Gatzel* suggests, for example, that the doctrine of an eternal world is due especially to ignorance of spiritual truth (lines 1002–44). Now he argues that this ignorance arises from the failure to recognize distinct lower and higher modes of knowledge. In his *Disputatio Raimundi et Averroistae* (1) and *Liber de fide sancta catholica* (1. 1–2) of 1310, he describes the two modes thus: the lower comes from the Senses and Imagination as corporeal powers, apprehends particulars, causes the liberal and mechanical arts, and denies any truth higher than itself; the higher comes from the Intellect itself with the Divine Dignities as spiritual beings, apprehends abstractions, causes Theology, and can recognize the lower mode as false with regard to its own higher truths. The lower mode 'disposes' the higher, but does not cause it, since this would make understanding not be the proper act of the Intellect itself. There are many possible objections to Llull's model, which relies on his view, consistent with his belief in plural substantial forms, of separate corporeal and intellectual essences in man, as expounded in his *Ars generalis ultima* (9. 45). It attempts to combine a sort of Neoplatonic gnoseology of ascent and descent through corporeal and spiritual levels of being with the Aristotelian faculty psychology of adequated cognitive powers and objects, an effort worked out most thoroughly in his *Liber de ascensu et descensu intellectus* of 1305. Llull's inability to integrate fully this ascent and descent with the faculty psychology of Aristotle is neatly evident in this passage from the *Liber lamentationis philosophiae* of 1311:

[Ait Intellectus] Confiteor, quod Deus est altius obiectum, quam ego possim intelligere. Et magis est per se intelligibilis sua bonitas, magnitudo, etc. et etiam suum agere intrinsecum et extrinsecum, quam ego possim intelligere, cum sim potentia inferior, et ipse obiectum superius. De istis autem aliis scientiis, quae sunt inferiores, non est sic, quae fiunt per sensum et imaginationem; quoniam ego sum magis dispositus et promptus ad intelligendum superiora, cum sim spiritus, quam sensus et imaginatio sint mihi sufficientes, quia sunt de genere corporeitatis. (10; p. 119)

The conjunction '*quoniam*' ('since') joins the two contending poles of Llull's scheme: God's unknowability to the Intellect in this life and the spiritual Intellect's urge to know other spiritual beings. This conjunction is itself Llull's moralization of Scholastic philosophy as *rectitudo* or the dynamic orientation of man to God. This conviction that man can and indeed must attain a higher spiritual or intellectual knowledge of God contributes the ultimate motive for his efforts to realign the roles of faith and understanding in that knowledge.

Psychology of faith and understanding

While Llull's recognition of a separate mode of spiritual knowledge assists his conception of the relationship between faith and understanding, it is not adequate justification for his explanations of their respective roles, a fact that Llull perhaps recognizes in the indecisive conclusion to his *Disputatio fidei et intellectus* of 1303; in this work the two contending allegorical figures of Faith and Understanding hand over their arguments to a hermit, who will carry them to the Pope, Cardinals, and Doctors of Theology at major universities for judgement (5. 40). One fundamental difficulty in Llull's accounts is that they cannot accommodate his suppositions as, in Scholastic terms, either the formal objective (the truth that is God) or material objective (the truths about God) of faith.[5] This failure results chiefly from his excessive emphasis on determining the psychological dynamics of faith and understanding, secondarily from his attempt to identify a common object for faith and understanding, and finally from his limited attention to the necessary role of grace. In order to appreciate the difficulties that Llull's approach creates, it is necessary to begin with his elaborate and frequent disquisitions on the psychology of faith and understanding.

A clear definition of the psychology of faith encounters an immediate impediment in Llull's varying use of the term 'faith' itself. The development in his later works of his full-fledged theory of supposition leads Llull commonly to use the three terms 'faith', 'belief', and 'supposition' interchangeably, even while recognizing the latter two as names for the act of the first. The couplet 'suppose or believe' is especially common, as in the first words of the *Liber de multiplicatione quae fit in essentia Dei* of 1314. Llull regards this belief largely as an act of the Intellect and Will, and thus does not repeat in his later works the laborious analyses of the influences of the Senses on faith that he offers in his earlier *Libre de contemplació*. Likewise, he

---

[5] On these distinctions see the very helpful presentation by T. C. O'Brien, *Summa Theologiae*, vol. 31 (New York: McGraw-Hill and London: Eyre & Spottiswoode, 1974), pp. 186–204.

rarely mentions the possibility of belief in non-spiritual matters. He none the less continues to recognize two functions of faith, one superior to the other. In his *Liber contradictionis* (1. Prol.) he speaks of two dispositions, one towards unintelligible falsehood and one towards intelligible truth; he exemplifies the second with Isaiah's dictum 'Unless you believe, you will not understand' (7. 9) and the first with the Psalmist's words 'the fool says in his heart there is no God' (13. 1; 52. 1). He generally seems to regard the inferior type of faith as that 'act of the Intellect moved to assent by the Will' recognized by Aquinas (2a. 2ae. 4, 2), and equates it with the faith that cannot attain understanding. This is the 'credulity' possessed by the Saracens who lack true faith (*DFI* 1. 2). It is an inferior form of knowledge, but necessary for the simple-minded (*DFI* 5. 40). In speaking of this type of belief he avers that what is known is more desirable than what is believed (*LNMD* Prol.); 'positive' belief based on authorities is opposed to demonstrative understanding based on reasons (*LP* 2. A. 5); belief corresponds to opinion and dialectical proof (*ABI* 4. 4); the irrational and merely credible have no place in philosophy (*LMNI* Prol.). Generally, faith is inferior to reason, yet Llull still insists that faith must assist reason in reaching God.

This assistance constitutes the superior function of belief that corresponds to Llull's supposition, or the doubt that 'assents to neither side of a question', in Aquinas's words (2a. 2ae. 2. 2). Supposition implies examination of both sides of a question in the search for truth, as in the *Liber lamentationis philosophiae*, where the allegorical figure of Intellect says:

Meus ordo est, quod sim primitivus in acquirendo species, distinguendo, concordando, contrariando. Et si non possum ipsas intelligere, faciam ipsas credibiles; et sic per accidens sum creditivus, positivus. Et quando sum in medio inter intelligere et credere, sum opinativus, dubitativus, et extra quietem et in labore positus, in tanto quod sum promptus ad concludendum verum aut falsum. (10; p. 118)

The supposition, positing, or belief of a proposition thus serves to engender doubt between it and its opposite, and this stimulates the Intellect to determine the true position. One position is, of course, always true and affirmable, the other false and deniable. In his earlier works Llull suggested that this supposition expresses man's natural desire for the truth, and he implies a similar tendency in the *Ars brevis de iure*, when he tells how quando ipse sequitur suam naturam mediocrem generat scientiam intellectam, dilectam et recolitam; sed quando magis est collateralis in una parte quam alia, tunc infirmatur et infuscatur et generat opiniones credulitates quibus ponitur in periculo et fortuna, quia subditus est voluntati atque memoriae et extra suam libertatem deductus. Intellectus quando se dirigit ad suum obiectum quod est intelligibile, primo se dirigit ad obiectum credibile, supponendo utramque partem esse possibilem, et sic est venativus et ascensivus et non quiescit usquequo pervenerit ad suum obiectum intellectum; sed quando intendit quiescere in credere, tunc ligat se et separat se a venatione sua. (5. 1; p. 186)

This passage implicitly identifies both inferior and superior functions of belief and suggests in the verbs *venari* and *quiescere* the soul's natural desire for the Supreme Truth. It is noteworthy, as will become apparent, that these accounts make no mention of divine grace. When Llull follows this procedure in the Second Distinction of the *Liber de fide sancta catholica*, he proposes to argue 'by contracting a position as a cause for faith, so that when a truth of Faith is supposed, the position will also be true' (Prol.). The Intellect naturally recognizes the supposition 'it is good that God exists' to be true because intelligible, since its opposite, 'it is good that God not exist', naturally is false because unintelligible. This appeal to the innate falsity of the unintelligible assumes the dictum that 'whatever is truly intelligible, its opposite cannot be truly believable' (*LEE* Prol.). Thus the Intellect's encounter with its proper object also presents a proper object to the Will that moves belief, in a way that fortifies the gnoseological model of supposition described above.

The habit of faith

The move from this belief to understanding is the basis for Llull's repeated definition of faith as a 'habit that disposes the Intellect to understand', as in the *Liber de convenientia fidei et intellectus in obiecto*:

Intellectus cum habitu Fidei supponit . . . et tunc transit ad intelligendum Deum, et deducit de ipso veras et reales affirmationes vel negationes, ex quibus facit scientiam, Fide permanente sine corruptione credendi et intelligendi concordante Intellectu et Fide in eodem Obiecto. (2. 8; p. 3)

Llull's formula superficially resembles Aquinas's 'habit of the mind . . . making the Intellect assent to things that appear not' (2a. 2ae. 4. 1), but lacks Saint Thomas's implicit recognition of the role of the Will, which is the critical difficulty in Llull's attempts to identify faith and supposition. Variations on this definition appear in all his later works from the *Disputatio fidei et intellectus* (Prol. and 1. 2) of 1303, *Liber de fide sancta catholica* (Prol.) of 1310, and *Excusatio Raimundi* (p. 357) of 1309 to the *Liber de minori loco ad maiorem* (Prol.) of 1314. Since Llull uses the terms faith and belief interchangeably in these passages, his new definition effectively restates the traditional *credo ut intelligam*, and he cites the Septuagint verse of Isaiah (7. 9) in support of his view (*LMLM* Prol.). Likewise, in the *Liber de convenientia* he explains that 'belief antecedes understanding and understanding is the consequent, when a supposition is made' because 'when faith is posited, the possibility for understanding is posited, with faith remaining, just as when the antecedent is posited, the consequent is posited' (2. 3). This rather deterministic analogy does show how the notion of faith as a habit resolves many of the problems described by Llull in his account of potential and actual faith and understanding in the early *Libre de contemplació*, especially the impossibility of simultaneous actual faith and understanding about the same object. Now both move together, in a staggered order that Llull describes using the metaphor of oil (faith) rising above water (understanding). He often speaks of 'ascending' from belief to understanding, as in the *Liber de potestate pura* of 1314, where he proposes to achieve this ascent 'by arguing in a new way and an old way; first through believing or supposing, and then by understanding' (1. Prol.). In the *Liber de convenientia* he compares faith to the foundation and understanding to the completion (*finis*) of a house (2. 9). In the same text he also offers this quaint analogy:

sicut cappatus homo ascendendo in montem, quanto magis ascendit, tanto magis ascendit cappa, quae est supra ipsum: a simili de Intellectu, quanto magis ascendit ad intelligendum DEUM et Articulos Fidei, tanto magis ascendit Fides, quae est suus habitus. (2. 10; pp. 3–4)

It is tempting to consider this analogy between the habit of faith and a hat as an expression of Llull's frequent vestimental interpretation of the category of habit, as explained in Chapter 12 above. Explanations such as these seek to refine the proportional relationship of faith and understanding expounded in his earlier works.

In many respects, the ascent from faith to understanding described thus far is entirely comprehensible within the bounds of natural theology. The mind is capable of conceiving and demonstrating truths such as God's existence, his oneness, his creation of the world, and so forth, as Aquinas argues (1a. 2, 2; 11, 3; 44, 1). Llull clearly believes that such truths fall within the scope of his theory of supposition and natural object of the Intellect, as already described. God is the 'maximal intelligibility' (*DFI* 1. 3). Llull assumes that God is naturally a proper object of the Will and Intellect, a position that Aquinas rejects (1a. 88, 3; 1a. 2ae. 9, 1 and 3; 109, 3). The highest truth necessarily yields the highest knowledge: the Divine Dignities are most certain and therefore arguments about them must be most certain as well (*LP* 1. C. 1. 2. 1. 18). Aquinas denies this, arguing that while Divine truths are indeed most certain, the limited human Intellect cannot grasp them as equally certain (2a. 2ae. 4, 8).

Llull accordingly conceives a hierarchy of truths, which faith and understanding ascend in their piggyback fashion, almost reaching to God himself: the truth of the Trinity is unknowable in its totality, but partially understandable through necessary reasons (*DFI* 1. 3). This scheme recognizes no real upward limit for the ascent of faith and understanding, only that faith is always able to believe a higher truth than the Intellect can comprehend (*DFI* 1. 4). It ultimately sets no obstacles to the mind's rise through what might be called the truth from God, the truth about God, and the truth that is God. For Aquinas, the last of these constitutes the formal objective of faith, to which all must first give assent; the second is the material objective, or content of faith, and includes not only the Articles of Faith or sheerly believable truths, but anything else that a person must accept on faith about God (2a. 2ac. 1, 1; 1, 5 ad 3; 5, 1). Because this other content varies depending on a person's capacity for understanding, it is useful to distinguish the first category as the knowledge of God accessible to natural reason, in the manner suggested by Saint Thomas (1a. 2, 2; 8, 3; 1a. 2ae. 109, 3; 2a. 2ae. 2, 3). Llull's failure to distinguish this dual character in the material objective of faith allows him to propound the Intellect's ascent to higher truths; for instance, in the example quoted earlier from the *Liber de fide sancta catholica*, he calls the proposition 'God exists' a 'truth of faith'. With faith the Intellect 'transits' from believing to understanding the truth of the Articles of Faith, and both faith and understanding 'attain' truths about God, with no distinction in the quality of these truths (*DFI* 1. 10). This indistinction reflects Llull's conception of all truth and intelligibility as participated. It also depends on his view of the spiritual Intellect's capacity to apprehend any spiritual object, and natural attraction to the highest intelligible truth. Moreover, in so far as the mind perceives the Divine Dignities through the *Principia*, which the Senses and Imagination find in things, then Llull also tends to efface the distinction between the formal and material objectives of faith themselves. Thus the Intellect understands the Trinity with faith and the sheerly intelligible Divine Dignities (*LMED* 1. 3). These come to the mind because 'It pleases God to act magnificently in the created subject, infusing his *Bonitas*, reducing that infused good to His good intelligibility.' (*DFI* 1. 4.) In this way, the Intellect can 'attain something from His Light of Truth' (ibid.). The participational import of the light metaphor makes recognition of a simply material objective alone difficult, as does the dual function of the Divine Dignities as both instruments and objects of thought in Llull's system.

Faith and grace

Now the mention of 'infusion' in the passages just cited obviously refers to divine grace, which Llull could not refuse to recognize as the cause of faith and stay within the bounds of orthodoxy. Just as in his earlier works, he mentions it occasionally in his later writings (e.g. *LMNI* 3; *LOFI* 5. 1. 5; *LCFI* 2. 1). The contribution of grace to faith in Llull's arguments would be wholly unremarkable were it not for the association of faith with the supposition that the mind naturally creates in pursuit of its proper intelligible object. This difficulty appears in Llull's remarks on grace itself as an attempt to attribute to grace both the impulse toward the act of belief, and presentation of the object of belief as well. For Aquinas, the initial act of grace, *gratia operans*, does only the former (2a. 2ae. 6, 1), while the subsequent influence of grace, *gratia cooperans*, contributes to the latter, because the Gifts of Faith, Understanding, and Knowledge, provide a sound grasp of the matters of Faith and correct judgement about what to believe (2a. 2ae. 9, 1). Again, qualifications such as this do not figure in Llull's account, which tends not to distinguish between the initial and subsequent acts of faith, since they all contribute to the Intellect's ascent. The infusion of the object of belief through grace is evidently a consequence of Llull's tacit appeal to illumination, and this confusion between the effects of grace, illumination, and the object of belief is apparent from his one major effort to explain grace in the *Disputatio fidei et intellectus*.

Llull describes grace as light (*lumen*) throughout the *Disputatio fidei et intellectus*, and this usage represents one of the few major references to illuminationism in his later writings (but see also the *Liber de essentia et esse Dei*, 10. Intro.). Most of his arguments in this work attempt to justify the dual illumination by grace of both the Will and Intellect. His arguments do not explicitly ‚assert for this illumination both the impulse to act and presentation of objects for each faculty, but rather allows both effects by failing to distinguish them, as the language of these passages show:

Fides vero est Lumen a DEO datum, cum quo Intellectus attingit extra suam naturam intelligendi, credendo de DEO, quod hoc sit verum, quod non attingit intelligendo. . . .

Sicut Divina Voluntas infundit in Via Charitatem ratione Gratiae in humanam voluntatem . . . quare non sic Divina Sapientia per Gratiam in me [Intellectum] possit infundere Scientiam, ut attingam de Divina Trinitate Veritatem? . . .

Sicut tu [Fides] per me [Intellectum], et ego per te credendo recipimus Lumen Gratiae a DEO, attingendo de eo aliquas Veritates, sic per idem Lumen possum intelligere aliquas Veritates de DEO; quia si non, Divinus Intellectus esset ligatus, quod non ita posset dare Lumen per intelligere, sicut per credere. . . .

[cum] sit scriptum quod Sanctus Spiritus, ubi vult, spirat, quis est ille, qui audeat dicere, quod non possit inspirare humanum Intellectum desiderantem habere notitiam de Divina Trinitate? . . .

Unde veniret, quod Divina Voluntas sit multum amabilis intensive per homines, et Divinus Intellectus non sit multum intelligibilis intensive, et quod ego [Intellectus] attingam in inferioribus veritates intensive et assertive, et non in Divina Trinitate? (Prol. and 1. 3, 10, 11, 16; pp. 1, 3, 5, 6)

What is perhaps most interesting about these proportional arguments for the illumination of both Will and Intellect is that by their very nature as analogical proofs they tend to assimilate and render indistinct the powers, acts, and objects that they compare. Whether the analogical form or the assimilation of terms is the cause or effect of Llull's moralizing mode of argument is difficult to determine in such cases.

This assimilation ignores a critical distinction between the Will and Intellect that bears directly on the very pragmatic application to Llull's own missionary goals of illumination of the Intellect: it allows intellectual comprehension and demonstration of Christian doctrine. Llull argues therefore that the Intellect must be able to respond to the infidel who does not wish to believe, 'since truth is above falsehood in understanding as in believing', otherwise the Intellect would not be held sinful for resisting falsehood, and therefore the Intellect must be able 'to attain as much about the Truth of the Divine Trinity' as it needs to resist falsehood (*DFI* 1. 4). This argument obviously appeals to the mind's natural attraction to its proper object, yet still confronts one fundamental difference that Llull cannot dismiss: the Intellect may naturally seek truth over falsehood, but the Will that refuses to believe or assent to understanding, simply does not. All Llull's psychological elaborations of the roles of faith and understanding ultimately return to the question of free will and the relation of the Will to the Intellect, whose mutually proportional influence he so often tries to express in formulas such as 'whatever is most intelligible, is most memorable and desirable'. Llull's inability to resolve this relationship in favour of the Intellect is explicit in the conclusion to the *exemplum* that he offers in support of the argument just cited. He tells the often-used story of the Saracen who came to understand the falsity of Islam and wished to be a Christian; he sought proof of Christian doctrine from a Christian, who replied that this was impossible; the Saracen asked for faith to believe, but heard in reply that only God gave faith. To the Saracen it thus seemed that he was trapped in an insuperable dilemma that could only result in his damnation. To this apparent paradox, the figure of Faith responds that the Saracen's desire was a result of divinely infused faith, but the Intellect objects that the Saracen 'wishes to be a Christian on one condition, namely that he understand the Trinity by necessary reasons, or because he believes that he cannot have Faith, unless given to him by God; and thus he feels in his mind that he does not believe the Trinity, but rather disbelieves and hates it' (1. 5). Llull is forced to conclude that the Saracen lacks belief, and therefore cannot understand. Even if necessary reasons were to convince him, he might still incur Aquinas's warning that reasoning lessens the merit of belief in those reluctant to believe without proof (2a. 2ae. 2, 10).

Llull never successfully resolves this dilemma in his own terms. In the *Liber de convenientia fidei et intellectus in obiecto* of 1309, he mentions neither illumination nor the Will, and the presentation there of faith disposing the Intellect to understanding, as in the man ascending the mountain, simply leaves the whole problem unspoken. Llull only recognizes it in so far as he argues another issue related to the dual illumination of Will and Intellect, the attainment of merit through understanding as well as faith. In the Prologue to this work, as in those of the *Disputatio fidei et intellectus* and *Liber de fide sancta catholica*, he cites and rejects Gregory the Great's famous dictum that 'faith to which human reason gives proof lacks merit' (*In Evang.* 2. 26). Llull argues in the *Liber de convenientia* that 'the greater intellectual act of understanding earns more merit than the lesser act of belief' (2. 12). Aquinas allows this with regard to understanding in the sense that it bears as a Gift of Faith or in matters accessible to natural reason (2a. 2ae. 2, 10). Llull's insistence that such understanding include proof of the Trinity and other Articles of Faith again conflicts with the origin of merit in acts of the free will. Aquinas explains that the decision simply to consider some truth is meritorious, but not the assent to conclusive proof of a truth (2a. 2ae. 2, 9 ad 2). The decision to consider some truth could perhaps serve to justify merit in Llull's suppositions, but he never develops such an explanation. Instead he insists on the habitual presence of faith in understanding, so that no act of the latter is ever without the former and, consequently, its merit as well.

The chief result of Llull's concern for faith and understanding in his later works is that it engenders an elaborate yet unworkable psychological model in order to explain the role of faith in understanding, and especially in order to accommodate his theory of supposition and the mind's natural attraction to its proper object. Integration of supposition into this model would effectively annex the act of belief to the Intellect's natural orientation to truth. His effort fails because it cannot successfully dismiss the orthodox doctrines of free will and the influence of grace on the Will. Llull's attempt to circumvent the Will probably marks him as a rationalist, even while his retreat from untenable positions saves him from the condemnation that those positions would incur. It is interesting that this rationalist orientation should arise from his adherence to the traditional Augustinian tenet of illumination of the Intellect. The peculiarity of his position may ultimately result from the pressure of his own evangelizing goals: he wishes to give one individual the capacity to induce this illumination in another.

Faith, understanding, and demonstration

This review of Llull's explanations of his notions of supposition, dual sense and intellectual knowledge, and the roles of faith and understanding is a requisite preparation for properly appreciating his specific references to demonstration in his later writings, because those other concerns embody the principles and convictions that most directly support Llull's ubiquitous claims to prove or demonstrate the truth of Christian Faith, and to establish a logical programme capable of expressing that proof or demonstration. As is by now obvious, these principles have very little to do with Aristotelian theories of demonstrative argument. Still, their very different character may not always be apparent amidst the proliferation of claims to prove the Faith and of references to propositions concerning Llull's *Principia* as 'true, necessary, and primary', as though these were in fact equivalent to the premisses of Aristotelian demonstration. In fact, Aristotelian concepts of demonstration play only an incidentally analogical role within the larger scheme of Llull's views on proof, which effectively moralize them as stages or particular manifestations of its one general method. The best way to recognize this moralization is to examine Llull's classifications of demonstration, analysing how they subordinate the Aristotelian modes of proof to Llull's supreme demonstration *per aequiparantiam* based on the metaphysics of coessentiality in the Godhead.

All Llull's classifications of demonstrative argument assume the axiom, noted already, that knowledge of God is most true, necessary, and primary because he is most true, necessary, and primary. The Divine Dignities found both the order of being and of knowledge, and indeed the latter is, thanks to the participational features of Llull's epistemology, a special case of the former. Thus he succinctly claims in the Prologue to the *Liber de fide sancta catholica* that 'just as if God does not exist, it follows that nothing exists, so if God is not understood as described in the Articles of Faith, nothing in or beyond the world truly exists or is understood'. The integration of this theocentric position into Aristotle's system of syllogistic reasoning is clearly a formidable undertaking, and the preceding chapters in this study have shown how close to, or rather far from, succeeding in it that Llull comes. His classifications of demonstration really comprise a series of moralizing comparisons of the truth value of divine and human knowledge. At best, his classifications serve to enclose Aristotelian demonstration within the context of his views on the function of supposition and roles of faith and understanding, as in this passage from the *Liber de praedicatione* of 1304:

Intendimus determinare de probatione. Et hoc duobus modis. Unus est per credere; alius per intelligere.

Per credere, sicut sermocinator qui allegat in sermone auctoritatibus sanctorum, et iste modus est positivus.

Per intelligere duobus modis. Unus modus est ostensivus; alius ducens ad impossibile. Et hoc est tribus modis, scilicet propter quid, et quia, et per aequiparantiam. (2. A. 5; p. 402)

Belief and understanding obviously establish the theological framework for considering the Aristotelian methods of ostensive and *ad impossibile* proof and demonstration *propter quid* and *quia* (*An. pr.* 1. 7 29a31; *An. post.* 1. 6 75a14). Yet Llull does not explain these methods or their interconnections; elsewhere in the same work he declares that his own demonstration is not merely persuasive, but most necessary, because it treats of God (1. C. 2. 1. 18). Few of Llull's classifications of demonstration show any greater concern for describing or explaining Aristotelian methods in themselves.

The most important purpose of these classifications is, as the preceding passage suggests, to establish Llull's demonstration *per aequiparantiam* at their summit and many of his comments, again like the preceding example, do no more than this. In the Prologue of his *Ars mystica* of 1309 Llull distinguishes demonstration *propter quid, quia*, and *per aequiparantiam* using his favourite scheme of positive, comparative, and superlative degrees, and goes on to explain how the latter employs the 'circulation' of convertible *Principia*, which he later applies in that work's Third Distinction through antecedents, consequents, enthymemes, syllogisms, and *exempla*, all constructed with convertible propositions about the Divine Dignities. He says nothing of demonstrations *propter quid* and *quia* themselves, but explains that these two modes found the arts and sciences, and have as their cause demonstration *per aequiparantiam* about God, thus affirming his axiom that no true knowledge is possible without knowledge of God. He emphasizes the proportional and participational character of this relationship when he observes in the Prologue that all things are rooted in the three degrees as lesser or greater.

The few instances in which Llull does attempt to define more exactly the respective principles or methods of the modes of demonstration that he classifies in these schemes are noteworthy as examples of his moralizing method. An unusual, but for that reason illustrative, passage in the *Ars brevis de iure* (4. 4) takes the basic divisions of 'positive' and 'natural' law, described in all encyclopaedic accounts, such as Vincent of Beauvais's (*SD* 7. 41–2), and identifies the former with belief or dialectical argument and the latter with understanding or demonstrative argument. He then distributes the topical proofs commonly attributed by the encyclopaedists to legal argument between these two divisions, giving to positive law the use of opinion, comparison, intention, custom, conjecture, testimony, bigamy [*sic*], and authority, and to natural law agreement (*convenientia*), disposition, proportion, and condition (i.e. consequence). The latter are not demonstrative arguments in themselves, but Llull's classification of them as such evidently indicates his own appreciation of their probative force within his own system of argumentation.

A definition of demonstration in more recognizably logical terms forms part of the Prologue to the Second Part of the Fourth Distinction of the *Liber de novis fallaciis* already discussed above. There Llull declares that demonstration has two types: the first is 'wholly most powerful', which employs universal major and minor premisses and therefore renders the mind more universal; the second is 'not wholly most powerful', which mixes universal and particular major and minor premisses. Both types employ true, necessary, and primary propositions, which may be Lullian suppositions, but the not wholly most powerful applies to particular beings, since there can be no universal conclusions about them. This scheme evidently alludes to Aristotle's explanation of how the three syllogistic figures employ universal or particular predications (*An. Pr.* 1. 7 29b1–25; 1. 24 41b6), but for Llull these expressions refer not to the quantification of terms, but to the ontological status of the beings themselves as either particulars or universals. As the previous analysis of Llull's remarks on syllogistics has shown, this terminological coincidence is in itself a moralization of the vocabulary of Aristotelian argumentation.

Even the account of demonstration that most clearly refers to received Aristotelian doctrine none the less revises it or organizes it in ways that assume Llull's own conceptions of the foundations of proof. Chapters 3 and 4 in the Fifth Distinction of the *Logica nova* treat demonstration and proof. The latter begins with a definition of proof, 'an argument in which truth is apparent', that loosely recalls Peter of Spain's (5. 2), and then specifies three types of proof: the first 'converts with the syllogism', that is, constitutes demonstration from wholly necessary premisses, as in the standard example 'Every animal is a substance . . . etc.'; the second uses one necessary and one non-necessary, or contingent, proposition, such as 'every lustful person is a sinner', which is contingent because man need not sin; the third uses two non-necessary propositions from authorities or testimony, as in law, and concerns what may possibly be or not be true (5. 4. 3). This account evidently derives from Algazel's classifications of possible, impossible, and necessary propositions in his *Logic* (3. 125–47), already noted as a source for Chapter 1 of the Fifth Distinction, and assumes as well Aristotle's distinctions between necessary and possible propositions (*An. pr.* 1. 13) and their combination in syllogistic argument (ibid. 1. 16, 19, 22). The relevance of these received doctrines to Llull's own practice is merely oblique, however, since he interprets propositions such as 'every lustful person is a sinner' as necessary or probable without reference to the quality of terms that they actually employ. The chapter on demonstration defines three types: *propter quid, quia,* and *per aequiparantiam.* Demonstration *propter quid* is from causes

quia A est ante B et B ante C. Adhuc 'Omne animal est substantia; omnis homo est animal; ergo omnis homo est substantia.', Quia substantia est super animal et animal super hominem. Iterum 'Nullum animal est lapis; omnis homo est animal; ergo nullus homo est lapis.' Ista demonstratio dicitur per causam eo quod animal est causa quare homo non est lapis. (5. 3. 1; f. 77va; p. 82)

The causal relationships that Aristotle finds in the middle term of any demonstrative argument (*An. post.* 2. 8, 11) tend in Llull's accounts to become simply proportional relationships defined by a being's relative position in the hierarchy of existence, especially as defined by the doctrines of Porphyry's *Isagoge.* Demonstration *quia* shows a cause from its effect as either wholly necessary or not wholly necessary. Llull illustrates the former with his correlatives, which always exist one from another, and the latter with the syllogism 'every good effect has a good cause; a castle is a good effect; therefore a castle has a good cause', where the castle may in fact result from evil intentions and thus the cause and effect 'are not conjoined by nature' (5. 3. 2). Llull's remarks assume Aristotle's distinction between the necessary and the generally true (*An. post.* 1. 30 87a18–26 or *Top.* 2. 6 112b1–20), as well as his critique of reasoning from cause to effect (*An. post.* 2. 16). However, the choice of Llull's correlatives as an example of wholly necessary relations of effect to cause tends to assimilate them to the three modes of demonstration *per aequiparantiam*: when several powers are demonstrated in the equality of their existence; demonstration of the equality of a power and its act; demonstration of the equality of the acts of those powers. Llull here makes no judgement regarding the respective degrees of necessity in these three modes of demonstration, perhaps because the difference between Llull's new mode and the two Aristotelian modes is in fact the difference between his *Art* and Scholastic Logic as a whole. The unsynthesized collocation of these three modes in this chapter of the *Logica nova* shows how they are perhaps comparable, but in no way compatible. The best that Llull can do is to order them relatively as a proportion, asserting his own methods as supreme.

Demonstration per aequiparantiam

The superiority of Llull's scheme is, as seen above, the pretended consequence of the superiority of its subject, God. The founding value of this claim is clear in Llull's *Liber de demonstratione per aequiparantiam*. Careful review of this work shows that it proposes his new method as a special kind of theological logic, as suggested already in regard to its use in Llull's earlier works. It is necessary to consider this aspect of the treatise in some detail in order to show how Llull's new demonstration *per aequiparantiam* is not simply an adaptation of received logical doctrine, but always remains, even in Llull's later development of his logical programme, the singular method most appropriate to expression of the Supreme Truth.

The Prologue of this work begins by opposing his new method to existing ones in this manner:

Quoniam quidquid demonstratum fuit ab antiquis, fuit demonstratum propter quid aut propter quia. Et subiectum huius libri sit investigare distinctionem in divinis personis per demonstrationem. Quae quidem demonstratio non potest fieri propter quid, ex eo quia Deus non habet supra se aliquid; et demonstratio quia non est potissima. Idcirco intendimus probare distinctionem in divinis per aequiparantiam et aequivalentiam actuum divinarum rationum. (Prol.; p. 216, lines 1–9)

It is obvious that Llull conceives his new method in relation and response to the two standard Scholastic divisions of demonstration, yet equally obvious that its foundation is the metaphysics of coessentiality found pre-eminently in the Godhead. In treating the divine nature demonstration *propter quid* is wholly inadequate because, as Aristotle acknowledges, it requires prior causes, which do not exist for God. Likewise, demonstration *quia* is insufficient since, as Aristotle explains, it lacks argument from a cause (*An. post.* 1. 13). The application of this new method to any other subject than God depends chiefly on the relationship of creature to Creator, which the *Principia* define. Thus Llull explains:

Cum igitur demonstratio, in quantum huiusmodi procedat ex primis veris inmediatis et necessariis principiis, ideo per talia principia volumus formare et invenire huiusmodi demonstrationem, quam aequiparantiam nominamus. Et sicut exemplificabimus in divinis, ita in aliis scientiis suo modo poterit demonstrari. (Prol.; p. 216, lines 10–14)

Even though Llull calls his *Principia* primary, true, and necessary, they are not Aristotelian premisses of demonstration, in the sense of essential and indemonstrable nexus or connections (*An. post.* 1. 2 71b9–72a8 and 1. 6 74b5–75a37), but rather transcendent universal forms of participation. His suggestion that demonstration *per aequipar-*

antiam is applicable to all fields of knowledge is therefore understandable as a consequence of the fact that the Dignities are *Principia* of any being that might be an object of knowledge, and serve to establish its truth in the manner explained above. The theocentric character of this truth and knowledge would therefore compel a reduction of all the arts and sciences to Theology, or better, theosophy, as their Lullian first intention.

In the subsequent lines of his Prologue, Llull proposes to explain how his *Principia* are primary, true, and necessary, perhaps imitating Aristotle's review of the same characteristics in the opening chapters of the *Posterior Analytics*, or some compendium of it. Llull's explanation turns out to be, however, an account of how his correlatives derive from the Divine Dignities, and this shows, even without acknowledging it, how his new demonstration *per aequiparantiam* describes and depends upon the coessential metaphysics of the Godhead. First, Llull explains that his *Principia* are primary

non in eo, quod alia ab eis descendant, sed ex eo, quia ipsa ab alio non descendunt. Et in hoc apparet, quod talis primitivitas retinet magis naturam primitivitatis, quam primitivitas causae ad effectum, quia est absoluta, illa vero respectiva. Verbi gratia: Sicut intellectus in Deo est primitivus per suum intelligere, et voluntas per suum velle ad omnes alias dignitates, ex eo quia aliae dignitates habent intelligi per intellectum et diligi per voluntatem. Non autem sicut effectus per causas, cum aliae dignitates sint eis aequivalentes in essentia et natura, et illis etiam primitivae per suos actus proprios suo modo. (Prol.; p. 217, lines 16–26)

The equivalence of the Dignities mentioned in the last lines here is both the namesake and the operative principle for Llull's demonstration *per aequiparantiam*. His new mode of demonstration has to do less with the conditions of demonstrative argument and more with trinitarian theology (the subject-matter of the treatise), especially the manner in which the Godhead embraces distinct powers and characteristics. Llull explains that this equivalence of the Dignities proceeds 'circularly according to their acts. We call this primacy (*primitivitatem*) circular because within the essence of God it is permanent and not external.' (Prol.; lines 31–3). This circularity of acts, which finds graphic expression in the circular Figures of Llull's *Art*, requires a definition of the Dignities' active and passive interrelations, which Llull proceeds to develop in his succeeding remarks. In this way, he introduces his innate correlatives, and ignores his original proposal to explain how the *Principia* are true, necessary, and immediate in themselves.

Next, Llull argues that the 'Principia, from which this [mode of] demonstration proceeds' are true because 'whatever truly is understood, truly has the state of being understood (*intelligi*) through the Intellect, and whatever truly is desired, truly has the state of being desired (*diligi*) through the Will, and similarly whatever truly is made good, truly has the state of being made good (*bonificari*) through *Bonitas*' and so on for the other Dignities (Prol.; lines 35–8). The formulation of this passage is noteworthy because it suggests that Llull extends a version of Anselm's ontological argument from a necessary concept of God to a necessary nature in God. The function of this argument is not, though, to prove the truth of the Divine Dignities, but rather to introduce their correlative passive aspect, by analogy to the metaphysics of intellection.

Llull then states that his *Principia* are immediate because no medium exists between the powers of Dignities and their proper acts. This expresses the same position that Aquinas affirms (1a. 3, 1; 9, 1–2). Llull appeals to this absolute actuality of God in order to argue that the *Principia* are necessary since the divine acts of understanding, willing, and making good necessarily follow from the Divine Dignities or powers of Intellect, Will, and *Bonitas*. This argument serves to introduce the correlative acts of the *Principia*. In the rest of his Prologue, Llull proposes to prove that the Divine Dignities have their proper acts, that from these acts results the *Principium* of *Concordantia*, and that from *Concordantia* results *Differentia*, and that from *Concordantia* and *Differentia* together results *Aequalitas*. These three are the *Principia* that, according to Llull, the demonstration *per aequiparantiam* will employ in the treatise (Prol.; lines 63–4). It is probably an exercise in elucidation of the obvious to say that Llull thus organizes within his demonstration *per aequiparantiam* the principles of identity and difference that are fundamental to his entire *Art* and all his methods of argumentation.

This review of Llull's remarks in the Prologue to his *Liber de demonstrationes* shows the inalterably theological, as opposed to logical, basis of his new mode of demonstration. As it happens, Llull mentions it by name only once more in the treatise: at the end of the Second Distinction, he concludes that he has proved the existence of the Trinity through demonstration *per aequiparantiam*, 'syllogizing' from his primary, true, and necessary principles of act, *Distinctio, Concordan-*

tia, and *Aequalitas* (2. 5). The broad relational value of these Relative *Principia* is implicit in Llull's interchangeable use of the terms 'distinction' and 'difference', although Aquinas notes that only the former is properly relevant to the Godhead (1a. 31, 2). Within the context of his entire logical programme, Llull's demonstration *per aequiparantiam* occupies a position at the summit of logical method that corresponds to the position of God in the hierarchy of being. It is the primary method, because its subject-matter is primary to the subjects of all other methods. Similarly, it is true and necessary because its subject is as well. Thus it stands to Logic as Llull's General Art stands to all other arts and sciences.

While Llull conceives of his method as general to all particular methods in other fields of knowledge, in fact it must replace them in order to fulfil his conception of its value and goals. Just as he applies his General Art to others by substituting its method for theirs, so he applies demonstration *per aequiparantiam* to logical discourse by substituting it for the procedures of Aristotelian demonstration. Yet Llull does not abandon the syllogism; he uses it always, and rarely in defective or imperfect forms. This is because demonstration *per aequiparantiam*, like so many of Llull's logical innovations, really concerns only the material value of logical terms, not their formal manipulation, and in this respect deserves better the label 'predication' *per aequiparantiam*. That material value depends on the broader gnoseological and epistemological issues defined by Llull's doctrine of supposition and view of the roles of faith and understanding. Where the analysis of Llull's earlier works observed that he is concerned less with Logic than with demonstration, this analysis of his later works might equally well conclude that he has less regard for demonstration than for psychology, conceived spiritually as the science of the soul. His theories regarding supposition do find formal expression in his use of affirmation and negation and attempted reform of the fallacies; yet it also finds material conception in his views concerning faith and spiritual knowledge. These latter concerns must ultimately be judged the ground for all Llull's attentions to proof and demonstration, because all demonstrative argument or reasoning for him consists in recognition and acknowledgement of the truth that is God. All his *Art* and all his schemes of argumentation seek to formalize the logic of the spirit in its pursuit of that truth.

Conclusion

THIS study has sought to show the manifold and various ways in which Ramon Llull strives to adapt Scholastic Logic to his own theological and metaphysical values, or, as he might say, to apply his own Great Universal Art to the art of Logic. It has suggested that Llull's efforts create a hybrid product that exemplifies a result common to all his exercises in application of his *Art* to another: it adopts the terminology and even some formal structures from received doctrine, sometimes almost wholly unrevised, but allows the practical use of these conventional elements only as they serve the strict spiritual ends of Llull's own projects. This conclusion will not attempt to summarize all his efforts and their consequences for logical doctrine, but simply recall their most basic principles, in order to consider, as a final point of enquiry, their bearing on the origin of Llull's logical programme as an art of argumentation.

First, it is not at all inappropriate to view Llull's logical programme, and the method of his *Art* that it adopts, from a totally non-logical perspective as something like a 'Christian phenomenology' or perhaps more exactly, a gnoseology of Anselmian *rectitudo*. That is, it offers a programme for comprehending the truth of any thing according to its agreement with the Supreme Truth that is God. This conception of truth assumes a participational ontology of particulars derived from universals, and projects a corresponding epistemology of universals apprehended from particulars. It ensures the mind's necessary recognition of Divine Truth in all particulars by deriving all universals from God, who is the mind's natural and proper object as the Highest Good and Truth. Llull's fundamental doctrine of intention, notions of supposition, and views on the roles of faith and reason all serve to support this programme. All this is obvious, and simply comprises a correlation of theocentric existence with theocentric knowledge. Llull's effort to specify every possible point of this correlation according to his Christian conception of that divine centre—the letter A surrounded by the letters B to K in the First Figure of his *Art*—produces innumerable secret significations that his moralizing procedures of interpretation and argument labour to reveal. The profusion of unmoralized real or rational beings whose existence remains unconverted to signifying Divine Truth never daunts Llull's conviction that all existence necessarily manifests not only the One God, but the Christian Revelation of him as well. Where his contemporaries were coming to accept a separation between what reason understands about this world and what belief accepts about the next, Llull still insists that 'just as if God does not exist, then nothing exists, so if God is not understood as described in the Articles of Faith, nothing is understood in this world or beyond'.

Llull's Logic

The details of the logical programme that Llull develops within this perspective can be summarized as follows. As one particular art, Logic must derive for Llull from his General Universal Art, and this derivation characteristically takes the form of a broadly comparative moralization that contrasts the whole Scholastic cult of dialectic to his own method as an inferior secular instrument to a superior sacred end. In his earlier works he simply asserts the derivation of all logical elements from the *Principia* and *Regulae* of his own *Art*; later, as he adopts a vehemently antagonistic posture toward his peers in the schools, he attempts to redefine the formal structures of Aristotelian argument according to his conception of their first intention. Llull rejects entirely the conception of Logic as an *ars sermocinalis* concerned with the truth in words and instead conceives it solely as an *ars realis*, or 'natural' art, as he says, concerned with the true natures of things, which necessarily reflect the Supreme Truth.

Thus he understands the predicables and categories as distinctions in the metaphysical and physical constitution of real beings. Llull is a 'super-Realist'. For him, the predicables name not class relationships but levels in the contraction of universals to particulars, conceived either physically as a relation of part to whole or more often metaphysically as limits of participation through resemblance. Likewise the categories name real, universal attributes of being. Llull's extreme essentialist ontology and strongly active conception of participation through resemblance lead him to posit his peculiar view of a substantial and accidental form or essence for *every* category; thus he sees in any being a substantial and accidental act, quantity, habit, and so forth, which are likenesses of each other and more or less direct expressions of the being's essential nature.

This natural conception of the basic categorematic terms manipulated in propositions obviously makes Llull's practice of predication very different from his contemporaries'. In fact, he generally ignores all predicative distinctions of categorematic and syncategorematic or quantifying and qualifying terms in order to interpret every proposition as expressing a mode of participation. Llull recognizes only the affirmation or negation of propositions, in so far as they correctly explain that participation by referring particulars to their relevant universals. Determining what is correct or relevant obviously depends on acceptance of Llull's favoured theological and metaphysical values. His own conviction of their truth leads him to assume, however, that any mind properly oriented to its first intention will, when it supposes or posits a proposition about those values, affirm them by virtue of the mind's natural attraction to the truth. Likewise, the properly ordered mind will deny any supposition that expresses the opposite of those values. Thus the formal mechanics of Llull's entire logical programme consists in the affirmation or negation of suppositions that the mind naturally accepts as its proper, or rejects as its improper, objects. In his earlier works, Llull attempts to develop plans of disputation based on the proper orientation of the mind and its consequent affirmation or negation of suppositions presented to it. Perhaps because of the limited practical success of these plans, Llull turned his attention in his later years to redefining the formal structures of Scholastic syllogistics and sophistics according to his method for affirming or negating suppositions.

From his earliest writings, Llull treats the entire syllogism more as an object, and less as an instrument, of knowledge. Following his basic metaphysical doctrines, he conceives that a particular syllogism expresses truth because it participates in universal truth, and attempts to explain its validity as the communication of an essential form of true necessity from premises to conclusion, rather than from the causal connections identified by Aristotle. Because syllogisms either do or do not express truth, Llull develops his procedure of 'contradictory syllogisms', which oppose each other because they use the affirmation and negation of the same supposition as their major premises, and thus necessarily lead to opposing conclusions. Llull regularly distinguishes superior syllogisms based on his criteria of truth, primacy, and necessity from inferior ones based on his Scholastic contemporaries' criteria; none the less, he often introduces syllogistic figures as analogous *exempla* for the truth in other beings or their relations, and thus recognizes in a popular sense the supreme status of the syllogism as the instrument of scientific knowledge.

With the fallacies, Llull attempts in his later period a much more ambitiously technical reformulation of their verbal structures. Drawing on Algazel's summary of the apparent contradictions caused by equivocal uses of terms, Llull restates all thirteen Aristotelian fallacies as instances of one equivocal contradiction. He understands contradiction as the affirmation and negation of a predication, and thus rewrites every fallacy in the form of a syllogism that concludes a compound contradiction ('Every A is B and not B') by combining two contradictory premisses. He resolves the contradiction by finding equivocal terms in the two premisses, and then rejects the premiss that uses a 'false' sense of the equivocal term. Formally, this produces a tautology, and Llull eventually abandons his efforts to develop it further. This conception of fallacy undoubtedly appealed to Llull because its conflation of equivocation and contradiction allowed him to interpret the opposing affirmations and negations of a position, as in his opponents' rejections of his views, as the 'fallacious' equivocation of truth and falsehood or perhaps of a higher and a lower truth.

It is Llull's concern for attaining that Supreme Truth that gives these peculiar adaptations of logical discourse demonstrative value for Llull. To him, demonstration is any argument that leads the soul to knowledge of the Supreme Truth and thereby fulfils man's first intention to know, love, and honour God. His whole missionary programme for 'proving' Christian truth to the infidels assumes that natural theology can accomplish this by tracing particular truths back to the universal Truth. Knowledge corresponds to being—both are modes of existence of truth—and the most certain knowledge, or demonstration, must correspond to the most certain being, God; hence Llull's supreme demonstration *per aequiparantiam* expresses the supremely coessential equivalence of God's attributes and Persons.

In earlier works such as the *Libre de contemplació*, Llull broadly treats demonstration as the properly ordered ascent from sense to intellectual knowledge; later he emphasizes the separation of sense from intellectual truth, which often contradict each other. Llull's insistence on this hierarchy of being and knowledge, which the soul ascends in striving to apprehend the Supreme Truth, is not immediately compatible with Christian doctrine regarding the roles of faith and under-standing, especially Anselm's *credo ut intelligam*, and Llull struggles throughout his career to reconcile his breed of natural theology with the tenets of dogma. The functions of grace and free will are particu-larly difficult to explain within his system, which already attributes to the mind a natural attraction to God as its highest proper object and assumes that the expression of this attraction in suppositions, even by infidels, actively realizes man's first intention. In his earliest works, Llull suggests a joint illumination by grace of the Will and Intellect in order to explain the contributions of faith and reason to those suppo-sitions, and defines a proportional scheme in which each faculty grows with the other. Llull always asserts that faith and reason have the same objects, including the Articles of Faith that his contemporaries consi-dered beyond the reach of reason, and always tends to denigrate faith as an inferior and unstable mode of knowledge. Later he abandons explanations through illumination, and attempts to describe a scheme where faith, in acts of supposition, leads the Intellect to attain higher and higher truths, and this use of suppositions is the basis for his reforms in syllogistics and sophistics as means of expressing this ascent to truth. Obviously this scheme neglects the roles of grace and free will and thus rightly incurs condemnation as rationalist, which Llull escapes by adding qualifications and appeals to the precedence of faith that in fact render his scheme unworkable. Overall, he seeks to combine the desire for truth and understanding of the truth into one desire for understanding as a necessary method of impelling the soul to accept truth. His spiritual Logic formalizes this method as the affirma-tive or negative understanding of naturally desirable or undesirable suppositions. Only the dynamic bond between the many and the one can ultimately sustain this method, and Llull's Logic serves above all to reveal that dynamic sustenance at work.

Llull's Logic and the arts of argument

A logical programme so obviously founded on spiritual principles might seem unlikely to serve very many practical purposes outside the cloister or choir. Many scholars have rightly regarded his entire system as a plan of mystical contemplation. None the less, the particular procedures that Llull develops in his programme, and in his Great Universal Art generally, have a real import for the arts of argumen-tation, conceived almost entirely apart from his spiritual values. This import consists in its very broad and very fecund exploitation of all forms of argument from comparison, analogy, proportion, congruence, correlation, or consequences as procedures of moralization, in the sense defined in the Introduction to this study. For Llull these arguments are the superlative, if not the necessary, means of expressing his theocentric conception of all existence according to a metaphysics of participation through resemblance, but its value as a method of argument is still recognizable independently of those theological and ontological foundations. Renaissance devotees of Llull's *Art* appreciated precisely this value, and the publication in those centuries of his own logical and rhetorical works, as well as apocryphal ones attributed to him, clearly testify to the perceived utility of his programme as a dialectical art. Many sixteenth-century authorities also appreciated Llull's *Art* as a possible system of universal knowledge or artificial memory, since these too include discursive aspects, especially in their inventional functions.

The ultimate consequence of the historical testimony to the value of Llull's method is that it serves to diminish the perception of his work as somehow wholly anomalous or singular in its historical context. The appreciation of its moralizing procedures by contemporaries or successors implies its accommodation to or derivation from others already known or practised by them. A sufficiently broad search for parallels to Llull's methods will probably show that they compare most easily to those used in the tremendous corpus of medieval devotional, exegetical, and sermon literature. Since this study emphasizes the spiritual character of Llull's programme for Logic and General Art as a whole, it readily supports the hypothesis that Llull's techniques of moralizing argument, evidently formed primally and immutably at the outset of his career, are products of a deep assimilation of that literature, where those techniques flourished abundantly, and probably owe much less than imagined to any special insights into the formal arguments from analogy defined by Aristotle or suggested in Arab or Latin authorities. The arguments of those religious genres are typically less formal than those of logical disputation, and therefore compare favourably with the popular character of Llull's work; they are typically exegetical or interpretative, rather than probative, a function that corresponds well to Llull's explication of a being's congruence with his *Principia*; finally, the purpose of that literature matches Llull's own original missionological goals, which, like his moralizing arguments, he never abandoned. Modern views of Llull's Great Universal Art as a mystical system, while largely inaccurate, none the less rightly recognize its function as a programme of 'spiritual exercise' and in this sense a legitimate precursor of another Spanish divine and proponent of the True Faith. Such a suggestion about the original inspiration of Llull's methods evidently serves to remove him even further from the ambit of the schools and academic philosophy or theology in his day; yet it by no means diminishes the extraordinary character of his contribution to modern understanding of medieval culture. For if the spiritual Logic of Ramon Llull does not earn a place for him among the great Scholastic masters such as Aquinas or Scotus, it surely wins his position in the first rank of the great moral teachers, such as Saints Bernard or Francis, and sets his *Art* apart as one of the Middle Age's most ambitious and enthusiastic projects for exhorting the soul to righteousness.

List of Works Cited

The note on References and Quotations at the beginning of this study explains the system of citations employed throughout this work. In the following list, each entry includes an indication of the abbreviation employed for a particular work (if any), and the pages or textual divisions designated by the reference numbers.

Classical and medieval authors

Albert the Great, *Liber de praedicabilibus*, in *Opera omnia*, ed. August Borgnet, vol. 1 (Paris: L. Vivès, 1890), pp. 149–304 (book, tract, chapter).

——, *Liber topicorum*, in *Opera omnia*, ed. August Borgnet, vol. 2 (Paris: L. Vivès, 1890) (*Top*. book, tract, chapter).

——, *Physicorum libri VIII*, in *Opera omnia*, ed. August Borgnet, vol. 3 (Paris: L. Vivès, 1890) (*Phys*. book, tract, chapter).

——, *Summa de creaturis*, in *Opera omnia*, ed. August Borgnet, vols. 34–5 (Paris: L. Vivès, 1890) (part, article, question).

Alexander of Hales, *Summa theologicae*, 4 vols. in 5 (Quaracchi: Collegium S. Bonaventurae, 1924–48) (book, chapter).

Algazel, *Logic*, in Charles H. Lohr, 'Logica Algazelis. Introduction and Critical Text', *Traditio*, 21 (1965), 223–90 (*LA* or *Log*. maniera, line).

——, *Metaphysics*, ed. J. T. Muckle, *Algazel's Metaphysics: A Medieval Translation* (Toronto: St Michael's College, 1933) (*M* part, tract, chapter, section).

Anselm, *De veritate*, in *Opera omnia*, ed. Franciscus S. Schmitt, vol. 1 (Edinburgh: T. Nelson, 1946), pp. 169–99 (*De ver*. chapter).

——, *Monologion*, in *Opera omnia*, ed. Franciscus S. Schmitt, vol. 1 (Edinburgh: T. Nelson, 1946), pp. 1–87 (*Monol*. chapter).

Aquinas, Thomas, *De ente et essentia*, in *Opuscula philosophica*, ed. Raimondo M. Spiazzi (Turin: Marietti, 1954), pp. 5–18 (chapter).

——, *In Aristotelis libros Peri hermeneias et Posteriorum Analyticorum*, ed. Raimondo M. Spiazzi (Turin: Marietti, 1955) (*In* Book *Post. An*. lectio, comment).

——, *In duodecim libros Metaphysicorum Aristotelis expositio*, ed. M. R. Cathala and R. M. Spiazzi (Turin: Marietti, 1950) (*In* Book *Metaph*. lectio, comment).

——, *In VIII libros Physicorum Aristotelis*, in *Opera omnia*, vol. 2 (Rome: Commissio Leonina, 1884) (*In* Book *Phys*. lectio, comment).

——, *Quaestiones disputatae De potentia Dei* and *De veritate*, in *Quaestiones disputatae et quaestiones duodecim quodlibetales*, 4 vols. (Turin: Marietti, 1927) (*De pot. Dei* and *De ver.* question, article).

——, *Summa contra gentiles*, Editio Leonina manualis (Rome: Libreria Vaticana, 1934) (*CG* book, chapter, paragraph).

——, *Summa Theologiae*, Blackfriars edn., 60 vols. (New York: McGraw-Hill and London: Eyre & Spottiswoode, 1964–76) (part, article, question).

Aristotle, *Aristoteles Latinus*, ed. Laurentius Minio-Paluello, 12 vols. to date (Bruges: Desclée de Brouwer for the Union Académique Internationale, 1953–) and *The Complete Works of Aristotle: The Revised Oxford Translation*, ed. Jonathan Barnes, 2 vols. (Princeton: Princeton University Press, 1984) (book, chapter Bekker pages—with these abbreviations: *An. post. Analytica posteriora*; *An. pr. Analytica priora*; *Cat. Categoriae*; *De an. De anima*; *De caelo*; *De gen. et corr. De generatione et corruptione*; *De interp. De interpretatione*; *De soph. el. De sophisticis elenchis*; *Eth.*, *Ethica Nicomachea*; *Metaph. Metaphysica*; *Phys. Physica*; *Rhet. Rhetorica*; *Top. Topica*).

Augustine, *De doctrina christiana*, ed. William M. Green, Corpus Scriptorum Ecclesiasticorum Latinorum, vol. 80 (Vienna: Hoelder–Pichter–Tempsky, 1963) (*Doc. christ.* book, chapter, paragraph).

——, *De ordine*, ed. P. Knoll, Corpus Scriptorum Ecclesiasticorum Latinorum, vol. 63 (Vienna: Hoelder–Pichter–Tempsky, 1922), pp. 119–85 (*De ord.* book, chapter, paragraph).

——, *De trinitate*, ed. W. J. Mountain, Corpus Christianorum, Series Latina, vols. 50 and 50A (Turnholt: Brepols, 1968) (*De trin.* book, chapter, paragraph).

——, *Soliloquia*, in Patrologia Latina, vol. 32 (Paris: J.-P. Migne, 1841), cols. 869–904 (*Sol.* book, chapter).

Avicebron, *Fons vitae*, ed. Clemens Baeumker, Beiträge zur Geschichte der Philosophie des Mittelalters, vol. 1, pts. 1–4 (Münster: Aschendorffsche Buchhandlung, 1891–5) (book, chapter).

Avicenna, *De anima, Logica* and *Sufficientia*, in *Opera philosophica* (Venice, 1508; repr. Louvain: Bibliotheca Societatis Jesu, 1961), paged separately (*De an., Log.* and *Suff.* part/book, chapter).

——, *Metaphysics*, ed. S. Van Reit, *Liber de philosophia divina sive scientia divina*, 2 vols. (Leiden: E. J. Brill, 1977–80) (*Metaph.* tract, chapter).

Bartholomeus Anglicus, *De rerum proprietatibus* (Frankfurt, 1601; repr. Frankfurt am Main: Minerva, 1964) (book, chapter).

Boethius, *De consolatione philosophiae*, in Patrologia Latina, vol. 63 (Paris: J.-P. Migne, 1882), cols. 579–870 (book, line).

——, *De differentiis topicis, De syllogismo hypothetico*, and *In Categorias Aristotelis*, in Patrologia Latina, vol. 64 (Paris: J.-P. Migne, 1891), cols. 1173–217, 831–75, and 159–293 (*De diff. top.*, *De syll. hyp.* and *In Cat.* part; column).

——, *In Isagogen Porphyrii Commenta*, ed. Samuel Brandt, Corpus Scriptorum

Ecclesiasticorum Latinorum, vol. 48 (Vienna: Tempsky, 1906) (*In Isag.* book, chapter).

Bonaventure, *Breviloquium*, in *Opera*, vol. 5 (Quaracchi: Collegium S. Bonaventurae, 1891), pp. 199–291 (part, chapter).

Cassiodorus, *Institutiones*, ed. R. A. B. Mynors (Oxford: Clarendon Press, 1937) (book, chapter, paragraph).

Cicero, *De inventione* and *Topica*, ed. H. M. Hubbell (London: Heinemann, 1949) (*De inv.* and *Top.* book, chapter, paragraph).

——, *De oratore*, ed. E. W. Sutton and H. Rackham, 2 vols. (London: Heinemann, 1948) (*De orat.* book, chapter, paragraph).

De natura accidentis (attributed to Aquinas), ed. Raimondo M. Spiazzi in Divi Thomae Aquinatis *Opusucula philosophica* (Turin: Marietti, 1954), pp. 169–74 (paragraph).

Dominicus Gundissalinus, *De divisione philosophiae*, ed. L. Baur, Beiträge zur Geschichte der Philosophie des Mittelalters, vol. 4, pts. 2–3 (Münster: Aschendorffsche Buchhandlung, 1903) (page).

Duns Scotus, John, *Ordinatio*, in *Opera omnia*, vols. 1–7 (Vatican City: Typi Polyglotti Vaticani, 1950–73) (book, distinction, part, question).

Eiximenis, Francesc, *Ars praedicandi*, ed. Martí de Barcelona, 'L'*Ars praedicandi* de Francesc Eiximenis', *Analecta Sacra Tarraconensia*, 12 (1936), 301–40 (chapter, section).

Fortunatianus, C. Chirius, *Ars rhetorica*, ed. Karl Halm, *Rhetores latini minores* (Leipzig: B. G. Teubner, 1863), pp. 79–134 (book, paragraph).

Gervais of Melkley, *Ars poetica*, ed. Hans-Jürgen Gräbener (Münster: Aschendorffsche Buchhandlung, 1965) (book, chapter, paragraph).

Glossa ordinaria (attributed to Walafrid Strabo), in Patrologia Latina, vols. 113 (Paris: J.-P. Migne, 1852) and 114 (idem), cols. 9–752 (book, chapter).

Gregory the Great, *Homiliae in Evangelia*, in Patrologia Latina, vol. 76 (Paris: J.-P. Migne, 1849), cols. 1075–311 (*In Evang.* book, homily).

Hugh of Saint Victor, *De sacramentis*, in Patrologia Latina, vol. 176 (Paris: J.-P. Migne, 1854), cols. 173–618 (book, chapter).

——, *Didascalicon*, ed. Charles Henry Buttimer, *Didascalicon de studio legendi* (Washington, DC: Catholic University of America, 1939) (*Didasc.* book, chapter).

Humbert of Romans, *De eruditione praedicatorum*, in *Opera de vita regulari*, ed. Joseph Berthier, vol. 1 (Rome: A. Befani, 1888), pp. 373–484 (part, chapter).

Introductiones montane minores, ed. Lambertus M. De Rijk in *Logica Modernorum*, vol. 2, pt. 2 (Assen: Van Gorcum, 1967), pp. 7–71 (page).

Isidore, *Etymologiae*, ed. W. M. Lindsay (Oxford: Clarendon Press, 1911) (book, chapter, paragraph).

John of Damascus, *Logic*, in Patrologia Graeca, vol. 94 (Paris: J.-P. Migne, 1864), cols. 518–78 (chapter, column).

Liber de causis, ed. Adriaan Pattin, *Le Liber de causis* (Louvain: Tijdschrift voor Filosofie, s.d.) (proposition).

Liber sex principiorum (attributed to Gilbert de la Porrée), ed. Laurentius Minio-Paluello and Bernard G. Dod in *Porphyrii Isagoge translatio Boethii et Anonymi Fragmentum vulgo vocatum 'Liber sex principorum'*, Aristoteles Latinus, vol. 2, 6–7 (Bruges: Desclée de Brouwer, 1966), pp. 33–59 (*Sex prin.* paragraph).

LLULL, RAMON

COLLECTED WORKS

Obres Originals del Illuminat Doctor Mestre Ramon Lull, ed. M. Obrador y Benassar (vols. 1–3), Comissió Editora Lulliana (vols. 4–6), Salvador Galmés (vols. 7–20), and Miquel Tous Gayà and Rafel Ginard Bauçà (vol. 21), 21 vols. (Palma de Mallorca: Comissió Editora Lulliana, 1906–17 and Diputació Provincial de Balears and Institut d'Estudis Catalans, 1923–50) (*Obres Originals*, volume, page).

Opera Latina, ed. Johannes Stohr (vols. 1–2), Abraham Soria Flores (vols. 3–4), Helmut Riedlinger (vols. 5–6), Hermogenes Harada (vols. 7–8), Aloisius Madre (vol. 9), Louis Sala-Molins (vol. 10), Charles Lohr (vol. 11), 11 vols. to date (Palma de Mallorca: Maioricensis Schola Lullistica del CSIC, 1959–67 and Turnholt: Brepols, 1978–), appearing since vol. 6 in the Corpus Christianorum, Continuatio Mediaevalis (*Opera Latina*, volume, page).

Opera omnia, ed. Ivo Salzinger, 9 vols. (Mainz, 1721–40; repr. Frankfurt am Main: Minerva, 1965), with each work separately paged (Mainz, volume).

INDIVIDUAL WORKS

Aplicació de l'Art General, in *Obres Originals*, 20. 209–54 (*AAG* line).

Arbre de sciència, in *Obres Originals*, 11–13 (tree, chapter, section/paragraph, etc.—with trees abbreviated 'Elem.' [Elemental], 'Veg.' [Vegetative], etc.).

Ars brevis, in *Opera parva*, vol. 1 (Palma de Mallorca, 1744; repr. in *Opuscula*, vol. 1 at Hildesheim: H. A. Gerstenberg, 1971), paged separately (*AB* part, chapter, paragraph).

Ars brevis quae est de inventione iuris, ed. E. Wohlhaupter, *Estudis Franciscans*, 29 (1935), 161–250 (*ABI* distinction, chapter, section).

Ars generalis ultima, in *Raymundi Lulli Opera . . .* (Strasbourg: L. Zetzner, 1617), pp. 218–663 (*AGU* part, chapter).

Ars mystica, in *Opera Latina*, 5. 259–466 (*AM* distinction, part, chapter, paragraph).

Art amativa, in *Obres Originals*, 17. 1–398 (part, chapter, paragraph).

Art demostrativa, in *Obres Originals*, 16. 1–288 (*AD* distinction, part, chapter, paragraph).

Compendium logicae Algazelis, ed. Charles Lohr, *Raimundus Lullus' Compendium Logicae Algazelis* (Freiburg im Breisgau: Albert-Ludwigs-Universität, 1967) (part, paragraph).

Compendium seu commentum Artis demonstrativae, in Mainz, 3 (*CAD* page).

Disputatio fidei et intellectus, in Mainz, 3 (*DFI* part, paragraph).

Disputatio Raimundi et Averroistae, in *Opera Latina*, 7. 9–17 (*DRA* question).

Doctrina pueril, in *Obres Originals*, 1. 1–199 (*DP* chapter, paragraph).

Excusatio Raimundi, in *Opera Latina*, 11. 339–75 (page).

Liber chaos, in Mainz, 3 (rubric, page).

Liber contradictionis, in *Opera Latina*, 7. 137–58 (chapter, paragraph).

Liber de accidente et substantia, in *Opera Latina*, 1. 138–47 (principle).

Liber de affirmatione et negatione, in *Opera Latina*, 2. 21–40 (distinction, chapter).

Liber de ascensu et descensu intellectus, in *Opera Latina*, 9. 20–199 (*LADI* distinction, chapter, paragraph).

Liber de concordantia et contrarietate, in *Opera Latina*, 1. 393–401 (distinction, chapter).

Liber de convenientia fidei et intellectus in obiecto, in Mainz, 4 (*LCFI* part, paragraph).

Liber de conversione subiecti et praedicati et medii, in *Opera Latina*, 6. 262–75 (distinction, paragraph).

Liber de conversione syllogismi opinativi in demonstrativum cum vicesima fallacia, in *Opera Latina*, 11. 327–9 (paragraph).

Liber de demonstratione per aequiparantiam, in *Opera Latina*, 9. 216–32 (distinction, chapter, paragraph).

Liber de Deo et de mundo, in *Opera Latina*, 2. 341–77 (distinction, chapter).

Liber de divina voluntate infinita et ordinata, in *Opera Latina*, 1. 461–83 (distinction, chapter/paragraph).

Liber de efficiente et effectu, in *Opera Latina*, 7. 273–91 (*LEE* distinction, paragraph).

Liber de ente reali et rationis, in *Opera parva*, vol. 4 (Palma de Mallorca, 1745; repr. as *Opuscula*, vol. 2 at Hildesheim: H. A. Gerstenberg, 1972), paged separately (distinction, part/chapter).

Liber de essentia et esse Dei, in *Opera Latina*, 1. 361–75 (*LEED* distinction, paragraph).

Liber de fallaciis, in *Opera Latina*, 6. 478–88 (chapter).

Liber de fide sancta catholica, in *Opera Latina*, 6. 328–73 (*LFSC* distinction, part, paragraph).

Liber de fine, in *Opera Latina*, 9. 250–91 (distinction, chapter).

Liber de inventione maiori, in *Opera Latina*, 2. 300–2 (distinction).

Liber de medio naturali, in *Opera Latina*, 1. 205–17 (principle).

Liber de minori loco ad maiorem, in *Opera Latina*, 1. 267–75 (*LMLM* distinction, paragraph).

Liber de modo naturali intelligendi, in *Opera Latina*, 6. 188–223 (*LMNI* distinction, chapter, paragraph).

Liber de multiplicatione quae fit in essentia Dei per divinam trinitatem, in *Opera Latina*, 2. 135–46 (*LMED* distinction, chapter, paragraph).

Liber de novis fallaciis, in *Opera Latina*, 11. 1–136 (distinction, part, chapter, section, paragraph).

Liber de novo modo demonstrandi, in Mainz, 4 (*LNMD* distinction, part, paragraph).

Liber de obiecto finito et infinito, in *Opera Latina*, 2. 101–16 (*LOFI* distinction, chapter, paragraph).

Liber de perfecto esse, in *Opera Latina*, 2. 84–95 (distinction, paragraph).

Liber de perversione entis removenda, in *Opera Latina*, 5. 467–506 (*LPER* question, paragraph).

Liber de possibili et impossibili, in *Opera Latina*, 6. 384–466 (distinction, part, chapter, paragraph).

Liber de potestate pura, in *Opera Latina*, 1. 407–35 (distinction, chapter).

Liber de praedicatione, in *Opera Latina*, 3–4 (*LP* distinction, part, chapter, paragraph).

Liber de quinque praedicabilibus et decem praedicamentis, in *Opera Latina*, 1. 333–45 (distinction, chapter).

Liber de significatione, in *Opera Latina*, 10. 11–100 (distinction, part, chapter, paragraph).

Liber de syllogismis contradictoriis, in *Opera Latina*, 7. 169–98 (distinction, chapter).

Liber de vita divina, in *Opera Latina*, 2. 75–9 (syllogism).

Liber facilis scientiae, in *Opera Latina*, 7. 303–17 (part).

Liber lamentationis philosophiae, in *Opera Latina*, 7. 85–126 (*LLP* chapter).

Liber novus physicorum, in *Opera Latina*, 6. 64–83 (*LNP* distinction, part/chapter, paragraph).

Libre de Blanquerna, in *Obres Originals*, 9 (*Blanquerna* chapter, paragraph).

Libre de contemplació en Déu, in *Obres Originals*, 2–8 (*LC* chapter, paragraph).

Libre de demostracions, in *Obres Originals*, 15 (*LD* distinction, chapter, paragraph).

Libre de intenció, in *Obres Originals*, 18. 1–66 (part, chapter, paragraph).

Libre de meravelles, ed. Salvador Galmés, 4 vols., Els nostres classics, Col-lecció A, 34, 38, 42, and 46–7 (Barcelona: Barcino, 1931–4) (*LM* chapter).

Lògica del Gatzell, in *Obres Originals*, 19. 1–62 (line).

Logica nova, in *Logica nova jam Valentiae impressa anno 1512. Et nunc Palmae cum libris Logica Parva . . .* (Palma de Mallorca, 1744; repr. Frankfurt am Main: Minerva, 1971), paged separately, used to assign textual divisions, only; all quotations are from the text in Paris, Bibliothèque Nationale MS latinus 6443c, ff. 58va–95va, which is free from the emendations of the 1512 editors (*LN* distinction, part, chapter, paragraph; MS folio; 1744 page).

Metaphysica nova et compendiosa, in *Opera Latina*, 6. 10–51 (*MN* distinction, part, chapter).

Mil proverbis, in *Obres Originals*, 14. 325–72 (*MP* chapter, proverb).

Proverbis de Ramon, in *Obres Originals*, 14. 1–324 (*PR* chapter, proverb).

Rethorica nova, from Paris, Bibliothèque Nationale MS latinus 6443c, ff. 95va–109va (distinction, chapter, paragraph).

Sermones contra errores Averrois, in *Opera Latina*, 7. 245–62 (part, paragraph).

Taula general, in *Obres Originals*, 16. 295–522 (*TG* distinction, part, chapter, paragraph).

Marius Victorinus, *Liber de diffinitione*, in Boethius, *Opera omnia*, Tomus posterior, Patrologia Latina, vol. 64 (Paris: J.-P. Migne, 1891), cols. 891–909 (column).

Ockham, William of, *Summa logicae*, ed. Philotheus Boehner, Gedeon Gál, and Stephen Brown (St Bonaventure, NY: Franciscan Institute, 1974) (part/sub-part, chapter).

Peter of Spain, *Summule logicales*, ed. Lambertus M. De Rijk, *Tractatus called afterwards Summule logicales* (Assen: Van Gorcum, 1972) (*SL* tractate, paragraph).

Porphyry, *Isagoge*, ed. Laurentius Minio-Paluello and Bernard G. Dod, *Porphyrii Isagoge Translatio Boethii*, Aristoteles Latinus, vol. 1, 6–7 (Bruges: Desclée de Brouwer, 1966), pp. 1–31 (page).

Priscian, *Institutiones grammaticae*, ed. Martin Hertz, in *Grammatici latini*, ed. H. Keil, vols. 2–3 (Leipzig: B. G. Teubner, 1855–9) (book, chapter, paragraph).

Pseudo-Augustine, *De dialectica*, ed. B. Darrell Jackson (Dordrecht: D. Reidel, 1975) (chapter).

——, *De rhetorica*, ed. Karl Halm in *Rhetores latini minores* (Leipzig: B. G. Teubner, 1863), pp. 135–51 (chapter).

Pseudo-Boethius, *De disciplina scholarium*, ed. Olga Weijers (Leiden: E. J. Brill, 1976) (chapter, paragraph).

Quintilian, *Institutio oratoria*, ed. H. E. Butler, 4 vols. (London: Heinemann, 1920–2) (book, chapter, paragraph).

Richard of Saint Victor, *De trinitate*, in Patrologia Latina, vol. 196 (Paris: J.-P. Migne, 1880), cols. 887–992 (*De trin.* book, chapter).

Richard of Thetford, *Ars dilatandi sermones*, published as Part 3 of *Ars concionandi* attributed to Bonaventure, *Opera omnia*, vol. 9 (Quaracchi: Collegium S. Bonaventurae, 1901), pp. 16–21 (paragraph).

Robert of Basevorn, *Forma praedicandi*, ed. Th.-M. Charland, *Artes praedicandi. Contribution à l'Histoire de la Rhetorique au Moyen Âge* (Paris: J. Vrin and Ottawa: Institut d'Études Médiévales, 1936), pp. 231–323 (chapter).

Tractatus de proprietatibus sermonum, ed. Lambertus M. De Rijk in *Logica Modernorum*, vol. 2, pt. 2 (Assen: Van Gorcum, 1967), pp. 703–30 (page).

Vincent of Beauvais, *Speculum doctrinale*, *Speculum morale*, and *Speculum naturale*, in *Bibliotheca mundi*, vols. 1–3 (Douay, 1624; repr. Graz: Akademische Druck- u. Verlagsanstalt, 1964–5) (*SD*, *SM*, and *SN* book/distinction, chapter).

William of Auvergne (attributed), *De faciebus*, ed. A. De Poorter, 'Un Manuel de prédication médiévale', *Revue Néo-scholastique de philosophie*, 25 (1923), 192–209 (chapter).

William of Sherwood, *Introductiones in logicam*, tr. Norman Kretzmann, *Introduction to Logic* (Minneapolis: University of Minnesota Press, 1966) (chapter, paragraph).

Secondary studies

Since this listing gives only the works cited in order to illuminate particular points in the present study, it can in no way be a comprehensive guide to the relevant literature on either medieval Logic or the work of Llull. For the former, consult the extensive bibliographies in *The Cambridge History of Later Medieval Philosophy*, ed. N. Kretzmann, A. Kenny, and J. Pinborg (Cambridge: Cambridge University Press, 1982); for the latter, see R. Brummer, *Bibliographia Lulliana. Ramon-Llull-Schrifttum* 1870–1973 (Hildesheim: H. A. Gerstenberg, 1976) and the additions noted by editors of Llull's *Opera Latina* (6. viii and 10. x).

Ashworth, E. J., *Language and Logic in the Post-Medieval Period* (Dordrecht: D. Reidel, 1974).

Bennett, R. F., *The Early Dominicans. Studies in Thirteenth-Century Dominican History* (Cambridge: Cambridge University Press, 1937).

Bird, Otto, 'The Tradition of the Logical Topics: Aristotle to Ockham', *Journal of the History of Ideas*, 23 (1962), 307–23.

Boehner, Philotheus, *Medieval Logic: An Outline of Its Development from 1250 to c.1400* (Manchester: Manchester University Press, 1952).

Brown, Stephen, 'Robert Cowton, O.F.M. and the Analogy of the Concept of Being', *Franciscan Studies*, 31 (1971), 5–40.

Bursill-Hall, Geoffrey, *Speculative Grammars of the Middle Ages* (Paris & The Hague: Mouton, 1971).

Carreras y Artau, Joaquín & Tomás, *Historia de la filosofía española: filosofía cristiana de los siglos XIII al XIV*, 2 vols. (Madrid: Asociación Española para el Progreso de las Ciencias, 1939–43).

Cruz Hernández, Miguel, *El pensamiento de Ramon Llull* (Madrid: Castalia, 1977).

De Rijk, Lambertus M., *Logica Modernorum. A Contribution to the History of Early Terminist Logic*, 2 vols. (Assen: Van Gorcum: 1962–7).

Eijo Garay, Leopoldo, 'La luz divina en la gnoseología luliana', *Estudios Lulianos*, 15 (1971), 153–73.

Fitzpatrick, Noel A., 'Walter Chatton on the Univocity of Being: A Reaction to Peter Aureoli and William Ockham', *Franciscan Studies*, 31 (1971), 88–126.

Gayà Estelric, J., *La teoría luliana de los correlativos. Historia de su formación conceptual* (Palma de Mallorca, 1979).

Geiger, Louis-Bertrand, *La Participation dans la philosophie de S. Thomas d'Aquin* (Paris: J. Vrin, 1953).

Gersh, Stephen E., *From Iamblichus to Eriugena: An Investigation of the Evolution of the Pseudo-Dionysian Tradition* (Leiden: E. J. Brill, 1978).

Gilson, Étienne, *Reason and Revelation in the Middle Ages* (New York: Scribner's, 1938).

Gracia, Jorge E., 'La doctrina luliana de las razones necesarias en el contexto de algunas de sus doctrinas epistemológicas y sicológicas', *Estudios Lulianos*, 19 (1975), 25–40.

——, 'The Structural Elements of Necessary Reasons in Anselm and Llull', *Diálogos*, 9 (1973), 105–29.

Heidegger, Martin, *Identity and Difference*, tr. Joan Stambaugh (New York: Harper & Row Torchbooks, 1974).

Henry, Desmond Paul, *The Logic of Saint Anselm* (Oxford: Clarendon Press, 1967).

Hillgarth, Jocelyn N., 'La biblioteca de La Real: fuentes posibles de Llull', *Estudios Lulianos*, 7 (1963), 5–17.

——, *Ramon Lull and Lullism in Fourteenth-Century France* (Oxford: Clarendon Press, 1971).

Howell, Wilbur Samuel, *Logic and Rhetoric in England, 1500–1700* (1956; repr. New York: Russell & Russell, 1961).

Hunt, Richard W., 'The Introduction to the "Artes" in the Twelfth Century', in *Studia Mediaevalia in honorem admodum Reverendi Patris Raymundi Josephi Martin* (Bruges: De Tempel, 1948), pp. 85–112.

Javelet, Robert, *Image et ressemblance au douzième siècle de Saint Anselme à Alain de Lille*, 2 vols. (Strasbourg: University of Strasbourg, 1967).

Johnston, Mark D., 'The Reception of the Lullian *Art*, 1450–1530', *Sixteenth Century Journal*, 12 (1981), 31–48.

——, 'The Treatment of Speech in Medieval Ethical and Courtesy Literature', *Rhetorica*, 4 (1986), 21–46.

——, 'Ramon Llull's Proposal of Speech as a Sixth Sense', Paper delivered at Twentieth International Congress on Medieval Studies, Kalamazoo, Mich., 11 May 1985.

Knowles, David, *The Evolution of Medieval Thought* (New York: Random House, 1962).

Kretzmann, Norman, 'Medieval Logicians on the Meaning of the *Propositio*', *Journal of Philosophy*, 67 (1970), 767–87.

Lauer, R. Z., 'St. Albert and the Theory of Abstraction', *Thomist*, 17 (1954), 69–83.

Leff, Gordon, *The Dissolution of the Medieval Outlook: An Essay on Intellectual and Spiritual Change in the Fourteenth Century* (New York: Harper & Row, 1976).

——, *Medieval Thought. St. Augustine to Ockham* (Harmondsworth: Penguin Books, 1958).

——, *Paris and Oxford Universities in the Thirteenth and Fourteenth Centuries* (New York: John Wiley & Sons, 1968).

Lloyd, A. C., 'Neoplatonists' Account of Predication and Medieval Logic', in *Le Néoplatonisme* (Paris: CNRS, 1971), pp. 357–62.

Lohr, Charles, 'Ibn Sab'in of Murcia and the Development of the Lullian Art', Segundo Congreso Internacional de Lulismo, Palma de Mallorca, October 1976.

——, 'Logica Algazelis. Introduction and Critical Text', *Traditio*, 21 (1965), 223–90.

——, *Raimundus Lullus' Compendium Logicae Algazelis. Quellen, Lehre, und Stellung in der Geschichte der Logik* (Freiburg im Breisgau: Albert-Ludwigs-Universität, 1967).

MacClintock, Stuart, *Perversity and Error: Studies on the 'Averroist' John of Jandun* (Bloomington: Indiana University Press, 1956).

McGovern, Thomas, 'The Division of Logic', *Laval Philosophique et Théologique*, 11 (1955), 157–81.

Minnis, A. J., 'Discussions of "Authorial Role" and "Literary Form" in Late-Medieval Scriptural Exegesis', *Beiträge zur Geschichte der deutschen Sprache und Literatur*, 99 (1977), 37–65.

Murphy, James J., *Rhetoric in the Middle Ages. A History of Rhetorical Theory from St. Augustine to the Renaissance* (Berkeley: University of California Press, 1974).

Pascual, Antonio Raymundo, 'Comparación de la lógica luliana con la aristotélica', *Revista Luliana*, 4, No. 29 (Feb. 1904), 13–16.

——, 'Comparación de la metafísica luliana con la aristotélica y la de otros', *Revista Luliana*, 4, No. 30 (Mar. 1904), 23–6.

——, 'Comparación del arte luliana con la Lógica de Aristóteles y la de los otros', *Revista Luliana*, 3, No. 25 (Oct. 1903), 251–60.

——, 'De las condiciones universales', *Revista Luliana*, 4, No. 33 (June 1904), 69–73.

——, 'De las definiciones de los principios universales', *Revista Luliana*, 4, No. 32 (May 1904), 51–5.

——, 'De las reglas generales', *Revista Luliana*, 4, No. 34 (July–Sept. 1904), 102–11.

——, 'Del sistema del Arte Luliana y la solidez e infalibilidad de sus principios de discurrir en todas las cosas', *Revista Luliana*, 4, No. 31 (Apr. 1904), 39–43.

Pelikan, Jaroslav, *The Growth of Medieval Theology (600–1300)* (Chicago: University of Chicago Press, 1978).

Perarnau i Espelt, Josep, 'Lo sisè seny, lo qual apel·lam affatus, de Ramon Llull', *Arxiu de Textos Catalans Antics*, 2 (1983), 23–103.

Platzeck, Erhard Wolfram, 'La combinatoria luliana', *Revista de filosofía*, 12 (1953), 575–609 and 13 (1954), 125–65.

——, 'Descubrimiento y esencia del Arte del Beato Ramon Llull', *Estudios Lulianos*, 8 (1964), 137–54.

——, *La evolución de la lógica griega en el aspecto especial de la analogía (desde la época de los Presocráticos hasta Aristóteles)* (Barcelona: Consejo Superior de Investigaciones Científicas, 1954).

——, *Raimund Lull. Sein Leben—Seine Werke. Die Grundlagen seines Denkens (Prinzipienlehre)*, 2 vols. (Rome: Editiones Franciscanae & Düsseldorf: Verlag L. Schwann, 1962–4).

——, 'Raimund Lulls Auffassung von der Logik (Was ist an Lulls Logik formale Logik?)', *Estudios Lulianos*, 2 (1958), 5–36 and 273–96.

Pring-Mill, Robert D. F., 'The Analogical Structure of the Lullian Art', in *Islamic Philosophy and the Classical Tradition: Essays presented to Richard Walzer* (Columbia, SC: University of South Carolina Press, 1973), pp. 315–26.

——, *El microcosmos lul·lià* (Oxford: Dolphin, 1961).

——, 'Ramón Lull y las tres potencias del alma', *Estudios Lulianos*, 12 (1968), 101–30.

——, 'The Trinitarian World-Picture of Ramón Lull', *Romanistisches Jahrbuch*, 7 (1955–6), 229–56.

Sala-Molins, Louis, *La Philosophie de l'amour chez Raymond Lulle* (Paris & The Hague: Mouton, 1974).

Smith, Margaret, *Al-Ghazali, the Mystic* (London: Luzac & Co., 1949).

Tusquets, Juan, *Ramón Lull, pedagogo de la cristiandad* (Madrid: Consejo Superior de Investigaciones Científicas, 1954).

Urvoy, Dominique, *Penser l'islam: les présupposés islamiques de l'"Art" de Lull*, Études Musulmanes, 23 (Paris: J. Vrin, 1980).

Van Steenberghen, Fernand, *The Philosophical Movement in the Thirteenth Century* (Edinburgh: Thomas Nelson, 1955).

Warren, Edward (ed. and tr.), *Isagoge* (Toronto: Pontifical Institute of Medieval Studies, 1975).

Washell, Richard F., 'Logic, Language, and Albert the Great', *Journal of the History of Ideas*, 34 (1973), 445–50.

Weinberg, Julius, *A Short History of Medieval Philosophy* (Princeton: Princeton University Press, 1964).

Wensinck, Arent Jan, *La Pensée de Ghazzali* (Paris: Adrien-Maisonneuve, 1940).

Yates, Frances A., 'The Art of Ramon Lull', *Journal of the Warburg and Courtauld Institute*, 17 (1954), 115–73.

Index

abstraction in Llull's epistemology, 169–72, 187, 236, 292
Abu Hafs Omar I, King of Tunis, 13
Acre, 13
activism of being in Llull's metaphysics, 19–20, 54, 60, 69, 113, 166, 188, 191, 194, 200, 204, 205–6, 223, 237, 280, 314
Affatus, 3
affirmation, doubt, and negation in Llull's *Art*, 76–93, 102, 107–8, 118, 130, 143, 161, 185, 192, 226, 232–3, 238–47, 248, 258–62, 267, 270, 272–3, 280, 282–8, 291–3, 297–8, 315
Albert the Great, 37, 63 n. 3, 104, 138, 189, 211
Alexander of Hales, 78, 130
Alfarabi, 168
Alfonso III of Aragon, 12
Algazel, 10, 11, 18, 19, 32–44, 94, 97, 107, 111, 149, 158–60, 216–19, 221, 223, 249–50, 254, 257, 263–6, 307, 316
Almería, 14
Almohadism, 9
analogy, as master method of Llull's *Art*, 5–6, 18, 78, 83, 103, 156, 183, 198, 220, 251, 261, 286, 299, 302, 305, 318
Anselm, Saint, Archbishop of Canterbury, 10, 11, 20, 82, 84, 118, 125–6, 128, 133, 233, 235, 311, 317
De veritate, 24, 83, 85, 86, 145
Monologion, 17, 81, 118
antecedent and consequent, in Llull's *Art*, 93, 96–8, 119, 132, 221–2, 251, 272, 284, 306
anti-Averroism, in Llull's work, 10, 12, 13, 14, 150, 240, 243–4, 258–62, 283, 286, 288, 294–5
Apulia, 12
Aquinas, Thomas, Saint, 9, 10, 37, 130, 319

In duodecim libros Metaphysicorum, 46, 154, 159, 182, 189, 198, 200, 239
De ente et essentia, 191
In VIII libros Physicorum, 213–14, 251
In libros Posteriorum Analyticorum, 104
De potentia Dei, 177
Summa contra gentiles, 121, 154
Summa Theologiae, 17, 47, 65, 66, 68, 69, 70, 72, 78, 83, 85, 86, 87, 89, 92, 102, 103, 105, 111, 116, 121, 123–6, 131, 135–6, 143–4, 161, 163, 166–7, 170–1, 173–4, 177, 179, 181, 188–9, 191, 193–4, 198, 200–1, 203, 205–6, 211–12, 215, 247, 259–60, 297–301, 311–12
De veritate, 91, 92
Aristotle and Aristotelian doctrines, 4, 26, 31, 43, 59, 62, 66, 80, 86, 100, 107, 135, 153, 156, 165, 186, 196, 233, 238, 248, 258, 287, 294, 312
Categories, 36, 41, 65, 66, 69–71, 78, 161, 180, 183, 195, 199–200, 202–4, 210, 214, 239, 241, 244, 246–7, 266, 278
Ethics, 17, 209
On Generation and Corruption, 65, 72, 181–2, 191, 202, 204
On the Heavens, 181, 212
On Interpretation, 75, 78, 79, 93, 167, 239, 241, 244, 245, 272
Metaphysics, 17, 42, 43, 56, 65, 66, 70–1, 76, 78, 90, 159–60, 166, 172, 179–80, 182–3, 186–9, 193–5, 198–200, 203–8, 210, 218, 221, 231–2, 241, 244, 286
Physics, 42, 65, 71–2, 102, 160, 166, 208, 211–14, 231–2, 250
Posterior Analytics, 53, 55, 85, 87, 91, 93, 94, 95, 98, 103, 104, 105, 108, 109, 113, 114–15, 117, 139, 144, 162, 165, 171–2, 190, 193, 208, 217–18, 223, 227, 229, 231–2, 245, 252, 256, 274, 308–10
Prior Analytics, 87, 89, 93, 95, 104, 106,